A PIONEERING COLLECTION

MASTER DRAWINGS FROM THE CROCKER ART MUSEUM

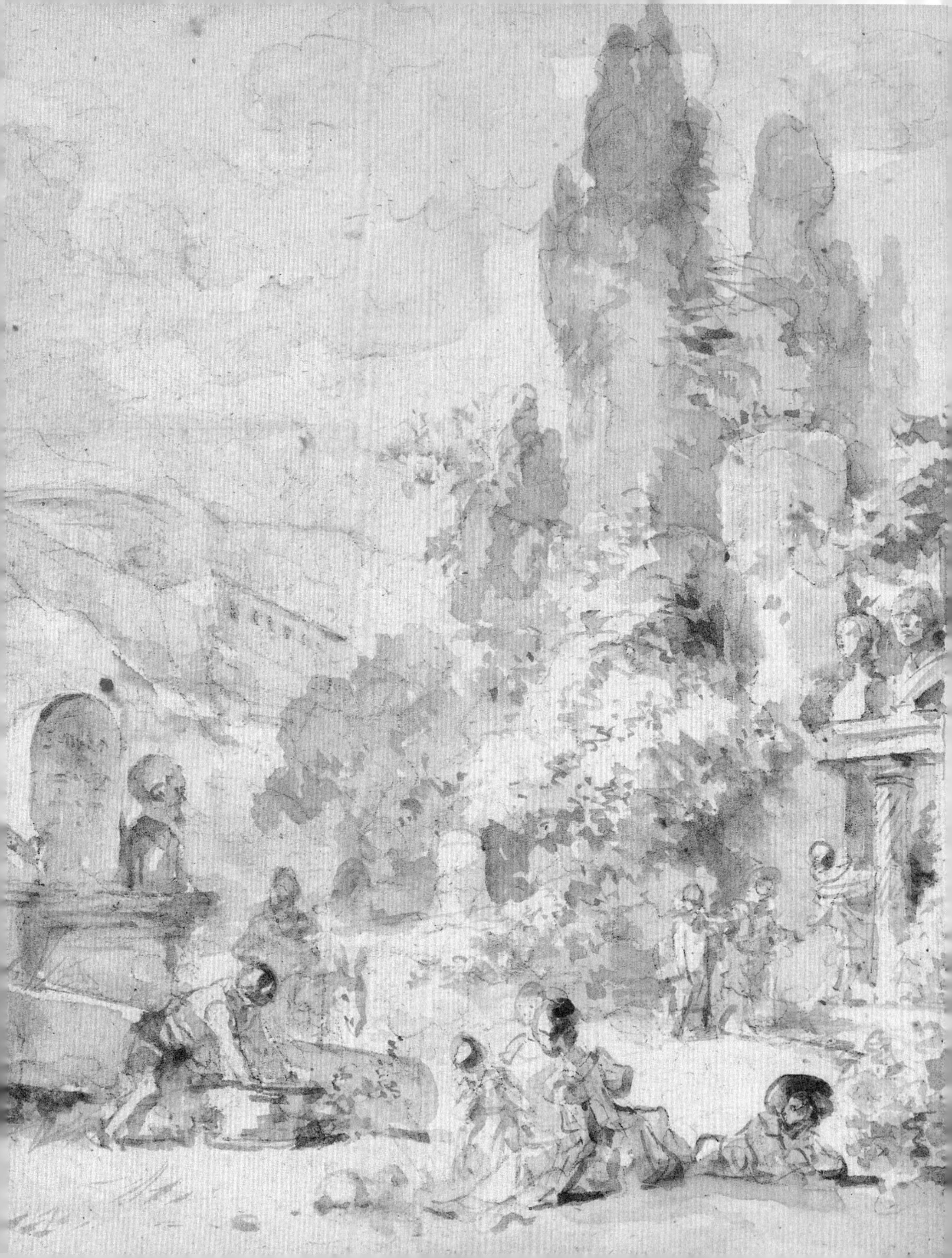

A PIONEERING COLLECTION

MASTER DRAWINGS FROM THE CROCKER ART MUSEUM

WILLIAM BREAZEALE

with CARA DENISON, STACEY SELL, *and* FREYDA SPIRA

PAUL HOLBERTON PUBLISHING

IN ASSOCIATION WITH

THE CROCKER ART MUSEUM, 2010

First published to accompany the exhibition

A PIONEERING COLLECTION
Master Drawings from the Crocker Art Museum

at the Crocker Art Museum
October 10, 2010–February 6, 2011

and at the Frances Lehman Loeb Art Center, Vassar College
September 16–December 11, 2011

Exhibition organized by William Breazeale

Authors for catalogue entries are indicated by initials.
Paper is off-white to buff laid paper unless otherwise
described. Mounts are described but simple linings and
secondary supports are not. Dimensions are given height
before width.

This exhibition is supported by a grant from the National
Endowment for the Arts.

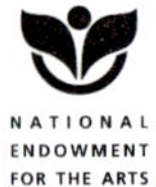

ISBN 978-1-884038-17-4

British Library Cataloguing in Publication Data

A catalogue record for this book is available from the
British Library

Produced by Paul Holberton publishing
89 Borough High Street, London SE1 1NL
www.paul-holberton.net

Designed by Peter Campbell

Origination and printing by
e-graphic, Verona, Italy

FRONT COVER: Cat. no. 2
BACK COVER: Cat. no. 41
FRONTISPIECE: Detail, cat. no. 38

TABLE OF CONTENTS

DIRECTOR'S FOREWORD

The drawings in this exhibition, dating from the late fifteenth to the mid-nineteenth centuries, represent a selection of the highest quality from an early and important American collection. Purchased for the most part in 1869–71 by the founders of the Crocker Art Museum, they are in some ways a time capsule that gives insight into the European art market and the taste of the patrons. Through this exhibition the Museum introduces many of these drawings to the public for the first time, and provides a splendid overview of this unique collection. One of the goals of mounting the exhibition is to provide a new picture of the collection's origin, an origin that, long mysterious from lack of documentation, is now beginning to emerge.

The second in a series of travelling exhibitions mounted by the Crocker, *A Pioneering Collection: Master Drawings from the Crocker Art Museum* marks an important step in the history of the institution. Concurrent with the opening of the Museum's new Anne and Malcolm McHenry Center for Works on Paper, the exhibition opens new opportunities for drawings study. We are pleased to share the exhibition with the Frances Lehman Loeb Art Center at Vassar College, and I wish to thank James Mundy, the Anne Hendricks Bass Director of the Art Center, for his commitment to this project. The work of William Breazeale, Curator at the Crocker Art Museum, in promoting study of the drawings shows his dedication to the collection and to the Museum. Both he and I believe the audience for drawings is much wider than the scholarly world of specialists, and we both hope through this exhibition, a broad public will come to share our enthusiasm for these works.

Lial. A. Jones

PREFACE

From the time of my arrival at the Crocker Art Museum, I have been drawn further and further into the fascinating questions that surround the Museum's master drawings collection. My focus here, as in so much else, has been on origins: the origins of the objects themselves, especially in regard to technique and authorship, and the origins of the collection as a whole, both in the founders' intent and in the nineteenth-century art market. The documents I have examined have created a very different picture from the one passed down through tradition, both of the drawings and of the patrons. Uncertainties remain, but I hope that the present exhibition will supply a proper introduction to an extremely fine American collection and its unusual history.

This exhibition is long overdue for the Crocker. Though the collection has regularly been included in exhibitions organized by other institutions, and its drawings of the nude were studied in our 2008 exhibition, this is the first time that the Crocker has been able to delve into the collection and its origin in a travelling exhibition and catalogue of its own. It is with the unflagging support of the Director, Lial Jones, the Associate Director and Chief Curator, Scott A. Shields, and a lively group of enthusiasts that this exhibition has now come to fruition, and it is my hope that it will serve as the foundation for future inquiry as well. This exhibition will for the first time allow audiences in other centers of drawings study to enjoy the riches of our collection, and will inaugurate the Anne and Malcolm McHenry Center for Works on Paper, both signal stages in the Museum's efforts on behalf of the collection.

ACKNOWLEDGEMENTS

In the process of study that has led to this exhibition and catalogue, the authors have incurred many debts. The support of the Director and Associate Director has been invaluable to the project, while the enthusiasm of the Sacramento community of arts supporters, especially Anne and Malcolm McHenry, Aj and Susana Molinet Watson, and Charles and Théa Givens has given us a sense of purpose, and a sense of humor, when our own were diminished by circumstances. Anne Rosenthal's skill in conservation and Jesse Bravo's in photography have made the exhibition and catalogue even more beautiful. The kindness of the staff at the Getty Research Institute, the Watson Library at the Metropolitan Museum of Art, the Morgan Library and Museum Reading Room, and the National Gallery of Art Library has been decisive to the outcome of the project, especially that of Ted Dalziel and Thomas McGill Jr. at the last. Many of our colleagues have been extremely generous in responding to requests for their time and attention, especially Bernadette Py, William Voelkle, Roger Wieck, Jennifer Tonkovich, Victor Carlson, Steen Alstijns, and Armin Kunz. Christine Giviskos and Wendy Thompson kindly critiqued a preliminary version of the catalogue essay. The often laborious process of collecting comparative photographs was made simpler and more pleasant by Bryony Kirby, Padre Luigi Pastoressa of S. Maria in Via, Rome, and Dekan Günter Hütter of the Pfarrkirche Tannheim, all of whose generosity is hereby gratefully acknowledged. On a personal level, I would like to express my gratitude to Greg Jecmen, whose patience and advice have made such a difference.
William Breazeale

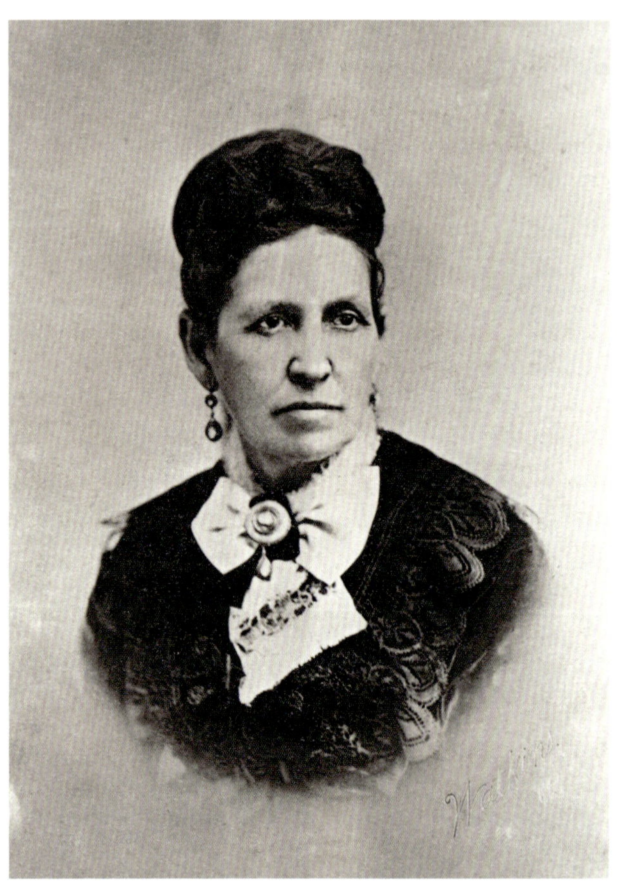 FIGURE 1 Carleton Watkins, *Margaret Rhodes Crocker*, n. d.
Albumen print, carte-de-visite. Crocker Art Museum

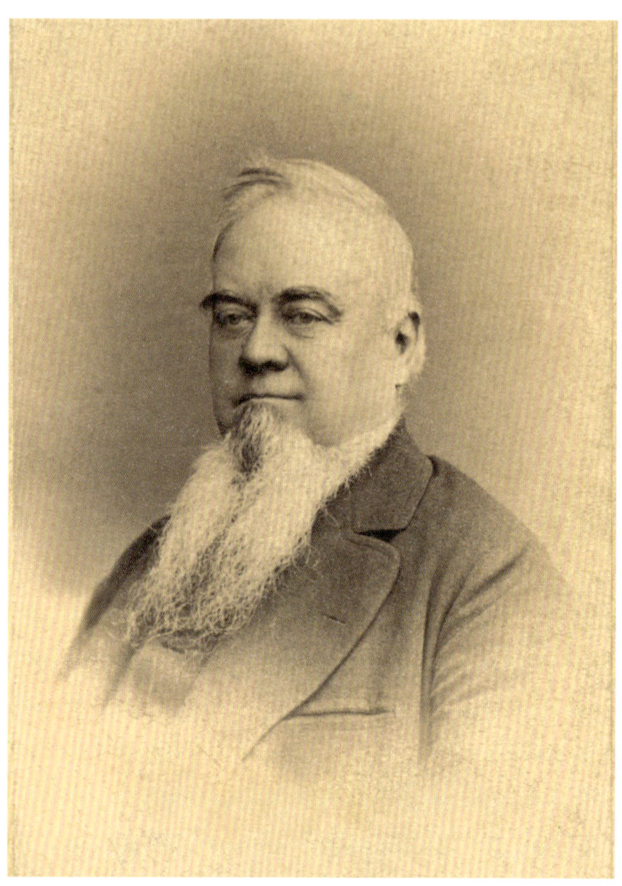 FIGURE 2 W. Lampmann, *Edwin Bryant Crocker*, 1869–71
Albumen print, carte-de-visite. Crocker Art Museum

PIONEERING COLLECTORS: THE E. B. CROCKER COLLECTION OF DRAWINGS AND ITS FOUNDERS

The master drawings at the Crocker Art Museum[1] form an unusually rich and historic collection, known to include many keystones of the history of art. Sheets by Carpaccio, Dürer, Callot and Boucher only scratch the surface of a collection whose sources include the great eighteenth-century collectors Pierre-Jean Mariette, Pierre Crozat, Joshua Reynolds, and Antoine-Joseph Dezallier d'Argenville, their seventeenth-century predecessors Evrard Jabach, Nicolas Lanier, Jan Pietersz. Zoomer, and Peter Lely, as well as nineteenth-century collectors like William Esdaile, Thomas Lawrence, and Dominique Vivant-Denon.[2] The high quality and composition of the collection show a methodical approach and degree of connoisseurship that raises many questions in the modern mind: why is it in Sacramento? why were the patrons interested in drawings? where and how did they acquire? what was the Crockers' purpose in doing so? was their purchase of such fine sheets an anomaly or part of a larger pattern of patronage? In addition to bringing a selection of the best drawings in the collection to a wider audience, one of the motivations of this exhibition is to shed a fuller light on the history of the collection and its context, in relation both to California events and to American patronage.[3]

Edwin Bryant Crocker and his wife Margaret Rhodes Crocker (figs. 1 and 2), the founders of the collection, were not born to the level of privilege they later attained. Edwin was the son of Isaac Crocker, a merchant in Jamesville, New York.[4] The eldest of five children, Edwin took his degree at the Rensselaer Institute in civil engineering. After their father moved to Indiana to take up farming, Edwin and his brother Charles joined him. Edwin studied law in South Bend and rose rapidly, practicing independently by 1847. His first wife, Mary Norton, died around 1850. Around the same time he became involved in a controversial legal suit involving runaway slaves.[5] These two events may have set Edwin on the path to a new life in California. With three of his brothers already settled as merchants serving gold miners, Edwin married again and set out to join them. His wife, Margaret Rhodes, was a close friend who had tended his first wife during her illness. They were married in New York by Henry Ward Beecher, the abolitionist preacher. The couple arrived in San Francisco on August 26, 1852.[6]

Though not initially wealthy, the Crockers shared a background that already made them likely patrons: the importance Edwin placed on education and social conscience is shown in his early activities in New York and Indiana, and perhaps the seeds of philanthropy were already sown in the East. After the couple's arrival in Sacramento, Edwin joined his brothers in business before returning to the practice of law in 1854. He was also active in politics and agricultural development, but his cultural interest led him to found the Sacramento Music Society in 1856 and, with others, the Sacramento Library Association the following year.[7] The city was ripe for such endeavors: as the capital of the new state and the gateway to the Sierra mining districts, Sacramento was on the way to becoming a booming metropolis. By 1861, plans for connecting California with the East by land had led to the formation of the Central Pacific Railroad Company, with

1. The Museum was known as the E. B. Crocker Art Gallery until 1978, when it became the Crocker Art Museum. To avoid confusion, for the purposes of this essay it will be known as the latter.

2. Mariette: 1871.372, 1871.415, 1871.421, 1871.503, 1871.507; Crozat: 1871.243, 1871.252, 1871.288, 1871.314, 1871.340, 1871.342–43, 1871.349, 1871.414, and possibly 1871.533, 1871.600, 1871.938, and 1871.1095; Reynolds: 1871.275; Dezallier d'Argenville: 1871.223, 1871.234; Jabach: 1871.2001; Lanier: 1871.278; Zoomer: 1871.328; Lely: 1871.305; Esdaile 1871.501; Lawrence: 1871.221; Vivant-Denon: 1871.231, 1871.1100.

3. There is a preliminary introduction to the collection by the present author: Breazeale 2008.

4. An account of the Crocker family with a focus on local history is Kurutz 1990.

5. The slaveowners forced Edwin to flee the courthouse after he pronounced the slaves free. See Kurutz 1990, p. 2.

6. Kurutz 1990, p. 3.

7. Kurutz 1990, p. 6.

Sacramento as the railroad's western terminus. The four principals—later known as the Big Four—were Leland Stanford, Mark Hopkins, Collis Huntington, and Edwin's brother Charles Crocker. Edwin continued in his legal career, being appointed Associate Justice of the State Supreme Court by Governor Stanford in 1863. Serving very actively for less than a year, he stepped down to become city commissioner for Sacramento and, soon, legal counsel for the Central Pacific Railroad Company. Such an appointment, like Leland Stanford's simultaneous service as governor and president of the railroad, must be put into context. In a new state founded by transient miners and speculators, there were few men with enterprise, capital, and sense of public service who would commit to the development of stable political and economic life. Though profit and personal power must have motivated them to the same degree as Eastern railroad families, the duties of powerful men were clear during the latter half of the nineteenth century. Edwin profited greatly from his involvment with the railroad and by the end of the 1860s he had begun collecting paintings by artists working in California.[8]

In 1868, Edwin purchased property at Third and O Streets and began making plans for a new, grand house which would include an art gallery. In the midst of these plans, in June 1869, he suffered a stroke which forced him to retire from public life. The evidence of his library, which included every volume of the *Art Journal* between 1849 and 1871 as well as reference works like the *Cyclopedia of Painters* and those by Gustav Friedrich Waagen, Anna Brownell Jameson, Luigi Lanzi, James Jackson Jarves and John Ruskin, indicates that the couple may already have begun their education in art.[9] Whether or not this is the case, the entire Crocker family left for Europe on August 9, 1869.

Few documents survive regarding the family's trip or their purchases, and newspaper accounts are both vague and unreliable.[10] It is known, however, that they rented rooms at 17 Lüttichaustraße in Dresden in 1870, and kept this address for at least a year.[11] The seat of the Saxon court, with its palaces, picture gallery, and art academy, Dresden was a lively center for the arts at the time and close to the dealers and auction-houses in Leipzig. The best evidence for travels further afield comes from the objects themselves. In the paintings collection, a large number of Munich and Düsseldorf artists are represented, while the presence of a painting almost certainly from the Berlin Kunstakademie exhibition in 1870 makes travel to the Prussian capital extremely likely as well.[12] The address of a copyist in Florence preserved on the back of a canvas after Salvator Rosa[13] and a mosaic table of the type made in the Vatican workshops in the collection[14] indicate that the family may have spent time in Italy. A series of prints no longer in the collection were catalogued in French,[15] indicating that, even with the 1870–71 war, the Crockers had contact with France.

The Crocker collection of Old Master drawings is one of the largest early collections in the United States to have been made public. Though an American collection of Old Master drawings became public as early as 1811, at Bowdoin College in Maine, it was not until 1887 that the Boston Museum of Fine Arts devoted a curatorial department to works on paper, and not until the twentieth century that the Metropolitan Museum of Art, the Pierpont Morgan Library, and the Fogg Art Museum became centers of systematic study in the field. The Vanderbilt gift of drawings to the Metropolitan dates from 1880, five years before the Crocker collection became public, while the John S. Phillips

8. Kurutz 1990, pp. 11–12.

9. The inventory of January 1924 lists these works as still in the library cases, as well as volumes of line-engravings of European paintings collections. Most of these survive in the Museum.

10. The earliest newspaper account (Sacramento Bee, July 11, 1871) mentions the collection but not the trip. The celebration of the Museum's donation to the public mentions that the Crockers "visited all the chief countries of the Old World" but contains other inaccuracies regarding the collection.

11. Letter from the Rat der Stadt Dresden to Richard Vincent West, 1980; see Kurutz 1990, p. 35.

12. 1872.506, Paul Bürde's *Preaching in the Woods by the Baltic Sea.*

13. *Harbor and Ships*, inv. no. 1872.521; Breazeale 2008 p. 225 n. 34.

14. Inv. no. 1885.38. The inventory number does not reflect the date it entered the collection.

15. In the 1924 inventory; see Breazeale 2008, p. 225 n. 35.

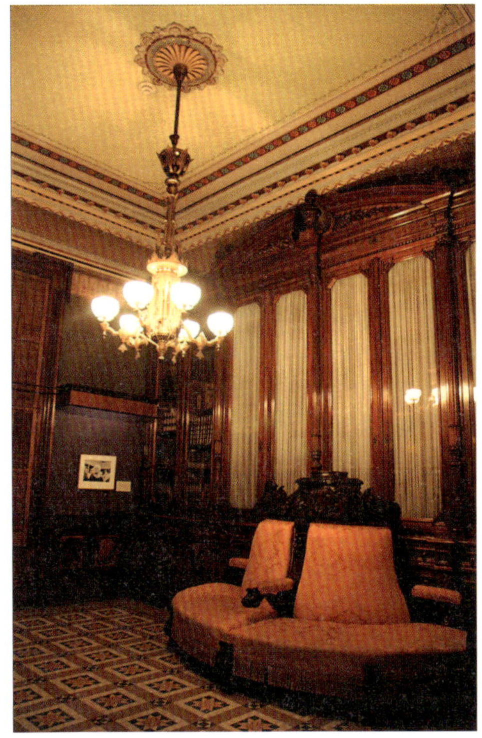

FIGURE 3 E. B. Crocker's library, now the Library Gallery, showing cabinets that originally housed the drawings collection. Crocker Art Museum

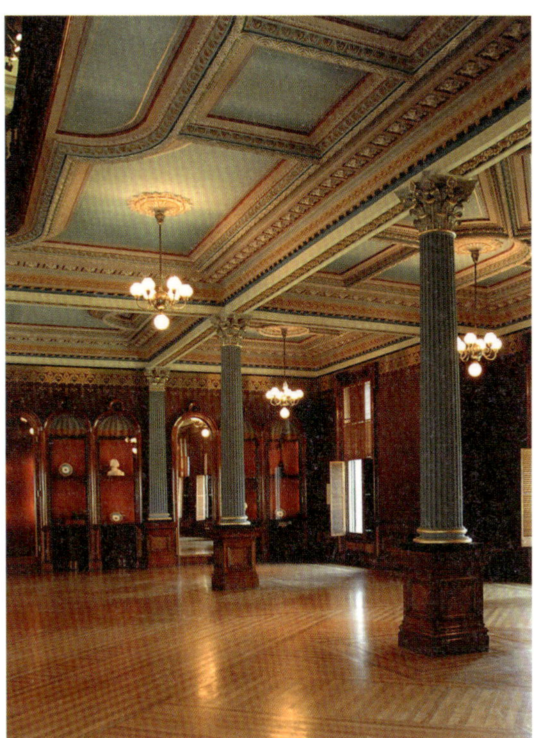

FIGURE 4 Ballroom of the Crocker Art Museum, meeting place of the Sacramento School of Design. Crocker Art Museum

16. The latter two points are the focus of Breazeale 2008.

17. 1871.940, van Thulden, is in Weigel's *Kunstlagerkatalog*, no. 1120, entered as Holzer; see Breazeale 2008, p. 225 n. 46; in addition 1871.284, most likely no. 19227 in the *Kunstlagerkatalog*, where it is listed as Cigoli, entered the collection as Fogolino, as is shown in the early inscription on its mount.

18. 1871.280 is stamped with Lugt 851, from the Gatteaux collection, a victim of the Paris Commune on May 23, 1871. The Crockers had returned to Sacramento on May 5.

bequest to the Pennsylvania Academy of Fine Arts dates to 1876. Though other private collections were formed in the decades before the Civil War, Old Master drawings collections in the United States tended to be formed by artists to aid them in their work, until industrialists began to collect them purely for enjoyment. As we shall see, the Crocker drawings collection may have combined these two purposes during its early history, especially in the period directly after becoming public in 1885.

Three old and contradictory ideas about the drawings collection may be laid to rest. Though the Franco-Prussian war may have made French collections more available, the largest part of the Crocker drawings whose sources are known was purchased in Germany. Nor is the entire collection likely to have come from the estate of the German dealer Rudolf Weigel (died 1867) as a single group, since well less than a third of the drawings can be connected with him directly. Finally, the drawings cannot have been purchased in bulk with paintings, since neither the dealer Weigel nor the firm of Boerner's (to whom his estate passed in 1871) dealt in paintings.[16] Though the drawings were certainly catalogued in Germany, it cannot have been by Weigel before his death in 1867 because several of the attributions under which the drawings entered the collection differ from those in his *Kunstlagerkatalog*.[17] Though the majority of the drawings whose sources are known, representing over a quarter of the collection, do seem to have come from Germany, a number of mid-nineteenth-century French collectors' marks, some of collections broken up after the Crockers' return to Sacramento,[18] point to the possibility of travel to France or at least contact with French dealers.

Why the Crockers purchased 1344 master drawings in addition to 700 paintings before they returned to Sacramento on May 5, 1871 can only be speculated upon (fig. 3). On the surface it seems an odd choice: an intimate medium that, however beautiful,

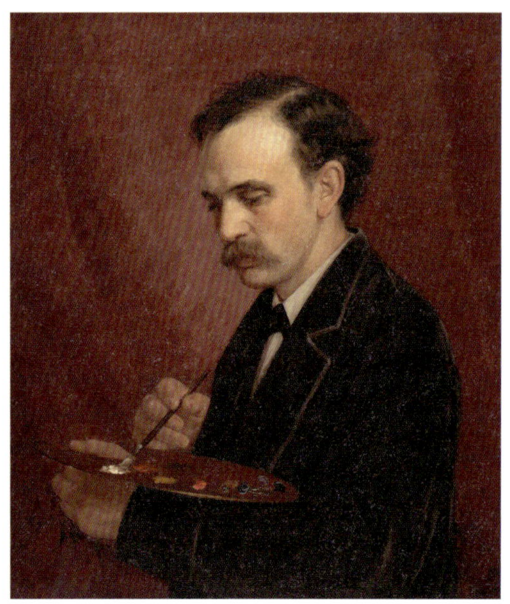

requires preparation and experience to appreciate fully, drawing has little grandeur or 'flash'. If the Crockers were boors who desired only to impress Sacramentans, their money would have been better spent on the paintings. However, that the Crockers were not the brash, uncultured innocents sometimes imagined is borne out by their activities in the 1850s and 1860s, which show a genuine concern for the welfare of their surroundings and, especially, development of cultural life. Even so, the purchase of a large collection which could be shared with a limited number of people certainly contributed little to the couple's fame. How the collection was employed in later years may give clues to the Crockers' original intent.

After its completion in 1872, the art gallery served not only as a private social center but also as a public one, hosting many benefit events for organizations like the Sacramento Library Association. This continued after Edwin's death in 1875, with visitors like the queen of Hawaii and former president Grant being received there.[19] In this period Edwin's widow became more active in public affairs, supporting many public organizations addressing social concerns between her travels to her daughter's home in San Francisco and to Europe. One of these, a conservatory, was opened directly across from the city cemetery and provided grave flowers for the poor, while another enterprise, the Marguerite Home for aged women, opened in 1884. Later that year Margaret Crocker began to make plans for the public administration of her private gallery, in accordance with the wishes of her late husband.

The California Museum Association, now known as the Crocker Art Museum Association, was officially formed to foster the arts and sciences in Northern California, though its immediate purpose was the administration of Margaret Crocker's collection. After its preliminary incorporation in December 1884, plans were made for a loan exhibition on the premises of the Crocker private gallery as a means to raise funds. Taking place in March 1885, the exhibition consisted of curiosities from citizens all over the state, including items of historical and scientific interest. Confederate swords, South Seas artifacts, and pioneer letters, along with Mrs. Crocker's own acorn from a tree

19. See Kurutz 1990, p. 20.

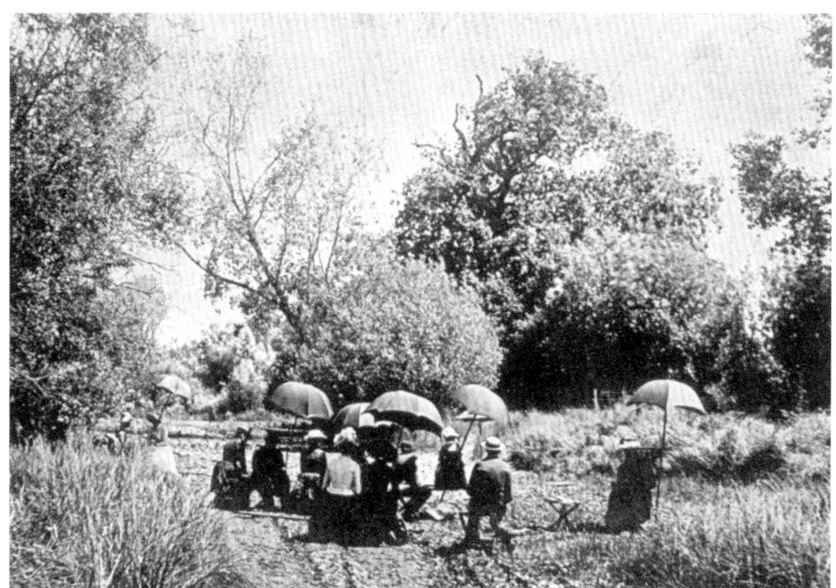

planted by George Washington, must have contrasted greatly with the collection of European and California paintings hanging nearby.[20] Over the course of the exhibition, the community's support for the idea of a public museum in Sacramento became clear to Mrs. Crocker, so much so that at its close she announced her intention that the art gallery become a public institution permanently. This was contingent upon the prospect that $100,000 be raised from Sacramento donors to ensure the health and administration of the gallery.

This fundraising effort did not meet its goal. Though merchants contributed significant amounts, the public's overwhelming support for the loan exhibition was not matched by donations of funds. In the presence of this impasse, the suggestion was made that the California Museum Association and the government of the city of Sacramento administer the collection jointly.[21] Mrs. Crocker accepted the new proposal, and May 5, 1885 was set as the date for the new arrangement to take effect, one which continues today. Enthusiasm and gratitude for the gift took the form of a floral festival in Mrs. Crocker's honor, with city organizations creating Greek temples, churches and other tributes entirely of flowers.[22] In the many newspaper accounts of the loan exhibition, the transfer of administration, and the celebration of the gift, no mention is made of master drawings in the Crocker collection.

Mrs. Crocker's life after 1885 expanded beyond Sacramento. Building houses in San Francisco, Los Angeles and New York, she began to take a greater part in the social life of those cities, while remaining a member of the board of directors of the California Museum Association. Continuing gifts of objects, funds, and reference works benefited the gallery, although, like her friends and rivals the Hopkinses, Huntingtons, and Stanfords, she had become a patron statewide.

The California Museum Association proved to be a dynamic organization, expanding its activities beyond gallery administration. In 1886, an art school opened with classes led by the Gallery's curator William F. Jackson (figs. 4, 5 and 6). An enthusiastic painter of landscapes, he was to remain as curator for the next forty-nine years. The

20. Newspaper accounts provide an exhaustive list, e.g. *Sacramento Bee,* March 17, 1885. An electric scarf pin made its appearance on March 19, according to the same paper.
21. *Sacramento Record-Union,* April 6, 1885.
22. A full account is in the *Sacramento Bee,* May 6, 1885, and the program survives in the Crocker curatorial files.

newly formed Sacramento School of Design, meeting regularly in the Crocker ballroom under Jackson's direction, provided the city with a counterpart to San Francisco's Art Association, which had begun operations over a decade earlier and had few collections of its own apart from casts.[23] Classes, held mainly in the Crocker ballroom, followed the curriculum of European and American academies.[24] A brochure of 1895 mentions the equipment and facilities then available to students:

The main studio is on the ground floor, a magnificent hall 58 × 52, of elegant design and elaborate finish. From models—after preliminary instruction and practice where necessary, in drawing from the flat, and from casts of hands, feet, masks, and torsi—the pupils work in charcoal or crayon. Instruction is also given in painting, always from natural objects, flowers, fruit, still-life, and landscape. Pupils well grounded in drawing from the cast, and who manifest sufficient skill, are encouraged to practice figure-drawing and portrait-painting from the living subject. In a smaller studio apart from the general classes, groups of students form life-classes where they draw and paint from models. The pupils under the personal care and direction of the instructors, make weekly excursions into the country, for instruction and practice in sketching from nature.[25]

For the academy to function properly, then, a set of casts had been made to supplement the "flats" or two-dimensional models for beginning students. If made from the original marbles, these would have been quite expensive (the French government had donated those at the San Francisco Art Association).[26] However, two-dimensional models were already available in the collection of Old Master drawings that had been in the Gallery since 1871, and were certainly in use by the school. A reporter's visit to the Sacramento School of Design, published on December 3, 1887, mentions the students' copies after "3000 studies from studios of Europe, gathered by the late Judge E. B. Crocker."[27]

Were the master drawings at the Crocker Art Museum purchased originally with the idea of serving a school of art? The thought is worthy of consideration. Part of the evidence comes from the collection's composition. Though drawings of the highest quality are distributed evenly among the main European schools—as seen in this exhibition—the collection has many characteristics that would seem incongruous in a collection assembled purely with private enjoyment in mind. Its strengths, allowing for the market and taste of the time it was purchased, still seem to follow unusually well the greatest periods of European draughtsmanship—the late sixteenth and seventeenth centuries in Italy, the seventeenth century in the Netherlands and Flanders, the eighteenth century in France, and the eighteenth and nineteenth centuries in Germany. Moreover, a bias towards Central Italian *disegno* may be present in the Italian collection, which contains fewer than ten Venetian drawings. In a collection this size, quality of course varies, but lesser works are often ruins still attributed to great draughtsmen. Likewise, copies of works by the greatest artists are present, but these are most often early copies and of very high quality.

Many groups of drawings seem to be present to showcase a technical point: the oiled-paper studies by Cades and the Macé tracings of compositional studies[28] have little appeal to the connoisseur's eye but much for the student of artistic practise. Similarly, large groups of figure studies, drapery studies, and animal studies, provide students with others' solutions to specific artistic challenges. The predominance of landscape in a

23. The Sacramento *Record-Union* of April 12, 1887 emphasizes the fact that these were the only two art schools in the state.
24. An article in the Sacramento *Record-Union* of December 3, 1887, while describing the entire curriculum, emphasizes the copying of "flat studies" and sculptural casts.
25. This brochure survives in the Crocker curatorial files.
26. Birgitta Hjalmarson, *Artful Players, Artistic life in early San Francisco*, Los Angeles, 1999, p. 31.
27. In the Sacramento *Record-Union* of that date. The number 3000 recurs in relation to the "flat studies" and later to the drawings themselves, but seems to be arbitrary as this author can find no physical evidence that the collection was ever so large.
28. Thanks to Bernadette Py for identifying this series in her visit of October 2006.

variety of media in the Dutch and German schools would have been especially welcome in California, where the surrounding landscape was a major subject for every painter. Beside these groups, and providing a unique object lesson in the training and development of a single artist, is a series of 279 studies of ancient sculpture, figure drawings, portraits and compositions by the Swiss artist Jacob Merz. These represent the majority of a lot of 471 items[29] listed in Weigel's *Kunstlagerkatalog* and may have been selected with specific criteria in mind. What little we know of the drawings' physical environment in early years shows that their use in the School of Design was facilitated, if not premeditated. They were stored in portfolios rather than the usual bound volumes, which made it possible to remove individual drawings when needed.[30]

The Crockers' trip provided them with the opportunity and likely the contacts that would lead them to consider an art school in association with their gallery. The Dresden Kunstakademie, founded just over a century before, was extremely active in training artists across Central Europe and was the home of a large and varied collection of drawings for the use of students as well as those by members of faculty, a collection now sadly reduced by war. The proximity of Leipzig, a center for auctions and dealers in the graphic arts for nearly a hundred years already, with the Weigel and Boerner families as well as other, smaller houses, provided a rich hunting-ground for works of art even without the further travel we have seen likely took place. It is possible that the large number of Crocker drawings directly connected with eighteenth- and nineteenth-century members of the Dresden Kunstakademie faculty comes not only from the opportunities provided by the Leipzig art market but also by the patrons' informed choice and desire to train students in the same tradition.

This tradition of solid academic training was gaining ground in the United States in the same years as the Crockers' trip. Collectors like the Philadelphian John S. Phillips bought drawings and prints at nearly the same time from the same Leipzig dealers and auction houses, objects which served the faculty and students of the Pennsylvania Academy of Fine Arts from 1876.[31] Collections of graphic arts for other academies were being formed across the country: the School of the Boston Museum of Fine Arts was to open in 1876, the Rhode Island School of Design in 1877, the Corcoran School of Art in 1878 and the School of the Art Institute of Chicago in 1882. Whether or not E. B. and Margaret Crocker had such a purpose in mind as early as 1869–71, the opening of the Sacramento School of Design in 1886 made a collection of the highest quality and remarkable appropriateness available to its pupils. By 1894 this training was bearing fruit, with a pupil preparing for study in Paris.[32]

In the early years of the Crocker as a public institution, a selection of drawings was available to the public as well. The question of public display was pursued by the California Museum Association as early as its June 1886 meeting[33] and, according to a much later account by William F. Jackson, was continued until the cases were in danger of being destroyed by people leaning on them.[34] He does not mention when this practise was dropped.

Margaret Crocker's decision to depart Sacramento in 1891 began a period of relative decline for the museum she had given to the city. The full reasons for her return to New York are unknown, though the fact that upon her death in 1901 her will made no

29. Weigel *Kunstlagerkatalog*, no. 5776b; Breazeale 2008 p. 223

30. This issue was unresolved in Breazeale 2008. The June 1886 meeting of the California Museum Association, however, pursued the possibility of hanging the "prints" (this term is used to refer to the entire collection of works on paper from the earliest times), making it almost certain that the drawings were not bound: minutes in Crocker curatorial files.

31. For a full account see Ann Percy, "Collecting Italian Drawings at Philadelphia: two Nineteenth-century Amateurs and a Twentieth-century Scholar," in *Italian Master Drawings at the Philadelphia Museum of Art*, exh. cat. Philadelphia Museum of Art; Bologna, 2004, pp. 11–101, esp. p. 35.

32. *Sacramento Record-Union*, October 2, 1894.

33. See note 30 above.

34. *Sacramento Union*, April 15, 1934.

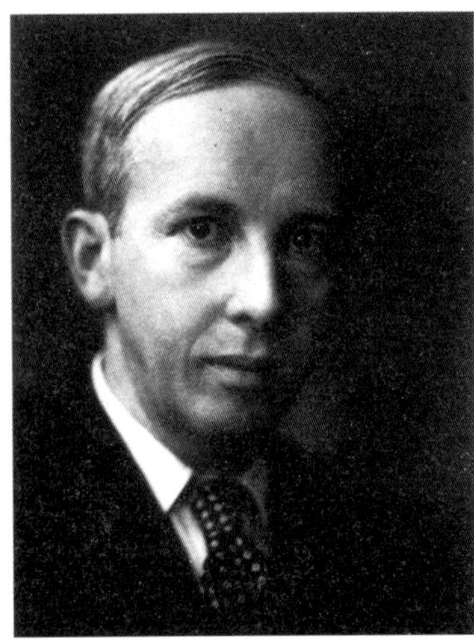

FIGURE 7 Unknown photographer, *Numa S. Trivas*, late 1930s. Gelatin silver print. Archives of American Art, Smithsonian Institution, Washington

35. In 1891 Margaret Crocker gave evidence in a legal suit involving the theft of jewelry from her daughter Amy. The result of the case implied that the jury did not believe her. A San Francisco newspaper account linked the trial, her rage, and her departure from Sacramento: see Duane Spilsbury, *California Territorial Quarterly*, no. 51, pp. 41–45.
36. See Katharine Baetjer, "Buying Pictures for New York: The Founding Purchase of 1871," *Metropolitan Museum Journal*, vol. XXXIX, 2004, pp. 161–245.
37. For example, Walter Liedtke recently stressed the importance of nineteenth-century American patrons' view of a similar Protestant democracy in Golden Age painting in his "Golden Age Painting in a Gilded Age: New York Collectors and the Metropolitan Museum of Art," given at the Frick Collection symposium *Holland's Golden Age in America: Collecting the Art of Rembrandt, Vermeer and Hals*, 16 May 2009.
38. *Sacramento Bee*, December 19, 1914.
39. *Sacramento Bee and Union*, June 5 and 6, 1925.
40. See Breazeale 2008, p. 224 n. 17.
41. *Sacramento News*, July 6, 1919.
42. *An Exhibition of Italian Paintings lent by Mr. Samuel H. Kress of New York to E. B. Crocker Art Gallery*, exh. cat. Crocker Art Museum; New York, 1933.

provision for the organizations she had begun in Sacramento may be related to events before her departure.[35] Sacramento, with the departure of the Big Four families, was no longer the seat of major patrons.

In many ways the Crockers, along with some of the other Big Four families, differed from the major Eastern art patrons. Their wealth created suddenly in California, they were not part of the Eastern upper merchant class that in the later nineteenth century provided the majority of art buyers, whose purchases represented only a small part of a lifetime of subtle jockeying for position in business and society. Moreover, they lived far from the cities of Boston, New York, and Philadelphia, where they would have had the opportunity closely to observe the implications of art patronage in action. The Metropolitan Museum's founding collection of 1871, for example—more or less contemporary with the Crocker purchase—drew upon major French collections and expertise, concentrating on the Dutch and Flemish seventeenth century, early Swiss and German masters, and a few pictures from eighteenth- and nineteenth-century France. Little contemporary art was part of this collection, brought together mainly through the efforts of two men, John Taylor Johnston and William Tilden Blodgett.[36] The idea that the Dutch Golden Age of merchant society served as a model for New York collectors, their aspirations and self-image, is a commonplace of museum lore.[37] Crocker taste may not have been such a case of self-mirroring, since it contrasted greatly: the real focus on Old Masters was in their forward-thinking purchases for the drawings collection, with the great majority of their paintings being nineteenth-century German; minor pictures from the seventeenth-century Netherlands and Flanders formed a much smaller group. On the other hand, the prevalence of emotional domestic scenes and a general air of *Gemütlichkeit* in the German paintings might have represented the Crockers' personal ideals.

In the first part of the twentieth century the Crocker Art Museum was isolated culturally, with its stable collection increasingly out of touch with changes in taste. Sacramento, however important as the seat of state government, remained in some ways a frontier town full of stories drawn as if from the pages of Bret Harte or Mark Twain. Newspaper accounts tell of the draping of the Museum's plaster cast of the Medici *Venus* with a nightgown for one occasion in 1914,[38] and a murderous rampage by a farmhand that left two bodies and a bullet hole in the foyer in 1925.[39] During this entire period William F. Jackson, appointed by Margaret Crocker in 1885, remained the curator and functioned as director. He retained the post until his death in 1935.

Jackson has suffered somewhat in later accounts of his tenure, especially at the hands of his successor, Harry Noyes Pratt. However, far from ignoring the drawings collection as Pratt assumed, Jackson was an advocate for it as much as his limited circumstances allowed. He sent photographs to a museum in Boston in 1918, with the result that Bernard Berenson was recommended to him as an expert, though through the inaction of the Museum board the matter was not pursued.[40] He welcomed the French expert Seymour de Ricci to the gallery for drawings study in 1919.[41] He kept in contact with his colleagues on the East Coast, hosting an exhibition of masterpieces of painting from the Kress collection in 1933,[42] and continually organized exhibitions of the drawings which garnered thorough, if local, attention. What may have been his last exhibition of master drawings took place beginning April 15, 1934, less than two years before Pratt arrived.[43]

What Harry Noyes Pratt brought to the collection in 1936 was a flair for publicity in keeping with his background as a poet, museum director, and journalist. Recognizing the collection's international importance, he began a campaign of publication, complete with a melodramatic story of the drawings' rediscovery in a mouldering basement, that served a greater purpose.[44] Not only was he determined that the drawings deserved greater study, he believed the entire collection deserved a new facility along modern lines. The neighborhood around Third and O Streets was by this time one of the most dangerous in the city, and the gallery had long been administered almost entirely by the government. Emphasizing the danger to the collection and its importance, he felt, would aid his plans for a new building in another location.

Pratt's campaign bore fruit in the form of visits by specialists in drawings. Especially in the late 1930s, with many European scholars uprooted by political events coming to serve as faculty in North American universities and colleges, American collections were receiving more informed visitors. Mills College in Oakland had secured the services of Alfred Neumeyer of the University of Berlin in 1935. Having published on subjects as varied as the Nazarenes, Michelangelo's frescoes in the Pauline Chapel, and Johann Anton Ramboux, he was also the author of the Dürer volume in the 'Maîtres d'autrefois' series published by Georges Besson and Jean Alazard.[45] His own expertise in drawings led the California Museum Association to invite him to organize the collection in December 1937, but it was his contacts with other scholars that proved invaluable. By 1939, Hans Tietze and Erika Tietze Conrat, János Scholz, Agnes Mongan, and Wilhelm Suida had visited the collection and scholarly publications featuring Crocker drawings had begun to appear.[46]

However, the greatest benefit to the Crocker drawings collection came from the Russian scholar Numa S. Trivas (fig. 7). He was trained at the Russian Institute of Art History in Saint Petersburg, where he wrote a dissertation on Baroque sculpture, and in following years attended the University of Berlin and the École du Louvre. Trivas then worked with the Rothmann galleries in Berlin and was a partner with V. Bloch & Co. until 1930. The author of seventeen exhibition reviews, letters, and articles between 1935 and his arrival in Sacramento, his main scholarly interests were Jean-Etienne Liotard and Frans Hals.[47] A friend of Neumeyer's from his days in Berlin, Trivas arrived in California in mid-1939 to cover the Golden Gate exposition in San Francisco for the Dutch newspaper *De Groene Amsterdammer*. His arrival in Sacramento to see the drawings was soon after 27 July.[48] It seems that the combination of impending war in Europe and the prospect of

43. See note 34 above.

44. The drawings were never stored underground, rather being in the Crocker library next to the ballroom. Pratt's journalistic bent as a museum director is seen best in his article in the San Francisco *Chronicle* of September 5, 1937.

45. Paris, 1929. He had also published the following before his arrival in the United States: "Beiträge zur Kunst der Nazarener in Rom," *Repertorium für Kunstwissenschaft*, vol. L, no. 2, 1929, pp. 64–80; "Schmiede-arbeiten von Andreas Moritz," *Kunst und Künstler*, vol. XXVII, July 1929, pp. 394–96; "Michelangelos Fresken in der Cappella Paolina des Vatikan," *Zeitschrift für bildende Kunst*, vol. XLIII, November 1929, pp. 173–82; "Die Pressestelle," *Jahrbuch der Berliner Museen*, vol. LII, no. 2, 1931, pp. 45–46; "Grenzendes Stilbegriff," *Repertorium für Kunstwissenschaft*, vol. LII, no. 6, 1931, pp. 201–12; "Johann Anton Ramboux: Rebekka und Eliesar," *Zeitschrift für bildende Kunst*, vol. LXV, March 1932, pp. 215–17; "Die Grenzen der Illusion: Hoffmanns Erzählungen im Grossen Schauspielhaus," *Kunst und Künstler*, vol. XXXI, March 1932, p. 108.

46. Tietze and Tietze-Conrat 1937–38, vol. II, no. 127a; Alfred Neumeyer, "Albrecht Dürer," *Old Master Drawings*, vol. XIII, 1938, pp. 16–17. Notes on mounts record scholarly visits: see Breazeale 2008, p. 207.

47. "Letter to the Editor: J. E. Liotard," *The Burlington Magazine*, vol. LXVI, no. 367, January, 1935, p. 300; "Liotard's Portraits of Frederick Lewis, Prince of Wales, and his Family," ibid., vol. LXVIII, no. 396, March, 1936, pp. 117–19; "Favray or Liotard?," *Old Master Drawings*, vol. X, 1935/36, pp. 61–63; "Les natures mortes de Liotard," *Gazette des Beaux-Arts*, ser. VI, vol. V, no. 15, May 1936, pp. 307–10; "Les répliques dans l'oeuvre de J. E. Liotard (1702-1789)," *Résumés*, 1936, pp. 127–28; "Les portraits de J. E. Liotard par lui-même," *Revue de l'art ancien et moderne*, vol. LXX, November 1936, pp. 153–62; "London Society portrayed by Liotard," *The Connoisseur*, no. 99, 1937, pp. 30–34; "Courrier de Hollande: exposition de l'art ancien," *Revue de l'art ancien et moderne*, vol. LXXI, April 1937, pp. 90–91; "Exposition des peintures divisionnistes de Seurat à Toorop," ibid., vol. LXXI, April 1937, pp. 91–92; "New Light on Rembrandt's So-called 'Hendrikje' at Edinburgh," *The Burlington Magazine*, vol. LXX, May 1937, p. 252; "L'exposition Frans Hals," *Revue de l'art ancien et moderne*, vol. LXXI, September 1937, pp. 201–02; "The Frans Hals Exhibition at Haarlem," *The Connoisseur*, no. 100, November 1937, pp. 227–31; "Pieter Saenredam," *Apollo*, vol. XXVII, March 1938, pp. 154–55; "Nineteenth-century French art at Amsterdam," ibid., vol. XXVIII, September 1938, p. 138; "Masterpieces from Dutch private collections at the Boymans Museum, Rotterdam," *The Connoisseur*, no. 102, September 1938, pp. 115–21; "Oude Kunst op de New Yorksche Wereldtentoonstelling," *Elseviers Geïllustreerd Maandschrift*, vol. XLIX, 1939, pp. 136–41; "Old Master Drawings at the Teyler Museum, Haarlem," *The Connoisseur*, no. 103, April 1939, pp. 209–14.

48. Letter of that date from Trivas to Harry Noyes Pratt in curatorial files.

an uncatalogued collection in California made him go to Amsterdam, pack his library and collection, and return to America before war was declared on 3 September. He arrived in Sacramento shortly after 7 February 1940[49] to begin cataloguing the drawings collection, serving without pay. It was not until 1941 that his contributions were recognized officially with the title of Curator of Drawings.[50]

Trivas breathed life into the Museum and its public: in addition to his catalogue work he organized imaginative and surely handsome exhibitions, including *Three Centuries of Landscape Drawings* and the inventive *Ten Problems/Nine Solutions*, which addressed issues in connoisseurship.[51] He also continued his frenetic pace of publication. In the space of just over a year, he authored four articles on California museums for *Apollo*, in addition to publishing individual Crocker drawings in *Old Master Drawings* and *The Art Quarterly*. At the same time he supervised the publication of his monograph on Frans Hals in London and the submission of one on Liotard in France, the latter sadly never brought out.[52] His scientific approach resulted in a considerable number of discoveries as well as great strides in the professional standards for the collection, including the housing and numbering system used today. Trivas must have functioned well on many levels, allowing him to connect the Museum and its collection with the public, and he appears in local newspaper accounts regularly. Having asked his friends in Sacramento to find him a less exotic name than Numa, he happily became Pete Trivas to them.[53]

The sudden deaths of both Trivas and Pratt within a short period dealt the Museum and the drawings collection a serious blow.[54] Its scholarly importance by now recognized, the drawings collection nonetheless lacked a specialist curator for many decades. The collection continued to be published and to be a part of a series of monographic and thematic exhibitions for other institutions, and a succession of drawings scholars continued to raise interest in the collection. Thomas daCosta Kaufmann's 2004 catalogue of the Central European drawings was the culmination of over twenty years' involvment with the collection.[55] The generosity of the administration allowed other scholars, especially Seymour Howard and Jeffrey Ruda of the University of California at Davis, to organize exhibitions from the drawings.[56] The first travelling drawings exhibition and full catalogue organized by a member of the Crocker curatorial staff, *The Language of the Nude*, opened in 2008.[57]

With the present exhibition, the Crocker will inaugurate the Anne and Malcolm McHenry Center for Works of Art on Paper, allowing the drawings finally to take their place among American collections. This facility, with study room and gallery space, will at last fulfil the desires of E. B. and Margaret Crocker for the collection's full appreciation.

49. Letter of February 7, 1940 from Trivas to Harry Noyes Pratt in curatorial files.

50. Minutes of California Museum Association meeting of April 2, 1941.

51. *Three Centuries of Landscape Drawings*, Sacramento, 1940. Brochures for *Ten Problems/Nine Solutions* survive in the curatorial files.

52. The manuscript is now in the Musée d'Art et d'Histoire, Geneva.

53. Sacramento *Union*, April 18, 1942.

54. Trivas died April 17, 1941; Pratt died in June 1944.

55. Kaufmann 2004

56. At first these were connected with university courses with heavy student involvement: Seymour Howard et al., *Classical Narratives in Master Drawings*, 1972; *Old Testament Narratives in Master Draiwngs*, 1973; *New Testament Narratives in Master Drawings*, 1976; and *Saints and Sinners in Master Drawings*, 1983. Jeffrey Ruda's own *The Art of Drawing*, Flint, 1992, travelled to the Flint Institute of Art.

57. William Breazeale, Susan Anderson, Christine Giviskos, and Christiane Andersson, *The Language of the Nude: Four Centuries of Drawing the Human Body*, exh. cat. Crocker Art Museum, John and Mable Ringling Museum of Art, and Douglas F. Cooley Memorial Gallery; London, 2008.

DRAWINGS FROM ITALY

1. **Vittore Carpaccio**, *Pope Alexander III Presenting a Ceremonial Umbrella to Doge Sebastiano Ziani at Ancona,* n. d.

Pen and brown ink, brush and brownish wash; verso: red chalk, pen and brown ink, 21.3 × 29.8 cm
Crocker Art Museum, E. B. Crocker Collection 1871.220

INSCRIPTIONS: dark-brown ink, upper right corner: DV; black chalk, lower margin at right: *Verte*[1]; dark-brown ink, lower left corner: *Carpaccio* [cancelled in graphite]; black chalk, lower margin at left: *Perugino*; verso, dark-brown ink, lower left corner: *Vittore Carpaccio*

MARKS: lower left corner: Lugt 2344 (Schumann)

PROVENANCE: Johann Gottfried Schumann, Dresden, before 1810; Edwin Bryant Crocker, Sacramento, by 1871; gift of his widow Margaret to the Museum, 1885

LITERATURE:
Breazeale 2008, p. 210; Cornelia Friedrichs, *Francesco Guardi, venezianische Feste und Zeremonien*, Berlin, 2006, p. 36; Peter Humfrey, *Carpaccio*, London, 2005, p. 118; Stefania Mason Rinaldi, *Carpaccio, The Major Pictorial Cycles*, Milan, 2000, p. 9; Ruda 1992, no. 1; Patricia Fortini Brown, *Venetian Narrative Painting in the Age of Carpaccio*, New Haven and London, 1988, pp. 85–86, 279; Rona Goffen, "Bellini, S. Giobbe and Altar Egos," *Artibus et historiae*, vol. VII, no. 14, 1986, p. 64, note 40; Wolfgang Wolters, *Der Bilderschmuck des Dogenpalastes*, Wiesbaden, 1983, p. 170; Edward Muir, "Images of Power: Art and Pageantry in Renaissance Venice," *The American Historical Review*, vol. LXXXIV, no. 1, February, 1979, p. 25; Michelangelo Muraro, *I disegni di Vittore Carpaccio*, Florence, 1977, pp. 76–77; Pignatti 1974, no. 5; White 1972, p. 167; Terisio Pignatti, *Vittore Carpaccio*, Milan, 1972, pp. 18, 21, 22; Norbert Huse, *Studien zu Giovanni Bellini*, Berlin, 1972, pp. 66, 70; Crocker 1971, no. 8, p. 3; Schultz 1968, no. 32; Guido Perocco, *L'opera completa del Carpaccio*, Milan, 1967, p. 104; Michelangelo Muraro, *Carpaccio*, Florence, 1966, pp. 10, 68, 82; Crocker 1964, p. 54; Terisio Pignatti, review of Lauts 1962, *Master Drawings*, vol. I, no. 4, Winter 1963, pp. 49–50; Michelangelo Muraro, *Treasures of Venice*, Geneva, 1963, p. 140; Jan

B EGINNING IN 1474, a campaign of historical decoration was created for the Sala del Maggior Consiglio, the Hall of the Great Council for the Palazzo Ducale in Venice. Depicting the city's triumphs of diplomacy and military might in a series of canvases by Giovanni Bellini and other artists, the cycle was destroyed by fire in 1577 and recreated by later hands. This drawing by Vittore Carpaccio is the only surviving evidence of a composition from this cycle.

Born between 1460 and 1466 to a member of the Venetian furrier's guild, Carpaccio was from the 1490s one of the chief Venetian painters of altarpieces and above all cycles of narrative paintings for the city's confraternities. Whether or not he trained with Gentile and Giovanni Bellini, as has been proposed, he collaborated with the latter even after he had been an independent master for over fifteen years. His major narrative cycles, for the Scuola di Sant'Orsola (1490-96), the Scuola degli Schiavoni (1502-08), the Scuola degli Albanesi (c. 1500-10) and the Scuola di Santo Stefano (1511–20), were renowned for their attention to visual variety, attention to detail, and naturalness of expression.[2] The fact that these were all small confraternities may have contributed to the fact that Carpaccio was chosen to collaborate with Giovanni Bellini in 1507 rather than leading the Sala del Maggior Consiglio project himself. Carpaccio served as part of the committee to evaluate Giorgione's frescoes for the Fondaco de' Tedeschi in 1508. He died between 28 October 1525 and 26 June 1526.

The Crocker drawing confirms Vasari's assessment of Carpaccio as a "*molto diligente e pratico maestro.*"[3] The moment depicted is a key event in Venetian historical mythography, related to the doge's intercession between pope and emperor in 1177. In the previous year, Frederick I Barbarossa had proclaimed an antipope and banished Alexander III from his lands. Taking refuge in Venice, the pope was received with great honors and Doge Sebastiano Ziani sent a delegation to Barbarossa to negotiate. The eventual result was that the emperor recognized the pope in a splendid ceremony in San Marco in Venice. In thanks, the Pope gave the doge dominion over the Adriatic (the origin of the annual wedding to the sea from the *bucintoro*) and symbols of his equality with the emperor and himself. These included the papal umbrella bestowed upon the doge in a ceremony at Ancona, as in the lost painting and the present drawing.[4]

In the scene in the recto drawing in dark brown ink and brown washes, Carpaccio isolates the narrative moment by placing the umbrella and the act of bestowal at the center of an x, formed by the wedge-shaped rows of attendant figures. The hands of pope, doge, and bearer rest upon its handle as the pope makes a gesture of blessing. The emperor witnesses this act at left. On the verso, in a much less detailed scene in red chalk and dark brown ink, the artist arranges the scene differently, the principal figures disposed about a semicircle with crowds of attendants radiating behind them in all directions. Though it has been proposed that the verso was used for Carpaccio's canvas

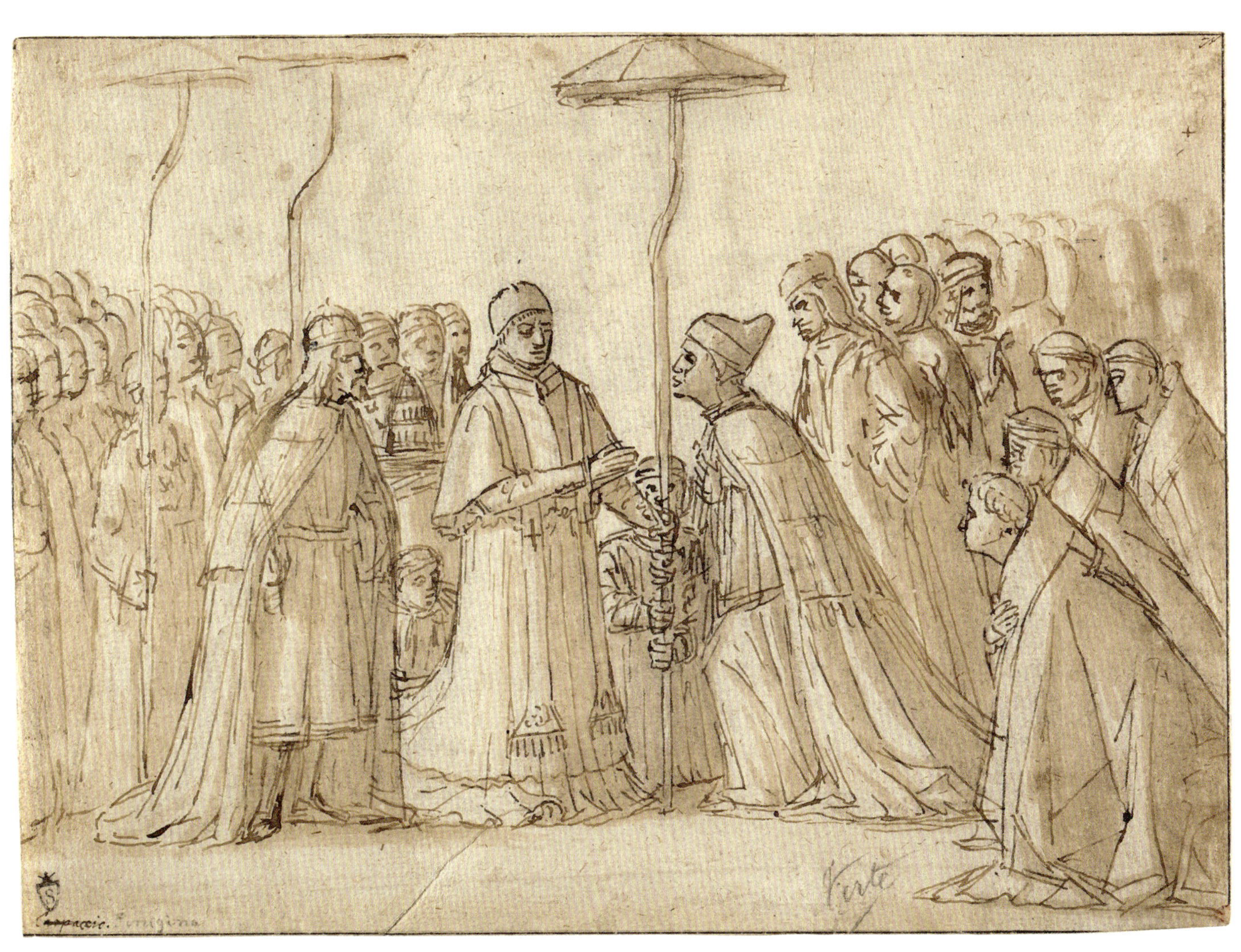

Lauts, *Carpaccio*, London, 1962, no. 49,
p. 277; Giuseppe Fiocco, *Carpaccio*, Novara,
1958, no. 8, p. 35; Bohr 1958, no. 34;
Edoardo Arslan, "Due disegni e un
dipinto di Carpaccio," *Emporio*, no. 116,
1952, p. 109; A. E. Popham and Philip
Pouncey, *Italian Drawings in the
Department of Prints and Drawings in the
British Museum, The Fourteenth and Fifteenth
Centuries*, British Museum Catalogues,
London, 1950, under no. 33; Hans Tietze
and Erika Tietze-Conrat, *The Drawings of
the Venetian Painters of the 15th and 16th
Centuries*, New York, 1944, no. 635 and
p. 143; Trivas 1940b, p. 137; Erika Tietze-
Conrat, "Decorative Paintings of the
Venetian Renaissance," *The Art Quarterly*,
vol. II, 1940, pp. 20–21

NOTES

1. "Turn the page" in Latin, indicating a
   double-sided composition.

2. Luigi Lanzi, *Storia pittorica della Italia dal
   risorgimento delle belle Arti fin presso al fine
   del XVIII secolo*, ed. Martino Capucci,
   Florence, 1968–74, vol. II, p. 27.

3. Vasari, ed. Milanesi, vol. VIII, p. 642.

4. See Giustina Renier Michiel, *Origine delle
   feste veneziane*, Milan, 1829, vol. I,
   pp. 125–29, for the history related to the
   Sala del Maggior Consiglio episodes. The
   historical basis for some of these has been
   questioned: see Filippo de Vivo, "Historial
   Justifications of Venetian Power in the
   Adriatic," *Journal of the History of Ideas*,
   vol. LXIV, no. 2, April 2003, pp. 159–76.

5. Huse 1972, as above, p. 66.

6. Lauts 1962, as above, no. 50.

7. Art Institute of Chicago, inv. no.
   1962.577R, formerly in the Colville
   collection; Lauts 1962, no. 31.

8. A note by Wilhelm Suida proposing
   Giovanni Bellini as author survives on the
   original mat in Crocker curatorial files.
   Norbert Huse (1972, p. 66) proposes Bellini
   or Carpaccio copying his design.

9. Inv. no. 1897-4-10-1; Tietzes 1944, as above,
   under no. 615; Popham and Pouncey as
   above, p. 21.

10. Pignatti 1974, p. 8.

11. Fortini Brown 1988, as above, p. 275.

on the basis of perceived similarities to its sixteenth-century replacement by Girolamo Gambarata,[5] surely the recto's focus and narrative clarity make it better suited to the subject than the verso, especially since the placement of the umbrella on the latter makes it seem that the doge bestows it upon the pope and not the other way round.

Stylistically the drawing fits well in Carpaccio's oeuvre, with similarities to figures in a scene for the Scuola degli Schiavoni composed in the same way, *The Funeral of Saint Jerome* of *c.* 1502, now in Uppsala.[6] The two monks kneeling at right are studied separately in a drawing now in Chicago.[7] It seems likely that the Crocker recto is close to the scene in the lost final canvas, if the few changes between the Uppsala drawing and the Scuola degli Schiavoni canvas are typical of Carpaccio's working habit.

The drawing, which entered the collection as the work of Carpaccio, was published first by Erika Tietze-Conrat in 1940 and has been connected to the Sala del Maggior Consiglio project from that time. The few doubts about its attribution have arisen not on stylistic grounds but from the assumption that Giovanni Bellini, by contract in charge of the decoration with Carpaccio and others assisting, would have made the compositional drawings.[8] However, the Crocker drawing must represent Carpaccio's studies of the small central section of a larger design, if the differently proportioned Gambarata painting indicates the original dimensions of the canvas it replaces. A drawing by Carpaccio in the British Museum (fig. 8) which bears the seventeenth-century collector Padre Resta's identification as the Port of Ancona may represent another section of the same larger design, as noted by the Tietzes and by Popham and Pouncey.[9] Though Pignatti once proposed a date of *c.* 1500 for the drawing on the basis of style,[10] it seems to this writer most logical to remain with a date of between 1507, when Carpaccio is documented as involved in the Sala del Maggior Consiglio project, and 1511, when his letter to the Marquis of Mantua mentions the completion of the "*historia del Ancona*."[11]   WB

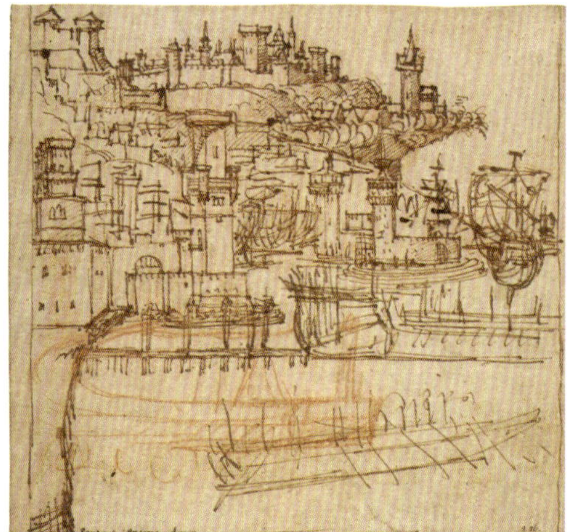

Verso of cat. no. 1

FIGURE 8 Vittore Carpaccio, *A Fortified Harbor with Shipping*, n. d. Pen and dark brown ink, red chalk, 17.2 × 19.1 cm. British Museum, London

2. **Fra Bartolommeo**, *Angel Playing a Lute*, n. d.

Black and white chalks on beige laid paper, squared in red and black chalks,
36.5 × 26.1 cm. Crocker Art Museum, E. B. Crocker Collection 1871.221

INSCRIPTIONS: dark-brown ink, lower left: *22*; secondary support, verso, black chalk, lower margin: *Fra: Bartolomeo*

MARKS: lower left corner: Lugt 2445 (Lawrence)

PROVENANCE: Sir Thomas Lawrence, London, before 1830; Edwin Bryant Crocker, Sacramento, by 1871; gift of his widow Margaret to the Museum, 1885

LITERATURE: Breazeale 2008, pp. 210, 215; Davidson 1982, no. 9; Reno 1978, no. 12; Crocker 1971, no. 9; Bohr 1958, no. 16; Alfred Neumeyer, "Fra Bartolomeo," *Old Master Drawings*, vol. XIII, June 1938–March 1939, p. 61

THOUGH PERHAPS LESS KNOWN than those he influenced, Fra Bartolommeo is a key figure in Florentine art at the turn of the sixteenth century. Acutely aware of the work of fellow artists across Italy, he both synthesized elements of their styles and constantly invented new forms and techniques. Among his innovations, a new type of *sacra conversazione* altarpiece, enlivened by the expression and gesture of those reacting to the central event, and the use of black chalk in drawings to capture the *sfumato* he had observed in Leonardo, had revolutionary and long-lasting effects. In this drawing of an *Angel playing a Lute*, Fra Bartolommeo employs expressive black chalk in a figure for his type of *sacra conversazione*, providing an instructive example of both.

Of humble origins, Baccio della Porta, as the artist was originally known, was first apprenticed to the painter Cosimo Rosselli in 1485 but seems to have learned more about technique from Piero di Cosimo, active in the same workshop. He was also in contact with other Florentine workshops, beginning a lifetime of observation and imitation of the best of other masters. Setting up shop with Mariotto Albertinelli, another Rosselli assistant, certainly before 1497, he was given the commission for a fresco of the Last Judgment for the hospital of Santa Maria Nuova, left unfinished in 1500 when he took Dominican orders. He resumed painting in 1504 and captured major commissions, including an altarpiece with the *Vision of Saint Bernard*, an altarpiece for the Cathedral of Lucca, and works for the monastery of San Marco, in sporadic association with Albertinelli. The most significant of these commissions, an altarpiece for the Great Council Hall in the Palazzo della Signoria in Florence in 1510, he left unfinished. Trips to Venice and Rome added the influence of artists like Giovanni Bellini and the mature Raphael to his fertile innovations. He died in 1517.

The Crocker *Angel with a Lute* shows well the possibilities of Fra Bartolommeo's pioneering work in the medium of black chalk, from the sharp, linear strokes defining the filmy undergarment to the bold upper contours of the beautifully textured wings, to the carefully modulated smoothness of the flesh. The angel's garment, of a type known to the artist from Botticelli and Filippino Lippi, is carefully highlighted in white chalk, a technique developed from the method of chiaroscuro drapery study he knew from Leonardo. Indecision as to the angle of heads seems to have plagued the artist occasionally, since drawings in the Boymans[1] and the Uffizi[2] share the superimposed solutions seen here.

Having entered the collection as the work of Fra Bartolommeo, the drawing was proposed by Alfred Neumeyer as a study for the music-making angel in the altarpiece for the Cathedral of Lucca, also known as the *Madonna del Santuario*, of 1509.[3] This proposal has great merit, since the distinctive angle of the legs and wings are extremely close. It is worth noting, however, that the present drawing is unlikely to represent Fra Bartolommeo's final resolution–even though it is squared for transfer in both red and black chalk similarly to a drawing in Rotterdam[4]–since in the painting the costume is

NOTES
1. Vol. N 77.
2. Inv. no. 396F verso.
3. Neumeyer 1939, as above. In addition to the opinions above, Philip Pouncey confirmed the attribution in a visit of November 1, 1983 (note in Crocker curatorial files).
4. Vol. N 65.

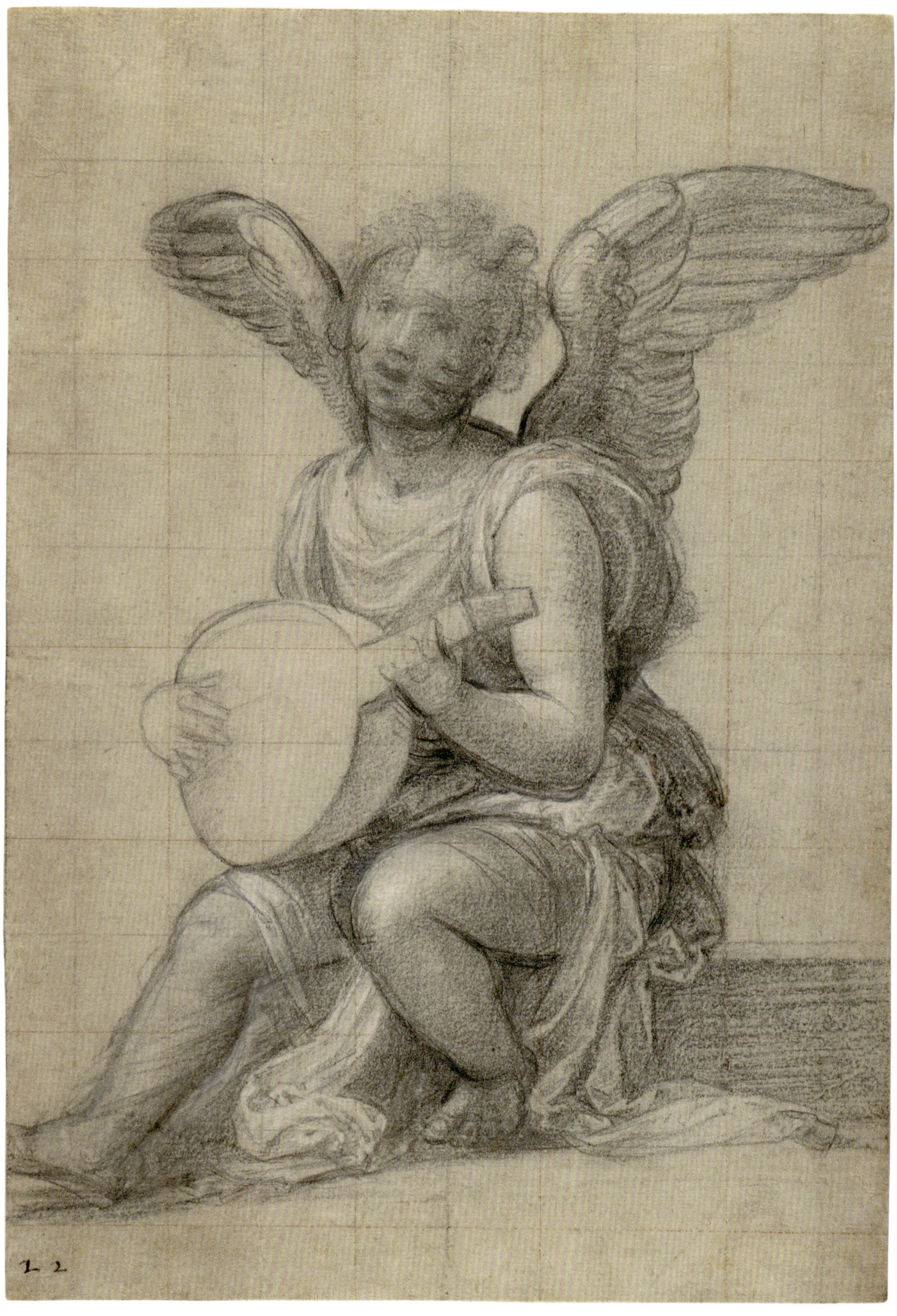

5. Chris Fischer, "Fra Bartolomeo als Zeichner," in *Zeichnungen aus der Toskana, das Zeitalter Michelangelos*, exh. cat. Saarland Museum; Munich 1997, pp. 33–35.

different, the position of the head differs from both those in the drawing, the figure does not lean forward, and the age appears younger. Moreover, a nearly identical angel plays a lute at the base of the steps in the *Mystic Marriage of Saint Catherine* or Pala Pitti of 1512-13. The angle of the head and the position of the hands are again changed.

Thanks to the long and thorough work of Chris Fischer, Fra Bartolommeo is known to have kept drawings in his studio for later use, the same figures being used several years apart and habitually transferred to one or more intermediary cartoons rather than directly to the prepared painting surface.[5] To this writer, the Crocker *Angel Playing a Lute* most likely represents a preliminary figure drawing, perhaps even one embellished from the waxen lay figures used by the artist, that was kept in the studio to be used with changes for many such figures in *sacre conversazioni*. As such, and given the archaizing drapery, it may date from even before 1509, its first known use.   WB

3. **Federico Barocci**, *Head of an Elderly Man*, n. d.

Black and white chalks and flesh-colored and ochre chalks on greyish-blue laid paper, 25.3 × 20.5 cm. Crocker Art Museum, E. B. Crocker Collection 1871.234

INSCRIPTIONS: dark-brown ink, lower right corner: *Barroche Ecole Romaine*; brown ink, lower right corner: *8966*

MARKS: lower right corner: Lugt 2951 (Dezallier d'Argenville, listed as Crozat in Lugt)

PROVENANCE: Antoine-Joseph Dezallier d'Argenville, Paris, before 1762; his sale, Rémy, Paris, 18-28 January 1779, part of lot 58; possibly Rudolph Weigel, Leipzig, by 1860;[1] Edwin Bryant Crocker, Sacramento, by 1871; gift of his widow Margaret to the Museum, 1885

LITERATURE: Breazeale 2008, p. 223; Jacqueline Labbé and Lise Bicart-Sée, *La collection de dessins d'Antoine-Joseph Dezallier d'Argenville*, Paris, 1996, no. 80; Edmund P. Pillsbury and Louise S. Richards, *The Graphic Art of Federico Barocci, Selected Drawings and Prints*, exh. cat. Cleveland and Yale, 1978, no. 57; Crocker 1971, no. 25; Vitzthum 1970, no. 9; Crocker 1959, no. 2; Bohr 1958, no. 14

NOTES
1. Rudolf Weigel, *Kunstlagerkatalog*, Leipzig, 1837-66, no. 3175 ("Männlicher Kopf, in farbigen Kreiden") may refer to this object: see Breazeale 2008 for this dealer and the Crocker collection (this object p. 223).

FEDERICO BAROCCI's importance to the history of art in the sixteenth century is belied by the relatively small number of his drawings in American collections and the complete absence of religious paintings, his most important output. This drawing, one of the first to enter an American public collection, captures well Barocci's renowned facility and expression in black, white and colored chalks. Related to a religious subject, it once belonged to the eminent French collector Dezallier d'Argenville.

Though many of its members were craftsmen, Barocci's family was well-placed. The artist's great-uncle, a sculptor, had come to Urbino from Milan to work for the ducal family, while Barocci's father and uncle were a maker of scientific instruments and a mathematician respectively. Apprenticed to the Venetian artist Battista Franco, the young Federico soon travelled to Pesaro to study perspective under Guidobaldo II della Rovere's architect Bartolomeo Genga, another of his uncles. In Pesaro he came to know the Titians in the ducal collection, while an early trip to Rome took him to stay with yet a third uncle, the head of the della Rovere cardinal's household. Even though he spent the next four years in Urbino, Barocci's reputation in Rome was such that he was called back to the city in 1560 to work on the Casino of Pius IV in the Vatican gardens. Upon completion of the decoration three years later he was struck down by an illness—perhaps poisoned by those jealous of his skill and advantages—which kept him in pain, and in Urbino, for the rest of his life. Nonetheless, he managed to have a fruitful and remunerative career based in the provincial city. His best-known works include the *Madonna di San Simone* for the church of San Francesco in Urbino and the glorious *Deposition* in Perugia, both of the late 1560s, the *Madonna della Gatta* of 1574 now in London, and the *Madonna del Popolo* of 1579, while the 1580s and 1590s brought a variety of commissions from outside Urbino, including a *Circumcision* for the confraternity of the Nome di Gesù in Pesaro. Barocci died in 1612.

2. Vitzthum 1970, as above.

3. Albertina, inv. no. 555; see Veronika Birke and Janine Kertész, *Die italienischen Zeichnungen der Albertina, Generalverzeichnis*, 4 vols., Vienna, Cologne and Colmar, 1992, vol. I, *sub voce*.

4. Pillsbury 1978, as above, p. 81.

5. Inv. no. 2849; see Nicholas Turner, *Federico Barocci*, Paris, 2001, fig. 29.

6. *Ibidem*, pp. 150–55, esp. p. 152.

Barocci's reputation as a draughtsman is enhanced by his sensitive treatment of heads in many shades of chalk and pastel, most often on tinted paper. In this example, the artist first lays in the clothing and outlines of the skull in black chalk, creating the features instead in red while building up the planes of the cheeks and balding forehead through the use of pinkish, ochre and white chalk, well stumped to create smooth volumes. The hair and beard are a fascinating study in textural variety, especially where the smooth darkness of the cheek is blended with wisps of white.

The drawing, which entered the Crocker collection as the work of Federico Barocci, was identified by Vitzthum in 1970 as a preparatory study for the head of Saint Joseph in the Louvre *Circumcision* of 1590.[2] Joseph's full head of hair in the altarpiece, as well as the existence of a drawing in Vienna showing a version identical to the altarpiece,[3] lent some doubt to the relationship. Explained by Pillsbury in 1978 as part of a series of studies documenting the transformation of Joseph's head from round and balding to thinner and hirsute,[4] the head may be related instead to another project, the *Madonna di San Simone*, for which a chiaroscuro study survives in the Louvre (fig. 9),[5] documenting an unexecuted design with a similar angle for the balding Joseph's head. If this association is correct, the drawing would date twenty years earlier, to the late 1560s.

However, regarded independently from Barocci's painted work, the Crocker drawing does not seem to be a study at all. A fully formed head placed before an indeterminate background, the drawing fits well into the category of auxiliary cartoon— a drawing made only after the full cartoon was finished—discussed recently and lucidly by Nicholas Turner.[6] As such it may possibly be independent both of the Louvre *Circumcision*, for which the Vienna drawing is not a study but rather the relevant auxiliary cartoon, and the *Madonna di San Simone*, recording a lost composition that used the same distinctive placement of the head.

WB

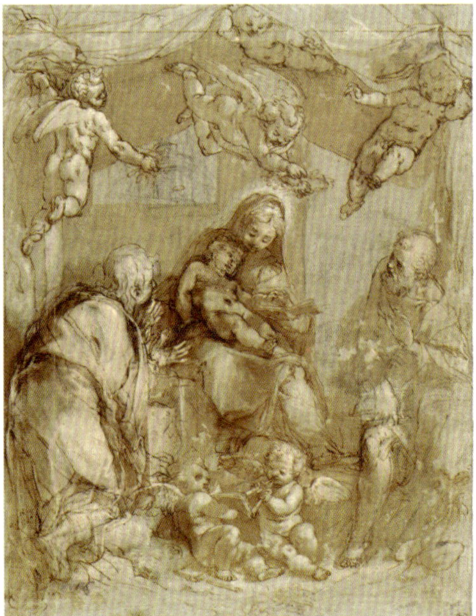

FIGURE 9 Federico Barocci, *Study for the Madonna di San Simone*, n. d. Pen and dark brown ink, brush and brown washes and white opaque watercolor on greyish-green paper faded from blue, 31 × 24 cm. Musée du Louvre, Paris

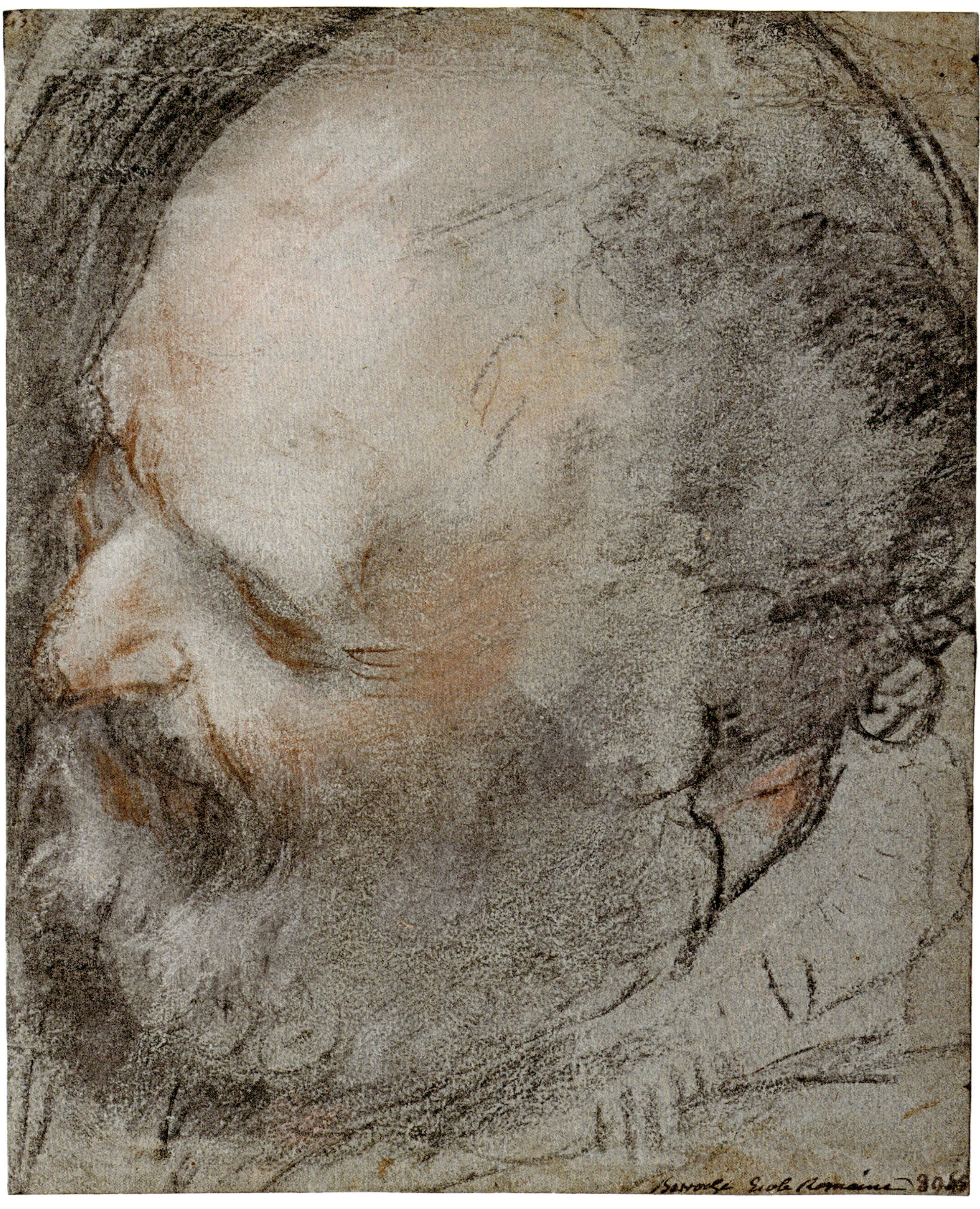

Barocci Ecole Romaine 30

4. **Domenico Campagnola**, *The Presentation of the Virgin*, n. d.

Pen and dark brown ink, black ink, 25.3 × 21.4 cm.
Crocker Art Museum, E. B. Crocker Collection 1871.1116

INSCRIPTIONS: verso, black chalk,
lower left: *…ssarotti; Maria im Tempel /
Tizian* [illegible]; verso, black chalk, lower
right corner: B

MARKS: lower right corner: Lugt 2092
(Lely)

PROVENANCE: Sir Peter Lely, before
1680; Edwin Bryant Crocker, Sacramento,
by 1871; gift of his widow Margaret to the
Museum, 1885

LITERATURE: Ruda 1992, no. 38; Crocker
1971, checklist p. 168

DOMENICO CAMPAGNOLA (1500–1564) belonged to a Venetian printmaking family. Originally born to a German artisan living in Venice, Domenico was adopted by Giulio Campagnola, under whom he received his first artistic training. He must have absorbed much from Giorgione in early years as well, for many of his first independent works, drawings predating his group of prints of 1517–18, share in the pastoral mystery of this artist's *poesie*—especially Domenico's *Landscape with Two Youths* in the British Museum.[1] The prints, on the other hand, show a more independent mind at work.

Domenico moved from Venice to Padua in the 1520s, being documented in the latter city in 1528. Though he has long been thought to have contributed to the frescoes in the Scoletta del Carmine, completed by 1520, doubts have emerged regarding this commission.[2] In Padua, Domenico worked more often as a painter than as a printmaker, it seems, and contributed to many of the fresco cycles underway in the city in addition to executing individual canvases. Nonetheless, his drawings and woodcuts of the 1530s and 1540s show strong and continuing development especially in regard to landscape. His best-known paintings include the *Holy Family with Saint John the Baptist* now in Bologna and the *Madonna with Saints George and Catherine of Alexandria* now in Philadelphia, both of 1533–35, the frescoes in the Sala dei Giganti in the Palazzo del Capitanio of 1540–41, and the frescoes of the Oratorio di San Bovo of 1550–55. In 1564 he received a religious commission as prestigious as the governmental one for the Capitanio—for two paintings for the sacristy of Padua's cathedral–but died on 10 December before it was well underway.

Among sixteenth-century Venetian draughtsmen, Domenico's style is distinctive for its linearity. As befits his early training under a printmaker, the artist preferred pen and ink almost exclusively, gradually leaving behind the Giorgionism of his early years in favor of precision and careful, studied hatching, as in the present drawing. This increasing boldness, perhaps less evident in his landscape drawings, comes through most of all in figural compositions placed in architectural settings.

The Crocker *Presentation of the Virgin* fits well with Domenico's later style exemplified in a series of drawings of the Life of Christ in Berlin and elsewhere.[3] In each case the group of figures is given legibility by its rhythmic integration into a boldly defined architectural setting. Here, the entire action is traced by the line of figures that ascends from Joachim and Anna up the staircase, given impetus by the Virgin's step, the drape of the attendant figure, and the welcome of the priest above.

Domenico's composition compresses Titian's horizontal canvas of the *Presentation of the Virgin* completed for the Scuola Grande della Carità in 1534–38, focusing the composition to the staircase itself and moving the attendant figures from the square Titian creates at its foot to distribute them along the Virgin's path upwards. The resulting sequence of heads and bodies creates a dynamic rhythm, a device Domenico had used as early as 1518 in his print of the *Massacre of the Innocents*.[4] Though many other possible precedents use the general device of a staircase seen diagonally, none shares the

NOTES

1. Inv. no. 1895-9-15-836.
2. Charles Hope, "The Attributions of Some Paduan Paintings of the Early Sixteenth Century," *Artibus et historiae*, vol. XVIII, no. 35, 1997, pp. 81–99, at pp. 85–90.
3. Kupferstichkabinett inv. nos. 432, 5147; Christie's, London July 3, 1984, lot 5.
4. Bartsch 3.

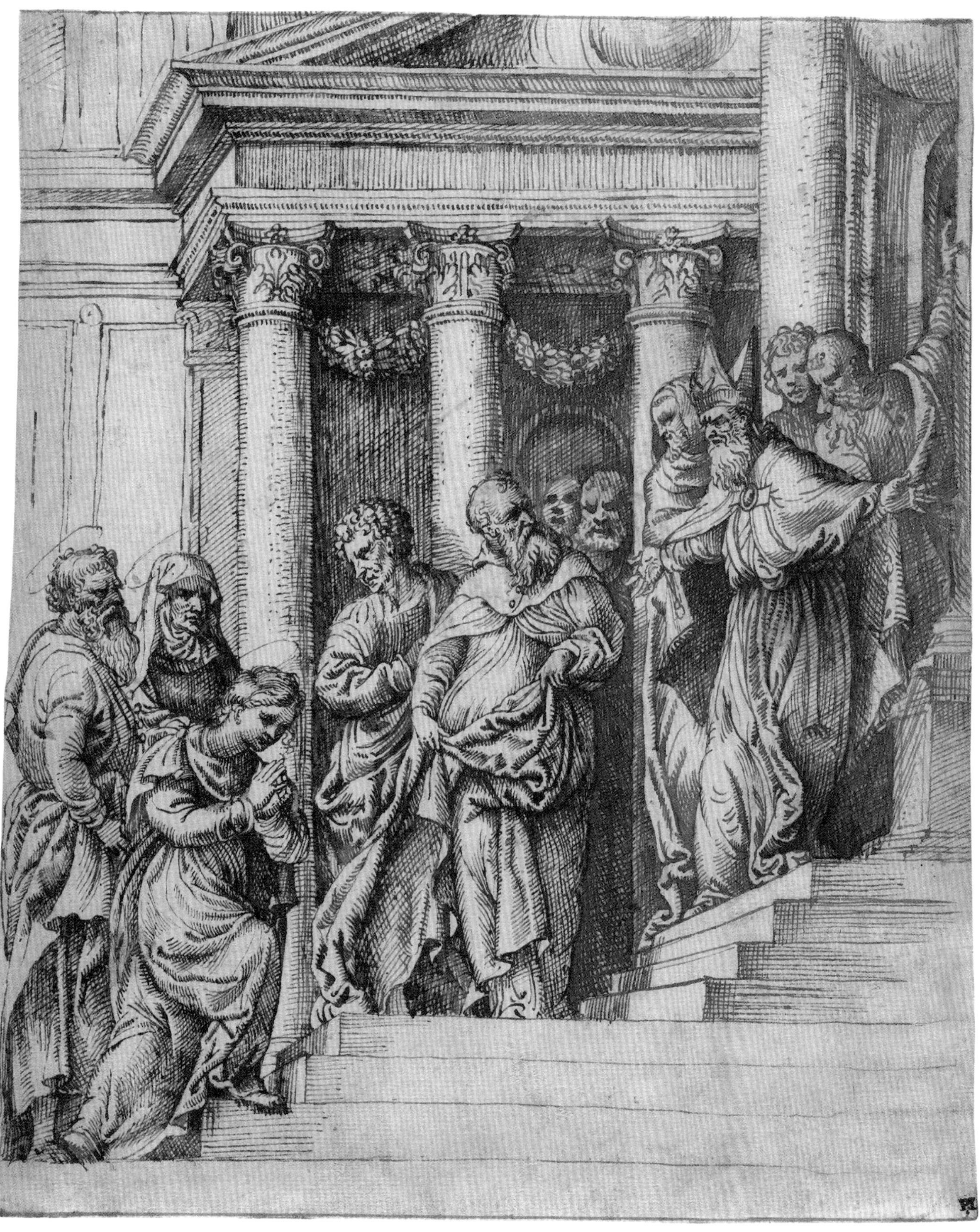

5. Ruda 1992, as above.

combination of a landing with three Corinthian columns seen directly behind found in Titian's canvas. Given this relationship, it seems most logical to date the drawing to after 1538, the date of the Carità project's completion.

The Crocker drawing, which belonged to the seventeenth-century Dutch collector and English court painter Peter Lely, bears later ascriptions to Titian and "…ssarotti," most likely the Bolognese Bartolomeo Passarotti, who shared with Campagnola a boldly hatched pen-and-ink style. Though the evidence for this is no longer in the Museum's curatorial files, Ruda reports that the drawing entered the collection as School of Titian and was first identified as Domenico Campagnola by Alfred Neumeyer.[5] The *Presentation* seems to have been unknown to the Tietzes, although they published six other Venetian drawings from the Crocker collection.   WB

5. Giacomo Franco (?), *Musicians in a Gondola*, n. d.

Pen and dark-brown ink, brush and brown washes, 22.6 × 17.2 cm.
Crocker Art Museum, E. B. Crocker Collection 1871.333

INSCRIPTIONS: none

MARKS: none

PROVENANCE: Edwin Bryant Crocker, Sacramento, by 1871; gift of his widow Margaret to the Museum, 1885

LITERATURE: Denys Sutton, "Sunlight and Movement: Splendours of Venetian Draughtsmanship", *Apollo*, vol. C, no. 152, October 1974, pp. 278–81; Pignatti 1974, no. 29, as Giacomo Franco; Crocker 1971, checklist p. 164, as Toeput; Trivas 1940a, no. 5, as 16th-century Venetian

GIACOMO FRANCO (1550-1620) engraved and published many works having to do with Venetian culture and tradition, especially towards the end of his life. Functioning as much as a publisher as a printmaker, he nevertheless preferred to be known as a "*desegnador*" or draughtsman, as in his will. In this drawing he captures a unique aspect of Venetian life as a young couple, witnessed by a *gondoliere* thankful for his rest, stops for a musical interlude far from the grandeur of the Piazza San Marco or the Grand Canal.

The illegitimate son of the painter and printmaker Battista Franco, Giacomo likely received his first training from his father before working for Cornelis Cort after 1565. His activity as a free-lance printmaker is attested by his many engravings published by others before he began his own book-publishing enterprise in 1595 at his father's address. This does not seem to have been his first ambition, since he never joined the guild of printers and booksellers. Even so, he is only documented in the perhaps more prestigious painters' guild in 1606. His most important works include eleven engravings for the first illustrated edition of Tasso's *Gerusalemme Liberata*, in 1590, on which he worked with Agostino Carracci, both interpreting drawings by the Genoese artist Bernardo Castello. His activity as a publisher, though varied, seems to have had a practical bent, including maps, books on penmanship, and records of ceremonial events. In 1611, his long history of collaboration with the artist Jacopo Palma il Giovane culminated in *De excellentia et nobilitate delineationis*, an illustrated manual for students of drawing.

The close collaboration between Giacomo and Palma Giovane, and their drawings' similarities with those of a third artist working in Venice, Lodewijk Toeput called Pozzoserrato, have led to difficulties when it comes to certain moments in their careers. In the case of the Crocker drawing, one of these points comes forward since, as Terisio Pignatti made clear, the female figure is related to the *Donna che sona di lauto*, a plate from

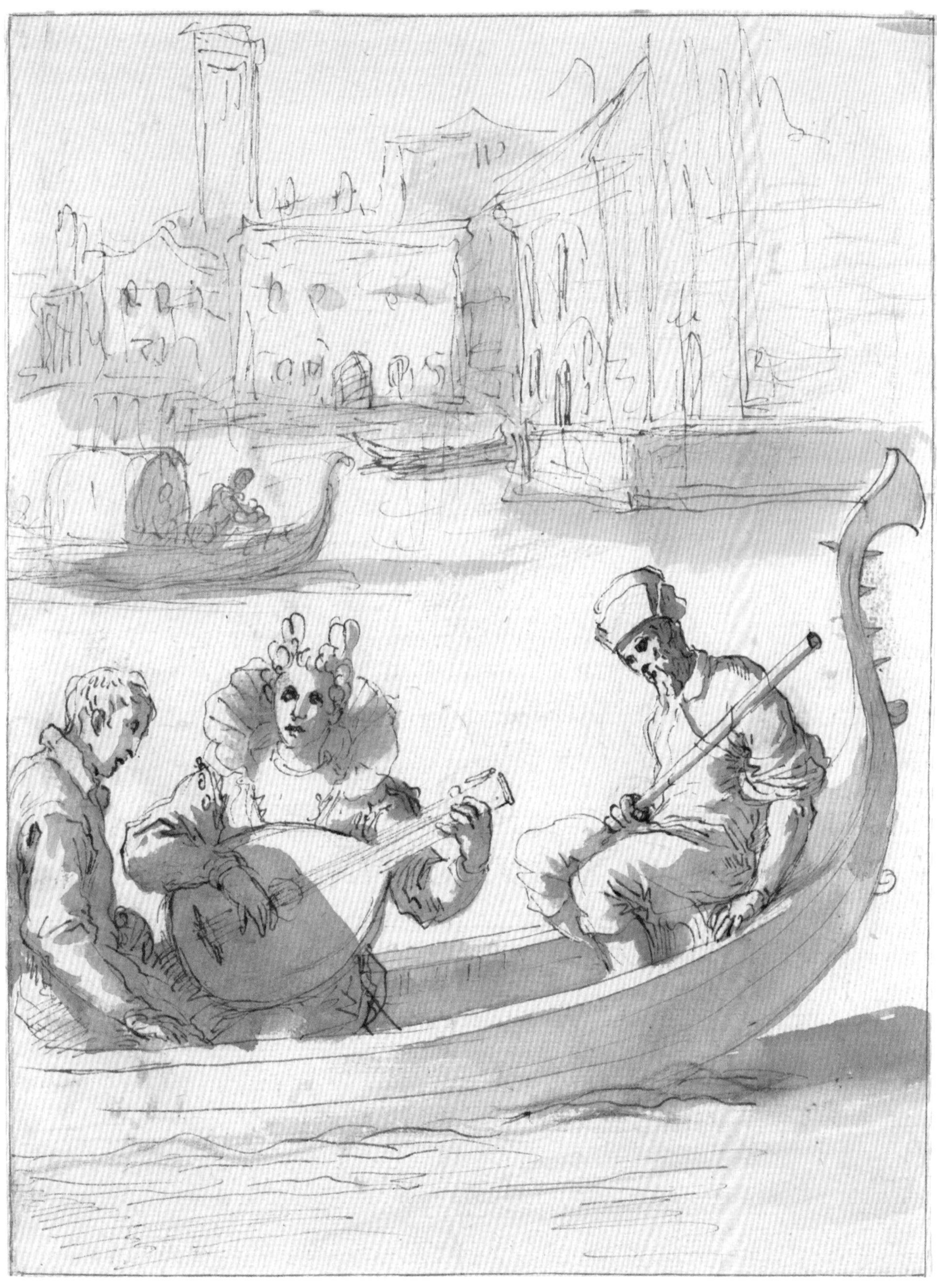

NOTES

1. *Habiti delle donne venetiane intagliate in rame nuouamente*, Venice, 1609.

the *Habiti delle donne venetiane* of 1609 for which both Franco and Palma designed plates.[1] Details of hair and costume, the winged coiffure, starched collar, and sleeves are similar, though the angle of the head differs and the setting is an interior scene. The words *Franco format* appear at the lower left of the engraving, making clear that the younger artist cut the plate.

Rather than being a close study of costume, however, the Crocker drawing represents a casual, charming vignette. It seems that this entertainment may not be entirely innocent, since the simply dressed man at left is not the grand "*sposo*" seen in Franco's other prints and courtesans were allowed to travel in gondolas with faces uncovered. The setting in one of Venice's many byways gives a sense of private enjoyment to the sunlit scene.

The drawing was first identified as Franco by Terisio Pignatti and has been contested among Franco, Palma and Pozzoserrato in the years since. To this writer, it seems best to retain Pignatti's attribution, especially given the relationship to Franco's print, since Palma's figures and Pozzoserrato's buildings do not share the heavy treatment of features and the nervous, graphic penmanship respectively.

WB

6. **Antonio Tempesta**, *Battle Scene*, n. d.

Pen and dark brown ink, brush and brown wash over black chalk, 15.4 × 26.6 cm.
Crocker Art Museum, E. B. Crocker Collection 1871.306

INSCRIPTIONS: black ink, bottom margin right: B.F. [cancelled]

MARKS: none

PROVENANCE: Edwin Bryant Crocker, Sacramento, by 1871; gift of his widow Margaret to the Museum, 1885

LITERATURE: Robbin et al. 2004, p. 40; Ruda 1992, no. 4; Crocker 1971, checklist p. 174; Bohr 1958, no. 157

OF HUMBLE ORIGIN, Antonio Tempesta was a pupil of Giovanni Stradano, the Flemish artist who collaborated with Giorgio Vasari on frescoes in Florence's Palazzo Vecchio, and later participated in the decoration himself. The experience of the triumphal frescoes in the Salone dei Cinquecento perhaps gave him the taste for the battle scenes for which he became renowned in later years. A member of the Accademia del Disegno in Florence from 1576, by that date he had already begun commissions for Roman patrons including Pope Gregory XIII, for whom he frescoed parts of the Vatican Loggie in the company of Matthijs Bril. In the late 1570s and early 1580s he decorated rooms in the country retreats of members of the papal court, returning to the city in

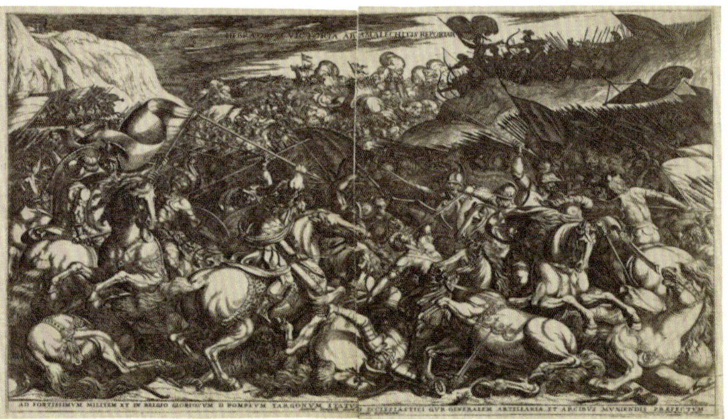

FIGURE 10 After Antonio Tempesta, *Battle of the Israelites and Amalekites*, 1609. Etching and engraving on two sheets, 50.8 × 79.9 cm. San Francisco, Achenbach Foundation for the Graphic Arts

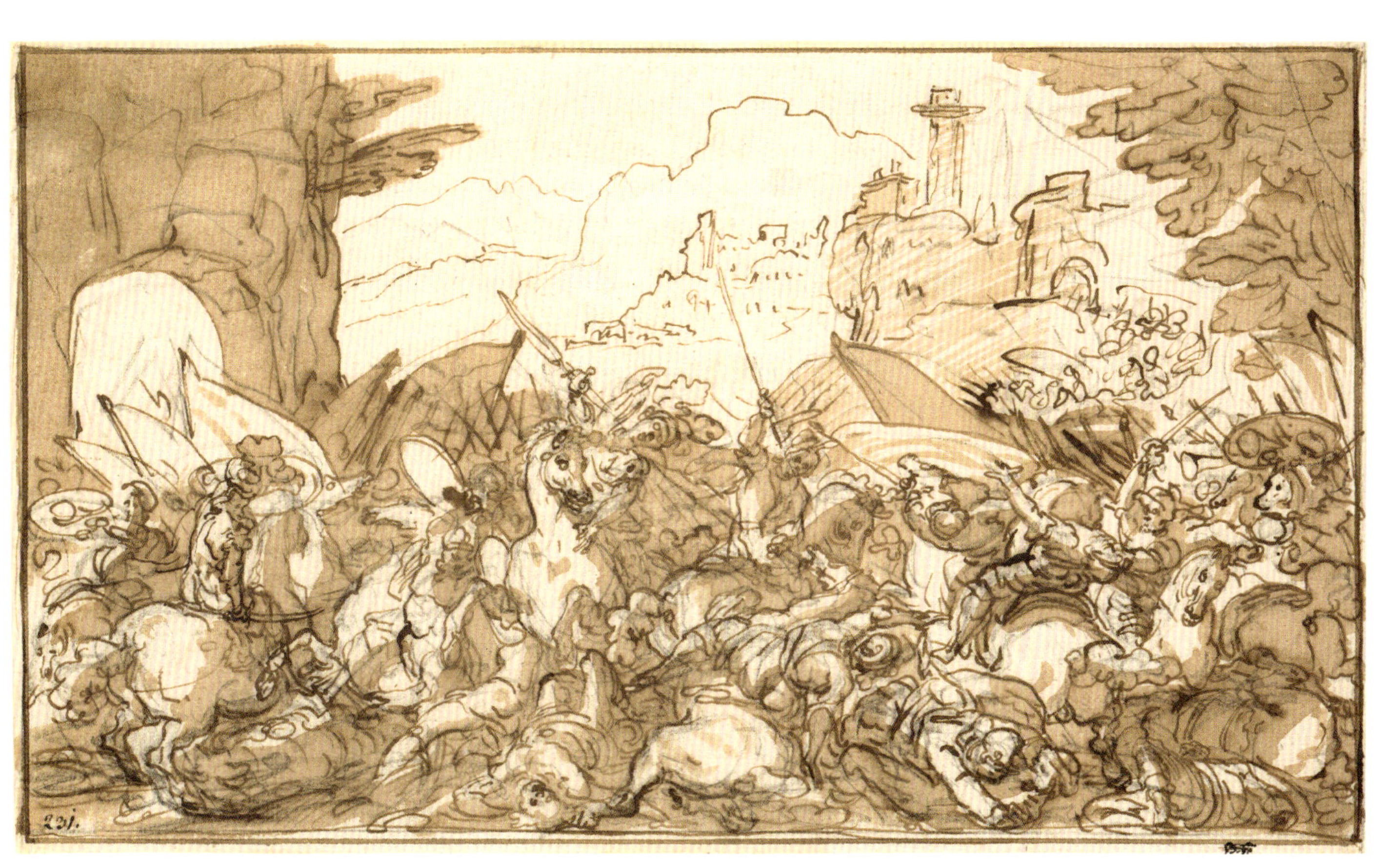

NOTES

1. Eckhard Leuschner, *Antonio Tempesta, ein Bahnbrecher des römischen Barock und seine europäische Wirkung*, Petersberg, 2005, p. 613.

2. Michael Bury, "Antonio Tempesta as Printmaker: Invention, drawing, and technique," in *Drawing 1400–1600, Invention and Innovation*, ed. Stuart Currie, Aldershot, 1998, pp. 189–205; Leuschner as in note 1 above.

3. Bartsch 234 (128), this impression San Francisco, Achenbach Foundation for the Graphic Arts, inv. no. 1963.30.36459-60.

4. Keith Andrews, *Catalogue of Italian Drawings, National Gallery of Scotland*, London, 1968, cat. and inv. no. D788.

5. Nicholas Turner, *Florentine Drawings of the Sixteenth Century*, London, 1986, no. 170, inv. no. 1946-7-13-535.

1583 to fresco walls and a chapel in the church of Santo Stefano Rotondo. From the late 1580s, however, his energies were directed towards panel paintings and, more importantly, prints, of which he made over a thousand before his death in 1630. Well-respected as examples for other artists, his *invenzioni* brought him membership in the Accademia dei Virtuosi al Pantheon and in the Accademia di San Luca late in his career.

"*All'occhio dei poco pratici appariscono strapazzati, confusi e del tutto informi*" (To inexperienced eyes they appear scrambled, confused and wholly without form).[1] Thus Filippo Baldinucci described Tempesta's drawings, while praising the depth of knowledge they transmitted to artists and connoisseurs. Though criticized for intermittent lighting in his prints, Tempesta nonetheless earned esteem for the visual variety he brought to his multi-figured compositions, especially battle scenes, and for his unique facility in depicting horses naturally from all angles and in all poses. For some time the perceived crudeness of some of his prints overshadowed the intellectual skill with which they and his frescoes were composed, though Michael Bury and Eckhard Leuschner have done much to reassess the importance of his *oeuvre*.[2]

In the case of Tempesta's drawings themselves, the preponderance of battle scenes and his often hard line have led to a somewhat one-sided view of his draughtsmanship. The Crocker drawing, however, is an exception: the open, gestural style and the skill with which the artist manipulates the masses of clashing horses and men in a still-legible whole go beyond their ultimate expression in his prints. Here the light, to the left and slightly behind the viewer, is unified; here too the legible jumble of chalk, ink and wash in the foreground contrasts with the spare lines that characterize the landscape beyond. Tempesta's *invenzione* is given shape by the compositional devices of arch and tree that channel the clash of armies winding back to the besieged fortress in the distance, armies themselves puncuated by soldiers falling almost into the viewer's space, rearing horses, and pikes and flags bristling in every direction. Tempesta's prints of battles rarely approach this complexity, since they are often part of narrative series requiring a visual hierarchy to distinguish the various characters.

A useful point of reference is the *Battle of the Amalekites and Israelites* print of 1613 (fig. 10).[3] Two drawings are related to the composition, one now in the National Gallery of Scotland.[4] Based on similarities with the warrior in left foreground attacked by a sword-wielding horseman, a second drawing now in the British Museum was proposed by Nicholas Turner.[5] The Crocker drawing, looser in execution than either of these, shares with both drawings the rearing horse at lower left serving as a repoussoir (seen in the print at right) and, a little closer to center, the supine warrior, while a prone figure at right appears in the same direction as in the print.

Given Tempesta's habitual reuse of certain motifs in his battle scenes, it is hazardous to propose the Crocker drawing as an early preparatory drawing for the *Battle of the Amalekites and Israelites*. To this writer it represents an *invenzione*, elaborated in part from motifs the artist found effective, which perhaps remained unused because of its visual complexity. It seems best, nevertheless, to date the drawing to the mid teens of the seventeenth century, close to the print with which it shares motifs.　　WB

7. **Agostino Ciampelli,** *The Visitation,* n. d.

Pen and dark brown ink, brush and brown washes and white opaque watercolor, partially darkened, on greenish-blue laid paper, 38.4 × 26.2 cm. Crocker Art Museum, E. B. Crocker Collection 1871.323

INSCRIPTIONS: dark-brown ink, lower right corner: *Agostino Ciampelli*

MARKS: none

PROVENANCE: Edwin Bryant Crocker, Sacramento, by 1871; gift of his widow Margaret to the Museum, 1885

LITERATURE: Breazeale 2008, p. 222; Milan Togner, *Agostino Ciampelli 1565–1630, Disegni,* Olomouc, 2000, no. B69, and under no. B64-65; Ruda 1992, no. 43; Simonetta Prosperi Valenti Rodinò, in *Dizionario Biografico degli Italiani,* Rome, 1960– (1982), *sub voce* Ciampelli, Agostino, p. 125; Christel Thiem, *Florentiner Zeichner des Frühbarock,* Munich, 1977, p. 309; Simonetta Prosperi Valenti Rodinò, *Disegni fiorentini 1560-1640,* exh. cat. Gabinetto Nazionale delle Stampe, Rome, 1977, under no. 68; Moir *et al.* 1977, no. 25; Simonetta Prosperi Valenti, "Ancora su Agostino Ciampelli disegnatore," *Antichità Viva,* vol. XII, no. 2, 1973, p. 9; Christel Thiem, "The Florentine Agostino Ciampelli as a Draughtsman," *Master Drawings,* vol. IX, no. 4, Winter 1971, pp. 362–63; Crocker 1971, no. 37; Vitzthum 1970, no. 24; Bohr 1958, no. 49

NOTES
1. Julian Brooks, *Graceful and True: Drawing in Florence c. 1600,* intr. by Catherine Whistler, exh. cat. Ashmolean; Oxford, 2003, p. 26.
2. Milan Togner, "Neznámé kresby Agostina Ciampelliho v olomoucké sbirke," *Umění,* vol. XLVI, nos. 1/2, 1998, pp. 101–08, and idem, *Agostino Ciampelli 1565-1630, Kresby,* exh. cat. Múzeum Umění; Olomouc, 2000, also published in Italian as Togner 2000 above.
3. Maria Cristina Terzaghi, "Bernini padre, figlio e cognato, nuovi dati ed aperture," in *Decorazione e collezionismo a Roma nel Seicento,* ed. Francesca Cappelletti, Rome, 2003, pp. 101–06.

THOUGH HE FREQUENTLY drew from life during his training, in his early career the Florentine artist Agostino Ciampelli often harked back to the tradition of elongated and stylized figures that was fading as reforms took hold in the city's artistic community. The Crocker *Visitation* exemplifies this period: combining elegant, almost Mannerist figures with clear storytelling antithetical to Mannerism itself, it preserves a moment not only of Ciampelli's career but also of the Florentine reform at the turn of the seventeenth century.

Agostino Ciampelli, born to a cobbler in 1565, trained under Santi di Tito, the Florentine Reform artist whose studio Julian Brooks has called the city's "real engine-room of life-drawing."[1] He entered the Accademia del Disegno in 1585, which led to Ciampelli's first court comission in 1586, a frescoed frieze for the Tribuna of the Uffizi, now destroyed. By 1594 he had secured the patronage of Alessandro de' Medici, the archbishop of Florence. After frescoing two rooms in the archbishop's palace in Florence, Ciampelli was called to Rome in late 1594 when his patron became a cardinal. His simple and direct narrative style, in the spirit of the reforms proposed by the Council of Trent, meant that he played a major part in the cardinal's renovation of the Church of the Lateran for the jubilee of 1600. The election of Alessandro de' Medici as pope in 1605 ironically led to Ciampelli's eclipse, as the pope was dead within three weeks. A new Florentine connection, the new pope's protégé Marcello Sacchetti, raised Ciampelli's fortunes again: by 1623 he was *principe* of the Accademia di San Luca and soon working on the renovation of the church of Santa Bibiana with Gian Lorenzo Bernini. The pinnacle of his career were his commissions at Saint Peter's for the Tuscan pope Urban VIII Barberini, who made him Soprastante alla Fabbrica di San Pietro alongside Bernini in 1629. Already failing in health, Ciampelli died the following year.

Recent scholarship by Milan Togner and Maria Cristina Terzaghi will continue to change our view of Ciampelli as a draughtsman and historical figure. Togner's 1998 discovery of sixty previously unknown drawings by the artist in the State Science Library in Olomouc in the Czech Republic has already helped to assess the artist's working method in his major commissions.[2] Terzaghi's archival work has located Ciampelli in 1609 in the household of his father-in-law Pietro Bernini, recently arrived from Florence.[3] This connection to the eleven-year-old future sculptor Gian Lorenzo Bernini sheds light on their later collaborations and raises the question of their relations during the sculptor's training and the painter's eclipse.

In the Crocker drawing, Ciampelli builds his composition of graceful figures into a legible whole. As Zacharias looks on at left, the Virgin greets the aged Elizabeth, soon to be the mother of John the Baptist. The shadowed space between them provides the background for the real focus of the composition, their joined hands and Elizabeth's gesture of welcome. A triangle of figures reinforces this focus through gesture and glance—Zacharias, the servant at right, and the foreground figure who points while

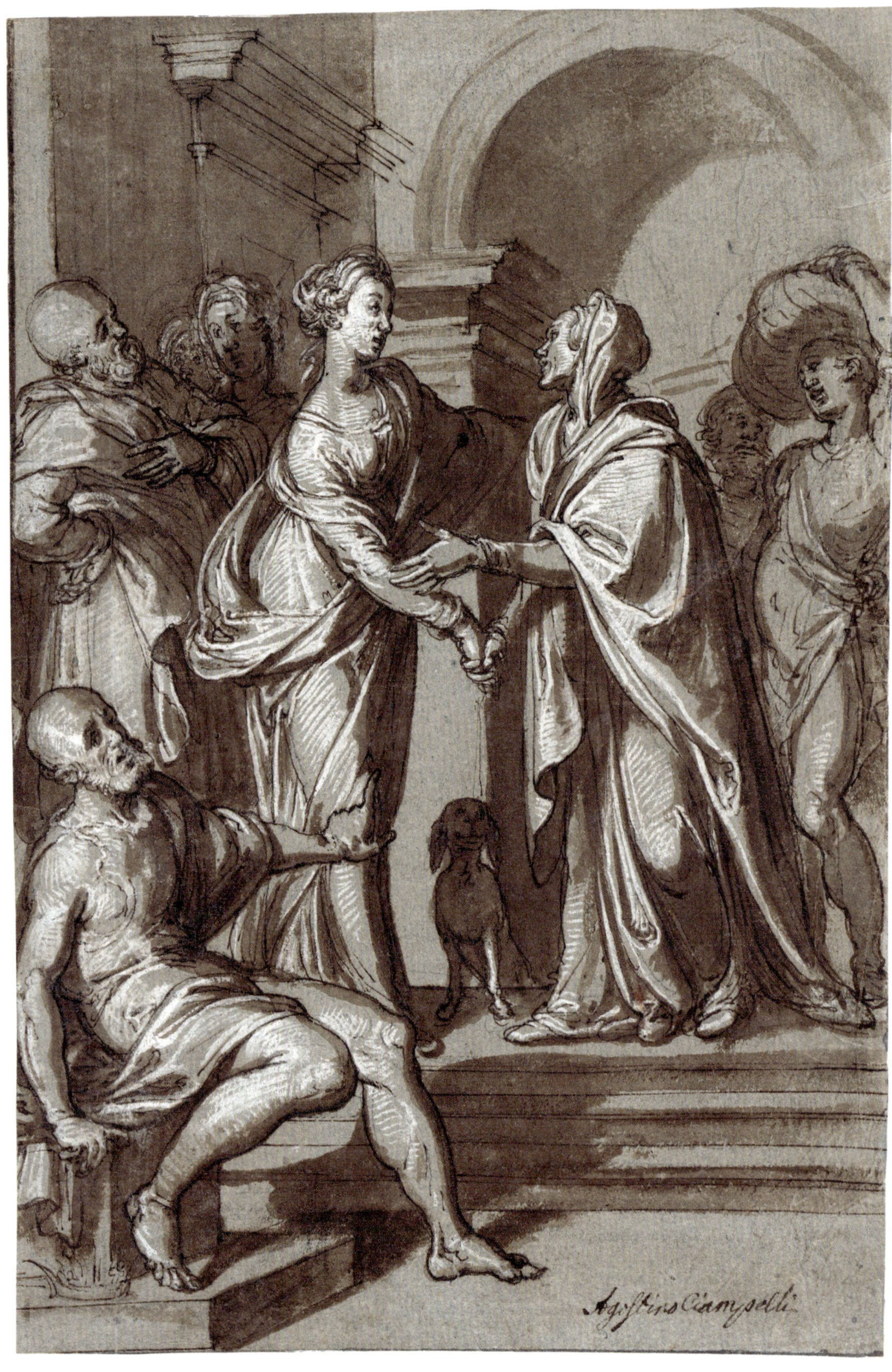

4. Thiem 1971, as above, p. 364 n. 18 and
   plate 5a.
5. Moir 1977, as above.
6. Thiem 1971. as above, pp. 362–63.

addressing the viewer. Even the dog gazes in curiosity. This narrative clarity is supported by Ciampelli's technique with its well-defined light source slightly to the left of the viewer, created with deep washes and shimmering white-lead highlights.

The drawing entered the Crocker collection as the work of Ciampelli. The near-contemporary inscription at lower right seems to share the hand of an inscription on a confirmed drawing in the Uffizi,[4] though the use of short and long s differs. The technique is consonant with Ciampelli's early pen-and-ink style, seen also in a *Christ before Herod* and a *Crowning with Thorns* now in the Gabinetto Nazionale delle Stampe in Rome—first connected with the Crocker *Visitation* by Christel Thiem in 1971. Both of these share as well the format of deep architectural background, side repoussoir figure and mid-ground central action emphasized by lighting. Perhaps because of the difficulty imposed upon stylistic research by the small number of confirmed drawings, the date of the *Visitation* has fluctuated between about 1594[5] and about 1600.[6] Until further assessment of the Olomouc drawings permits a more nuanced view of the artist's development, the present writer prefers the latter, implied by the relationship to the drawings in Rome.
WB

8. Giuseppe Cesari, called il Cavaliere d'Arpino, *Mystic Marriage of Saint Catherine,* n. d.

Black chalk, 22.5 × 16.8 cm. Crocker Art Museum, E. B. Crocker Collection 1871.313

INSCRIPTIONS: verso, black chalk: *Co…tona*

MARKS: none

PROVENANCE: Edwin Bryant Crocker, Sacramento, by 1871; gift of his widow Margaret to the Museum, 1885

LITERATURE: Breazeale 2008, p. 219; Robbin *et al.* 2004, no. 1; Ruda 1992, no. 72; Howard 1984, pp. 353–54; Westins 1981, no. 6; Moir *et al.* 1977, no. 1; Herwarth Röttgen, *Il Cavalier d'Arpino*, exh. cat. Palazzo Venezia; Rome, 1973, p. 85; Crocker 1971, no. 34; Bohr 1958, no. 10

THOUGH HIS ASSISTANT Caravaggio is better known today, at the turn of the seventeenth century Giuseppe Cesari, later known as the Cavaliere d'Arpino, enjoyed the patronage of pope and court, receiving major commissions throughout Rome. His position at the cusp between Mannerism and the Baroque is shown well in this drawing, where the elegance and grace of the sixteenth century are combined with the emotional and narrative clarity of the seventeenth.

Born in 1568 in Arpino, the hill town south-east of Rome, Cesari learned the art of painting from his father before travelling to the papal city in 1582. The fourteen-year-old artist assisted Niccolò Circignani, known as il Pomarancio, with his work on the final stages of the Vatican Loggie decoration and by the following year had received both a regular papal stipend and membership in the Accademia di San Luca. His star rose quickly, so that he soon gained the patronage of Cardinal Alessandro Farnese, for whom he painted frescoes in San Lorenzo in Damaso. Under Pope Clement VIII Aldobrandini (pope 1592–1605) he was favored highly, in 1593 painting the ceiling of the Contarelli chapel in San Luigi dei Francesi (for which Caravaggio, his assistant at the time, later provided the side canvases), as well as the entire Olgiati chapel in San Prassede. In 1599–1600 the artist was honored with the *principato* of the Accademia di San Luca and the papal knighthood that gave him the title of Cavaliere. The pope's death in 1605 ended

NOTES

1. This trial is examined in detail in Lothar Sickel, "Künstlerrivalität in Schatten der Peterskuppel: Giuseppe Cesari d'Arpino und das Attentat auf Cristoforo Roncalli," *Marburger Jahrbuch für Kunstwissenschaft*, vol. XXVIII, 2001, pp. 159–89.

2. This collection forms the core of the present Galleria Borghese.

3. Recorded by Herwarth Röttgen in his entry on the artist for *Saurs Allgemeines Künstlerlexikon*, vol. XVIII, 1998, p. 4.

4. Röttgen 1973, as above.

5. Ibidem; Herwarth Röttgen, *Il Cavaliere Giuseppe Cesari d'Arpino, un pittore nello splendore della fama e nell'incostanza della fortuna*, Rome, 2002, p. 532.

6. Moir *et al.* 1977, as above.

his favor at court, so that by 1607, when he was briefly imprisoned on a weapons charge,[1] Scipione Borghese, the new pope's nephew, seized his collection of 105 paintings.[2] Paul V was not entirely unreachable, however, restoring him to his previous commissions for Saint Peter's by 1608. Over the following decades—though taste was changing around him—Cesari continued to receive commissions from popes and cardinals and was twice more *principe* of the Accademia di San Luca (1615, 1629). He died a highly respected and wealthy artist in 1640.

"[H]a in sé quella vaghezza che in un tratto rapisce l'occhio e diletta" (He has the kind of charm that captures the eye and at the same time fills it with delight).[3] The critic Giulio Mancini's words about Cesari's paintings written in the early seventeeenth century can be applied to the Crocker drawing as well: the composition's focus on the ring draws the viewer's attention, which is then informed by the experience of pleasurable looking as it turns to figures and drapery. Stylistically the sheet fits best with drawings from the artist's early maturity, of which the parallel shading in drapery and background is typical. It seems, however, that the composition may be related to another subject in which Cesari depicted the Child turned outwards, the *Adoration of the Magi* in the Aldobrandini chapel in Santa Maria in Via of 1594–96. Though in the fresco the Child rests on the Virgin's knees rather than on her lap, the turn of her head, her bodice and her glance are nearly identical (fig. 11).

Bearing an inscription to the later seventeenth-century artist Pietro da Cortona, the drawing was first published with relation to Cesari in 1973.[4] It seems that the artist was not satisfied with his original composition, since nearly the entire current figure of Saint Catherine, with the exception of her hand, appears on a second sheet of paper carefully cut to the outline left by its predecessor, both being laid down to a third sheet. The artist was certainly responsible for the change, since the shading lines are broken at the edge of the paper above, while they extend across the edge below.

In 1973, Herwarth Röttgen related the drawing to a *Holy Family* in the Prado which he has since given to Morazzone.[5] Four years later Moir placed the drawing near a panel of the *Mystic Marriage* in Apsley House of uncertain attribution.[6] The drawing itself being certainly from Cesari's hand, to this writer the relationship of the Virgin to the figure in the fresco in S. Maria in Via remains significant. It seems best to date the drawing near that work, between 1594 and 1596, rather than earlier as some authors have preferred.

WB

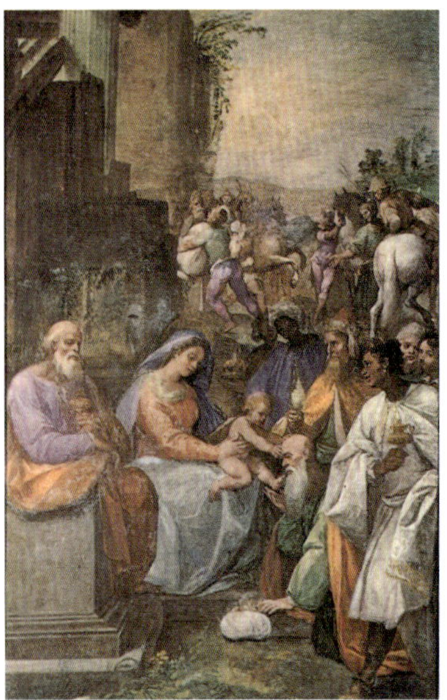

FIGURE 11 Giuseppe Cesari, called il Cavaliere d'Arpino, *Adoration*, 1594–96. Fresco. Santa Maria in Via, Rome

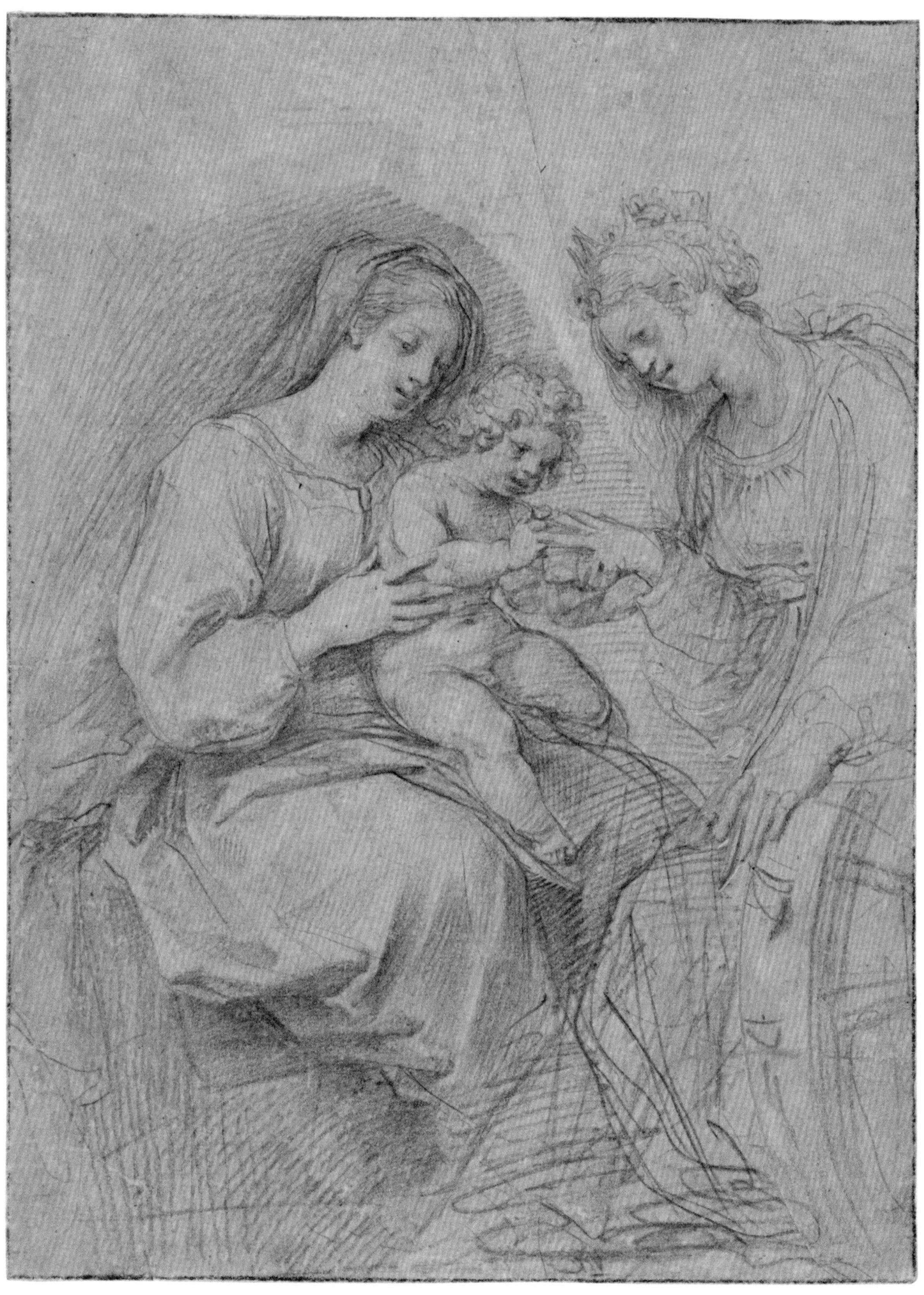

9. **Pier Francesco Mola**, *Christ in the Garden of Gethsemane*, n. d.

Pen and dark-brown ink, brush and brown washes over traces of red chalk, laid down, 25.2 × 20.6 cm.
Crocker Art Museum, E. B. Crocker Collection 1871.245

INSCRIPTIONS: dark-brown ink, lower left corner: *Mola*

MARKS: Lugt 2464a (Johann Jacob Faesch, listed in Lugt as Hugford)

PROVENANCE: Johann Jacob Faesch, Basle, before 1796; Edwin Bryant Crocker, Sacramento, by 1871; gift of his widow Margaret to the Museum, 1885

LITERATURE: Ruda 1992, no. 15; Howard 1984, p. 372; Westins 1981, no. 22; Howard et al. 1976, no. 11; Crocker 1971, checklist p. 158; Rosenberg 1970, p. 37 n. 4; Crocker 1964, pp. 22 and 84; Crocker 1959, no. 10; Bohr 1958, no. 96

NOTES

1. Now in the Metropolitan Museum of Art.
2. In her review of Richard Cocke's monograph, *Art Bulletin*, vol. LVI, no. 2, June 1974, p. 289.
3. Now in the J. Paul Getty Museum.
4. Nicholas Turner, in *Pier Francesco Mola 1612–1666*, exh. cat. Lugano and Rome, pp. 103–20, discusses the artist's technique and subject in detail.
5. Though the evidence does not survive in the Crocker curatorial files, Bohr 1958, as above, records the original mat inscription.
6. Note in the Crocker curatorial files.
7. Ruda 1992, as above.
8. Sonia Brink, *Disegnatore virtuoso, die Zeichnungen des Pier Francesco Mola und seines Kreises*, exh. cat. Düsseldorf, 2002, pp. 108–09.
9. In the Hendricks Collection in Arnhem in 1972; see Richard Cocke, *Pier Francesco Mola*, Oxford, 1972, no. 1, where he discusses the related drawings in Princeton and Haarlem as well.

THOUGH HE ABSORBED MUCH from the style of painters throughout Italy, Pier Francesco Mola developed and retained a distinctive drawing style based less on line than on colorism achieved with various shades of wash. In the Crocker *Christ in the Garden of Gesthemane*, natural and holy light coincide, with the source located behind the Cross, symbol of the coming Passion and Resurrection.

Mola, son of the architect Giovanni Battista Mola, was born in the town of Coldrerio in the Ticino and moved to Rome with his family at the age of four in 1616. It seems that his first artistic training was under his father. An album of Giovanni Battista's drawings includes a few sketches his son added, one dated 1631.[1] His real formative years, however, were between 1633 and 1647, when, though few documents trace his movements, he is known to have travelled to northern Italy, Venice, Bologna, and Lucca. A letter by the Bolognese artist Francesco Albani records Mola's two-year presence in his studio some time during this period. The artist learned much from his contemporary Guercino and earlier Venetian artists as well.

Upon his return to Rome in 1647, Mola, described as a "slow starter" by Ann Sutherland Harris,[2] began his career in a style that synthesized his North Italian experience with Roman styles. His work for the Costaguti family included frescoes of Bacchus and Ariadne, completed around 1650 for their Roman palace, which still betray the challenges of this synthesis. Religious commissions, frescoes of the lives of Saints Peter and Paul in the Ravenna chapel in the church of the Gesù, and of Joseph for the papal palace on the Quirinal followed later in the decade. At the same time he completed portraits, saints and literary subjects for other patrons, who grew to include Queen Christina and the Colonna family, though his dispute with the Pamphilj family led to the destruction of his work rather than payment for services rendered. The most compelling of his single canvases is probably the *Vision of Saint Bruno* painted for Pope Alexander VII's nephew Agostino Chigi.[3] Mola was made *principe* of the Accademia di San Luca in 1662, having been a member since 1655. It seems likely that his drawings were already prized during his lifetime, especially since he received a visit from the collector Padre Sebastiano Resta shortly before his death in 1666.[4]

The Crocker *Christ in the Garden of Gesthemane* entered the collection as the work of Mola,[5] and was confirmed as such by Ann Sutherland Harris in 1988.[6] The subject, Christ praying alone before his coming Passion, is unknown in Mola's surviving paintings. Mola's composition relies on two ideas he explored in paintings of other subjects, however. A figure similar to the angel appears as Saint Michael in an altarpiece in the church of San Marco in Rome, as Jeffrey Ruda pointed out in 1992,[7] though its oil *bozzetto* now in Düsseldorf and especially a study for the archangel's head now in Budapest seem even more closely tied to the Crocker drawing.[8] The pose of Christ, on the other hand, relates to a painting of Saint Jerome kneeling in worship of the Crucifix.[9] Drawings in Princeton and Haarlem show the saint in the same direction as Christ in the Crocker

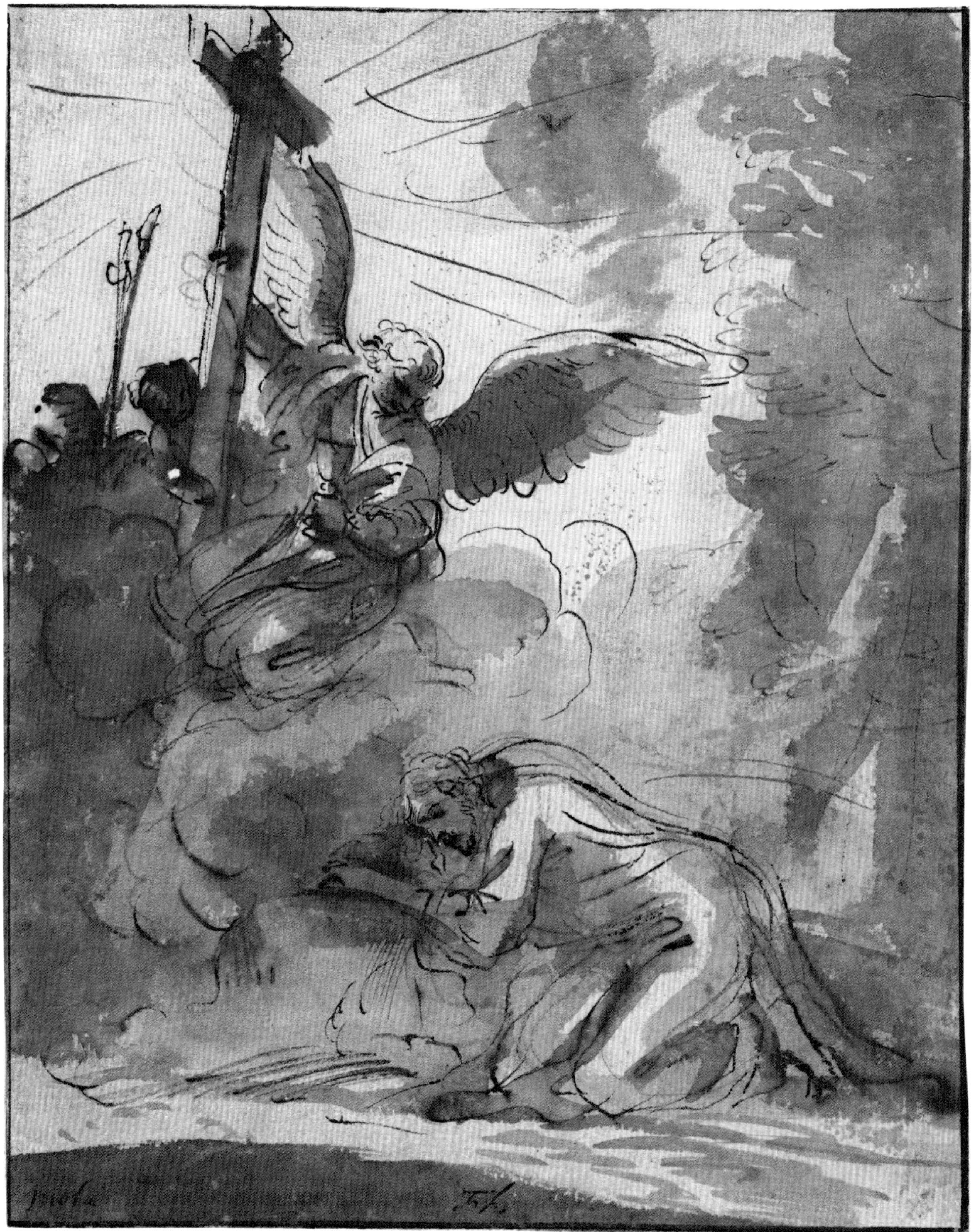

drawing, though the reversed figure in the finished painting is closer to the Crocker Christ, who is more thoroughly draped. Such later reuse was perhaps inspired by the common element in each subject, the Cross: just as Jerome contemplates Christ's suffering, Christ has earlier contemplated his coming Passion.

Both of the sources for the Crocker drawing date from the 1650s, the altarpiece in San Marco to 1658 or later. However, a document places the San Marco commission to 1655, so that its oil *bozzetto* must have followed shortly afterwards. The present writer believes that the Crocker drawing, with its angel so closely related, should be dated near this time. WB

10. Simone Cantarini, *Holy Family and Figure Studies*, n. d.

Red chalk, laid down to heavy cream laid paper mount with yellowish and blue framing-pieces, 17.4 × 11.9; 11.9 × 17.8 cm. Crocker Art Museum, E. B. Crocker Collection 1871.348-49

INSCRIPTIONS: on 1871.348, dark-brown ink, lower margin: *Simone Cantarini da pesaro* [corrected to capital P in black ink]; on 1871.349, dark-brown ink, lower right corner: 62 (Crozat numbering); verso of mount, black ink, lower margin at left: *Scuola di Bologna*

MARKS: on 1871.348: dark-brown ink, lower right corner: Lugt 2951 (Dezallier d'Argenville, listed in Lugt as Crozat), with number: 1211; lower left corner: Lugt 1015 (Flury-Hérard) with number: 13; on 1871.349: lower left corner: Lugt 1015 (Flury-Hérard) with number: 14; verso, graphite, lower left corner: circle and stroke; on mount, graphite, center right: circle and stroke

PROVENANCE: (1871.349): Pierre Crozat, before 1740; (both): Antoine-Joseph Dezallier d'Argenville, Paris, before 1762; Lenglier, Paris, before 1788; Jean-Baptiste-Marie Bourguignon de Fabregoules, Aix-en-Provence; Charles-Joseph-Barthélemi Giraud; Flury-Hérard; Edwin Bryant Crocker, Sacramento, by 1871; gift of his widow Margaret to the Museum, 1885

LITERATURE: Breazeale 2008, p. 208; Andrea Emiliani et al., *Simone Cantarini detto il Pesarese 1612–1648*, exh. cat. Pinacoteca Nazionale, Bologna; Milan, 1997, under no. I.10; Andrea Emiliani et al., *Simone Cantarini nelle Marche*, exh. cat. Musei Civici, Pesaro; Milan, 1997, under nos. 82 and 92; Maria Cellini, *Disegni di Simon da Pesaro, l'album Horne*, Cinisello Balsamo, 1996, p. 22; Ruda 1992, no. 14; Moir et al. 1977, no. 45; Crocker 1971, no. 60a

THE DYNAMIC USE of red chalk made Simone Cantarini's drawings some of the most sought-after by eighteenth-century collectors. The mount and collector's marks present with these sheets by the artist, a *Holy Family with Saint Anne* above and *Saint John the Evangelist Writing and Standing Women* below, provide insight into the provenance shared by many Crocker drawings: the *Holy Family* was once owned by the eighteenth-century French collector Pierre Crozat, then was joined by the other drawing in the collection of the courtier and lawyer Antoine-Joseph Dezallier d'Argenville, the two passing to the dealer Lenglier and then to the nineteenth-century Aixois lawyer de Bourguignon de Fabregoules and the Parisian banker Flury-Hérard.[1] The sale of this last was in 1861, fewer than ten years before the drawings' purchase by the Crockers.

Born in Pesaro in 1612 to a merchant family, Simone Cantarini trained—after overcoming parental opposition—under the painters Giacomo Pandolfi and Claudio Ridolfi. He seems to have limited himself to learning the rudiments of their art since he took on little of their style, profiting more from seeing the works of artists like Federico Barocci and Orazio Gentileschi. At the age of twenty, however, he was enraptured by Guido Reni's altarpieces in Pesaro and Fano, and resolved to meet the artist. He entered Guido's studio in 1635, absorbing as much as he could while concealing his real talent. Upon discovery, he proclaimed himself Reni's rival rather than pupil, which, though the elder master still supported his talent, exploded their relationship by 1638, when Cantarini left Bologna. Documented in Pesaro in 1639 for the marriage of his sister, the artist went to Rome in the next years, where he discovered the works of Raphael. At Guido's death in 1642 Cantarini sought to replace him in Bologna, opening his own studio and finding patrons among those whom he had not previously alienated. In 1647, invited by Carlo II Gonzaga to paint his portrait in Mantua, Cantarini managed to lose both favor and the commission. Falling ill shortly afterwards, he travelled to Verona for a change of air, where he died the next year of his bitterness or, perhaps, poison.

"*Il più corretto disegnatore ch'abbia mai avuto il nostro secolo*" (The most proper draughtsman of our century).[2] Malvasia's assessment of Cantarini's talent as a draughtsman is based on his probable first-hand knowledge of his working method. As he tells us, Cantarini

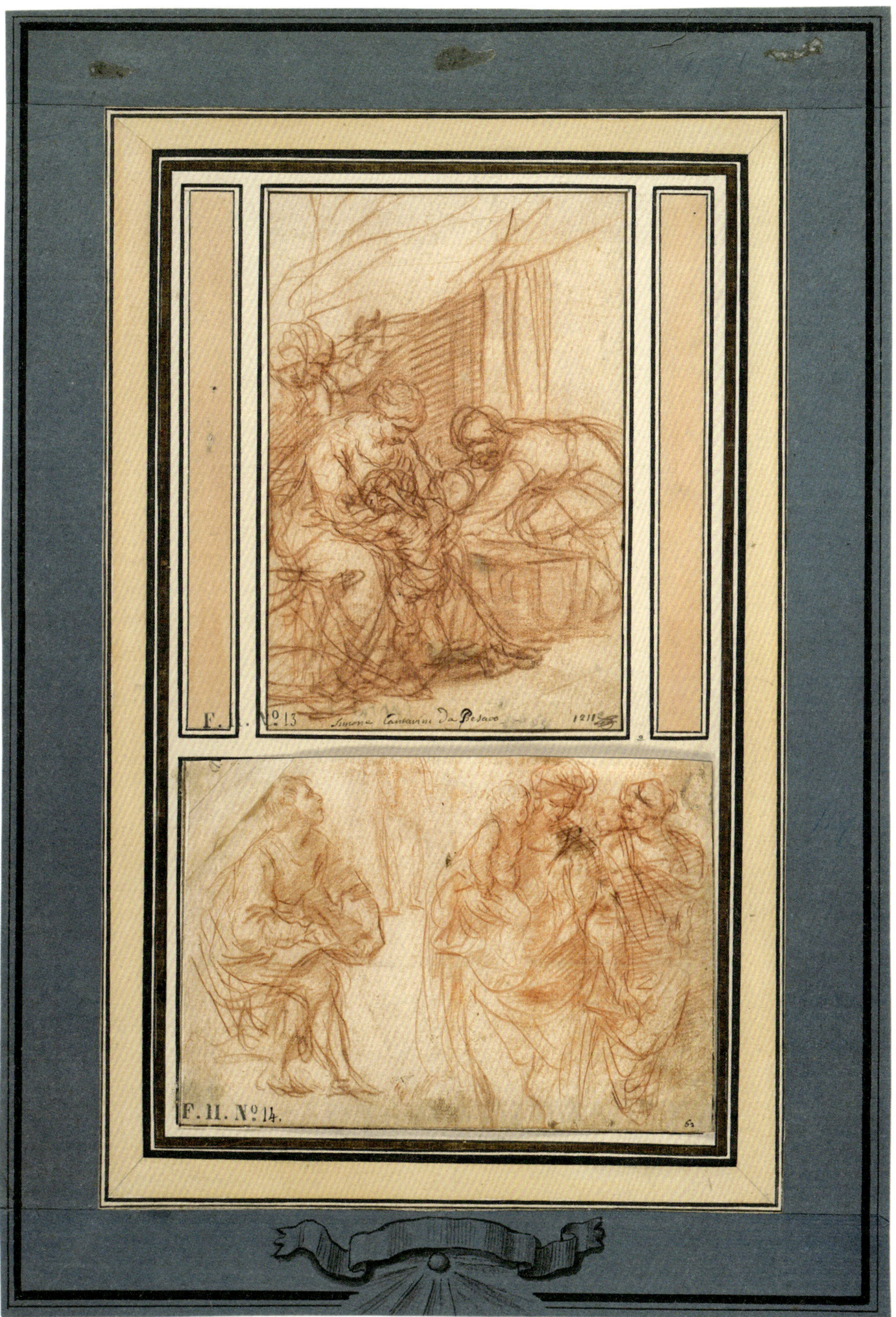

F. I. N.° 13   Simone Cantarini da Pesaro   1211
F. II. N.° 14.

NOTES

1. Thanks to Bernadette Py for her kind correspondence regarding this drawing and French collections: email of March 2, 2007.

2. Carlo Cesare Malvasia, *Felsina Pittrice, vite dei Pittori Bolognesi*, ed. Marcella Brascaglia, Bologna, 1971, p. 601.

3. Emiliani il Pesarese 1997, as above, no. III.4.

4. Rome, Gabinetto Nazionale, inv. no. F. C. 125847

5. Brera, inv. no. 86; Emiliani Marche 1997, as above, no. 92.

6. Bartsch 14(131); Emiliani il Pesarese 1997, as above, no. III.3.

7. *Ibidem*, no. I.10.

8. Franklin 2003, no. 30, inv. no. 23212 verso.

9. Moir *et al.* 1977 above.

created sculptural models to draw from, not only the heads which the biographer saw repeated in several paintings but also clay figures upon which he arranged drapery made of dampened paper. He would have then made many drawings, which he corrected and copied before making a full, dynamic version of the composition.

It seems that Malvasia's description of Cantarini's working method may have merit, since nearly every figure in the Crocker *Holy Family with Saint Anne* is shared with at least one other work, though no finished painting or print is known. One print (not in Bartsch), a simpler *Holy Family*, employs the motif of the Child climbing into the Virgin's lap identically, with the Crocker drawing recording a superimposed alternate position for the Child's head.[3] The difference between the latter and the print's incised *modello*[4] points to a common ancestor rather than a direct relationship. The figure of the carpenter Joseph planing a board is shared by a drawing in Milan,[5] with differences in the position of the leading leg. The pose of Anne holding up the curtain is similar to that of Joseph in another print.[6]

In the lower drawing, on the other hand, seemingly unrelated figures are juxtaposed on the same sheet. At left, the figure of John the Evangelist writing is related to the altarpiece of the *Immaculate Conception with Saints John the Evangelist, Nicholas of Tolentino and Euphemia* of 1632-34 now in the Pinacoteca Nazionale in Bologna.[7] Another preparatory drawing for the figure, which likely preceded the Crocker drawing since it includes elements of the composition that do not appear in the finished version, is in the National Gallery of Canada.[8] The female figures on the right have been related to the subject of the infant Hippomenes and Atalanta,[9] though this does not explain the third, kneeling figure at lower right, perhaps better seen in a religious context. The standing figure in the background seems unrelated to either of the other motifs. WB

11. ## Pier Francesco Cittadini, *Landscape with Herder and Animals*, n. d.

Pen and dark brown ink, brush and brown and greyish-brown washes, laid down, 18.9 × 28.8 cm. Crocker Art Museum, E. B. Crocker Collection 1871.1095

INSCRIPTIONS: dark-brown ink, lower right corner: *n.ftt 34* (Crozat numbering)

MARKS: none discernible

PROVENANCE: Pierre Crozat, before 1740; Edwin Bryant Crocker, Sacramento, by 1871; gift of his widow Margaret to the Museum, 1885

LITERATURE: Howard 1984 p. 372; Crocker 1971, checklist p. 167 as Zilotti; Bohr 1958, no. 262 as Zilotti

LANDSCAPE as an independent genre did not flower in Italy until the seventeenth century, though individual artists like Fra Bartolomeo had explored it much earlier. Pier Francesco Cittadini's fresh and atmospheric scene at the Crocker, once part of a famous French collection, combines several currents in mid-seventeenth-century Rome.

Cittadini, born in Milan probably in 1616, received his early training under the painter Daniele Crespi, then moved to Bologna at the age of seventeen to work under Guido Reni. At his maturity in the mid 1630s he received religious commissions, including an altarpiece for the church of Santo Stefano in Bologna depicting the stoning of the Protomartyr. By the mid 1640s Cittadini was in Rome, where he encountered a very different scene: in addition to painters like Pierfrancesco Mola and Simone Cantarini, both of whom seem to have influenced his work, Cittadini surely knew the community of

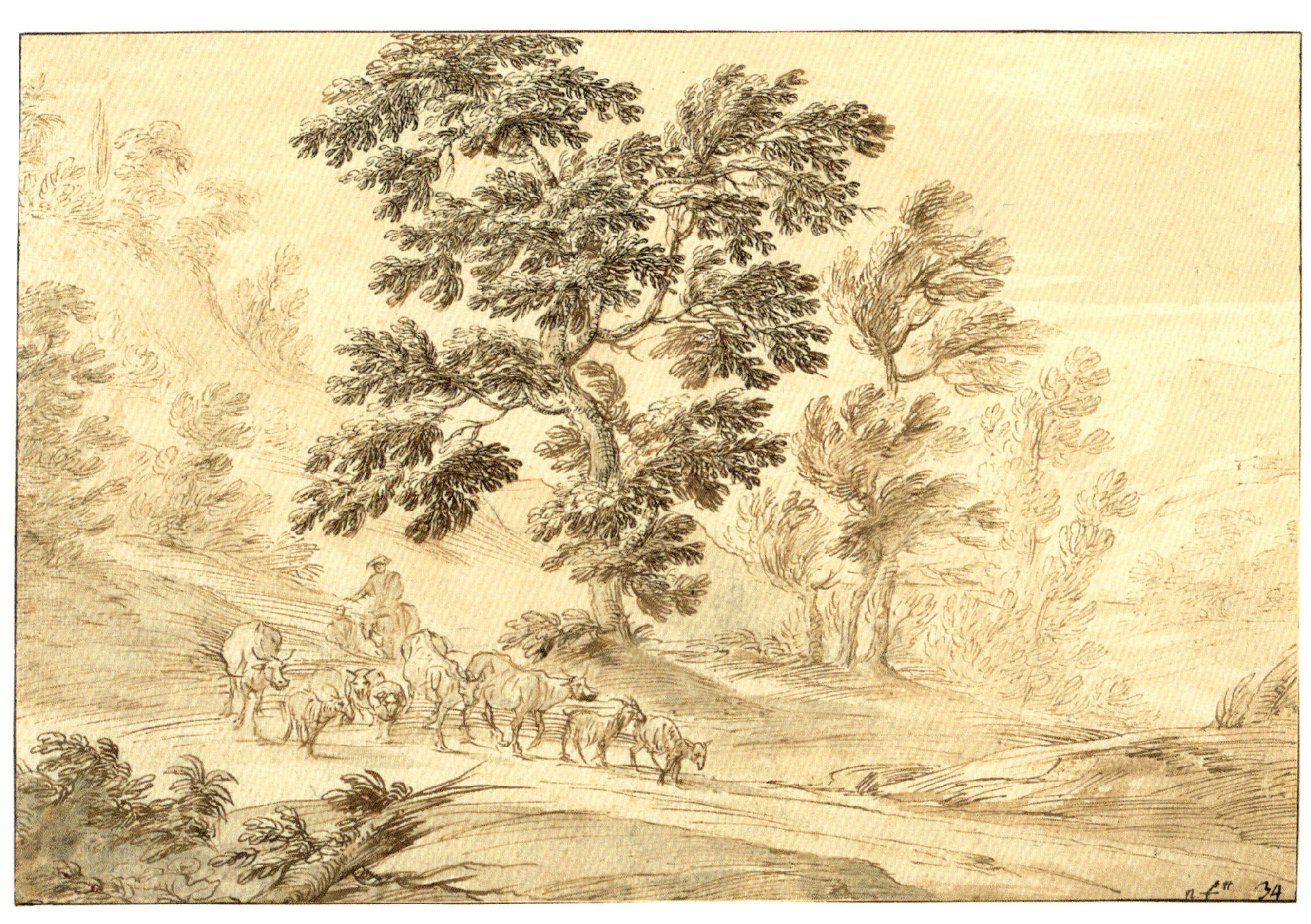

NOTES

1. Many of these artists were not well-liked: see letter of the Marchese Giustiniani to Dirk Amayden, in Gian Alberto Dell'Acqua, *Il Caravaggio e le sue grandi opere di San Luigi dei Francesi*, appendix by Mia Cinotti, Milan 1971, p. 166. Northern landscape drawings have been examined by Peter Schatborn in *Drawn to Warmth, 17th century Dutch Artists in Italy*, exh. cat. Rijksmuseum, Amsterdam; Zwolle, 2001.

2. Franklin 2003, no. 27.

3. Otto Kurz, *Bolognese Drawings of the XVII and XVIII Centuries in the Collection of Her Majesty the Queen at Windsor Castle*, London, 1955, nos. 151–56, inv. nos. 3268–73.

4. Inv. no. 1930.203; Mimi Cazort and Catherine Johnston, *Bolognese Drawings in North American Collections 1500-1800*, exh. cat. National Gallery of Canada, Ottawa, 1982, no. 66.

5. Franklin 2003, no. 27.

6. Note in Crocker curatorial files.

7. Thanks to Bernadette Py for her kindness in identifying the numbering during her visit of October 2006.

Dutch and Flemish artists in the city. Working in genres disdained by the Italians, for whom history painting was the highest expression of art, they had created their own market in scenes of daily life, still lifes, and especially landscapes depicting the country around Rome, which captivated them.[1] Cittadini spent the rest of his career working in the latter two genres and as a portraitist, supplying a ready market for such paintings in northern Italy. He had left Rome by 1650 for Sassuolo, where he supplied landscapes and garlands for the Este villa in the town, and returned to Bologna in 1653, where he married. He lived in Bologna and Milan for the rest of his life except for 1662–63, when he worked for the Este family in Modena. He died in Bologna in 1681.

The Crocker drawing depicts a herder in a deep and hilly landscape driving his animals—cattle, sheep, and goats—to market. Among Cittadini's surviving drawings are many graceful landscapes of this type, some of which include biblical subjects, such as the *Flight into Egypt* now in the National Gallery of Canada.[2] The artist's treatment of trees and landscape details in a manner similar to those in the series of the Prodigal Son in Windsor[3] makes clear the authorship of Cittadini rather than Zilotti, the name under which the drawing entered the collection. The wind-blown trees in the middle ground animate the drawing and contrast with the bold penmanship of the foreground tree and vegetation at lower left, devices used by Northern landscapists to anchor compositions while providing depth.

Except for its size, a drawing at Bowdoin College (fig. 12)[4] could be seen as a pendant to the Crocker landscape. Along a path which seems to continue from the left, shepherds, cattleherds, and a donkey driver readjusting his animal's burden follow each other to market. Though paintings of such subjects are known in pairs, especially those by Northern artists, the two drawings may not be different preparations for a pair planned by Cittadini, since he is thought to have made some landscapes as independent works of art.[5]

Once thought to be the work of the eighteenth-century Veneto landscapist and printmaker Domenico Zilotti, the Crocker drawing was identified as Cittadini's by Noel Annesley, probably at the time of his visit in 1982.[6] The inscription and numbering at lower right are those of the eighteenth-century collector Pierre Crozat.[7]   WB

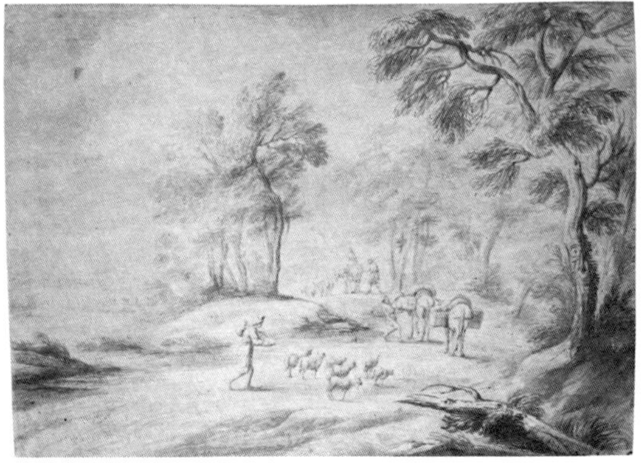

FIGURE 12 Pier Francesco Cittadini, *Landscape with Travellers*, n. d. Pen and point of brush and brown ink, brush and brown washes over graphite or black chalk, 29.2 × 41.7 cm. Bowdoin College Museum of Art, Brunswick, Maine

12. **Donato Creti**, *Virgin and Child*, n. d.

Pen and brown ink, 22.7 × 20.7 cm. Crocker Art Museum, E. B. Crocker Collection 1871.375

INSCRIPTIONS: none

MARKS: none

PROVENANCE: Edwin Bryant Crocker, Sacramento, before 1871; gift of his widow Margaret to the Museum, 1885

LITERATURE: Ruda 1992, no. 34; Howard 1984, p. 372; Moir et al. 1977, no. 46; Crocker 1971, no. 77; Vitzthum 1970, no. 77; Rosenberg 1970, p. 37 n. 4; Bohr 1958, no. 57 (misnumbered as 439)

A LETTER FROM Johann Adam, Prince of Liechtenstein, to the artist Marcantonio Franceschini shows how at the age of twenty-two Creti's fame as a draughtsman had already spread to powerful foreign patrons: *"sentiamo ancora che si trova là un tal chiamato Ragazzino e deve essere un grandissimo disegnatore"* (We hear that there is a certain man there named Ragazzino and that he is a very great draughtsman).[1]

Creti, born in Cremona in 1671, received his nickname of Ragazzino (little boy), when he was training in the Bolognese studio of Lorenzo Pasinelli, because he was the youngest and most talented student. Pasinelli's teaching was supplemented by the study of prints by his master Cantarini and Guido Reni himself, which may have facilitated Creti's development of a linear, subtly hatched style. While still in Pasinelli's studio, Creti was discovered by the patron Alessandro Fava, whose son Pietro was also Pasinelli's student. By 1708 Creti was working for other patrons, including the Pepoli family, for whom he created frescoes including *Alexander Cutting the Gordian Knot*. In 1713 the Sbaraglia family began their decisive support, commissioning canvases with stories of Achilles and perhaps influencing his founding membership in the Accademia Clementina. Creti was the academy's director seven times between 1713 and 1727, becoming *principe* in 1728. He turned to religious painting in a serious manner only in the 1730s and 1740s, producing a series of altarpieces for major Bolognese churches before his death in 1749.

The Crocker *Virgin and Child* entered the collection as the work of Francesco Amato, the early seventeenth-century Neapolitan printmaker, before being identified as Creti's by Wilhelm Suida.[2] It is an especially attractive example of the artist's unique draughts-manship, with the long curved lines that record drapery and flesh forming a counter-point to the shorter, carefully angled crossed and parallel lines that create volume. The composition is related to the *Saint Ignatius Adoring the Virgin and Child in Glory* of 1737,[3] painted for the cathedral church of San Pietro in Bologna and itself indebted to Guido Reni's *Madonna with Three Saints* of 1620-21 now in Dresden[4] for the central group, as Walter Vitzthum pointed out in 1970.[5] Vitzthum also pointed out a drawing in the British Museum (fig. 13) which shares elements with the Crocker sheet.[6] This drawing is more closely related to the altarpiece's central group, sharing the setting on clouds, the Virgin's drapery and pose, the Child's body and the crown-bearing putti above, though the gestures of Child and putti differ. This sheet is also quicker and more gestural than the more highly worked Crocker drawing, and both its *mise-en-page* and the autograph inscription *Di me Donato Creti* suggest that, as Renato Roli pointed out, it is a record of the finished group perhaps meant as a gift.[7]

The present writer sees the Crocker drawing as the artist's further development of the British Museum drawing rather than of the painting, especially since such details as the position of the feet correspond so closely. Creti enthrones the Virgin on a raised plat-form, thereby creating new rhythms in the composition, with a diagonal traversing the throne's finial and the heads of Virgin and Child and a harpy-like creature, perhaps meant to be part of the throne, echoing the latter's pose at right. Other changes animate

NOTES

1. Dwight Miller, review of Renato Roli, *Donato Creti*, *Burlington Magazine*, vol. CXI, no. 794, May 1969, pp. 306–07, at p. 306.

2. Mat note preserved in Crocker files. Suida's visit took place before the end of 1939; see Breazeale 2008, p. 224 n. 25.

3. Renato Roli, *Donato Creti*, Milan, 1967, no. 43.

4. Dresden, Gemäldegalerie, inv. no. 328; Stephen Pepper, *Guido Reni*, Oxford, 1984, no. 79.

5. Vitzthum 1970, as above.

6. Inv. no. 1920-11-16-5; *ibidem*.

7. Renato Roli, "Drawings by Donato Creti: Notes for a Chronology," *Master Drawings*, vol. XI, no. 1, Spring 1973, pp. 25–32, at p. 30.

8. As pointed out by Jeffrey Ruda in a mat note, a derivation from the 1737 altarpiece, oil on copper, 11 x 14 cm, was exhibited in the *Mostra del Settecento Bolognese* in 1935 as in the Maccaferri collection in Bologna but is unillustrated in the catalogue; see also Roli 1967, as above, note 3. To this writer it seems unlikely to be related directly to the Crocker drawing because it is a horizontal, not a vertical, composition and is much smaller.

the new composition: the Virgin is turned further away from the viewer and grasps her bodice with closed hand as she gazes at the Cross now held by the Infant; the light source now streams from upper left; and the Virgin's shoulder is now revealed above the folds of her heavy cloak. By creating this self-contained pyramidal composition, Creti has gone far beyond the drawing and altarpiece that precede it. Though Creti's works were occasionally engraved, it seems that the new subject was more appropriate for a small devotional painting, perhaps one never executed.[8] The most logical date for the Crocker drawing is after the British Museum sheet from which it derives, both post-dating the altarpiece of 1737.

WB

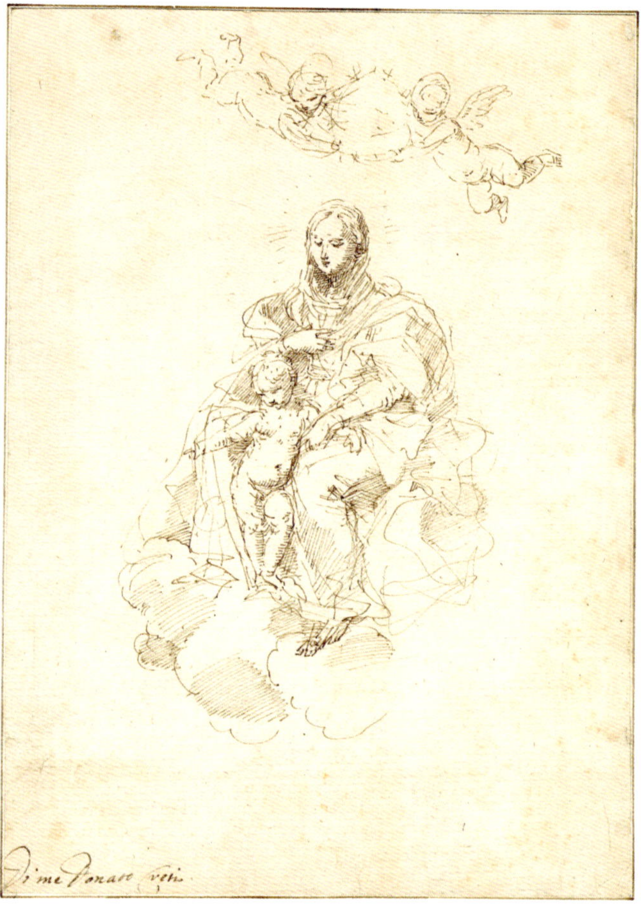

FIGURE 13 Donato Creti, *Virgin and Child Seated on Clouds*, c. 1737. Pen and dark-brown ink, 28.2 × 20.8 cm. British Museum, London

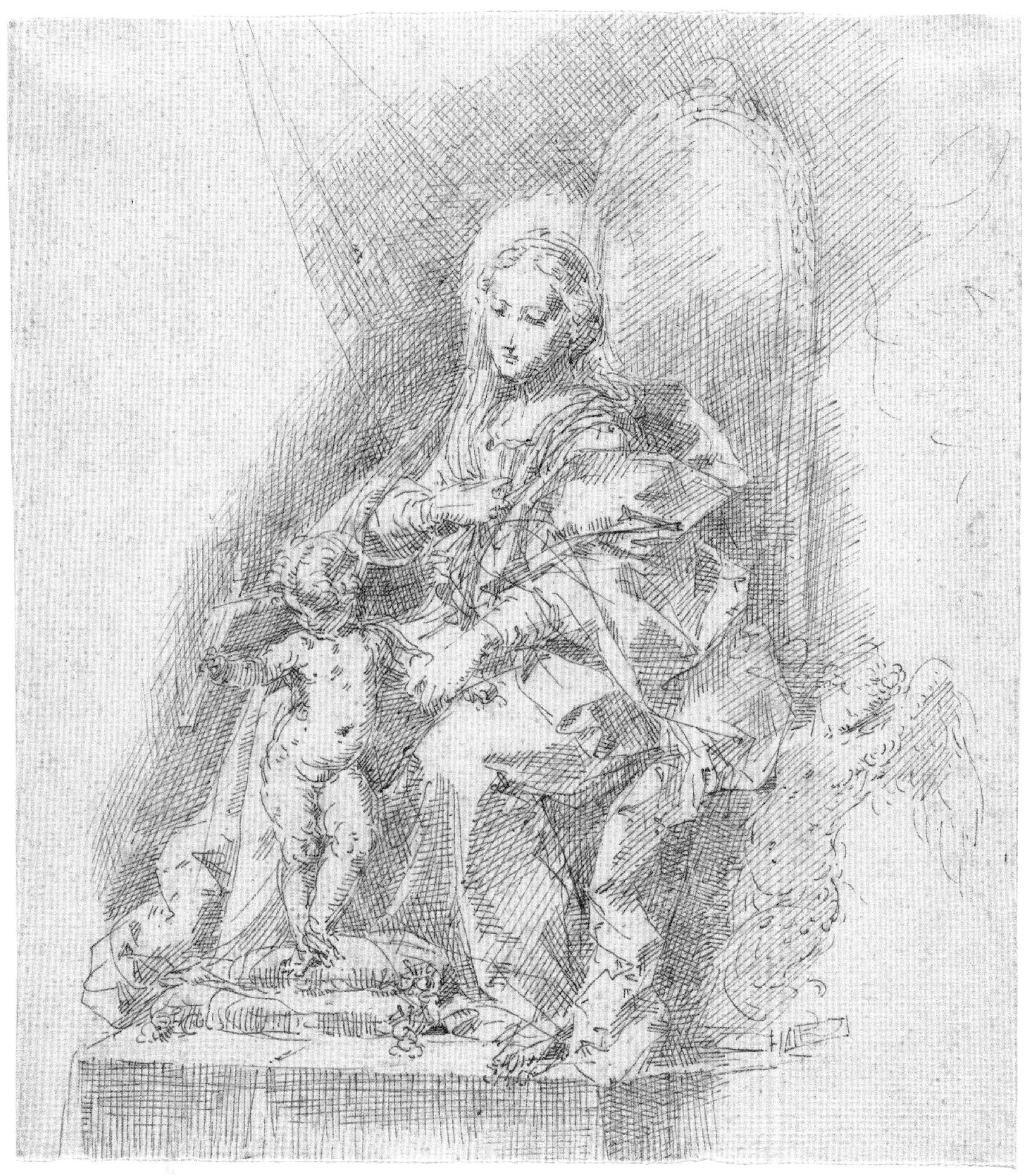

13. **Ubaldo Gandolfi,** *Education of the Virgin,* n. d.

Pen and dark brown ink, brush and brown washes over traces of black chalk, laid down, 12.1 × 9.6 cm.
Crocker Art Museum, E. B. Crocker Collection 1871.607

INSCRIPTIONS: none discernible

MARKS: none discernible

PROVENANCE: Edwin Bryant Crocker, Sacramento, before 1871; gift of his widow Margaret to the Museum, 1885

LITERATURE: Crocker 1971, checklist p. 167, as German

NOTES

1. See Mimi Cazort, *Bella Pittura, the Art of the Gandolfi,* exh. cat. National Gallery of Canada, Ottawa, 1993, and Prisco Bagni, *I Gandolfi, affreschi dipinti bozzetti disegni,* Bologna, 1992.
2. Mimi Cazort, "Some Early Drawings by Mauro Gandolfi," *Master Drawings,* vol. XXXIII, no. 2, Summer 1995, pp. 144–51; her introduction to Cazort 1993, as above, pp. 11–21; both following her early article, Mary Cazort Taylor, "The Pen and Wash Drawings of the Brothers Gandolfi," *Master Drawings,* vol. XIV, no. 2, Summer 1976, pp. 159–65; Andrea Czére, "Four Drawings by the Gandolfi Brothers and the 'scuola del nudo' in Bologna", *Master Drawings,* vol. XXXI, no. 4, Winter 1993, pp. 463–69.
3. Undated mat note by Alfred Neumeyer.
4. "Around Gaetano Gandolfi", undated mat note perhaps during his visit of 1982.
5. Now in the Collegiata; Donatella Biagi Maino, *Ubaldo Gandolfo,* Turin, 1990, no. 165; Bagni 1992, as above, no. 185.
6. Cazort 1993, as above, p. 21.
7. The oval format must be original to the drawing since lines at the edges are not cut off.
8. Inv. no. 1880.3.501; Bagni 1992, as above, no. 186; Jacob Bean and William Griswold, *Eighteenth-Century Italian Drawings in the Metropolitan Museum of Art,* New York, 1990, no. 62.
9. Inv. no. 4470S; Bagni 1992, as above, no. 512.
10. Inv. no. 4452S; Bagni 1992, as above, no. 604.

THIS DRAWING depicting the Education of the Virgin, with Anne emphasizing a point while embracing her devoutly attentive daughter, is an especially fresh survival of the eighteenth-century Gandolfi family's activity in Bologna. Once seen as the last gasp of the city's great painters dating back to the sixteenth century, they are now recognized as independent and original, if historically conscious, artists.[1] This author sees the drawing as the work of Ubaldo rather than his brother Gaetano or his nephew Mauro.

Ubaldo Gandolfi was born in San Matteo della Decima, ten miles north-west of Bologna, in 1728. He trained at the larger city's Accademia Clementina from 1745, where he studied under Ercole Graziani the Younger, himself a pupil of Donato Creti; Felice Torelli; and the anatomist and sculptor Ercole Lelli. Attention to the teachings of the last allowed him to gain the skills to win three medals for figure drawing in his first four years. In 1759, the church of Santa Maria Maggiore in the town of Castel San Pietro commissioned an altarpiece of the Assumption from him. This achievement marked the real start of his career, followed swiftly by his marriage and his appointment as director of figure drawing at the Accademia Clementina. Major private patrons began to support him in the late 1760s, though his portraits and depictions of saints for them did not allow him to avoid inactivity. Major mythological canvases and frescoes date from the late 1760s and 1770s. Especially in the 1770s, these commissions were supplemented by a series of altarpieces for religious communities in small towns, the kind of work that had begun his career. *Principe* of the Accademia Clementina in 1772, Ubaldo died suddenly in 1781 during his work on the frescoes for the cupola of San Vitale in Ravenna.

Drawings by all three Gandolfi were prized during their lifetimes. Connoisseurship was long notoriously difficult but has been greatly facilitated by the careful work of Mimi Cazort and others assessing the graphic habits of all three artists.[2] The name under which the Crocker drawing entered the collection is not recorded. By the 1930s, it was thought to be eighteenth-century German[3] and was first related to the Gandolfi family by Noel Annesley.[4] The Crocker drawing in pen and wash is loosely related to one of Ubaldo's best-known altarpieces, the *Education of the Virgin* for the church of San Francesco of the Minorite Friars in San Giovanni in Persiceto, painted in 1779 (fig. 14),[5] but is not preparatory to it.

According to Cazort, a greater number of independent compositional drawings survive for Ubaldo than for either Gaetano or Mauro, "suggest[ing] that the elder brother, chronically lacking commissions, often fulfilled his creative urges and 'kept his hand in' by making drawings."[6] The Crocker *Education of the Virgin* may be one of these. The painting in San Giovanni in Persiceto is conceived in a different, grander format, with the Virgin standing at the top of a staircase, Anne kneeling beside her. As Joachim reads in the background, the Virgin gazes towards God the Father in the clouds above. The drawing retains the physiognomy and gestures of mother and child. Setting and intent have

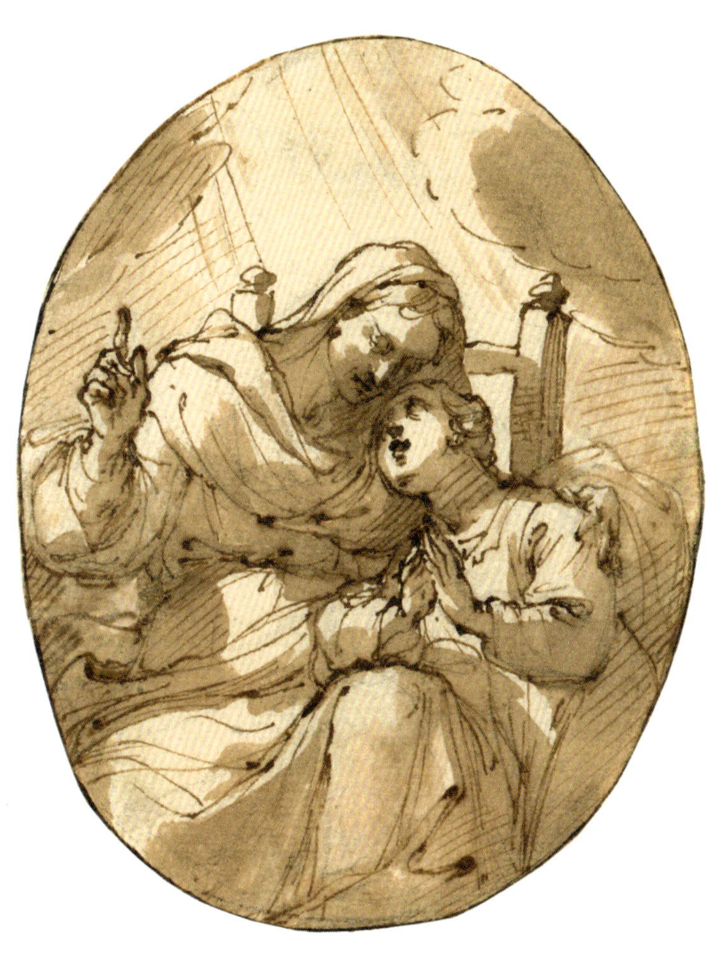

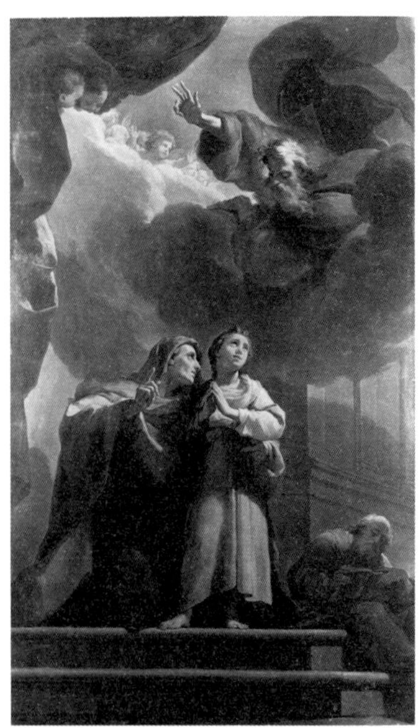

FIGURE 14 Ubaldo Gandolfi, *Education of the Virgin*, 1779. Oil on canvas, 285 × 185 cm. San Giovanni in Persiceto, Collegiata

changed radically, however, with the seated Anne embracing her daughter, while God is represented only by light streaming from above. This domestic scale and intimate tone are accented by the oval format,[7] which guides the eye to follow the curve of Anne's embrace. By transposing the altarpiece's composition into this domestic mode, Ubaldo creates a cousin to it, one whose intimacy and reduced dimensions would make an appealing focus for private devotions.

A drawing by Ubaldo in the Metropolitan Museum[8] which is preparatory to the altarpiece shares the graphic quirks evident in the Crocker drawing, especially in the Virgin's head, in the application of wash, and in the drapery, where Ubaldo's slight hesitation when he changes the direction of his stroke leaves distinctive pools of ink, a characteristic shared by few of Gaetano's or Mauro's own drawings. The Crocker drawing shares a bold and decisive line with other drawings by Ubaldo as well, for example the Uffizi *Holy Family*[9] and *Diana*.[10] It should be dated after the San Giovanni in Persiceto painting, to the last two years of his life.

WB

14. Giuseppe Bernardino Bison, *Capriccio Landscape with Classical Monuments*, n. d.

Pen and dark-brown ink, brush and green, yellowish-brown, reddish watercolor and grey wash, over black chalk; verso: dark-brown ink over graphite, 12.7 × 15.4 cm. Crocker Art Museum Purchase 2007.41

BORN IN THE Friulian town of Palmanova in 1762, Giuseppe Bernardino Bison was one of the most accomplished decorative painters of the turn of the nineteenth century, creating theater set designs and palace frescoes across north-eastern Italy. He studied first in Brescia, then moved at the age of fifteen to Venice, where he met the painter Antonio Maria Zanetti the Younger. Zanetti perhaps eased his admission into the city's Accademia in 1779, where he remained ten years. Friendships among architects led to his work for theaters in Venice, Treviso, Trento, and Gorizia. At the same time, specific commissions, like that for the Obizzi family in 1790, allowed him to apply his skills to private dwellings. Though he was based in Trieste in the years around 1800, the wanderings of his middle years brought him as far afield as Udine in Friuli and Zara in Dalmatia. In 1831 he settled permanently in Milan, where he took part in exhibitions at the Brera, until his death in 1844.

Bison's engaging and imaginative style drew upon the legacy of the great Venetian painters, though he concentrated not on weighty subject matter but rather on their shimmering, graceful technique. Here, the artist creates a vision assembled from a variety of architectural elements, with pyramids, temples, equestrian monuments, and columned porches arranged along a meadow. Bison's use of watercolor and wash captures well the humid heat and languor of the Veneto midday.

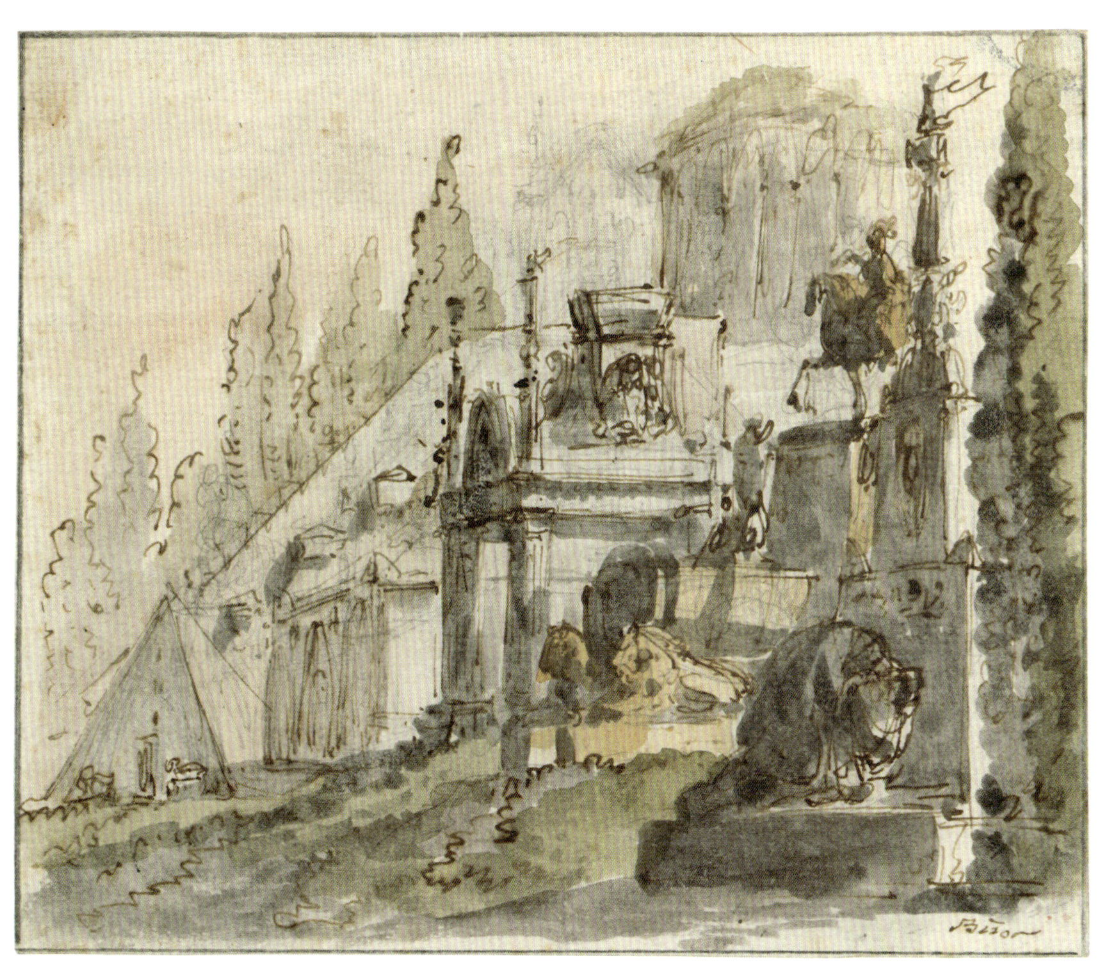

NOTES

1. E.g. Aldo Rizzi, *Disegni del Bison*, Udine, 1976, nos. 54, 95, 174.

2. E.g. Rizzi 1976, no. 42.

Imaginary buildings and landscapes were of course important in the repertoire of an artist who designed stage sets, but Bison's composition is not necessarily theatrical. A prolific, nervous draughtsman, the artist created many such landscapes as independent works of art, whether for personal pleasure or, certainly in the case of his many drawings in tempera on cardboard, for sale. The pure pleasure of creation may have motivated him here as elsewhere.

A recent purchase, the Crocker drawing is very much in the spirit of the artist's views of monuments, sharing details in plant forms as well as the brilliant pen- and brush-work.[1] A second, figural motif occupies the verso, its dynamic, gestural pen over graphite in keeping with known drawings.[2] The signature at lower right recto may indicate intent to sell.

It is possible that the scene depicts a view in the real world. Each of the architectural forms we see—pyramid, monument, and temple—was used for mausolea (the pyramid most memorably for Canova's recently completed monument to the Archduchess Maria Christina in Vienna). The columned portico at center is reminiscent of tombs in Venice and the Veneto. Such a jumble of styles and periods in monuments enclosed by a wall with cypresses beyond is typical of cemeteries especially in north-eastern Italy.   WB

DRAWINGS FROM THE LOW COUNTRIES

INSCRIPTIONS: brown ink, lower margin at left: *bosch*

MARKS: none

PROVENANCE: Edwin Bryant Crocker, Sacramento, by 1871; gift of his widow Margaret to the Museum, 1885

LITERATURE: Elsig 2004, p. 143; Koldewij et al. 2001, p. 133 ; *Caricature, Its Role in Graphic Satire*, exh. cat. Rhode Island School of Design, Providence, 1971, no. 2; Schulz 1968, p. 67; *Jheronimus Bosch*, exh. cat. Noordbrabants Museum, 's Hertogenbosch, 1967, no. 54; Charles de Tolnay, *Hieronymus Bosch*, London and New York, 1966, no. 24; Charles de Tolnay, "The Paintings of Hieronymus Bosch in the Philadelphia Museum of Art," *Art International*, vol. VII, no. 4, 1963, p. 26; Colin T. Eisler, *Corpus de la peinture des anciens Pays-Bas méridionaux au quinzième siècle*, vol 4: *New England Museums*, Brussels, 1961, p. 37; K. G. Boon, "Hieronymus Bosch," *The Burlington Magazine*, vol. CII, no. 691, October 1960, p. 458; Ludwig Baldass, *Hieronymus Bosch*, Vienna, 1959, under no. 114; Crocker 1959, no. 2; Hans Swarzenski, "An Unknown Bosch," *Bulletin of the Museum of Fine Arts Boston*, XIII, no. 291, February 1955, p. 5; Trivas 1942, no. 12

NOTES

1. Koreny, Pokorny, and Zeman, for instance, accept only fifteen drawings: Koreny et al. 2002, p. 164.
2. See, for instance, J. P. Filedt Kok, "Underdrawing and Drawing in the Work of Hieronymus Bosch; a Provisional Survey in Connection with the Paintings by Him in Rotterdam," *Simiolus*, vol. VI, 1972–73, pp. 133–62.
3. For discussions of Bosch's draughtsmanship, see Koreny et al. 2002, pp. 164–67, and Stephanie Buck, *Die niederländischen Zeichnungen des 15. Jahrhunderts im Berliner Kupferstichkabinett: kritischer Katalog*, Berlin, 2001, pp. 197–237.
4. Elsig 2004, p. 143.
5. See, for instance, the *Ecce Homo* in the Museum voor Schoone Kunsten, Ghent.
6. James H. Marrow, *Passion Iconography in Northern European Art of the Late Middle Ages and Early Renaissance*, Kortrijk, 1979, pp. 33ff.

15. Circle of Hieronymus Bosch, *Christ Carrying the Cross*, n. d.

Pen and brown ink, black and white chalk, 25.3 × 20.2 cm. Crocker Art Museum, E. B. Crocker Collection, 1871.126

DESPITE THE VAST amount of scholarship devoted to Hieronymus Bosch (c. 1450–1516), he remains one of the most mysterious artists of the northern Renaissance. The facts of his life can be established through documents: born in about 1450, he spent his career in 's Hertogenbosch. He married a wealthy woman and enjoyed high standing in his community. By the early sixteenth century, his moralizing and religious paintings had attracted the attention of some distinguished patrons, including Philip the Fair of Burgundy. Many of his works have been lost, leaving us with about twenty-five securely attributed paintings and even fewer drawings, all undated.[1] The precise meanings of many of his works remain elusive: the monstrous creatures and often bizarre iconography of his art are without precedent, though he had countless imitators throughout the sixteenth century.

The drawings that have been attributed to Bosch over the years vary wildly in style. Art historians have attempted to define the character of his draughtsmanship by studying the underdrawings in his most securely attributed paintings,[2] but even his underdrawings differ, encompassing a more finished and delicate technique as well as a rougher, sketchier approach that was highly unusual among northern artists of his time.[3] The Crocker drawing exhibits none of the expressive use of line found in Bosch's work, however, and appears to be the work of a follower. Although Bosch evidently ran a workshop, its size and the identity of the people who worked with him remain unknown.

In addition to the main subject matter in the foreground, the artist depicted other scenes from the Passion in the background, including the suicide of Judas and Christ presented to the people in the upper left. The latter scene paraphrases a painting, sometimes attributed to Bosch but more likely by a follower, now in the Philadelphia Museum of Art. On the basis of this relationship, Frédéric Elsig has attributed the drawing to the 'Maître du panneau double-face de Valenciennes.'[4] This attribution seems tenuous, however: there is no reason to assume that the Crocker drawing is a preparatory study for the painting. In fact, its somewhat tentative draughtsmanship would suggest the work of a copyist.

The delicate lyrical lines of *Christ Carrying the Cross* form a striking contrast with the cruelty of the subject matter. As in paintings of the same subject by Bosch and his followers,[5] the figures are crammed into the foreground, creating a sense of immediacy, as though the viewer is a participant in the event rather than an observer. This, combined with the freakish appearance of the crowd, lends a hallucinatory quality to the drawing, as Christ is completely engulfed by monstrous faces. Although the drawing participates in a long tradition in Northern Renaissance art of depicting Christ's tormentors as bestially ugly,[6] the fanciful costumes, the figure types, and the nature of the demons in the background make it clear that this artist was looking specifically at Bosch's art.   SS

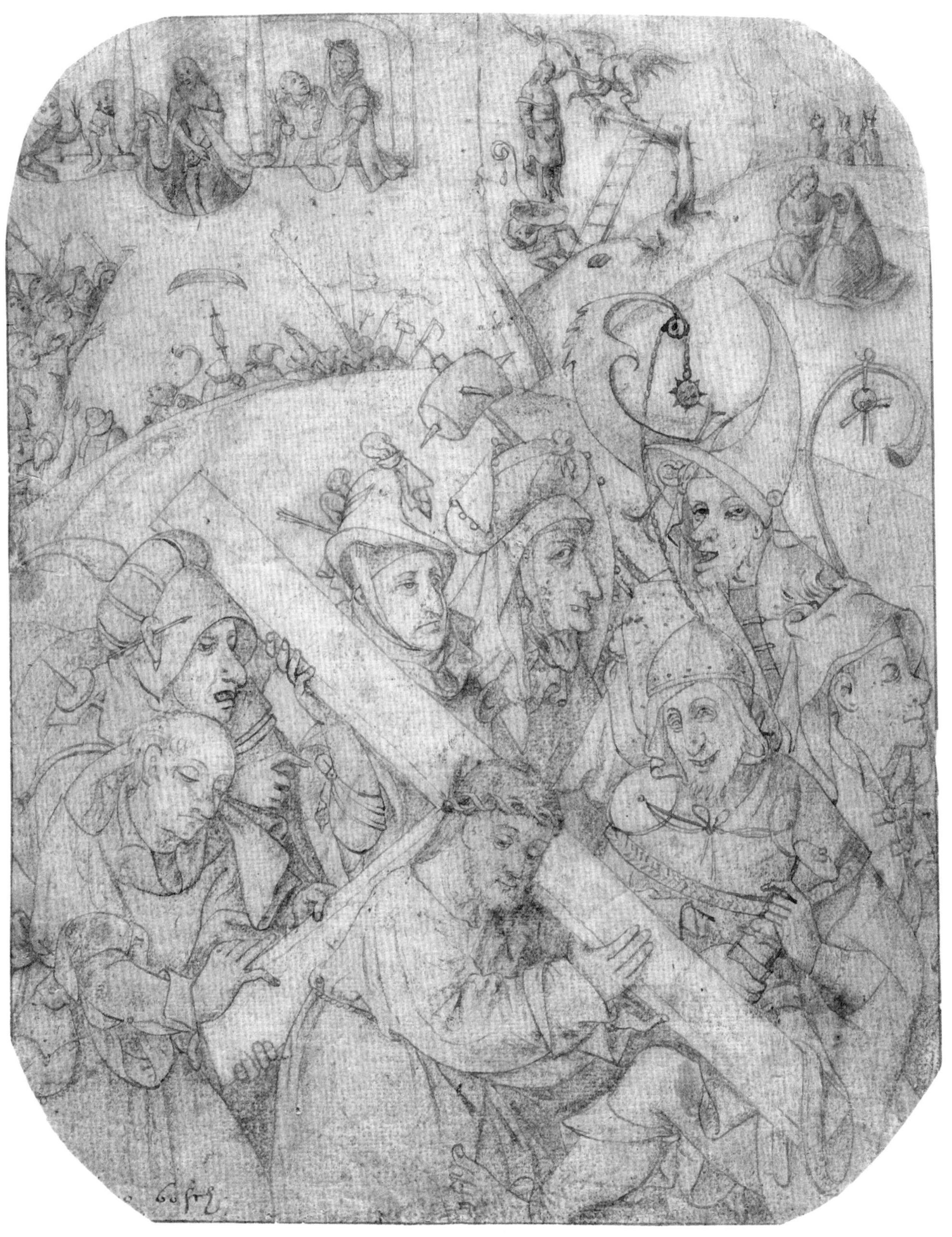

16. Jan Steven van Calcar, *Studies of Human Bones*, c. 1543

Red chalk, incised, verso: black chalk, 29.3 × 19.6 cm. Crocker Art Museum,
E. B. Crocker Collection 1871.127

INSCRIPTIONS: red chalk, lower right corner, possible monogram: JSK; dark-brown ink, center of bottom margin: *Jan van Kalkar*; verso, graphite, lower margin: *Geschenk des Herrn v. Amstetten, Breslau / copirt in Holzschnitt v. A. Kretzchmer für Choulant's Buch*; verso, dark-brown ink, upper margin, numbered: *No. 15*

MARKS: none

PROVENANCE: Baron von Amstetter, Breslau; Rudolph Weigel, Leipzig, by 1852;[1] Edwin Bryant Crocker, Sacramento, by 1871; gift of his widow Margaret to the Museum, 1885

LITERATURE: Kaufmann 2004, pp. 17–20; Ruda 1992, no. 22, p. 60; Rosand and Muraro 1976, p. 215 n. 14; Crocker 1971, no. 15; Schulz 1968, no. 22; Trivas 1942, no. 22; Choulant 1920, p. 417; Choulant 1852, p. 179, no. 43

NOTES

1. Based on a statement in Choulant 1852, as above, p. 179, that the drawing was given by Amstetter to Weigel. By 1920, when the English edition was published, the drawing was described as "lost."
2. Van Mander 1994, ff. 217v and 218r. Cited in Rosand and Muraro 1976, as above, p. 212.
3. Vasari, ed. Milanesi, vol. V, p. 434, and vol. VII, pp. 462 and 582; cited by Rosand and Muraro 1976, p. 212.
4. For a review of scholarship on this issue, see Röhrl 2000, pp. 77–78.
5. See, for instance, Röhrl 2000, p. 78, and Rosand and Muraro 1976, pp. 214–15.
6. Quoted in Rosand and Muraro 1976, p. 214.
7. Reproduced in Saunders and O'Malley 1950, p. 51. A skull related to that in the drawing appears in the same sense in Plate V of the same treatise (reproduced by Saunders and O'Malley 1950, p. 53).
8. Andrea Vesalius, ed. Hermann Boerhaave and Berhard Siegfried Albini, Leiden, 1727, p. 5. Here, the bones have been rearranged yet again, with most of them appearing in

BORN IN CALCAR, Westphalia, Jan Steven van Calcar (c. 1499–c. 1546) spent his career in Italy. In Venice, he studied with Titian and absorbed the Italian master's style so thoroughly that Karel van Mander claimed that their drawings could barely be distinguished.[2] The artist's life ended in Naples, where he had befriended Giorgio Vasari. Vasari mentioned Calcar several times in his *Vite*, praising the northerner's rare ability to work in an Italian style and naming him as the designer of woodcut illustrations for the works of the pioneering anatomist Andreas Vesalius.[3]

Although Calcar certainly contributed to Vesalius's earlier work, *Tabulae anatomicae sex* (1538), the artist's precise role in the illustration of Vesalius's most famous treatise, the *De humani corporis fabrica libri septem* (1543) is a matter of much debate.[4] Vasari mentioned only Calcar in connection with the treatise, but most art historians have concluded that probably a number of artists were involved.[5] Vesalius's lament that he had "to put up with the bad temper of artists and cutters who made me more miserable than did the bodies I was dissecting" corroborates the view that a number of artists were involved, but their identities are unknown.[6] The Crocker drawing was not reproduced directly in the treatise, but most of the individual bones appear reversed and rearranged into a tidier composition in Plate IV in Book I of the *Fabrica*.[7] The drawing, or more likely its related woodcut, was further adapted by the famous anatomical illustrator Jan Wandelaar (1690–1759) for a later edition of the collected works of Vesalius.[8]

The scarcity of secure comparative material, whether related to Calcar or to the *Fabrica*, makes it extremely difficult to evaluate the Crocker sketch.[9] As a result, despite the monogram on the drawing, the attribution to Calcar must remain tentative. As Thomas DaCosta Kaufmann has noted, the reversals in the finished woodcuts as well as the presence of incised lines in the drawing suggest that it was a working preparatory study. His description of the drawing as "an accumulation of studies relatively close to the final cutting of the block" is perhaps as close as we can come at the present time to pinpointing its role in the preparatory process.[10] Variations in both composition and details between the drawing and the woodcut as it appeared in the treatise imply the existence of at least one other preliminary step between the two. For example, the femur is shown at the left of the drawing as a whole and in rough sketch to the right with its head detached. It appears twice in the illustration, once intact and once with the head labeled and detached. The careful delineation and modeling of the bones as well as the small sketches investigating the relationships of the working parts are all in keeping with Vesalius's belief in direct experience with human anatomy and his rejection of traditional, theoretically based medicine. This study provides a tantalizing glimpe into the working methods behind some of the most groundbreaking scientific illustrations ever published.

SS

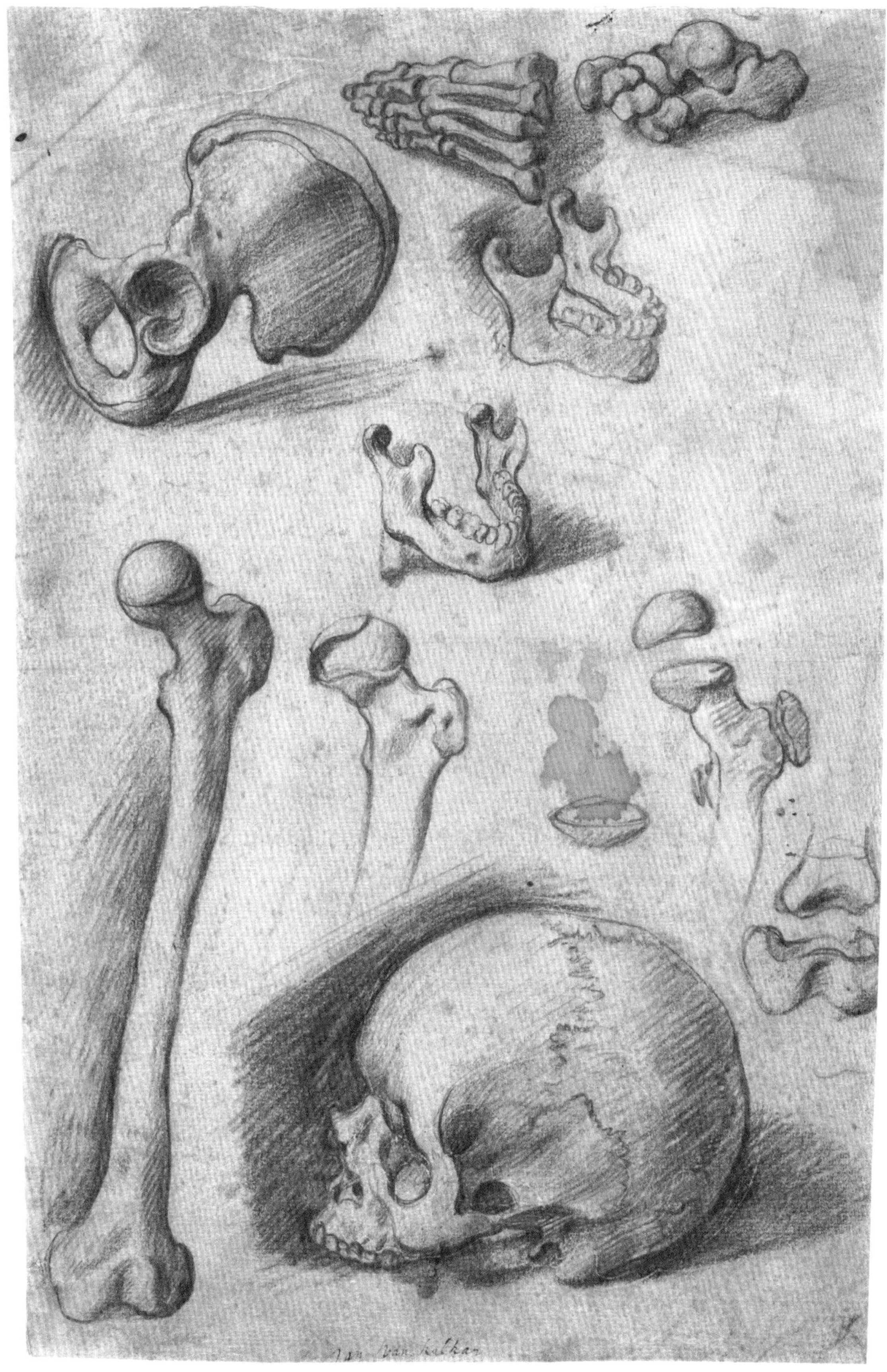

a single image. The Crocker drawing was
also reproduced in a print by Albert
Kretschmer (1825–1891) in Choulant 1852.

9. For other possible attributions to Calcar,
see Nicole Davos, "Jan Stephan van Calcar
en Italie: Rome Florence, Venise, Naples,"
in Napoli, l'Europa: Ricerche di storia dell'arte
in onore di Ferdinando Bologna, ed.
Francesco Abbate and Fiorella Sricchia
Santoro, Naples, 1995, pp. 145–48, and
Marta Ausserhofer, *Johann Stephan van
Calcar. Das Porträt des Melchior van
Brauweiler von 1540*, Kleve, 1992. See also
Martin Kemp, "A Drawing for the *Fabrica*;
and Some Thoughts upon the Vesalius
Muscle-Men," *Medical History*, XIV, 1970,
pp. 277–88. Kemp attributed a red chalk
drawing for one of the muscle men in the
Fabrica to Calcar, noting that the artist's
use of chalk was more Northern than
Venetian and admitting that "the
existing clues do not indicate any wholly
feasible alternatives" (p. 286).

10. DaCosta Kaufmann 2004, p. 19. The
incised lines do not follow the forms
precisely and may indicate the existence
of another preparatory stage.

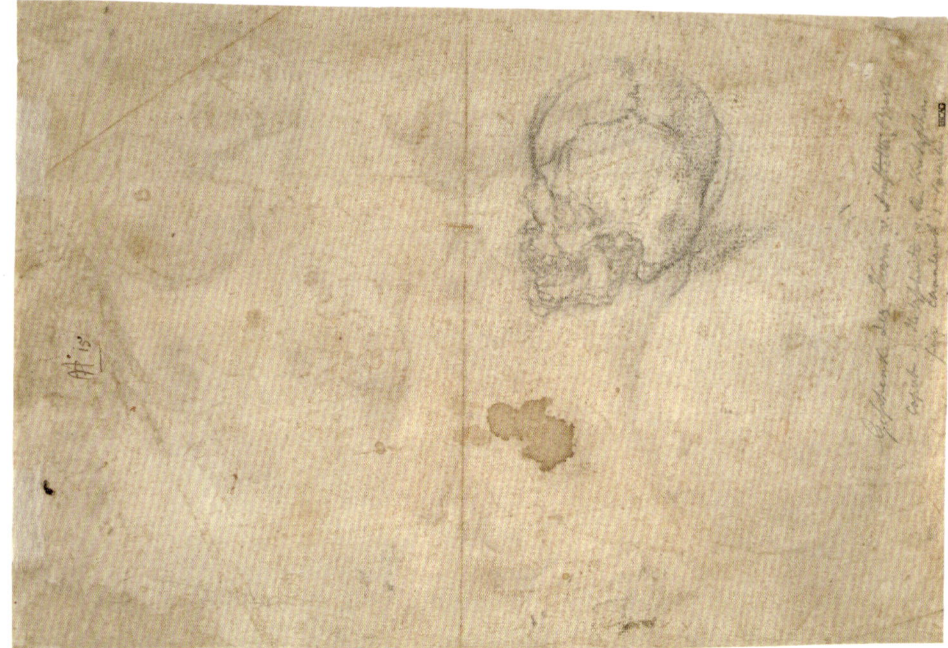

Verso of cat. no. 16

17. Hendrick Goltzius, *Judith with the Head of Holofernes*, early 1590s

Pen and dark-brown ink, brush and gray wash and blue and white opaque watercolor, partially darkened, on brown laid paper, 20.3 × 16.6 cm. Crocker Art Museum, E. B. Crocker Collection 1871.142

INSCRIPTIONS: dark-brown ink, upper right corner: HG [monogram]

MARKS: verso, graphite, lower left: Lugt 2315 (Stiglmeier)

PROVENANCE: Johann Stiglmeier, Straubing, by 1856; Edwin Bryant Crocker, Sacramento, by 1871; gift of his widow Margaret to the Museum, 1885

LITERATURE: Breazeale 2008, p. 212; Ruda 1992, no. 70; Ruda 1985, no. 6; Bionda 1983, p. 96; Frima Fox Hofrichter, *Haarlem: The Seventeenth Century*, exh. cat. Zimmerli Museum, New Brunswick, 1982, no. 50; Reno 1978, n. p.; Howard *et al.* 1973, no. 17; Crocker 1971, no. 32; *Dutch Mannerism, Apogee and Epilogue*, exh. cat. Poughkeepsie, 1970, no. 51; Reznicek 1961, no. 20, p. 243, fig. A 138; Trivas 1942, no. 42

INTERNATIONALLY FAMOUS for his dazzling technical skill as an engraver, the Haarlem artist Hendrick Goltzius (1558–1617) was equally accomplished as a draughtsman. He spent much of his early career establishing the thriving printmaking business that spread his distinctive Mannerist style throughout Europe. In 1590, Goltzius traveled to Italy, visiting Venice, Bologna, Florence, and Naples, but spending most of his time in Rome, where he made dozens of drawings after antique monuments and sculpture. After his return to Haarlem, he initially concentrated on engraving but turned instead to painting for the last seven years of his life.[1]

Judith with the Head of Holofernes depicts the moment after the Old Testament heroine Judith has beheaded the drunken Assyrian leader, saving her fellow Israelites from defeat and her city of Bethulia from invasion. Probably executed around the time of Goltzius's trip to Rome, the study demonstrates his intense study of Italian art. While Judith's sinuous pose and the effortless grace with which she has dispatched Holofernes both recall Goltzius's earlier, more mannered style, the monumentality of the figure and the simplicity of the composition demonstrate his new familiarity with classical sculpture and High Renaissance painting. His handling of pen and ink recalls the swelling and tapering lines of his engraving technique. Here, he used the variation in line to express the passage of light: for instance, he used thinner contours to delineate Judith's arm on the lightstruck side and thicker ones on the shadowed side.

The style and technique of this drawing both suggest that it was intended to serve as a model for an engraving, apparently never executed. The use of pen and brown ink shaded with gray wash and heightened with opaque watercolor is consistent with the working methods of Goltzius and his contemporaries when producing drawings for experienced printmakers, who were entrusted with the task of translating these painterly sketches into the linear vocabulary of engraving.[2] A drawing of *The Penitent Magdalene* by Goltzius now in the Fitzwilliam Museum (fig. 15), so closely related in composition, size, and technique as to suggest that the two drawings were intended as pendants, was incised for transfer and reproduced in an engraving by Jacob Matham (1571–1631).[3] Series of half-length biblical figures enjoyed a surge of popularity among Haarlem printmakers around this time and it is possible that Goltzius planned to include both compositions in a similar series.[4]

Although Goltzius's reputation suffered in the centuries following his death, his drawings continued to appeal to collectors. In about 1795, the Amsterdam artist Jacob Ernst Marcus (1774–1826) made a careful copy of this drawing for the *album amicorum* of his friend and fellow artist Jacob Smies.[5] The meticulous nature of the copy suggests that Smies had the original before him as he worked, indicating that the Crocker drawing was probably still in a Dutch private collection at the time. Goltzius's popularity with foreign collectors increased during the following decades, as nineteenth-century critics

NOTES

1. For Goltzius's drawings, see Rezniceck 1961. For his career as a whole, see Huigen Leeflang et al., *Hendrick Goltzius (1558–1617): Drawings, Prints, and Paintings*, exh. cat. Rijksmuseum, Amsterdam, 2003.

2. Karel Van Mander's *modelli* for prints, for example, employ a similarly painterly technique.

3. Inv. no. PD-164-1963; see E. K. J. Reznicek, "Drawings by Hendrick Goltzius, Thirty Years Later: Supplement to the 1961 catalogue raisonné," *Master Drawings*, vol. XXXI, no. 3, Autumn 1993, no. K78a.

4. Hollstein, p. XXI. See also Goltzius's drawing *Rachel and Leah* (Reznicek 15), which was also engraved by Matham for his series of Old Testament women.

5. Bionda 1983, pp. 96–97.

6. Jan Piet Filedt Kok, "De wisselvallige reputatie van Hendrick Goltzius," *Bulletin van het Rijksmuseum*, vol. 52, no. 1, 2004, pp. 47–48.

drew a distinction between the extravagant mannerism of Goltzius's early career and the more classical approach he adopted after his trip to Italy, praising the latter. By the middle decades of the century, when Crocker acquired this study, Goltzius drawings had been dispersed and were considered crucial to major European collections of Dutch drawings.[6] The Dutch themselves were somewhat slower to value him, and by time of the late nineteenth-century "rediscovery" of Goltzius drawings, many fine examples of his draughtsmanship, like this drawing, had already left the Netherlands.	55

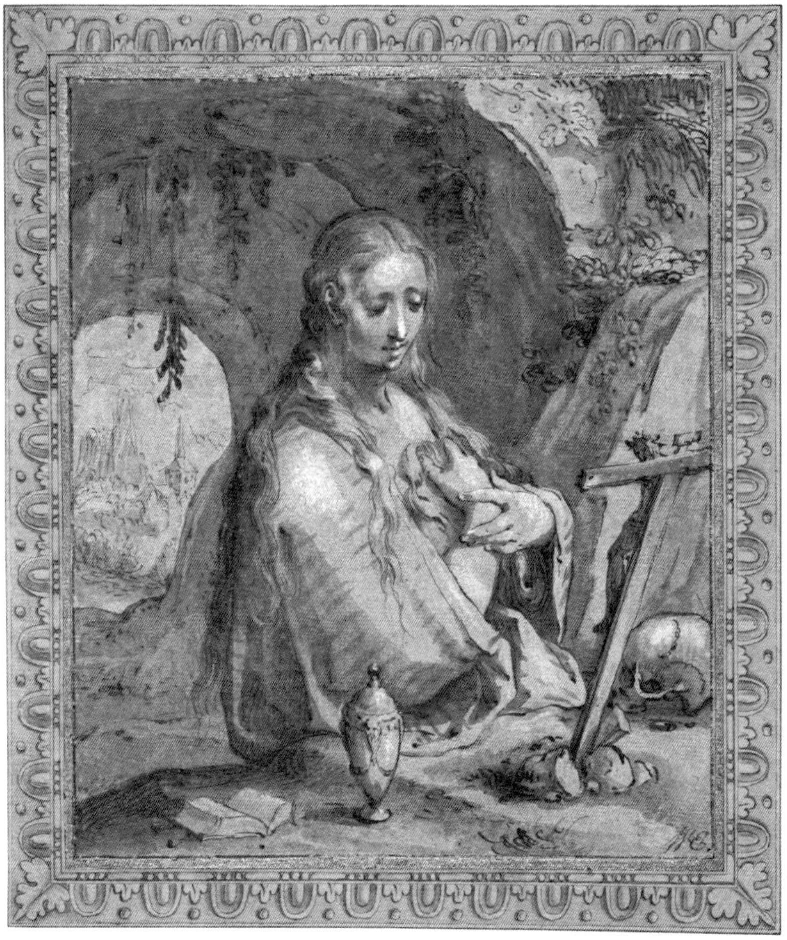

FIGURE 15 Hendrick Goltzius, *The Penitent Magdalene*, n. d. Pen and dark-brown ink, brush and brown washes and white opaque watercolor on buff prepared paper, 16.1 × 13.8 cm. Fitzwilliam Museum, Cambridge

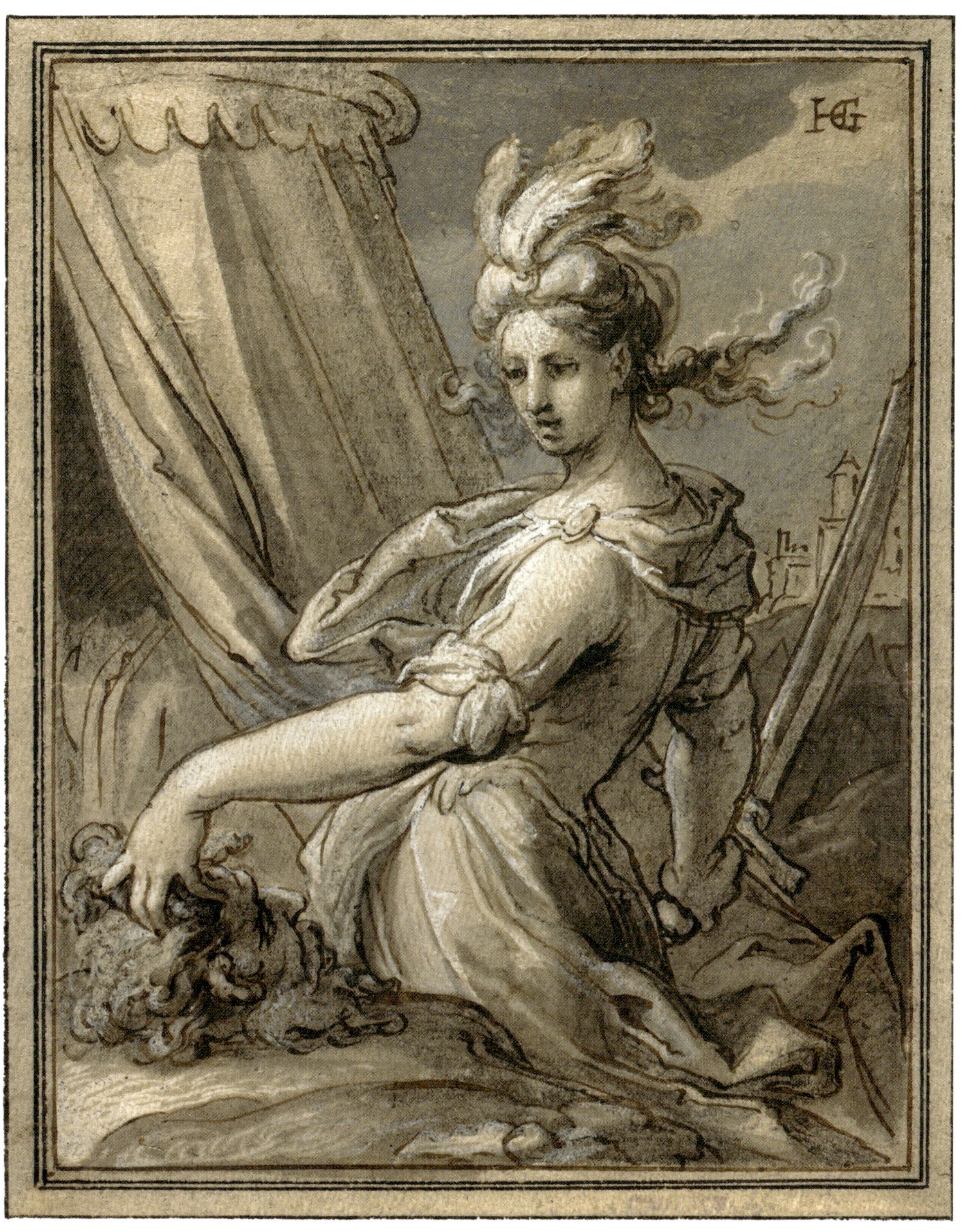

18. Pieter Stevens, *The Month of February*, 1604–07

Pen and dark-brown ink, brush and brown, red, and blue washes, 20.6 × 28.6 cm.
Crocker Art Museum, E. B. Crocker Collection, 1871.141

INSCRIPTIONS: none

MARKS: lower left corner: Lugt 2237
(Rolas du Rosey)

PROVENANCE: Franz Graf von
Sternberg-Manderscheid; his sale,
Dresden, 10 November 1845, no. 742; Carl
Freiherr von Rolas du Rosey, before 1862;
his sale, Leipzig, Rudolph Weigel, 13 June
1864, no. 4826 (as Sadeler); Edwin Bryant
Crocker, Sacramento, by 1871; gift of his
widow Margaret to the Museum, 1885

LITERATURE: Katritzky 2006, p. 173, 181,
and fig. 278; Rollová 1993–94, p. 117;
Kaufmann 1985, p. 106; Kaufmann 1982,
no. 58; An Zwollo, "Pieter Stevens, nieuw
werk, contact met Jan Brueghel, invloed
op Kerstiaen de Deuninck," *Leids
Kunsthistorisch Jaarboek*, vol. I, 1982,
pp. 108–10, fig. 17; Trivas 1942, no. 116;
Rolas du Rosey sale, Weigel, Leipzig,
13 June and 5 September 1864, no. 4826
(as Sadeler); Sternberg-Manderscheid sale,
Carl Heinrich, Dresden, 10 November
1845, vol. V, no. 742

ALTHOUGH LITTLE is known of the earliest years of this Flemish artist's career, Pieter Stevens (c. 1567– after 1624) was established in Prague by 1594, when he became court painter to Emperor Rudolf II. He was still in imperial service in 1612, the year of the emperor's death, and apparently remained in Prague until at least 1624. In this thriving artistic environment, he came in contact with the work of a wide range of Mannerist landscape artists, including Roelandt Savery (1576–1639) and Jan Brueghel the Elder (1568–1625). Steven's own landscapes range from busy populated scenes like *The Month of February* to deserted woodlands. His drawings, especially those dating from the early 1600s, often demonstrate the sensitivity to atmospheric perspective evident in the present work, while the division of the composition into distinct planes and the anchoring presence of trees in the center of the scene are Mannerist devices typical of many of his landscapes.[1]

The theme of the Twelve Months, usually depicted in series of six or twelve images, was so popular among Stevens and his Flemish contemporaries that one art historian has described their production as taking place in "almost industrial quantities."[2] The Crocker drawing functioned as a model for the month of February in a series of twelve engravings by Aegidius Sadeler (c. 1570–1629), the main engraver of Stevens's designs and an important Rudolfine artist in his own right; the drawing is incised for transfer even in minor details.[3] Another drawing for the series survives: *January* (fig. 16), now in the National Gallery in Prague, is closely related to the Crocker drawing in size and composition. In addition, both drawings are surprisingly colorful, featuring Stevens's characteristic red and blue wash as well as brown ink.[4] The colors help to define space, create a sense of atmospheric perspective, and unify the composition in this complex scene, teeming with diverse activities. The artist's taste for these delicate washes may

NOTES

1. For an overview of Stevens's drawings, see *Praga Magica 1600, L'art à Prague au temps de Rodolphe II*, exh. cat. Musée national Magnin, Dijon, 2002, pp. 98–103.

2. Hans J. van Miegrot, "'The Twelve Months' Reconsidered: How a Drawing by Pieter Stevens Clarifies a Bruegel Enigma," *Simiolus: Netherlands Quarterly for the History of Art*, vol. 16, 1986, p. 33.

3. Hollstein 130.

4. Inv. no. K26962; Rollová 1993-94, p. 117. The colored washes appear in many of his other drawings, including, for instance, *A Wooded Landscape with Travelers by a Stream, a Town Beyond*, now in the Getty (84.GG.807).

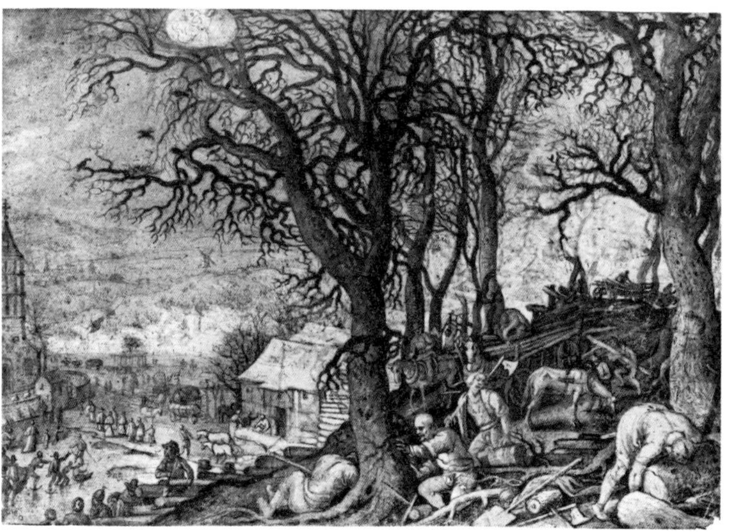

FIGURE 16
Pieter Stevens, *January*, n. d. Pen and dark-brown ink, brush and brown and red-brown washes, 20.1 × 28.8 cm. National Gallery, Prague

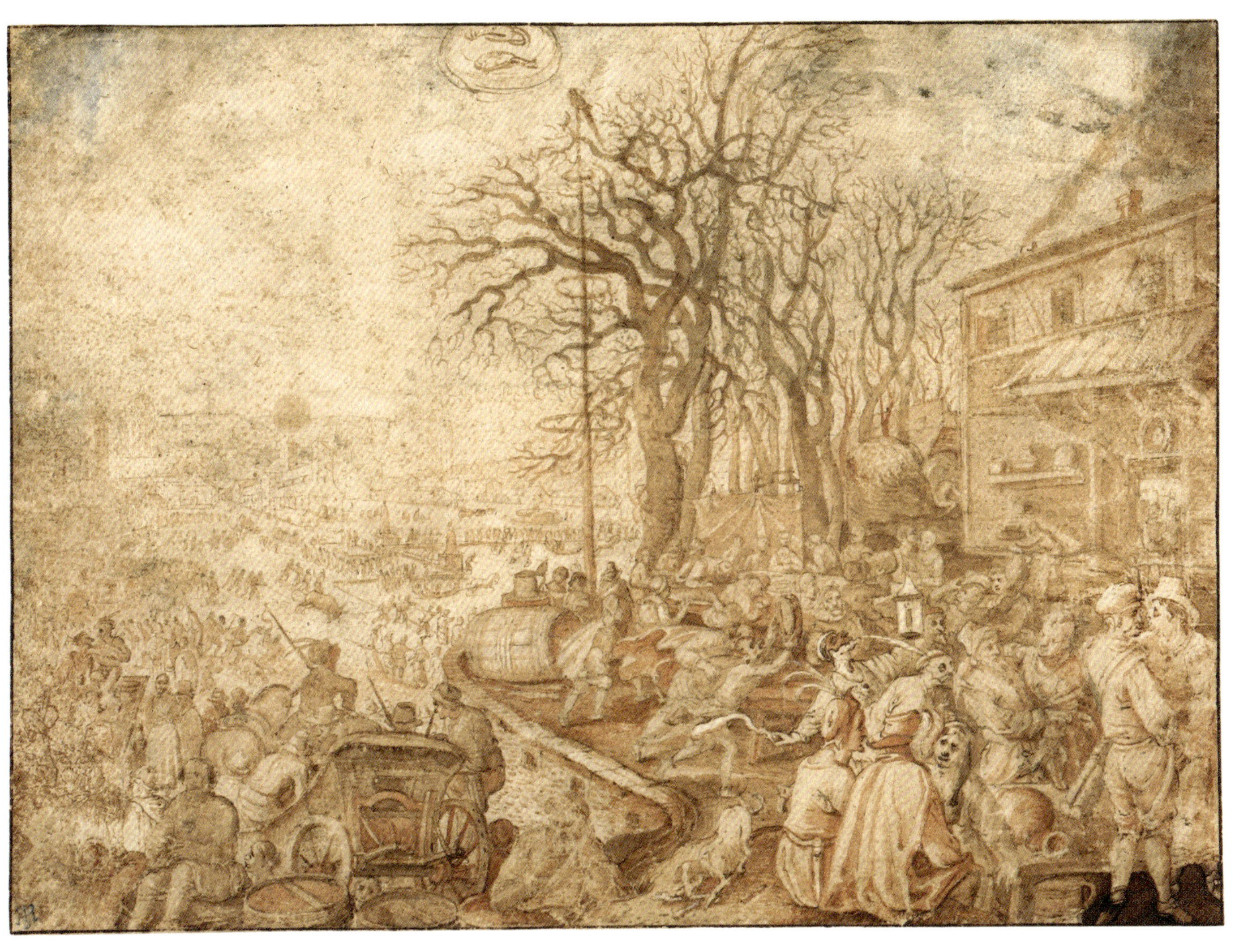

5. For the place of Stevens's design in this tradition, see Charles de Mooij et al., *Vastenavond–Carnival, Feesten van de omgekeerde wereld*, Zwolle, 1992, especially pp. 80–85 and no. 3, and Gaignebet 2004, no. 45. The depiction of Carnival to represent a time of year was a relatively recent development: earlier cycles of the months and seasons in manuscripts generally featured the labors of the months instead: Iain Buchanan, "The Collection of Nicolaes Jongelinck II: The 'Months' by Pieter Bruegel the Elder," *The Burlington Magazine*, vol. CXXXII, August 1990, p. 545.

6. See Katritzky 2006, p. 180.

7. For similar activity in carnival scenes, see Gaignebet 2004, pp. 63–67.

8. The bird on top of the pole could be decorative, as shown here, or real: sometimes, competitors climbed to the top of the pole to win their dinners. See, for instance, Gaignebet 2004, pp. 69–70, and Alison G. Stewart, *Before Bruegel: Sebald Beham and the Origins of Peasant Festival Imagery*, Burlington, 2008, p. 110.

9. Ibidem, pp. 194–96.

10. Kaufmann 1982, p. 160.

have been influenced by the drawings of Jan Brueghel the Elder, who visited Prague around the time of the execution of the present drawing.

Carnival celebrations, taking place in the period before Lent, often represented January and February in depictions of the months.[5] The Crocker drawing is crowded with revelers celebrating with typical carnival activities: in addition to the amorous couples and drinkers in the foreground, a troupe of *commedia dell'arte* actors appears on the outdoor stage in the lower left.[6] A bull running takes place in the distance.[7] The pole in the center of the composition was used for a competition long associated with carnival – the climbing of the greased pole.[8] The feast taking place in the center of the sheet may be a wedding, which were sometimes held during winter carnivals. Not only does the banner behind the party resemble those traditionally erected behind the bridal couple, but the woman's pose, with her demurely clasped hands, demonstrates ideal bridal behavior as depicted in German and Flemish art for over a century.[9] The sign of Pisces at the top indicates that this carnival scene was intended to depict February.

As noted by Thomas DaCosta Kaufmann, *February* must date from before 1607, when Sadeler's series of prints was published, but demonstrates sufficient affinity to Jan Brueghel's drawings to suggest that it was created after his arrival in Prague in 1604.[10] ss

19. **Jan Savery,** *Dodo Birds*, n. d.

Black chalk and brown wash, 14 × 20.9 cm. Crocker Art Museum,
E. B. Crocker Collection 1871.102

INSCRIPTIONS: black chalk, lower left:
SAVERŸ

MARKS: in blue, lower left corner: Lugt
2237 (Rolas du Rosey)

PROVENANCE: possibly Jungmeister;[1]
Rudolf Weigel, Leipzig, by 1849,
Kunstlagerkatalog, no. 1096; Carl Freiherr
von Rolas du Rosey, before 1862; his sale,
Leipzig, Rudolph Weigel, 13 June 1864,
no. 4836; Edwin Bryant Crocker,
Sacramento, by 1871; gift of his widow
Margaret to the Museum, 1885

LITERATURE: Breazeale 2008, p. 212;
Spicer 2004, p. 91, under no. 34; Hume and
Cheke, pp. 66, 69, and 74, as Roelandt;
Clara Pinto-Correia, *Return of the Crazy
Bird, the Sad, Strange Tale of the Dodo*, New
York, 2003, p. 78, as Roelandt; Ruda 1992,
no. 53, as Roelandt; Colin Eisler, *Dürer's
Animals*, Washington, D.C., 1991, pp. 265
and 356, fig. 10.30, as Roelandt; Joy
Kenseth, *The Age of the Marvelous*, exh. cat.
Hood Museum of Art, Hanover, NH, 1991,
p. 34, fig. 3, as Roelandt; Ruda 1985, n.p.,
as Roelandt; Kaufmann 1985, p. 101, as
Roelandt; Joaneath Spicer, review of
Kaufmann 1982, *Master Drawings*, vol. 22,
no. 3, 1984, p. 328, as Roelandt; Kaufmann
1982, p. 170, note 4 under no. 63, as
Roelandt; Joaneath Spicer, *Drawings of
Roelandt Savery*, PhD diss., Yale University,
1979, no. C 143 F 141, pp. 174, 185–86, as
Roelandt; Reno 1978, no. 2, as Roelandt;
Robinson 1977, no. 11, as Roelandt;
Crocker 1971, no. 39, as Roelandt; Schulz
1968, no. 71, as Roelandt; Reznicek 1961,
p. 207, as Roelandt; Walther Berndt, *Die
niederländischen Zeichner des 17. Jahrhunderts*, 2 vols., Munich, 1958, vol. II,
no. 533, as Roelandt; Jan Bialostocki, "Les
bêtes et les humains de Roelandt Savery,"

ALTHOUGH HE WAS A MEMBER of an important artistic family in Amsterdam, relatively little is known of the life of Jan Savery (1597–1654). After his father's death, Jan became close to his more famous uncle, the artist Roelandt Savery (1576–1639). Although Roelandt worked as a court painter in Prague from 1603 to 1613, he returned to Amsterdam at the end of his imperial service and took Jan as his assistant. The two artists also worked in Utrecht. Jan was so strongly influenced by his uncle that their styles can be difficult to distinguish: in fact, *Dodo Birds*, like its companion sketch *Elephants with a Monkey* (also in the Crocker; see fig. 17), is part of a large group of chalk drawings of animals that were all attributed to Roelandt until quite recently.[2] Joaneath Spicer has separated the chalk drawings into two categories: the first, by Roelandt, probably drawn from life at the imperial menagerie at Prague, is typified by a more naturalistic and "dignified" characterization of the animals. The second, by Jan, is notable for its expressive, often humorous depiction of animal personalities and relationships. Both Crocker drawings fall into this second category and both drawings are signed with only the artist's last name, a signature that Roelandt apparently did not use.[3]

First recorded by Western explorers on the island of Mauritius around 1600, dodos were extinct before the end of the seventeenth century. Early depictions of the birds show them as chubby or slim, colored or white, with webbed feet (as seen here) or without, leading to centuries of consternation in the world of dodo scholarship. Accuracy was probably a secondary concern for most artists depicting the birds, especially in the case

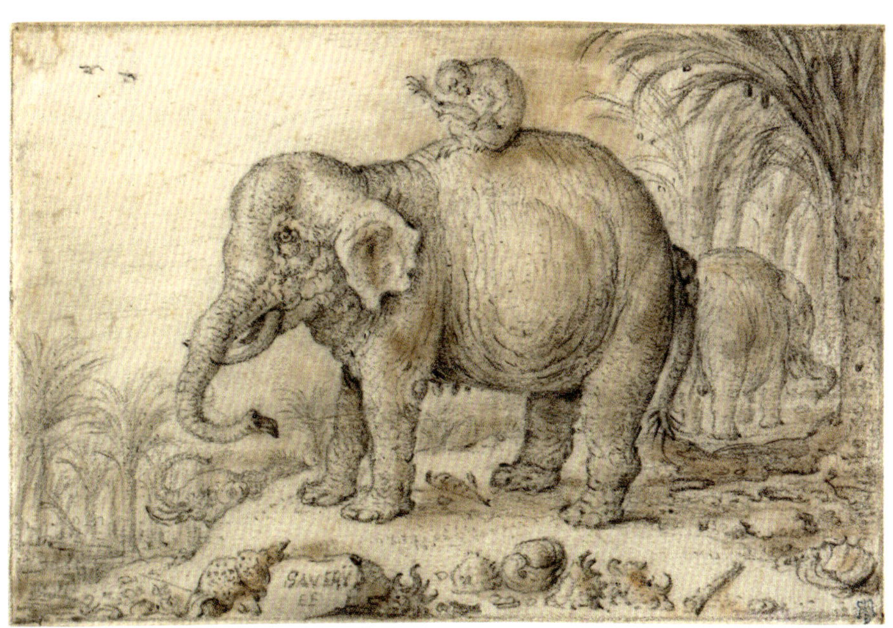

FIGURE 17 Jan Savery, *Elephants and
Monkey*, n. d. Black chalk and brown
wash, 14 × 21.1 cm. Crocker Art
Museum, E. B. Crocker Collection

*Bulletin, Musées royaux des beaux-arts de
Belgique*, vol. VII, no. 2, 1958, p. 87, as
Roelandt; H. Friedman, "New Light on
the Dodo and its Illustrators," *Smithsonian
Report*, 1956, pp. 475–81, as Roelandt;
Roelandt Savery 1576–1639, exh. cat.
Museum voor Schone Kunsten, Ghent,
1954, no. 107, p. 31, and under no. 75, as
Roelandt; Trivas 1942, no. 112, as
Roelandt; Rudolph Weigel, *Kunstlager-
katalog*, Leipzig, 1838–66, no. 1096, as
Roelandt; Rolas du Rosey sale, Leipzig,
Rudolph Weigel, 13 June 1864, no. 4836,
as Roelandt

NOTES
1. Notation in Rolas du Rosey sale catalogue,
   as above.
2. Related drawings include the *Lion
   Attacking a Horse* in Ottawa (Spicer 2004,
   no. 34), as well as drawings in Rotterdam
   and Berlin (Kaufmann 1982, p. 170).
3. Spicer 2004, p. 91.
4. For some of these variations, see Hume
   and Cheke 2004, pp. 66 and 74 n. 33.
5. *Ibidem*, p. 66.
6. Kaufmann 1982, p. 170.

of this comical and endearing image. The Crocker birds reappear, sometimes slightly
altered or reversed, in numerous paintings, drawings, and prints, not only by both of the
Saverys and their contemporaries but by illustrators well into the nineteenth century.[4]
According to an inscription on a drawing by Adriaen de Venne (1589–1662), a live dodo
appeared in Amsterdam in 1626, but there is no reason to suppose, as one dodologist has
posited, that this bird is depicted in the Crocker drawing, or even that the Crocker sheet
was drawn from life.[5] The difficulty of establishing a Savery chronology, or even of
separating the hands of the two artists, makes it impossible to determine whether the
present drawing was the source of the many other dodos, or simply one version among
many.

As Thomas DaCosta Kaufmann has noted of the Crocker *Elephants with a Monkey*, the
detailed if fanciful settings and the signatures on both drawings suggest that they were
part of a series of finished drawings intended for a collector.[6] Other animals depicted in
the series include lions, monkeys, and camels. The early seventeenth-century fascination
with natural wonders from distant lands would have made these drawings appealing
additions to any number of collections or *Wunderkammern*.   SS

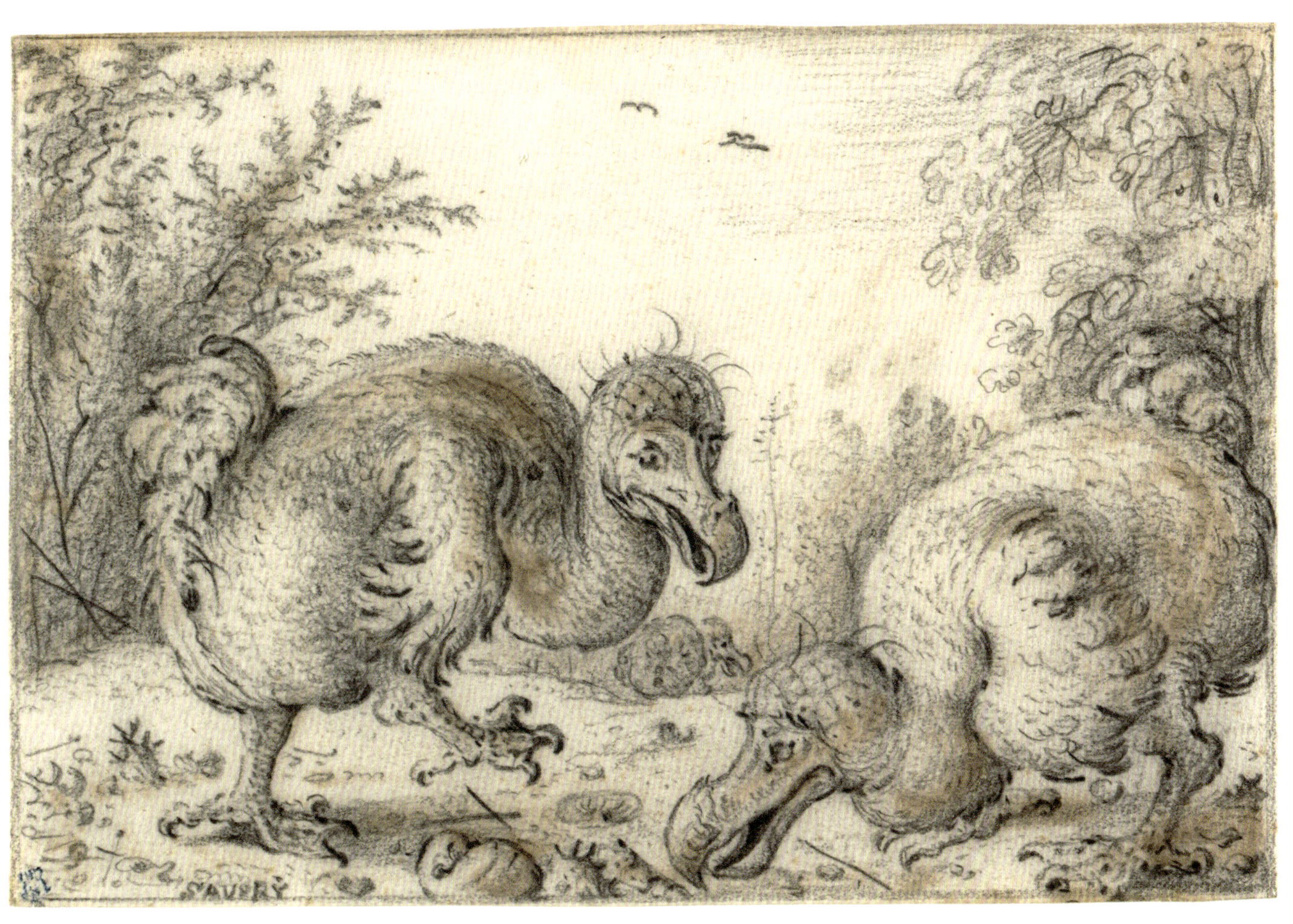

SAVERY

20. **Anthony van Dyck**, *Portrait of Paulus Halmalius*, n. d.

Black and white chalk, touches of red chalk, corner mounted to heavy cream laid-paper mount, laid down in its turn to grayish wove card, 22.8 × 20.3 cm. Crocker Art Museum, E. B. Crocker Collection 1871.106

INSCRIPTIONS: verso, dark-brown ink, lower left along bottom margin: *A: Van Dyck fe:*; mount, recto, black chalk, center bottom margin: *Anton van Dyck f.*

MARKS: verso, lower left corner: Lugt 474 (?) (pseudo-Crozat) (also resembles Lugt 1893 and 481)

PROVENANCE: Edwin Bryant Crocker, Sacramento, by 1871; gift of his widow Margaret to the Museum, 1885

LITERATURE: Jaffé 2002, no. 50; Vey 1962, p. 320, under no. 254 (as "*eine Kopie met Veränderungen*"); Crocker 1959, no. 5; Alfred Neumeyer, "Anthonie van Dyck," *Old Master Drawings*, vol. XIV, nos. 54–56, September 1939– March 1940, pp. 56–57; Trivas 1942, no. 35

ONE OF THE FOREMOST Flemish painters of the seventeenth century, Anthony van Dyck (1599–1641) was a prodigy, demonstrating great promise during his early years in the studio of Peter Paul Rubens (1577–1640) and already internationally famous by his early twenties. In 1620, he moved to England to work for King James I, leaving for Italy the next year. He returned to Antwerp in 1627 and divided the remainder of his career between the Southern Netherlands and England, attracting honors and royal and noble patronage in both places.

Like Rubens, Van Dyck recognized the value of printmaking as a means of disseminating a painter's works and of spreading his fame throughout Europe. His portraits were particularly well known, and from the late 1620s Van Dyck embarked on the first stage of a long-term project intended to highlight this aspect of his oeuvre – the series of portrait engravings known today as the *Iconography*.[1] The Crocker drawing is closely

NOTES

1. The literature on the complex history of the *Iconography* is extensive. For the best reconstruction of Van Dyck's changing intentions and preparatory techniques, with extensive bibliography, see Spicer 1994, pp. 327–58. For a concise discussion of the series and its art historical context, see Ger Luijten, "The Iconography: Van Dyck's Portraits in Print," in Carl Depauw and Ger Luijten, *Anthony van Dyck as a Printmaker*, New York, 1999, pp. 73–103. For states and editions, see Mauquoy-Hendrickx 1956 and Simon Turner, *The New Hollstein: Dutch and Flemish Etchings, Engravings, and Woodcuts, 1450–1700, Anthony Van Dyck, Part I*, Rotterdam, 2002.

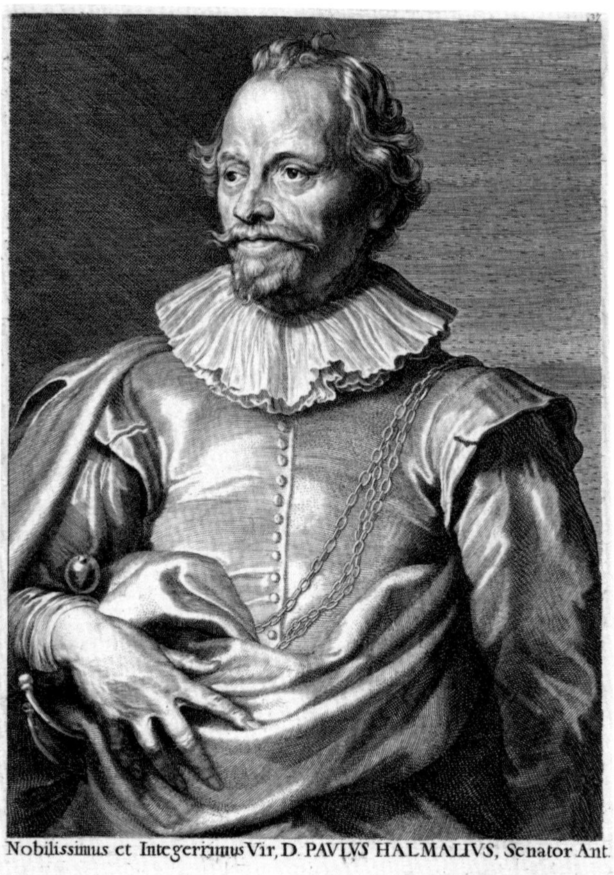

FIGURE 18 Pieter de Jode II after Anthony van Dyck, *Paulus Halmalius*, n. d. Engraving, 24.5 × 17.3 cm. British Museum, London

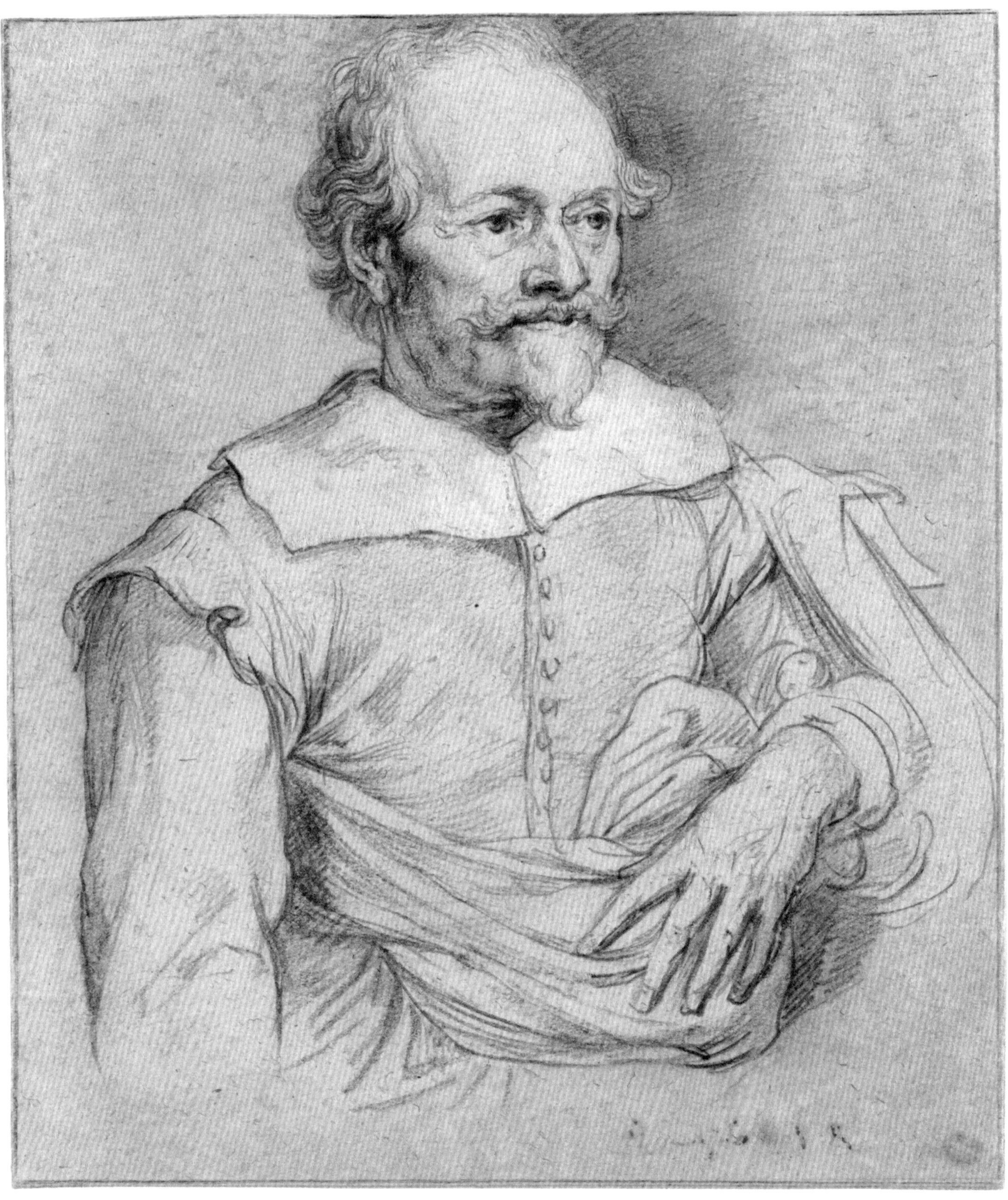

related to the *Iconography*'s portrait of Paulus Halmalius, or Paul van Halmale (1562–1648), a senator, magistrate and art collector.[2] Van Dyck may have intended to etch the portraits in the *Iconography* himself, but he made only eighteen plates, arranging for professional printmakers to engrave the rest. Pieter de Jode II (1601–1674?), the engraver of the portrait of Halmalius (fig. 18),[3] executed twelve plates for the series.

It is difficult to situate the Crocker drawing within the preparatory steps Van Dyck followed for most of the *Iconography* portraits. Most of the engravings in the series reproduce paintings by Van Dyck, with the intermediary steps of a black-chalk drawing and then a carefully modeled wash or oil sketch or a touched counterproof.[4] The present drawing, however, differs from the other black-chalk sketches, which tend to anticipate details of costume and features as seen in the engraving quite closely. In contrast, the collar, the arrangement of drapery, and even the shape of Halmalius's face all vary between the Crocker drawing and the finished engraving. Instead, a second drawing of Halmalius now at Chatsworth is more typical of the preparatory drawings, anticipating the engraving in the sitter's elegant proportions and in details of costume.[5] Moreover, the combination of red and black chalk as well as the nearly square format of the Crocker drawing set it apart from the other preparatory chalk sketches.

The painting of Halmalius, if it ever existed, has been lost.[6] In only one other case in the *Iconography* do two chalk drawings survive, one more closely related to the etching than the other. In that instance, as with the *Paulus Halmalius*, no associated painting is known, and Joneath Spicer posits that Van Dyck made the more distantly related sketch from life.[7] Although Horst Vey viewed the Crocker drawing as a copy with changes from the Chatsworth version, Michael Jaffé considers the present sketch "an original ... of high quality drawn by Van Dyck, with numerous pentimenti." These pentimenti, as well as the sitter's comparatively unidealized appearance, suggest that the Crocker version may have been made from life, with the Chatsworth sketch an intermediate step in refining the image for publication in the *Iconography*.   SS

2. *Ibidem*, p. 152, and Mauquoy-Hendrickx 1956, p. 128.

3. This impression British Museum inv. no. 1863-5-9-855.

4. Spicer 1994, p. 334. Although a counterproof for this print does exist in the British Museum (inv. no. 1841-12-11-42), it is not touched with oil or wash. For a summary of varying views of the preparatory steps, see Spicer 1994, p. 353 n. 65, with bibliography. There is also an oil sketch in Hamburg, and others "of lesser quality" (E. Larsen, *The Paintings of Anthony van Dyck*, Freren 1988, no. 534).

5. Vey 1962, no. 254, and Jaffé 2002, p. 33.

6. As Spicer points out, Van Dyck's use of the term "*pinxit*" in the published engravings appears to be a deliberate choice, indicating the existence of a painting.

7. Spicer lists two preparatory drawings for the portrait of Pieter Brueghel the Younger (Mauquoy-Hendricx 1956, no. 2): Spicer 1994, pp. 33 and 357.

21. **Bartholomaeus Breenbergh**, *Temple of the Tiburtine Sibyl at Tivoli, 1627*

Pen and brown ink, brush and brown and grayish-brown washes, 32.5 × 31 cm.
Crocker Art Museum, E. B. Crocker Collection 1871.155

INSCRIPTIONS: black chalk, lower right: BB [monogram] *f. Ano 1627*; dark-brown ink, lower right corner: *Tempio della Sybilla Tiburtina a Tivoli*

MARKS: lower right corner: Lugt 2237 (Rolas du Rosey)

PROVENANCE: Rudolph Weigel, Leipzig, by 1849, *Kunstlagerkatalog*, no. 1109; Carl Freiherr von Rolas du Rosey, before 1862; his sale, Leipzig, Rudolph Weigel, 13 June 1864, no. 4395; Edwin Bryant Crocker, Sacramento, by 1871; gift of his widow Margaret to the Museum, 1885

LITERATURE: Dittrich 1997, under no. 78; Ruda 1992, no. 56; Ruda 1985, no. 4; Stampfle 1979, under no. 62; *Remnants of Things Past*, exh. cat. Museum of Fine Arts, Saint Petersburg, Florida, 1971, no. 8; Roethlisberger 1969, no. 88; Schulz 1968, no. 65; Malcolm Waddingham, "Adam Elsheimer and His Circle at Frankfurt," *The Burlington Magazine*, vol. CIX, no. 766, January 1967, p. 48 n. 8; *The Changeful Earth*, exh. cat. UCLA; Los Angeles, 1955, no. 15; Trivas 1942, no. 17; Trivas 1940a, no. 25; Rolas du Rosey sale, Rudolph Weigel, Leipzig, 1864, no. 4395; Weigel, *Kunstlagerkatalog*, no. 1109

BORN IN DEVENTER and apparently first active as an artist in Amsterdam, Bartholomaeus Breenbergh (1598-1657) was among the earliest of the flood of Dutch artists who would study in Rome during the seventeenth century. He was a founding member of the Schildersbent, the society of Dutch painters working in Rome. Although he remained in Rome for about a decade, from *c.* 1619 to *c.* 1629, relatively few of his paintings from this period are known, and his artistic development can be traced mainly through his drawings. During this time he worked with the Dutch painter Paul Bril (1554–1626), who exerted an important influence on the younger artist. Breenbergh's draughtsmanship also resembles that of his contemporary Cornelis Poelenberg (1594 or 1595–1667), a fellow student of Bril's.[1] After Breenbergh's return to Amsterdam, he turned for inspiration to an earlier generation of Dutch artists, the "Pre-Rembrandtists," in particular to Pieter Lastman (1583–1633). During this later stage of his career, Breenbergh favored biblical scenes set in somewhat mannered landscapes, peppered with classical ruins of the type he had seen in Rome, though he also painted portraits.[2]

In contrast to his sparse output of paintings during his Roman period, Breenbergh's production of drawings from this decade was prodigious and forms the largest part of his oeuvre. He mined these drawings for motifs for the rest of his life, repeating the ruins he sketched in both etchings and paintings. While he sometimes drew pure landscapes, he favored views of the Roman countryside that included architecture, such as scenes from the Orsini park at Bomarzo and the classical ruins at Tivoli. In technique and subject matter, the Crocker drawing is typical of his draughtsmanship: most of his Roman drawings, like this one, consist of black chalk underdrawings overlaid with brown ink and wash. Clearly fascinated by the dramatic effects of the bright Italian sunlight passing over crumbling ruins, the artist used a wide variety of touches, ranging from broad areas of smooth wash through a range of different pen strokes, to capture the fall of light and shadow.

The town of Tivoli, located about twenty miles outside of Rome, over centuries attracted artists to its Roman ruins, dramatic waterfalls, and views of the surrounding *campagna*. Breenbergh returned to the area a number of times during his years in Rome. Although he sketched a variety of views, here he chose to concentrate on the most popular of the ruins, the circular Temple of the Sibyl, or Temple of Vesta. Dating from the first century BC, the temple was later used as a Christian chapel: a lunette of the Madonna is visible through the door in the present drawing. The same temple appears in a number of other drawings by Breenbergh.[3] An unsigned drawing in Dresden (fig. 19) is another version of the Crocker sheet, which Christian Dittrich regards as a workshop copy.[4] Dittrich points out that the irregularities and weak areas in the Dresden sketch are corrected in the Crocker version, resulting in a less spontaneous,

NOTES

1. Their drawings are often confused: see, for instance, Marian Bisanz-Prakken, *Rembrandt and His Time: Masterworks from the Albertina*, exh. cat. Milwaukee Art Museum, 2005, no. 262.

2. For overviews of Breenbergh's career, see M. Roethlisberger, *Bartholomeus Breenbergh: The Paintings*, Berlin, 1981; Roethlisberger 1969; and Peter Schatborn, *Drawn to Warmth, 17th-century Dutch Artists in Italy*, exh. cat. Rijksmuseum, Amsterdam, 2001, pp. 66–73.

3. The attribution of the drawing in the Morgan Library is a matter of some controversy (Turner and Stampfle 2006, no. 286, as "attributed to Swanevelt"); so is attribution of the version in Dresden (Dittrich 1997, no. 78).

4. Inv. no. C1898-30; Roethlisberger, 1969, no. 87, on the other hand, attributed the Dresden version to Poelenburgh.

more careful drawing. Indeed, the precision with which the draughtsman followed the black chalk guidelines with pen and wash suggests that the Crocker drawing may be a later version completed in the studio rather than *in situ*. The liveliness of handling and sparkling contrast between sun and shade, however, are characteristic of Breenbergh's Roman drawings, and there is no reason to believe the Crocker drawing is a workshop copy rather than a second version by the artist, who sometimes repeated his own compositions.

ss

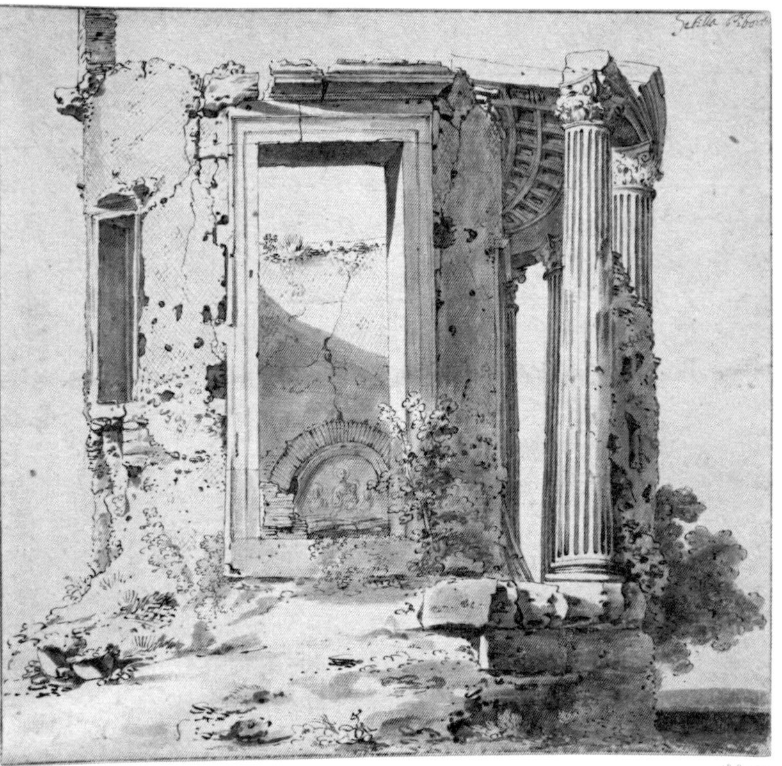

FIGURE 19 Bartholomaeus Breenbergh, *The Temple of the Tiburtine Sibyl at Tivoli*, n. d. Pen and dark-brown ink, brush and brown washes over black chalk, 26.1 × 27.8 cm. Kuperstichkabinett, Dresden

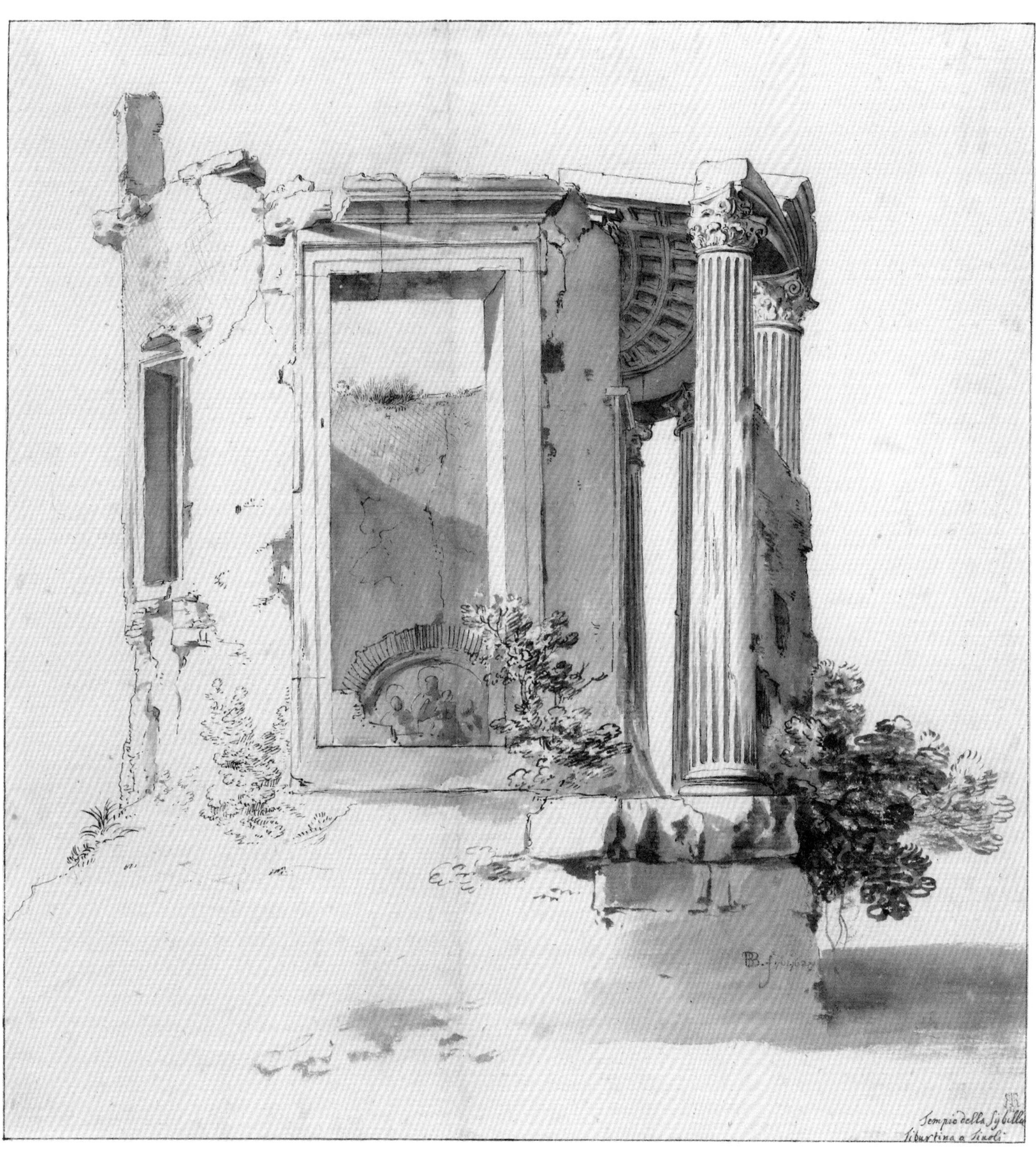

Tempio della Sybilla
Tiburtina a Tivoli

 Simon de Vlieger, *Landscape,* n. d.

Black and white chalks, brush and point of brush and gray wash on blue laid paper, 38.4 × 53.4 cm.
Crocker Art Museum, E. B. Crocker Collection 1871.352

INSCRIPTIONS: verso, graphite, lower left: *No. 129;* dark-brown ink, lower left: *180 z*

MARKS: none

PROVENANCE: Edwin Bryant Crocker, Sacramento, by 1871; gift of his widow Margaret to the Museum, 1885

LITERATURE: Trivas 1942, no. 136; Trivas 1940a, no. 52

NOTES

1. In Spicer 2004, 136. Similar drawings survive in collections all over the world: see, for example, Spicer 2004, no. 57; Schapelhouman and Schatborn 1987, p. 34; Hautekeete 2007, no. 41; Michiel Plomp, *The Dutch Drawings in the Teyler Museum, Haarlem,* 1997, nos. 513–17; Stampfle 1979, no. 65. For de Vlieger's pen drawings, see Christiaan P. van Eeghen, "Simon de Vlieger as a Draftsman, I: The Pen Drawings," in *Master Drawings,* vol. XLIV, no. 1, 2006, pp. 3–47.
2. For Van der Haagen and de Vlieger, see Hautekeete 2007, p. 129. For Jan van Kessel, see Farr and Bradford 1986, no. 67, p. 158.
3. Hautekeete 2007, 132, and [no author listed], "Keuze uit de aanwisten," *Bulletin van het Rijksmuseum,* 1986, no. 1, pp. 37–38 and 44–45.
4. Schapelhoumann and Schatborn 1987, p. 34.
5. Hautekeet 2007, no. 42.
6. Bonebakker in Spicer 2004, no. 57.
7. Both drawings are attributed to de Vlieger by Charles Dumas and illustrated in Budapest 2007, p. 162.
8. *Ibidem,* p. 162.

A S A PAINTER, Simon de Vlieger (1601–1653) specialized in marine scenes ranging from stormy shipwrecks to ceremonial parades. Although he also occasionally painted forest scenes, it was as a draughtsman that he most fully explored the genre of landscape, and the Crocker drawing typifies this important aspect of his career. As Odilia Bonebakker has noted, de Vlieger's finished landscape studies fall into two categories— smaller vertical scenes and larger horizontal compositions like this one.[1] These detailed black- and white-chalk drawings on blue paper, often touched with gray wash, were finished works of art in their own right, not studies for paintings or for the landscape etchings that de Vlieger also produced.

While de Vlieger sometimes signed these drawings, many lack signatures, including the Crocker work. The similarity of de Vlieger's draughtsmanship to that of his contemporaries Anthonie Waterloo, Jan van Kessel, and Joris van der Haagen has led to recurring confusion, as have monograms or signatures added by collectors over the past three centuries.[2] A group of signed landscapes by de Vlieger, acquired by the Rijksmuseum in 1985, has clarified some aspects of his draughtsmanship and assisted in the attribution of many of the unsigned drawings.[3] Even now, however, the hands of de Vlieger and Waterloo are difficult to differentiate, though some scholars believe that Waterloo only rarely used blue paper.[4] The linear treatment of the distant landscape in the Crocker drawing, for instance, resembles the view of Haarlem in the background of a drawing in Brussels, but scholars are divided on the attribution of that sheet.[5]

Several aspects of the Crocker drawing's style point toward Simon de Vlieger as the artist. The use of white chalk to suggest patches of dappled sunlight as well as the strong contrast between patches of sun and shade on the ground both resemble the description of light in de Vlieger's drawings, including the example in Ottawa.[6] The serpentine tree branches also recall those in a number of drawings by de Vlieger, and the motif of the path winding into the distance recurs in several of his landscapes. Although de Vlieger used a variety of techniques to evoke different types of foliage, the spiky bunches of leaves and broad areas of wash seen here both appear in his other drawings. The composition of the Crocker drawing is especially close to that of an example now in Budapest, while the gentle hills recall the terrain in the Budapest drawing and one in The Hague.[7]

Because most of de Vlieger's landscape sketches are undated, it is difficult at the present time to establish a chronology for these drawings. In addition, the artist moved several times during the course of his career, living at various times in Delft, Amsterdam, and Rotterdam. Both factors complicate any attempt to pinpoint the settings of his landscape drawings. Two sheets, however, bear inscriptions locating the landscapes in the woods outside of The Hague, offering one possibility for their inspiration whether or not they were actually drawn from life.[8]

SS

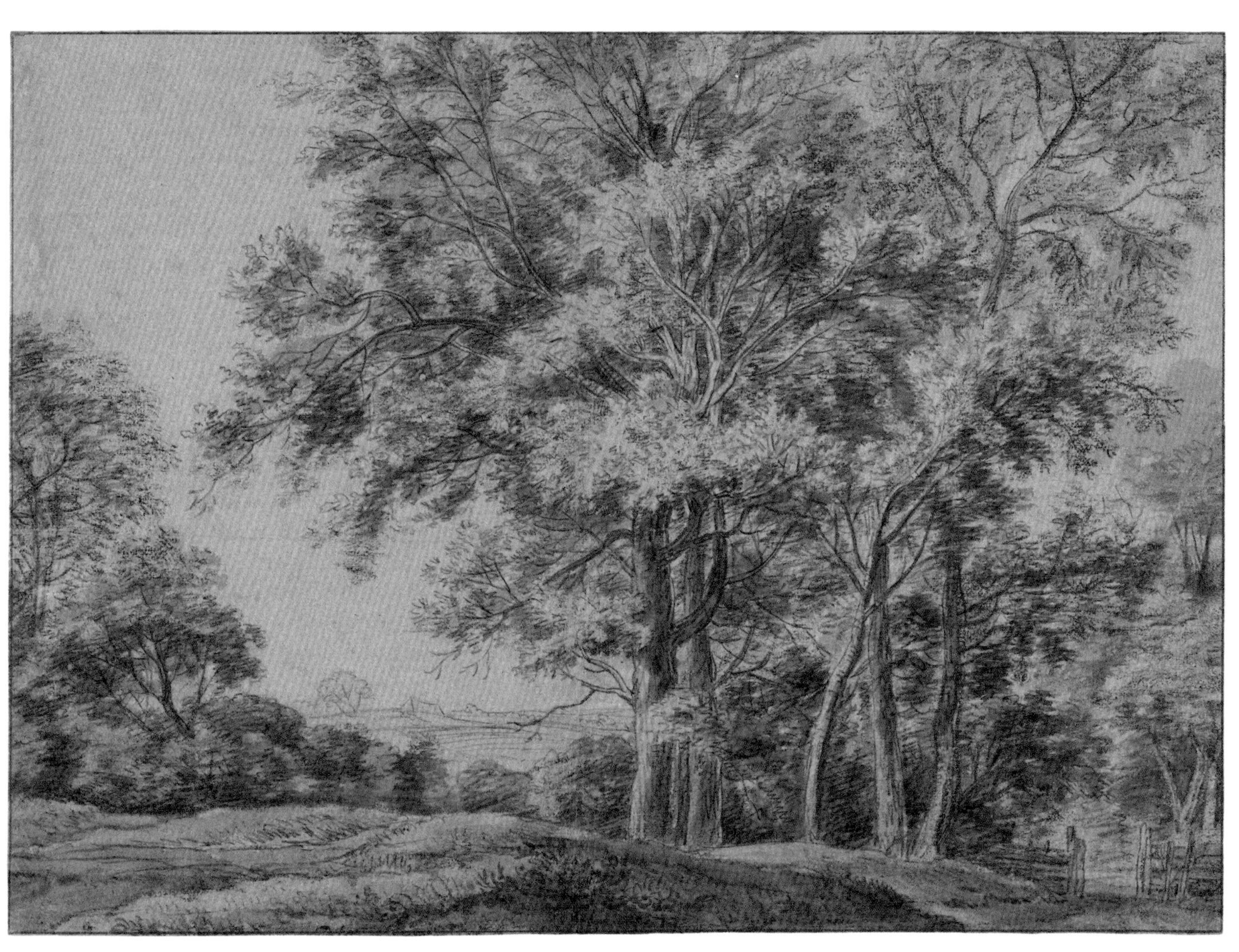

23. **Rembrandt van Rijn** (?), *Liberation of Saint Peter*, mid 1630s

Pen and dark-brown ink, brush and blue-gray wash, 9.6 × 8.5 cm. Crocker Art Museum,
E. B. Crocker Collection 1871.134

INSCRIPTIONS: none

MARKS: none

PROVENANCE: Edwin Bryant Crocker, Sacramento, by 1871; gift of his widow Margaret to the Museum, 1885

LITERATURE: Howard et al. 1983, no. 30; Reno 1978, no. 18; Benesch 1973, no. 126, fig. 146; Crocker 1971, no. 57; Crocker 1964, pp. 22, 69; Crocker 1959, no. 4; Henle 1940, no. 84; Trivas 1942, no. 99; Trivas 1940b, pp. 135–37; Numa S. Trivas, "Rembrandt van Rijn (1606–1669)," *Old Master Drawings*, September – March 1939–40, pp. 57-58

NOTES

1. William W. Robinson, "Rembrandt's Sketches of Historical Subjects," in *Drawings Defined*, Walter Strauss and Tracie Felker, eds., New York, 1987, pp. 241–57.

2. See, for instance, *The Rape of Ganymede*, Dresden (Benesch 92), where the figures of the parents are roughed in and surrounded by a chaotic tangle of lines.

3. Benesch 100 and 133 respectively. For a thorough discussion of these drawings, see Bevers 2006, nos. 9 and 10.

4. See, for instance, *Ruth and Boaz* (Benesch 133); *Lot and His Daughters* (Benesch 128); and two student drawings in the Rijksprentenkabinet, in Schatborn 1985, nos. 74 and 75.

5. See, for instance, both versions of *Jacob Blessing Josephs' Sons* in the Rijksprentenkabinet (Schatborn 1985, nos. 74 and 75). In addition, the *Old Man in Profile* (Benesch 1106) at the Metropolitan Museum of Art exhibits a similar lack of modeling and is now assigned to "Rembrandt (?)": Carolyn Logan, in Lietdke et al. 1995, no. 67.

6. Compare, for example, the more coherent use of hatching in the equally abbreviated *Ruth and Boaz* (Benesch 133).

ONE OF THE MOST prolific and accomplished draughtsmen in the history of art, Rembrandt van Rijn (1606–1669) viewed drawing as a matter of central importance to his own work as well as to that of his many students. He made direct preparatory studies relatively rarely, and most of his surviving drawings do not relate directly to a painting or print. Instead, many of his sketches appear to have functioned partly as exercise for the imagination, independent of finished works of art.[1] Leader of a thriving workshop even early in his career, he passed on this habit to his students, apparently setting them the assignment of drawing a particular subject as a way of learning to compose and to express emotion and narrative. Like other masters of the time, Rembrandt also used his own sketches as teaching tools. His students made careful copies of his drawings, transcribing even the scribbles and pentimenti characteristic of his rough draughtsmanship. They absorbed his style so thoroughly that many of them continued to draw in Rembrandt's manner long after they left his workshop. For all these reasons, the task of separating Rembrandt's own drawings from those of his pupils is a particularly arduous task.

In many ways, *The Liberation of Saint Peter* fits into Rembrandt's draughtsmanship of the mid 1630s, as it was dated by Otto Benesch. Rembrandt drew in an especially sketchy style at this point, sometimes simply indicating subsidiary figures.[2] He clearly reveled in the expressive possibility of the pen line, varying the pressure to create thick and thin lines, leaving pentimenti clearly visible, and shading with scribbles rather than with the neater techniques more common among his Dutch contemporaries. The Crocker drawing fits this pattern: an earlier version of the angel, positioned higher on the page than the final version, remains clearly visible, and his finely delineated face forms a striking contrast with the rough, heavy lines on the lower part of the sheet. This same contrast appears in a number of Rembrandt's drawings from the mid 1630s, such as the *Lamentation under the Cross* or *Ruth and Boaz*, both in Berlin.[3] Compositionally, the Crocker sketch also has a great deal in common with several drawings by Rembrandt and his school from the mid 1630s.[4]

Nevertheless, other aspects of the Crocker drawing deviate from Rembrandt's style of draughtsmanship. Most notably, The *Liberation of Saint Peter* exhibits a lack of clarity in both form and expression. Even in Rembrandt's roughest drawings, elements crucial to the narrative content of the drawing, such as facial expression or gesture, are generally described with a lucidity absent from this sketch. Not only are the attitudes of the two figures here difficult to read, but their poses are also indistinct: the angel's body and wings are left almost totally blank, leaving its pose unclear, and the vaguely defined limbs, including the awkward foreshortening of the angel's arm and its claw-shaped hand, are more typical of student drawings than of those by Rembrandt himself.[5] Finally, the almost calligraphic scribble in the lower foreground serves no clear purpose: Rembrandt was more likely to use this rough shading to darken areas thrown into shadow, again contributing to the weight of the forms.[6]

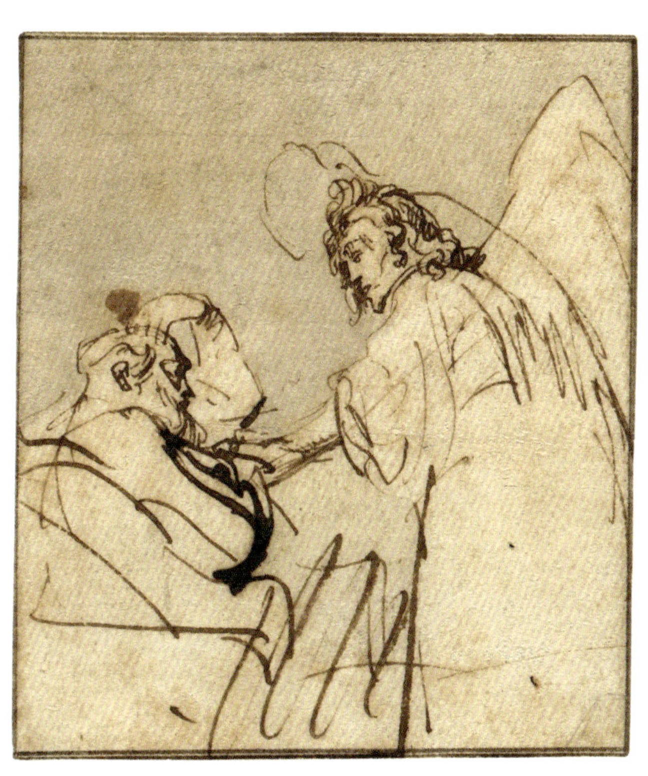

7. Josua Bruyn et al., *A Corpus of Rembrandt Paintings*, Boston, 1982–.

8. Among the most important of these are Schatborn 1985; Martin Royalton-Kisch, *Drawings by Rembrandt and His Circle in the British Museum*, London, 1992; Jeroen Giltaij, *The Drawings by Rembrandt and His School in the Museum Boymans-van Beuningen*, Rotterdam, 1988; Thea Vignau-Wilberg, *Rembrandt auf Papier: Werk und Wirkung*, Munich, 2003; and Bevers 2006.

9. Bevers 2006, p. 6. Other re-evaluations have had similar results: the Rijksmuseum and the Museum Boijmans-van Beuningen, for instance, have both reduced the number of secure attributions to Rembrandt to about half of those accepted by Benesch (Bevers *et al.* 1991, p. 11). In America, the Metropolitan Museum of Art owns nineteen drawings attributed to Rembrandt by Benesch, but now accepts only eleven as secure attributions (Logan in Liedtke *et al.* 1995, pp. 155–56).

10. For example, Benesch himself compared the Crocker drawing to *Jacob's Dream* in Berlin (Benesch 125), which is apparently not among the fifty-five drawings to survive the re-evaluation of the collection by Bevers. Additionally, *The Prophet Elijah and the Widow Sarepta* in the Louvre (Benesch 112) is also now considered the work of a follower (Schatborn 1985, p. 16 n. 3; and Bevers *et al.* 1991, p. 194 n. 7).

In the same way that the Rembrandt Research Project, formed in 1968, has attempted to separate the hands of Rembrandt and his followers in paintings,[7] similar efforts are taking place as major museums reconsider their collections of drawings attributed to the artist.[8] The results have been startling: in Berlin, for example, the collection of 126 drawings once believed to be the work of Rembrandt has been pared down to a group of fifty-five.[9] Among the casualties of these re-examinations have been several of the drawings once compared to the Crocker sketch.[10] Because of the scarcity of signed or preparatory sketches by Rembrandt and the proximity of his hand to those of his many students and followers, his style of draughtsmanship is redefined with each generation of scholarship, and it is likely that in decades to come the current definition will be viewed as too narrow. At this time, however, the possibility must be considered that the Crocker sketch is the work of a follower rather than of Rembrandt himself.

24. **Otto Marseus van Schrieck**, *Morning Glory and Butterflies*, n. d.

Brush and watercolor with applied decoration on three separate fragments of cream laid paper,
19.4 × 15.3 cm. Crocker Art Museum, E. B. Crocker Collection, 1871.467

INSCRIPTIONS: dark-brown ink, lower left corner: O.M.S.

MARKS: none

PROVENANCE: Edwin Bryant Crocker, Sacramento, by 1871; gift of his widow Margaret to the Museum, 1885

LITERATURE: Breazeale 2008, p. 212; Breazeale 2007, pp. 527–33, fig. 1; Steensma 1999, no. A110, p. 105; Trivas 1942, no. 72; Trivas 1940b, p. 137

NOTES

1. For Van Schrieck's years in Italy, see Hildebrecht 2004, pp. 47–71 and 250–282, and Fausta Franchini-Guelfi, "Otto Marseus van Schrieck a Firenze, contributo alla storia dei rapporti fra scienza e arti figurative nel Seicento toscano," in two parts in *Antichità Viva*, vol. XVI, no. 2, March–April 1977, pp. 15–26, and no. 4, July–August 1977, pp. 13–21.

2. Steensma 1999, pp. 10–22.

3. For a detailed account of this technique and its use by other artists, see Steensma 1999, pp. 61–67; see also Hildebrecht 2004, pp. 137–40. The technique was first discovered by Bodo Beier in the work of Johann Falch.

4. Steensma 1999, p. 61. Among the other artists to incorporate butterfly wings into paintings was Van Schrieck's follower Elias van den Broeck, whose biographer claimed he was driven out of Antwerp by angry customers for the practice. See Fred G. Meijer, *The Collection of Dutch and Flemish Still-life Paintings Bequeathed by Daisy Linda Ward*, Oxford, 2003, pp. 184–85.

5. Breazeale 2007, pp. 527–33.

6. For the allegorical content of other still lifes by Van Schrieck, see Ingvar Bergström, "Marseus, peintre de fleurs, papillons, et serpents," *L'Œil*, vol. 223, December 1974, pp. 24–29. For varying interpretations of the *sottoboschi*, see Steensma 1999, pp. 77–79.

7. Breazeale 2007, pp. 529–33.

8. Steensma 1999, p. 105.

FAMOUS FOR HIS development of the *sottobosco*, a specific type of still life depicting lizards, frogs, and creatures of the forest floor, Otto Marseus van Schrieck (1619/20–1678) also painted more conventional flower pieces. The Dutch painter traveled widely, spending time in England and France before moving to Italy in the company of his pupil Willem van Aelst (1627– after 1687) before 1652. Once there, he worked in Rome for several years before he moved on to Florence, where his meticulous botanical and zoological paintings attracted the interest of the more scientifically minded members of the Medici family.[1] Upon his return to Amsterdam in about 1656, Van Schrieck settled down to paint, collect art, and raise the reptiles, amphibians, and insects that feature so prominently in many of his works.[2] His followers, including Rachel Ruysch (1664–1750), carried his subject matter and techniques well into the eighteenth century.

While at first glance the *Morning Glory and Butterflies* appears to be a simple watercolor, microscopic examination reveals Van Schrieck's use of an unusual technique: he pressed real butterfly wings onto a prepared ground on paper, leaving a powdery colored residue in the pattern of the original butterfly. He then cut out these counterproofs and glued them to the sheet seen here, filling in any losses in the pattern with watercolor.[3] Van Schrieck used this technique in a number of his oil paintings, sometimes supplementing the counterproofs with real insect parts, ranging from butterfly wings to fly legs.[4] Similar practices have been detected in the works of a number of artists in Van Schrieck's circle, including Ruysch. *The Morning-Glory and Butterflies* proves that he used the same technique in his drawings, which are extremely rare.[5]

In contrast to the meticulous delicacy of the butterfly wings, the flowers and vine are summarily executed. Clearly this watercolor was not intended to provide the artist with an accurate visual record of the plant for later use in his paintings. Instead, it was probably conceived as a finished work of art in its own right. Van Schrieck may have considered the morning glory a prop for the butterflies, leading the viewer to focus on his unusual technique. As flowers that bloom and fade within a day, however, morning glories could have contributed to the meaning of the image as a whole, working in harmony with the fragile butterflies to remind the beholder of the transience of life. In his larger, more elaborate *sottoboschi* and flower pieces, Van Schrieck returned a number of times to this theme, though the meanings of his still lifes are often complex and open to multiple interpretations.[6]

In addition to the present drawing, the Crocker owns a small watercolor of a frog, only recently re-attributed to Van Schrieck. The *Froglet* and the *Morning Glory* were once mounted together, along with several watercolor studies of insects by other artists.[7] The presence of similar watercolors and drawings in Van Schrieck's inventory (*"een party teeckeningen wesende Schetsen soo van bloemen, kruyden als anders"*) indicates that he made other such sketches.[8] Additionally, he made watercolor studies of plants for the famous plant

9. See C. Catherina van de Graft, *Agneta Block, Vondel's Nicht en Vriendin*, Utrecht, 1943, pp. 135–52, for the inventory of Block's collection.

10. Hildebrecht 2004, p. 76. Hildebrecht was unable to obtain photographs of the drawings, but notes that they depict "plants growing out of the soil," like the Crocker watercolor. In addition, he cites a more vaguely worded reference to an album of Van Schrieck's studies mentioned in the diary of Balthasar de Monconys (Hildebrecht 2004, p. 70).

collector and gardener Agneta Block, who built up a collection of about four hundred botanical studies recording her specimens.[9] Although the Crocker drawing is not listed in her inventory, Douglas Hildebrecht notes that several of Van Schrieck's watercolors for Block survive in the collection of the Earl of Derby, including a bindweed (a wild type of morning glory) with caterpillar and chrysalis.[10] The summary treatment of the plant in this watercolor diverges from the more carefully descriptive botanical illustrations by other artists that comprised most of Block's collection. If the Crocker sheet was not intended for the collection of a such horticulturalist, it attests to the burgeoning interest in natural history in seventeenth-century Europe.

SS

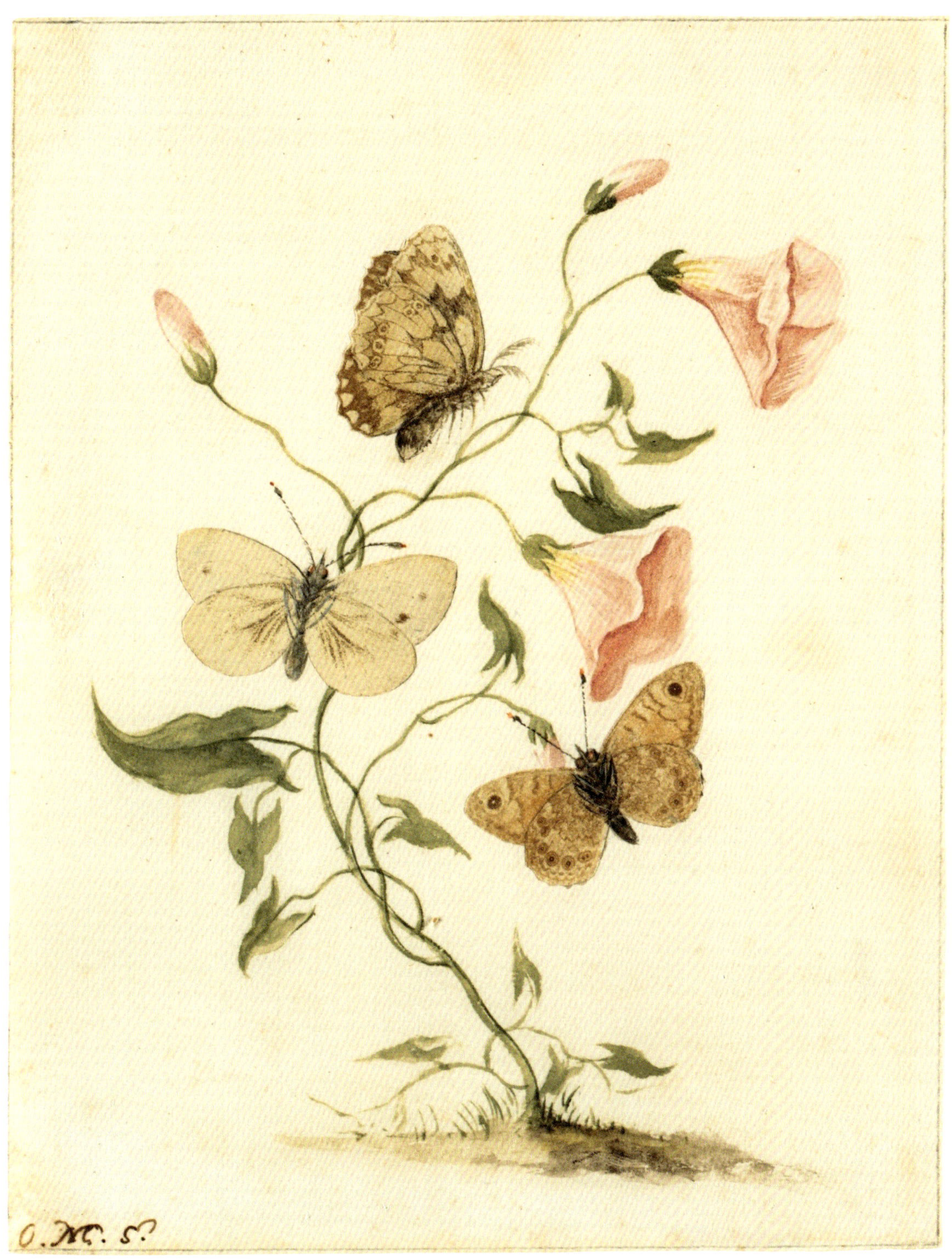

O. M. S.

25. Frederick Bloemaert, *Landscape with Tree Trunks and a Shepherd Resting*, n. d.

Pen and dark brown ink, brush and brown washes over black chalk, incised, on buff laid paper rubbed with charcoal verso, 15.9 × 20.3 cm. Crocker Art Museum, Collector's Guild purchase with contributions from the F. M. Rowles Fund 2003.5

INSCRIPTIONS: verso, dark-brown ink, lower left: *179-*; verso, black chalk, lower left corner: *8-*; verso, black chalk, center bottom margin: *A Bloemaart*; verso, graphite, lower right: *5*; verso, dark brown ink, lower right corner: *no. 326*

MARKS: none

PROVENANCE: Nicolaas Nieuhoff, by 1777; his sale, Philippe van der Schley, Hendrick de Winter and Jan Yver, Amsterdam, 14 April 1777, no. 145; private German collection; Thomas Le Claire, Hamburg, by 2002; Crocker Art Museum purchase, 2003

LITERATURE: Bolten 2007, under no. 1613; Thomas Le Claire, *Master Drawings: Recent Acquisitions, a Review of the Years 1982 – 2002*, vol. XIV, 2002, no. 4 (as Abraham Bloemaert)

NOTES

1. For Bloemaert's biography and the careers of his sons, see Roethlisberger and Bok 1993.
2. Van Mander 1994, f. 297r–97v.
3. Jaap Bolten, "Abraham Bloemaert (1564–1651) and his Tekenboek," *Delineavit et Sculpsit*, vol. IX, 1993, pp. 1–10.
4. Although there are approximately six hundred prints after Bloemaert's designs, the artist made only one etching himself, *Juno* (Hollstein 4).
5. This impression British Museum inv. no. D. 7. 139; Roethlisberger and Bok 1993, nos. 463–77; Hollstein 279–93.
6. The back of the drawing is blackened, as is that of the Washington drawing (National Gallery of Art, no. 1978.81.1). See also British Museum no. SL, 5224.85 and, for the example at Windsor, White and Crawley 1994, no. 312.

A POPULAR AND INFLUENTIAL teacher, the Utrecht painter Abraham Bloemaert (c. 1565–1651) was the son of a sculptor and the father of four painters and printmakers.[1] According to Van Mander, Bloemaert claimed that he had suffered as a boy under the direction of incompetent masters, an experience he often recalled to his own students.[2] Along with Paulus Moreelse, he established an academy of art in his native city, contributing greatly to its reputation as one of the most thriving artistic centers of the Dutch seventeenth century. This may account in part for the importance teaching played in his own career. His pupils included such major painters as Gerrit von Honthorst and Hendrick ter Brugghen. Drawing played a major role in Abraham's busy studio, not only as preparation for paintings or prints but also as a teaching aid, a necessity in a large workshop where students learned to emulate the master's style by copying his work. In 1650, working in collaboration with his son Frederick, Bloemaert published the *Tekenboek*, a collection of Abraham's designs intended for students to copy as they learned to draw.[3]

Bloemaert disseminated his style not only through his many pupils but also via the hundreds of prints for which he provided designs.[4] The present landscape was reproduced in an etching by his son Frederick (c. 1616-1690), as part of a series of fifteen large landscapes (see fig. 20).[5] By far the most prolific of the printmakers reproducing Abraham's work, Frederick was particularly successful at evoking his father's light, calligraphic touch of the pen with etched lines, which he sometimes supplemented with chiaroscuro woodcut. As is the case with other drawings Frederick etched for this series, including examples in Washington, London, and Windsor, the Crocker drawing is incised with a stylus for transfer.[6]

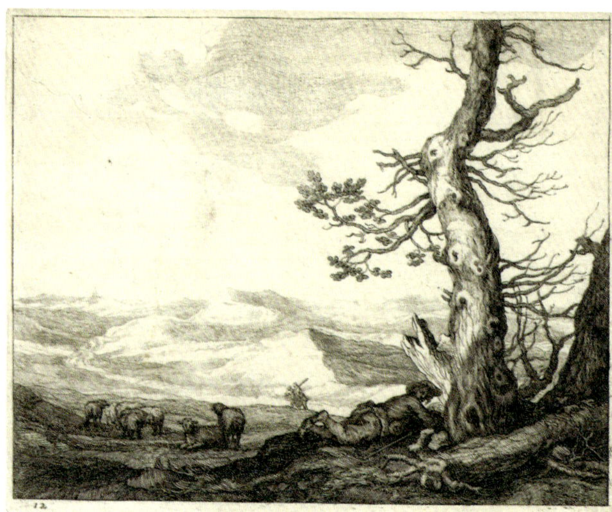

FIGURE 20 Frederick Bloemaert after Abraham Bloemaert, *Landscape with Shepherd and Tree*, c. 1635. Etching, 17.2 x 21.5 cm. British Museum, London

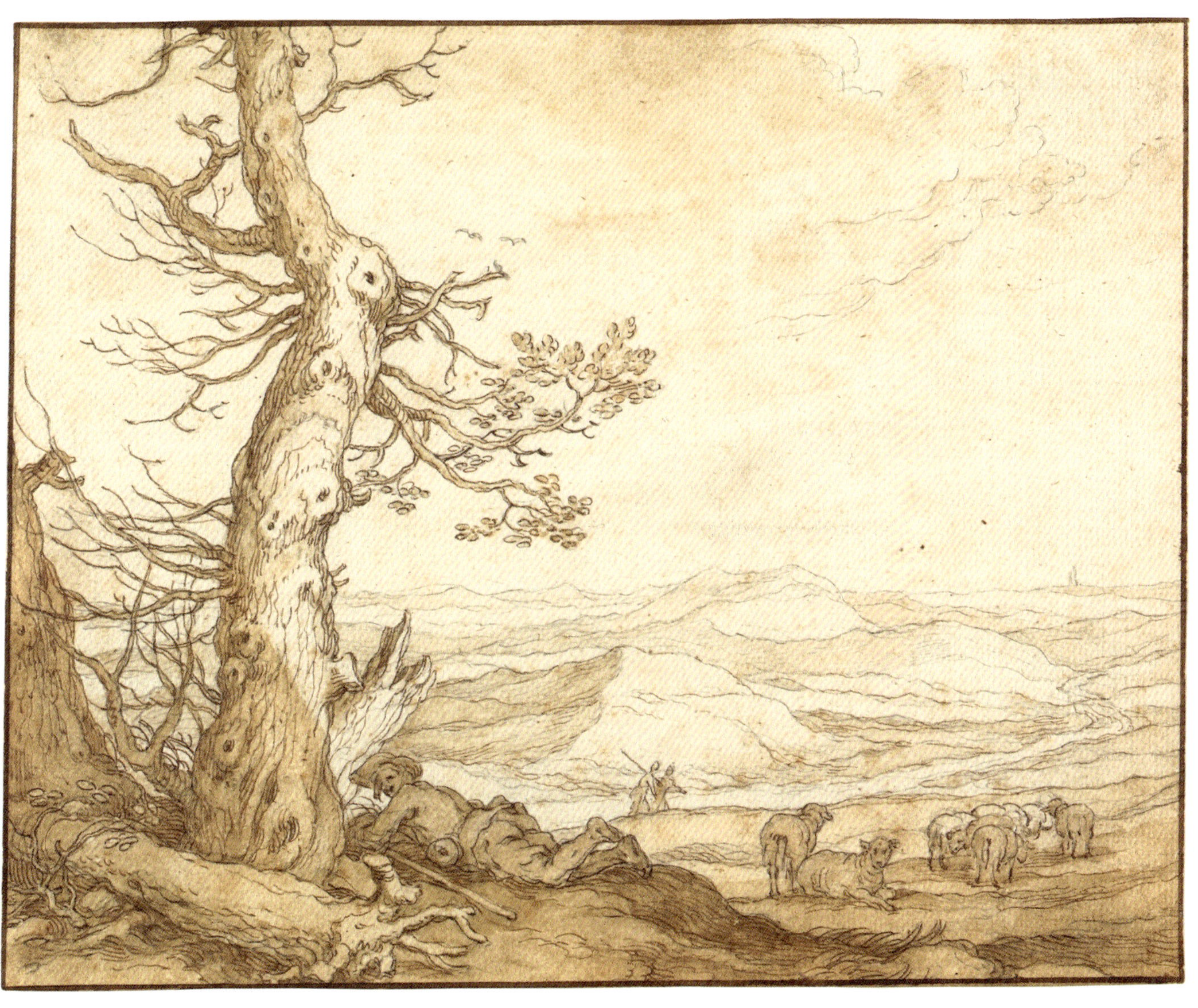

7. Bolten 2007, p. 479, and White and
Crawley 1994, nos. 312 and 313. Although
the *modello* in London has been published
only as Abraham's work (A.E. Popham,
*Dutch and Flemish Drawings of the XV and
XVI Centuries*, London, 1932, no. 13), the
British Museum has changed the
attribution to Frederick in their database,
citing Bolten. Confusingly, Bolten
describes the Crocker drawing as
"Frederick's engraver's model," but
elsewhere notes that only in the case of
this print has a drawing by Abraham
"been preserved that was actually used as
an engraver's model" (p. 479). Evidently
he is referring to the Metropolitan
Museum drawing, the only other
drawing he lists in connection with this
print, but this is very unclear.

8. Bolten 2007, p. 475.

9. Van Mander 1994, f. 298r, lists a wealth of
such motifs displaying Bloemaert's skills,
ranging from peasants' houses to "algae-
covered waters."

10. White and Crawley 1994, p. 202. See also
Bolten in Luijten *et al.*, 1993, no. 319.

11. For Frederick's biography, see
Roethlisberger and Bok 1993, pp. 527–28.

12. Marcel George Roethlisberger,
"Bloemaert's Series of Genre Prints," in
Gazette des-Beaux-Arts, vol. CXIX, January
1992, p. 30, note 41.

Long regarded as the work of Abraham Bloemaert himself, these *modelli* have more recently been attributed to Frederick.[7] The younger artist drew upon the vast supply of his father's sketches, combining or adapting them using Abraham's style of draughts-manship, which he would have learned thoroughly. A black-chalk sketch by Abraham now in the Metropolitan Museum of Art, for instance, provided the panoramic landscape of hills or dunes in the background of the present drawing.[8] Abraham made hundreds of these sketches of landscape motifs, often from life, as described by van Mander.[9] Frederick apparently adapted motifs from Abraham's sketches for other prints in the series, and his tidier style of draughtsmanship is demonstrated by a comparison of a drawing in Windsor with the looser, more painterly quality of Abraham's original sketch.[10]

Despite his close collaboration with his father on such projects as the *Tekenboek*, Frederick remains a shadowy figure, and little is known about his life or artistic style: his many prints are undated, he left no signed drawings, and he appears to have devoted his entire career to reproducing or elaborating upon his father's designs.[11] Drawings have in the past been tentatively assigned to Frederick, such as the *modelli* for the *Tekenboek*.[12] Like the engravers' models for the Large Landscape series, these drawings both copy and elaborate upon Abraham's motifs. With the publication of Jaap Bolten's catalogue raisonné of Abraham's drawings and the re-examination of the models for Frederick's prints, the son's role in his father's workshop is likely to come into clearer focus.   ss

26. **Peter Lely** *Two Clerics, from a Procession of the Order of the Garter*, n. d.

Black and white chalks on blue laid paper, laid down, 48.7 × 41.5 cm. Crocker Art Museum, E. B. Crocker Collection, 1871.167

INSCRIPTIONS: verso of secondary support, black chalk, upper left: *N. 20 uit De Leths Verk. / te Amst. In Maart 1763. / Twee Geestelijke Ridders / door Peter Lely;* verso of secondary support, graphite, upper left, by Alfred Neumeyer: *on auction in March 1763 / two noble clergymen / by Peter Lely / N.*

MARKS: none discernible

PROVENANCE: anonymous collection; sale, Amsterdam, Hendrick de Leth, 23 March 1763, no. 20; Johan Vandenmarck, Leiden; Rudolph Weigel, Leipzig, by 1860, *Kunstlagerkatalog*, no. 2975; Edwin Bryant Crocker, Sacramento, by 1871; gift of his widow Margaret to the Museum, 1885

LITERATURE: Breazeale 2008, p. 212; Ruda 1992, no. 26; Rodgers 1978, no. 97; Feinblatt 1976, no. 232, p. 220; Edward Croft-Murray and Paul Hilton, *Catalogue of British Drawings, Sixteenth and Seventeenth Centuries*, London, 1960, vol. I, p. 409; Michel N. Benisovich, "Some Drawings by European Masters in United States Museum Collections," in *Art Quarterly*, vol. XXII, Spring 1959, pp. 60–62, fig. 5; Anthony Blunt et al., *Drawings from the Robert Witt Collection at the Courtauld Institute of Art*, exh. cat. Courtauld Institute, London, 1953, p. 13, under no. 23; John Woodward, *Tudor and Stuart Drawings*, London, 1951, p. 49; Michel Benisovich, "Two Drawings by Peter Lely," *The Burlington Magazine*, vol. XCI, March 1949, pp. 79–80; Trivas 1942, no. 67; Pratt 1937, p. 33; Rudolph Weigel, *Kunstlagerkatalog*, no. 2975

NOTES

1. For the early years of Lely's career, see Jacques Foucart, "Peter Lely, Dutch History Painter," *Hoogsteder-Naumann Mercury*, vol. VIII, 1989, p. 17–26.
2. Lely may have been emulating Venetian artists in his use of this technique: from the time of his arrival in England, he built up a major collection of prints, drawings, and paintings, including a large number of drawings by Venetian artists.

ORN IN THE HAGUE and trained in Haarlem, Peter Lely (1618–1680) followed in the footsteps of his Flemish predecessor Antony van Dyck (1599–1641), moving to London and becoming one of the most important artists in Stuart England. Although his earliest works suggest that he aspired to be a history painter, Lely made his career in the far more lucrative field of aristocratic portraiture.[1] Throughout the years of the Commonwealth, he maintained ties with both Royalist and Parliamentarian families, a strategy that resulted in enormous success after the Restoration.

The demand for Lely's portraits dictated the employment of a large number of studio assistants, which in turn required the artist to use drawings as an important part of his working methods: detailed drawings allowed him to pass on to apprentices and assistants the painting of drapery or backgrounds. Lely's drawings are among his most widely admired works today. Many, like the *Two Clerics* exhibited here, are black or red chalk drawings executed on blue paper and heightened with white chalk, a painterly technique that would have served well in preparatory sketches.[2]

The Crocker drawing is part of a now-disassembled series that forms one of Lely's most famous works, the Procession of the Order of the Garter (figure 21).[3] This procession, held on the Feast of Saint George, had been discontinued during the Civil War (1641-51) but was revived under Charles II, when the chivalric order assumed a new political significance and provided an important link with the past. The exact dates of drawings and procession are unknown, though the identity of the participants points to a date between 1663 and 1671.[4] Although it has been suggested that the drawings were

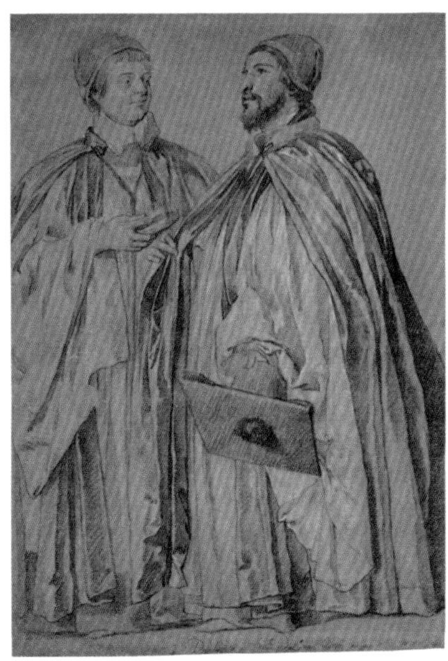

FIGURE 21 Peter Lely, *Two Canons*, n. d. Black and white chalks on blue laid paper, 53.2 × 37.8 cm. British Museum, London

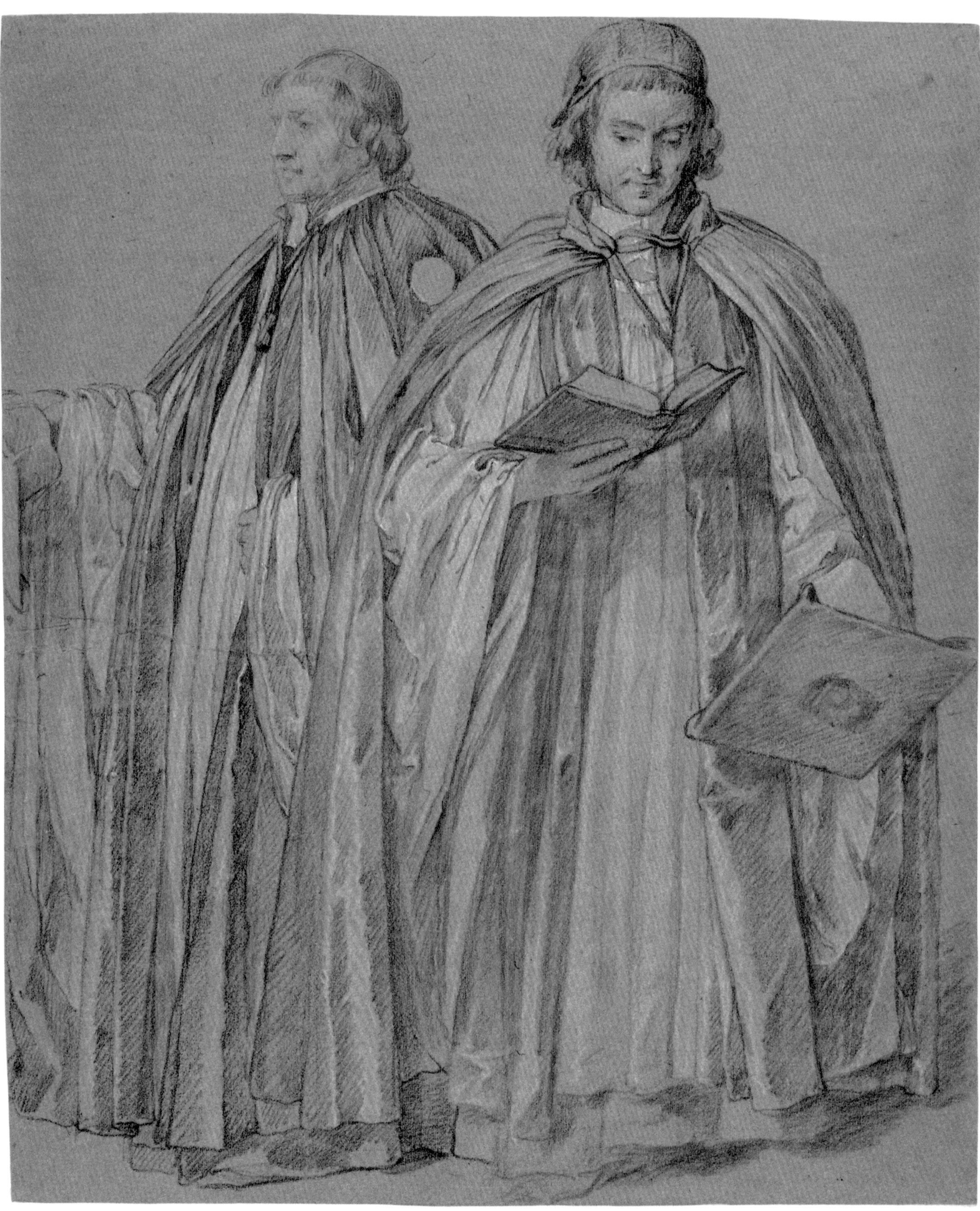

3. British Museum inv. no. 1862-7-12-652. For all the known surviving drawings in the series, see Oliver Millar in Rodgers 1978, pp. 80–87. Millar succeeded in reuniting all but two of the drawings for an exhibition.

4. Lindsay Stainton and Christopher White, *Drawing in England from Hilliard to Hogarth*, Cambridge, 1987, p. 129.

5. Millar in Rodgers 1978, p. 81. Van Dyck's oil sketch of the procession is the only surviving design for the paintings. Stainton suggests that Lely may have been preparing for a series of paintings at Windsor, home of the Order's chapel. The castle was undergoing extensive renovations and redecoration at the time (Stainton 1987, as in note 4, p. 129).

done from life, the level of detail and the lack of pentimenti makes this seem unlikely. However, the coherence of the series and the liveliness of the participants, who in many of the drawings gesture or speak to one another or to spectators leaves the viewer with the impression that Lely witnessed the procession. Perhaps he made quick sketches on the scene and then brought the sitters to his studio for these more finished drawings.

The purpose of this cycle of drawings remains unknown. They may have been preparatory in nature: Charles I planned an elaborate cycle of tapestries for Whitehall illustrating the history of the Order of the Garter, including a scene of the Saint George procession, and it is possible that his son intended to emulate him with a similar decorative scheme.[5] Furthermore, several of the Garter drawings in the British Museum are counterproofs, suggesting that Lely had in mind a composition that dictated the directions of the figures' poses. Whether or not the drawings were intended as works of art in their own right, the Crocker sketch demonstrates Lely's dazzling abilities as a draughtsman. His coloristic use of black and white chalk captures the shimmer of silk or satin as persuasively as his use of oil paint does in his portraits, an effect enhanced here by his use of moistened or oiled black chalk to achieve the darkest shadows. The flickering lights and darks, carefully individualized portraits, and virtuoso technique combine to make the Garter series one of the most impressive examples of draughtsmanship in Britain in the seventeenth century.

ss

27. Adriaen van de Velde, *A Young Woman as Pomona*, c. 1670

Black and white chalks on cream laid paper prepared with tan, 42.4 × 29.5 cm. Crocker Art Museum, E. B. Crocker Collection 1871.186

INSCRIPTIONS: black chalk, lower right at margin, cut off: *A v d Velde fe.*

MARKS: lower left corner: Lugt 1853 (Mouriau); preserved from original mount: Lugt 1829 (Mouriau)

PROVENANCE: A. Mouriau, Belgium, before 1858; Edwin Bryant Crocker, Sacramento, by 1871; gift of his widow Margaret to the Museum, 1885

LITERATURE: Frensemeier 2001, p. 147, under no. 14; Bruce Davis, *Master Drawings in the Los Angeles County Museum of Art*, Los Angeles, 1997, p. 64; Robinson 1993, no. 2, p. 65 n. 5; Ruda 1992, no. 27; Robinson 1979, pp. 11–12, 22, D-15; Robinson 1977, no. 80; Crocker 1971, no. 73; Crocker 1959; no. 9; Trivas 1942, no. 129; Trivas 1940b, p. 137

ONE OF THE FOREMOST Dutch painters of the seventeenth century, Adriaen van de Velde (1636–1672) was also a highly accomplished draughtsman, producing a large number of figure studies like this one. Son of the famous marine artist Willem van de Velde I (1611–1693), Adriaen specialized instead in landscapes, usually populated with figures and livestock. Although he is not known to have traveled to Italy, many of his paintings have a strongly Italianate flavor, while others depict more local views. He was also a talented etcher, favoring cattle and other animals as subjects for his prints.

Many of the artist's surviving drawings, including the *Pomona*, were preparatory: the Crocker's drawing is a study for one of the figures in the painting *Vertumnus and Pomona* of 1670 (fig. 22).[1] William Robinson's study of Van de Velde's studio practice reveals that the artist's preparation for his landscape paintings was fairly elaborate.[2] The artist made a rough compositional sketch, followed by a more detailed *modello*, as well as careful chalk studies of figures and animals. Although Van de Velde's drawing practice has been reconstructed in far more detail than those of his contemporaries, a number of his fellow Italianate landscape painters made similar chalk figure studies.[3]

NOTES

1. Kunsthistorisches Museum, Vienna, inv. no. 6446; Frensemeier 2001, no. 14.
2. Robinson 1979, pp. 3–23 and 57–69.
3. For a thorough overview of the subject, see Peter Schatborn, *Dutch Figure Drawings*, The Hague, 1981. The drawings of Nicholas Berchem and Jan Baptist Weenix, for example, sometimes demonstrate a painterly handling of chalk much like the technique in the Crocker *Pomona*.
4. Robinson 1979, D 14 (location unknown). A pen-and-ink composition sketch is in the British Museum (Hind 1915, no. 26).
5. Robinson 1993, pp. 53–66.
6. Ibidem, pp. 6off.
7. Ibidem, p. 60.
8. Van de Velde made similar drawings and counterproofs of livestock for his landscapes.

The Crocker's study is the second of two known preparatory drawings for this figure. Van de Velde first concentrated on Pomona's pose and anatomy in a meticulous study from a nude model.[4] In the Crocker *Pomona*, he turned his attention to the fall of drapery across the woman's body, maintaining the pose he established in the original sketch. Possibly intending to focus on the arrangement of the skirt, he apparently first roughed in the figure to the upper right of the page: the finished Pomona leans her elbow against a rock that closely resembles the lower half of her own body, and traces remain of her left foot at the right edge of the page. Evidently still dissatisfied with the finished drawing, he made a number of changes to the figure in the painting. While the figures play a major role in *Vertumnus and Pomona*, Van de Velde sometimes followed this painstaking process even for small figures that played a far less important part in his landscapes.[5]

Although many of Van de Velde's figure studies, like the *Pomona*, were made with a specific painting already in mind, some of these drawings had other purposes.[6] He appears to have drawn from the nude in part as practice. In addition, a number of carefully finished studies of clothed figures survive which do not appear in any of Van de Velde's paintings, indicating that he maintained a stock of figures for later use in his paintings. The presence of his signature on many of his figure studies (mostly cut off on the present drawing) suggests that he sold them to collectors.[7] His choice to draw figures in chalk probably stemmed not only from tradition but also from the practical reason that he could make counterproofs from them: by moistening the paper and pressing a second sheet onto the drawing, he could reproduce his original study in reverse, providing himself with twice as many options for later use of the figure.[8] His thorough understanding of the nude and his command of the medium of chalk make his figure drawings some of the finest in Dutch seventeenth-century art.   SS

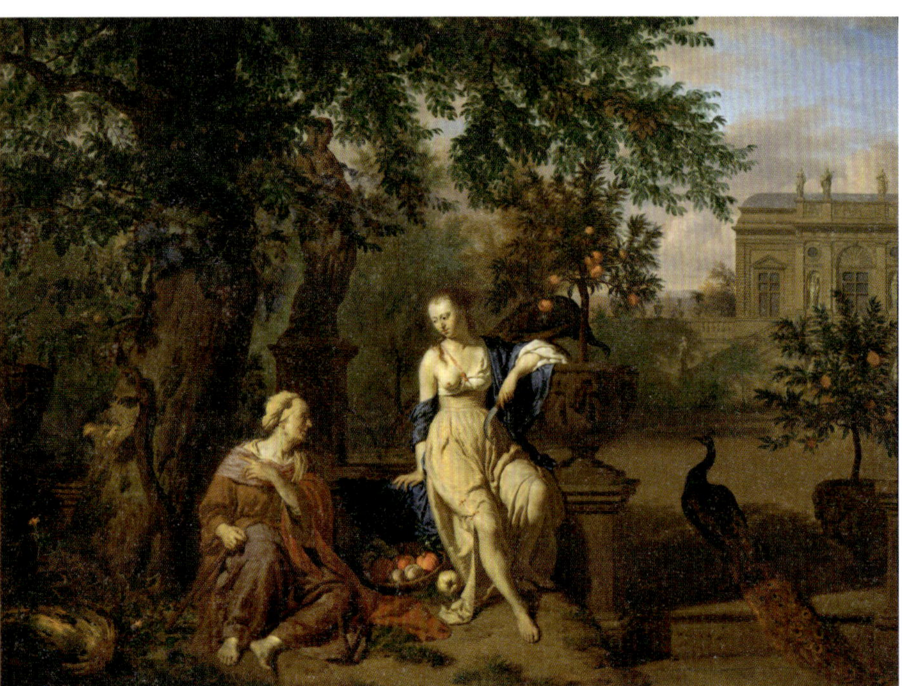

FIGURE 22 Adriaen van de Velde, *Vertumnus and Pomona*, 1670. Oil on canvas, 76.5 × 103 cm. Kunsthistorisches Museum, Vienna

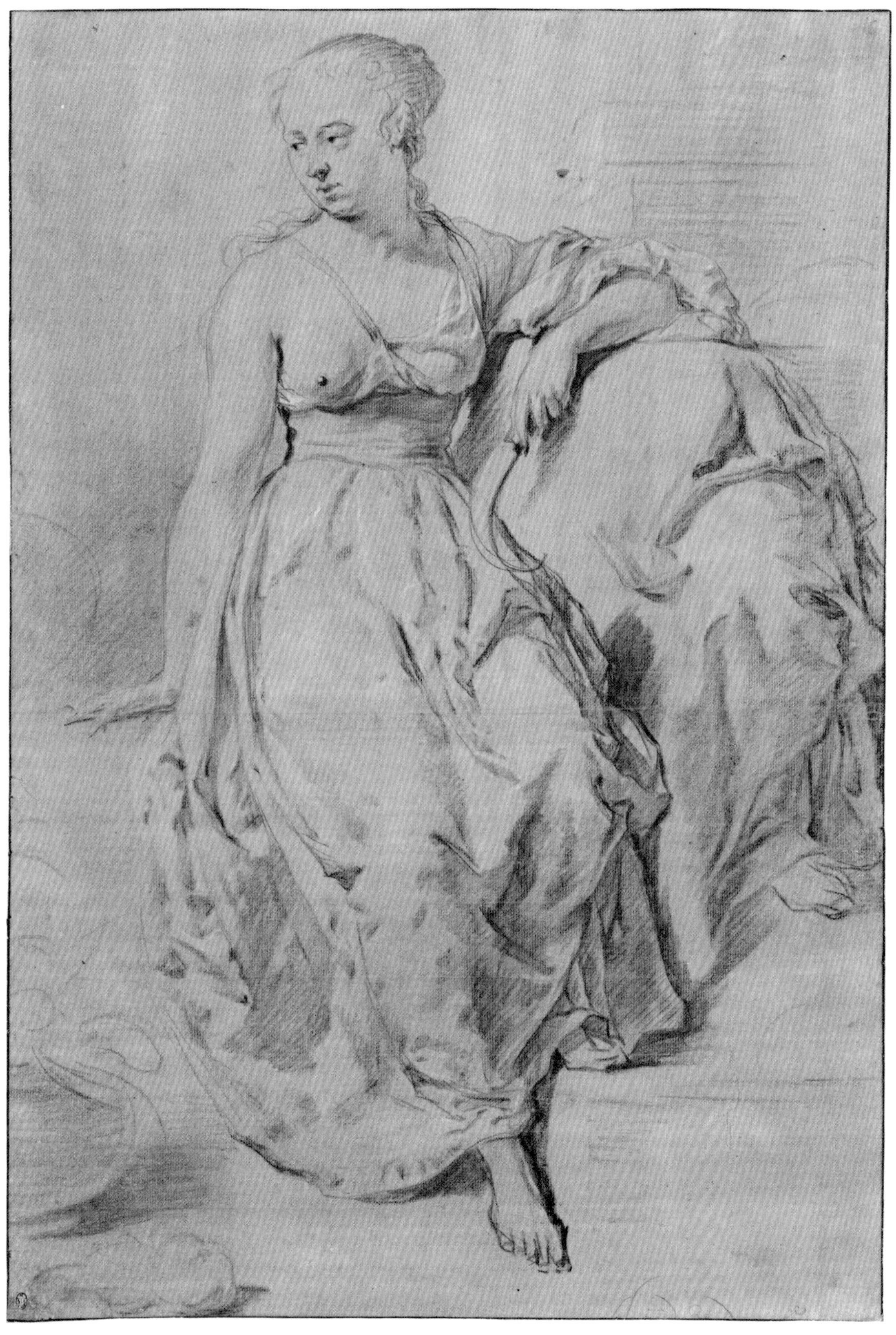

28. **Gérard de Lairesse,** *Expulsion of Hagar,* c. 1675

Pen and reddish-brown ink, graphite, and brush and grey washes, 31 × 22.5 cm. Crocker Art Museum, E. B. Crocker Collection 1871.217

INSCRIPTIONS: brown ink, lower center: *G. Lairesse inv. F.*

MARKS: none

PROVENANCE: Edwin Bryant Crocker, Sacramento, by 1871; gift of his widow Margaret to the Museum, 1885

LITERATURE: Roy 1992, no. D. 33 and p. 122; Howard et al. 1973, no. 16; Trivas 1942, no. 66

NOTES

1. For Lairesse's life and critical reception, see Roy 1992, pp. 44-56, and Lyckle de Vries, *Gerard de Lairesse, An Artist between Stage and Studio,* Amsterdam, 2002. See also Claus Kemmer's review of Roy in *Simiolus,* vol. 23, 1995, pp. 186-96.

2. Roy 1992, pp. 120-21.

3. See, for example *Allegory: The Apple of Discord,* gray ink and wash over red chalk, British Museum, inv. no. 1943, 1113.72.

4. Hollstein 16. Because the location of the grisaille (Roy no. P 90) is unknown, there is no way to ascertain whether the technique is related to that of the Crocker drawing. Roy convincingly dates both grisaille and wash drawing to c. 1675 on stylistic grounds.

5. Hollstein 17.

6. For an overview, see Christine Petra Sellin, *Fractured Families and Rebel Maidservants: The Biblical Hagar in Seventeenth-Century Dutch Art and Literature,* New York, 2006.

Blamed since the late nineteenth century for the "decline" of Dutch art as it moved toward classicism at the end of the seventeenth century, Gérard de Lairesse (1640–1711) was one of the most exalted artists of his time and is the subject of a new wave of scholarly reappraisal. After spending his early career in his native Liège, Lairesse made brief stops in 's Hertogenbosch and in Utrecht before moving to Amsterdam in about 1665. He spent the next twenty-five years building a career as one of most successful painters in the city, particularly noted for his decorative paintings in both public institutions and private homes. He was also a prolific printmaker and closely connected with the group of intellectuals known as *"Nil Volentibus Arduum,"* whose ideas about theater and literature helped to shape Lairesse's own art theory. In 1690, shortly after earning a commission to help decorate the new town hall in Amsterdam, Lairesse went blind. He devoted the rest of his career to lecturing and writing, publishing several influential treatises on art.[1]

In his catalogue raisonné for this artist, Alain Roy divides Lairesse's drawings into three groups – rapid pen and ink studies, ink-and-wash drawings made mainly in preparation for paintings, and more highly finished pen and wash drawings, executed over chalk or ink sketches.[2] *The Expulsion of Hagar* belongs to this final group. The prominence of the red underdrawing, which peeks out so clearly through the wash that it reads as a deliberate accent, is somewhat unusual but not unique among drawings by or attributed to Lairesse.[3] While no known print can be associated with this drawing, Lairesse may have intended to publish one: many of the other drawings in this category served as models for printmakers and in general Lairesse appears to have viewed his drawings as models or preparatory tools, making relatively few of them as independent works of art. In particular, the composition of the present drawing resembles that of Lairesse's grisaille *Jael and Sisera,* which served as a model for a mezzotint executed by Wallerant Vaillant.[4] *The Expulsion of Hagar* and *Jael and Sisera* are so similar in format and dimensions that they were likely originally planned as a pair. Even locations and wording of the signatures (in both cases, *G. Lairesse inv. f.*) are closely related. Although Vaillant did not make a mezzotint version of the Crocker drawing, he did engrave a Guido Reni *Judith and Holofernes* as a companion to the *Jael and Sisera.*[5] While the two prints are neatly related thematically, the composition of the Reni does not correspond as closely to the *Jael and Sisera* as does that of the present drawing.

The Old Testament subject of the expulsion of Hagar was exceptionally popular in seventeenth-century Dutch art.[6] As related in Genesis (16: 1–16 and 21: 8–21), Abraham's barren wife, Sarah, gave her servant Hagar to her husband so he could have children. Hagar and Abraham had a son, Ishmael, but, when Sarah herself later bore a child, she insisted that her husband banish Hagar and the boy from their home. Initially reluctant, Abraham agreed to cast the pair into the wilderness when God promised to make a great

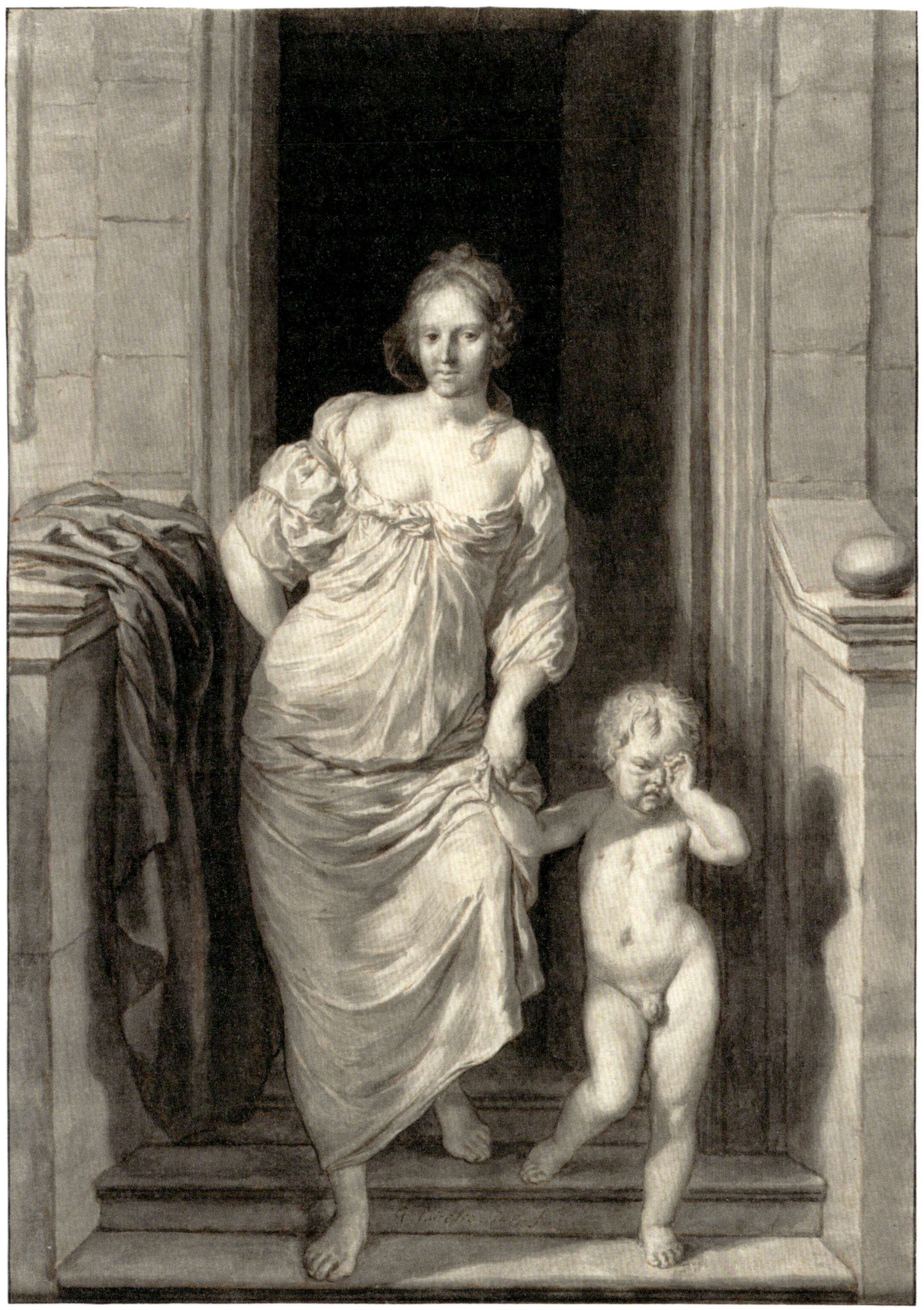

7. *Ibidem*, p. 144–45. The painting, Roy 1992,
   P. 120, is now in the Hermitage.

nation of Ishmael. The mother and son were eventually rescued by an angel and Ishmael
lived to father many children, finally dying at the age of 137. The overwhelming majority
of seventeenth-century depictions of the Expulsion of Hagar include various props and
attributes specific to the story: the water bottle mentioned in the biblical account,
Abraham, and Sarah all appear regularly. Hagar herself is often depicted weeping. Her
serene smile and the absence of attributes set this version apart from others of the time,
though her classically inspired pose and dress as well as her sensual appearance are in
keeping with contemporary trends, as seen in Lairesse's own painting of *Hagar in the
Wilderness*, executed at about the same time as this drawing.[7]   ss

DRAWINGS FROM FRANCE

29. **Burgundian School (?)**, *Two Magistrates with a Shield*, n. d.

Pen and brown ink with traces of black chalk, bottom made up, laid down, 17 × 13 cm. Crocker Art Museum, E. B. Crocker Collection 1871.2

INSCRIPTIONS: graphite, center of lower margin: 10 [...] 16; mount, dark brown ink, center of lower margin: No. 4; mount, graphite, lower right corner: 1132; verso of mount, graphite, lower left and right corners: w-

MARKS: none discernible

PROVENANCE: Edwin Bryant Crocker, by 1871; gift of his widow Margaret to the Museum, 1885

LITERATURE: Breazeale 2008, p. 214; Ruda 1992, no. 19, as Master of Mary of Burgundy; Reno 1978, no. 10; Crocker 1971, no. 2, as Burgundian School; Crocker 1964, no. 2, as German master of 15th century; Crocker 1959, no. 17, as unknown German master; Montreal 1953, no. 93, as unknown German master; Trivas 1940b, p. 137, as Master of the Playing Cards; Crocker 1939, no. 2, as unknown German master

NOTES

1. Winkler, in a letter of 1957 of which record survives in Crocker curatorial files but which is not extant.
2. School of Jan van Eyck, inv. no. 20674. It was Roger Wieck, Curator of Medieval and Renaissance Manuscripts at the Morgan Library and Museum, who drew my attention to this resemblance.
3. The *houppelande* is basically an outer garment with a long full body and flaring sleeves that was worn by both men and women in Europe in the late medieval period. Sometimes it was lined with fur, and it was later worn by the professional classes. It appeared around 1380 and remained fashionable well into the next century.
4. An illuminator active in and around Ghent late in the century who is named for the patron of a manuscript of *c.* 1480.
5. Inv. no. 12512, repr. Elfried Bock and Jakob Rosenberg, 'Die Niederlandischen Meister II', in Max Friedlaender, *Die Zeichnungen Alter Meister im Kupferstichkabinett, Staatliche Museen zu Berlin*, Berlin, 1930, pl. 5.
6. *Ibidem*, inv. no. 1983, repr. pl. 5.

A FTER YEARS OF STUDY the identity of the artist of this work as well as the school to which he belongs remain elusive. From the late 1930s through much of the 1950s the drawing was considered to be German mid-fifteenth century, most likely the work of a printmaker for a woodcut or engraving. As early as 1957, however, Friedrich Winkler suggested that the work must date to 1480–90, somewhat later than originally thought, and was most likely by a Flemish artist working in the School of Ghent.[1] By 1978 most scholars essentially subscribed to this opinion. Even before Winkler, however, Agnes Mongan had gone a little further (in a 1938 handwritten note on the mount of the drawing) and suggested that the drawing might be Burgundian.

In looking at the drawing, the viewer is almost immediately aware that the costumes of the two men clearly date to the first decade of the fifteenth century rather than either the middle or late fifteenth century. Their clothes are very close to those worn by the people represented in manuscript illuminations like the *Très Riches Heures* by the Limbourg brothers, which dates to the early 1400s, as well as to costumes worn in Van Eyck's paintings. The man on the left stepping forward wears a short tunic, cape and beret not unlike the costume of the kneeling figure in the so-called *Fishing Party* in the Département des arts graphiques of the Louvre.[2] He steps forward as does the man on the far right of the *Fishing Party*, except that his pose reverses that in the Crocker drawing. In the latter, the two figures are somewhat unrelated in the space of the drawing, connected to each other only at the top of the image where they both grasp the escutcheon. The man on the left wears a short costume with dagged sleeves and edges, while the man on the right wears a long outer garment with full sleeves called a *houppelande*.[3] Moreover, the sword or short stick worn by the man in the beret is incomplete in the drawing and intersects the long walking pole held by the other figure in a meaningless way. Details like this as well as the late fifteenth-century style of the penwork itself suggest that these two figures are not original but most likely were copied from an earlier composition or compositions such as the *Fishing Party*.

The name of the Master of Mary of Burgundy,[4] an illuminator who was active in and around Ghent late in the century, was the suggestion of Jeffrey Ruda (1992). Professor Ruda compares the features of the men in the Crocker drawing with a sheet of head studies by the Master of Mary of Burgundy in Berlin.[5] There is a much greater resemblance between the Crocker drawing and another sheet in Berlin attributed to the Master of Mary of Burgundy, *Allegory with Venus as Vanity*, in which the profile features of two men are similar to the men in the present drawing, executed in pen and brown ink as well.[6] Professor Ruda's suggestion that the Crocker drawing might be a miniaturist's design for a genealogy (book or scroll?) with ancestor images is ingenious and might account for the archaic costumes as well as the empty escutcheon supported by both figures.

CD

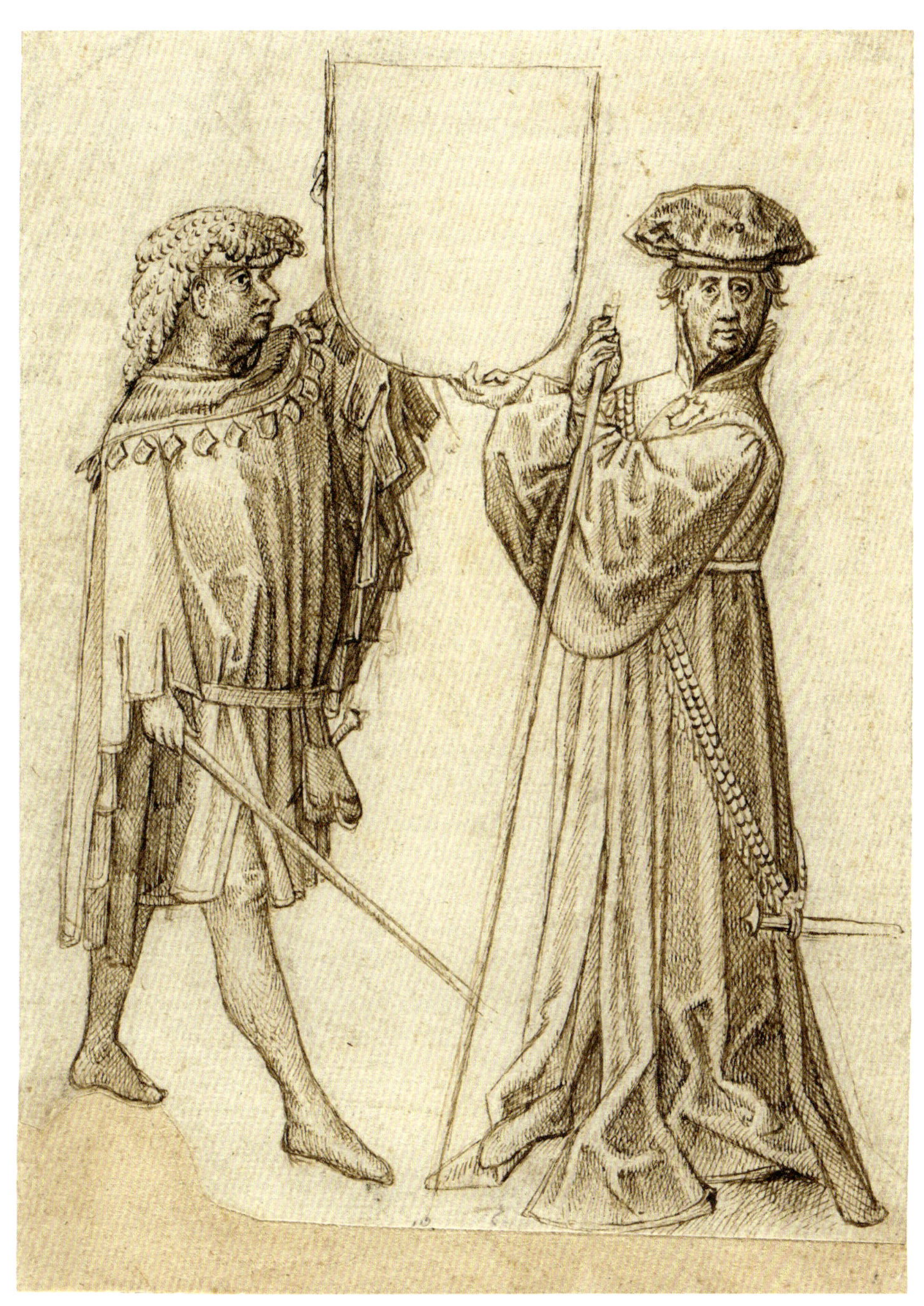

30. **Jacques Callot**, *Martyrdom of Saint Sebastian*, *c. 1630*

Brush and brown wash over black chalk, incised, overlay at right. 20.4 × 34.4 cm. Crocker Art Museum,
E. B. Crocker Collection 1871.392

NOTES
1. Édouard Meaume, *Recherches sur la vie et les
ouvrages de Jacques Callot, cat. raisonné*,
Paris, 1860, no. 137; Jules Lieure, *Jacques
Callot, catalogue raisonné de l'oeuvre gravé*,
Paris, 1924–27, no. 670. The etching
measures 16.1 x 32.7 cm., considerably
smaller than the preparatory drawings.
2. This impression British Museum, inv. no.
1861-7-13-258.
3. Album Jullienne (Hermitage, St.
Petersburg); Ternois 1962, nos. 1176–91.
4. Inv. no. D. 20.1887.

FIGURE 23 Jacques Callot, *Martyrdom of
Saint Sebastian*, 1630. Etching, 16.3 ×
33.0 cm. British Museum, London

BORN IN LORRAINE, Jacques Callot (1592-1635) began his artistic studies with a gold-smith and engraver in Nancy. By 1608 he was in Rome studying drawing under Antonio Tempesta (*q.v.*) and then, when his finances ran out, he began working as an engraver for the printmaker Philippe Thomassin as well as for Tempesta, his master. In 1611 Tempesta sent Callot to Florence to deliver some plates and etchings to the Grand Duchess of Tuscany, who persuaded her husband to sponsor Callot. He remained in Florence until 1621, when he returned to Nancy. There he produced many religious prints and recorded court pageants in numerous prints and drawings.

In 1630 he began preparations for the print of *Saint Sebastian*,[1] an early Christian martyr who was the patron saint of Nancy (fig. 23).[2] He made three preparatory com-positional drawings for this etching as well as numerous figure sketches in red chalk.[3] The earliest and least detailed sketch is in the collection of Jacques Dupont Paris. The Crocker drawing is the second study for the print, while the third and latest study is in the Victoria and Albert Museum, London.[4]

All three compositional drawings are in the reverse sense of the etching. In the first study Callot blocked out the principal groups and organized the general layout, in which the foreground is established with spectators at the left and archers at the right. In the second—the Crocker drawing—Callot centered the figure of Saint Sebastian, still seen at some distance, and the crowd has become more numerous in the left foreground, including a few horsemen and an especially dense concentration of figures, creating a diagonal from the right corner to the middle distance. The architecture has become more complex, with an arch at the left, while antique ruins including the Colosseum have been added to the middle distance. Standards add further diagonal accents to the left and right foreground. Overall, the second compositional sketch is much more

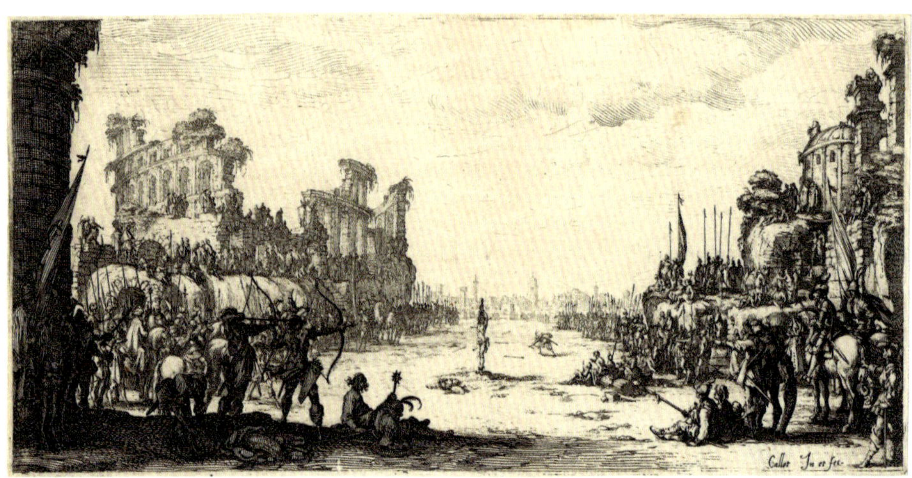

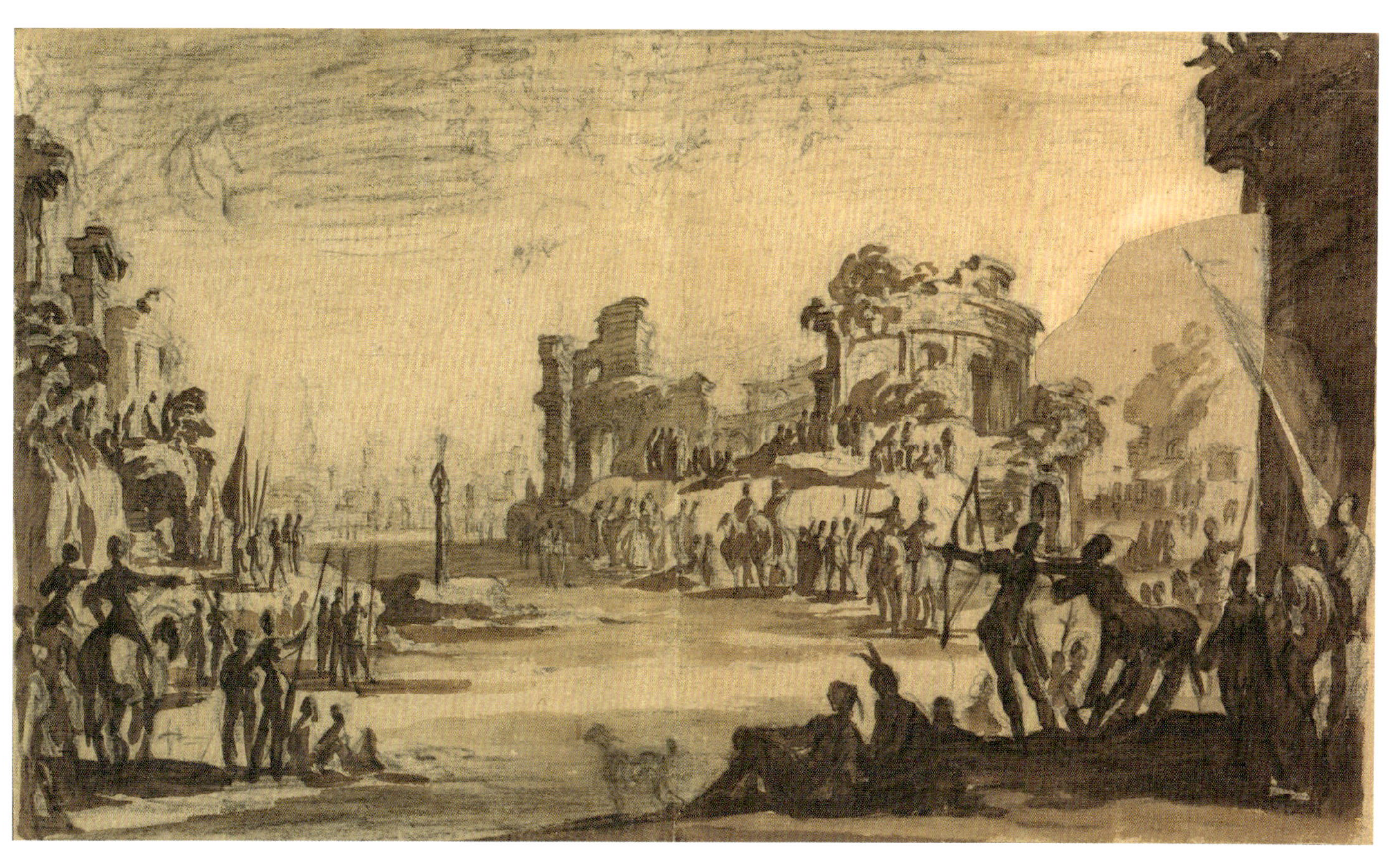

complex than the first. While the third and last compositional drawing is very close to the Crocker sheet, Callot tightens up the structure of the composition, strengthening the diagonals leading to the small central figure of the saint. The subject gains dramatic impact as the composition extends deeper into the background with the view of the city in the distance. It has often been remarked that Callot conceived this composition theatrically. The setting is wide and deep like a stage, the immediate foreground taken up with what at first appear to be dominant figures of the archers and lounging spectators seen in strong silhouette. These are turned towards the miniscule figure of Sebastian in the middle distance and serve to emphasize his martyrdom and the significance of the event.

CD

31. Pierre Patel the Elder, *Classical Landscape*, n. d.

Black and white chalk on gray laid paper pieced together and lined, 15.1 × 22.9 cm. Crocker Art Museum, E. B. Crocker Collection 1871.394

INSCRIPTIONS: none

MARKS: none

PROVENANCE: Edwin Bryant Crocker, by 1871; gift of his widow Margaret to the Museum, 1885

LITERATURE: Goldfarb 1989, under no. 81; Harrison 1986, under no.3, note 3; Christian Dittrich, "Zeichnung von Pierre Patel des Älteren: Drei unbekannte Werke im Kupferstich-Kabinett Dresden," *Dresdener Kunstblätter*, vol. V, no. 23, 1979, p. 147; Crocker 1979, no. 31; Rosenberg 1972, no. 106; Crocker 1971, no. 66; Rosenberg 1970, no. 1; Schulz 1968, no. 14; Trivas 1940a, no. 58

MARIETTE CALLED PATEL (1605–1676), the artist of this exceptional drawing, the "*Claude Lorraine de la France*."[1] Its composition is close to the painting *Landscape with the Journey to Emmaus* in the Chrysler Museum in Norfolk[2] and it is one of a number of drawings by Patel employing the device of a colonnaded structure seen from the side which leads the eye back into the landscape. The receding colonnade device is used also in works in Dresden such as *Rebecca Going from Bethuel and Laban* of a similar size and technique.[3] The painting in the Chrysler to which this drawing is connected was executed in 1652, the same year that Patel collaborated with Eustache Le Sueur on the Hotel Lambert paintings. However closely connected the Crocker sheet is to the Chrysler drawing, it has been suggested that it may be closer still and perhaps a preparation of some sort for the 1650 painting *Landscape with Antique Ruins* in the Kunstmuseum, Basle.[4] Another drawing in the Ecole des Beaux-Arts, Paris, shows the same study in reverse.[5]

Drawings by Patel are rather rare. There are six landscapes by him in the Louvre, four of which are executed in the familiar black and white chalks on gray paper,[6] while two others are in gouache on vellum.[7] The four landscapes in chalk on gray paper were in the Mariette collection. Mariette thought very highly of Patel, noting that his sense of perspective was perfect and that his paintings and drawings reveal a sureness of touch. Another three drawings in the same technique as the Crocker sheet are in the Kupferstichkabinett, Dresden, and are published in Christian Dittrich's article of 1979.[8]   CD

NOTES

1. *Abécédario de P. J. Mariette et autres notes inédites de cet amateur sur les arts et les artistes, ouvrage publié d'après les manuscrits autographes au cabinet des estampes de la bibliothèque impériale, et annoté par MM. Ph. de Chennevières et A. de Montaiglon*, vol. IV, Paris, 1857–58, p. 88.

2. Harrison 1986, no. 3, repr.

3. 14.0 x 22.3 mm., black and white chalk with pen; see Dittrich 1979, as above, pp. 146–51, figs. 1–3.

4. Harrison 1986, no. 3, note 3.

5. Schulz 1968, under no. 14.

6. Inv. nos. 32282, 32283, 32284, 32255, all executed in black and white chalk on gray paper, larger than the Crocker sheet, measuring c. 26 x 38 cm. All four are from the collection of P. J. Mariette and were acquired for the Cabinet du Roi in 1775.

7. Inv. nos. RF 1958 and 1959.

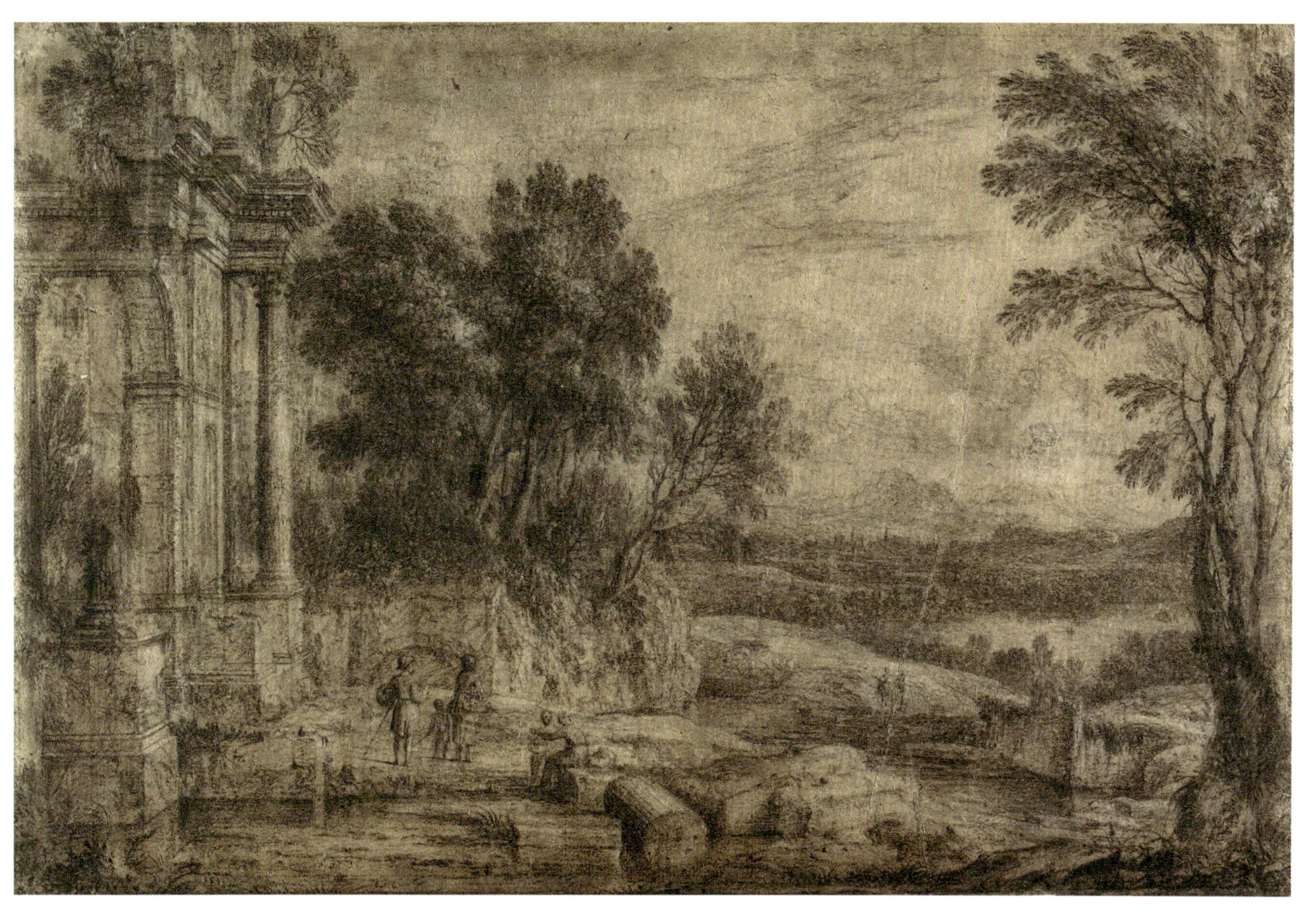

32. Eustache Le Sueur, *Kneeling Woman Seen in Profile, Arms Upraised*, n. d.

Black and white chalks on brown laid paper, 27.6 × 21.2 cm. Crocker Art Museum,
E. B. Crocker Collection 1871.414

INSCRIPTIONS: pen and brown ink,
lower left: *i36*; lower right: *29*

MARKS: none

PROVENANCE: Edwin Bryant Crocker,
before 1871; gift of his widow Margaret to
the Museum, 1885

LITERATURE: Alain Mérot, *Eustache Le
Sueur (1616–1655)*, Paris, 1987, p. 249,
fig. 322; Crocker 1979, no. 26; Marguerite
Sapin, "Contribution à l'étude de
quelques oeuvres d'Eustache Le Sueur,"
Revue du Louvre et des Musées de France,
vol. IV, 1978, p. 246 n. 21; Rosenberg 1970,
no. 6

DURING THE EIGHTEENTH CENTURY especially, Le Sueur (1616–1655) was greatly admired and was considered "the French Raphael." In his own rather short lifetime he occupied a major position in French seventeenth-century art. By the time he was sixteen he was apprenticed to Simon Vouet, then the busiest and most famous artist in Paris. He was to remain in Vouet's studio until 1642, at which time he was able to establish his own career. By 1644 he was admitted as a master in the painters' guild in Paris and in 1645 he was commissioned to paint a cycle of twenty-two paintings depicting the Life of Saint Bruno for the cloister of the Charterhouse in Paris (now in the Louvre), a project that occupied him for three years. By 1649 he was appointed Peintre Ordinaire du Roi and was chosen to paint the *May of Notre-Dame de Paris*, the large painting presented annually to the Cathedral of Notre-Dame by the guild of goldsmiths. He was also among twelve painters appointed to teach at the Académie Royale de Peinture et de Sculpture, founded the previous year. He worked without interruption during the time of the Fronde, and during difficult economic times worked for a private clientele, for whom he often painted subjects drawn from the Bible or ancient history. His style became more serious and somewhat austere and he came to rely on his drawings for details as well as for overall compositional study. The largest holdings of his drawings are in the Louvre and in Besançon, Chantilly and Montpellier.

As was customary, Le Sueur made many figure and drapery studies in preparation for his paintings. The figure drawings are usually executed in black and white chalks on

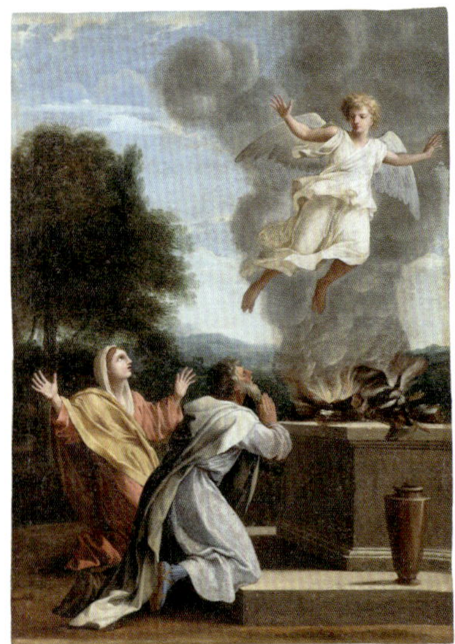

FIGURE 24 Eustache Le Sueur, *Sacrifice of Manoah*, n. d. Oil on canvas, 118 × 84 cm. Musée des Augustins, Toulouse

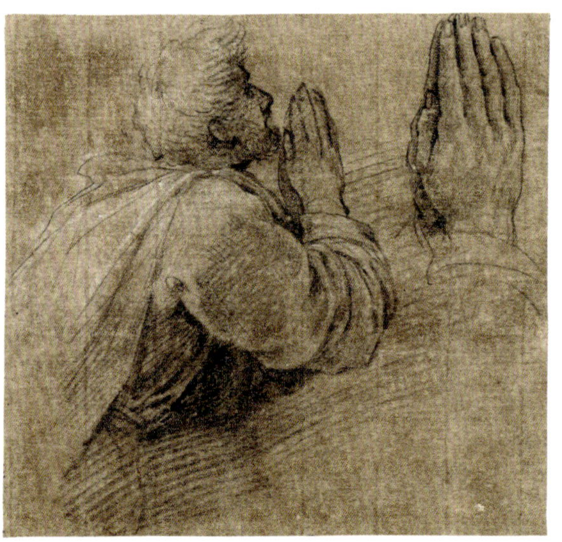

FIGURE 25 Eustache Le Sueur, *Study of a Man at Prayer*, n. d. Black and white chalks on brown paper, 17.2 × 18.8 cm. British Museum, London

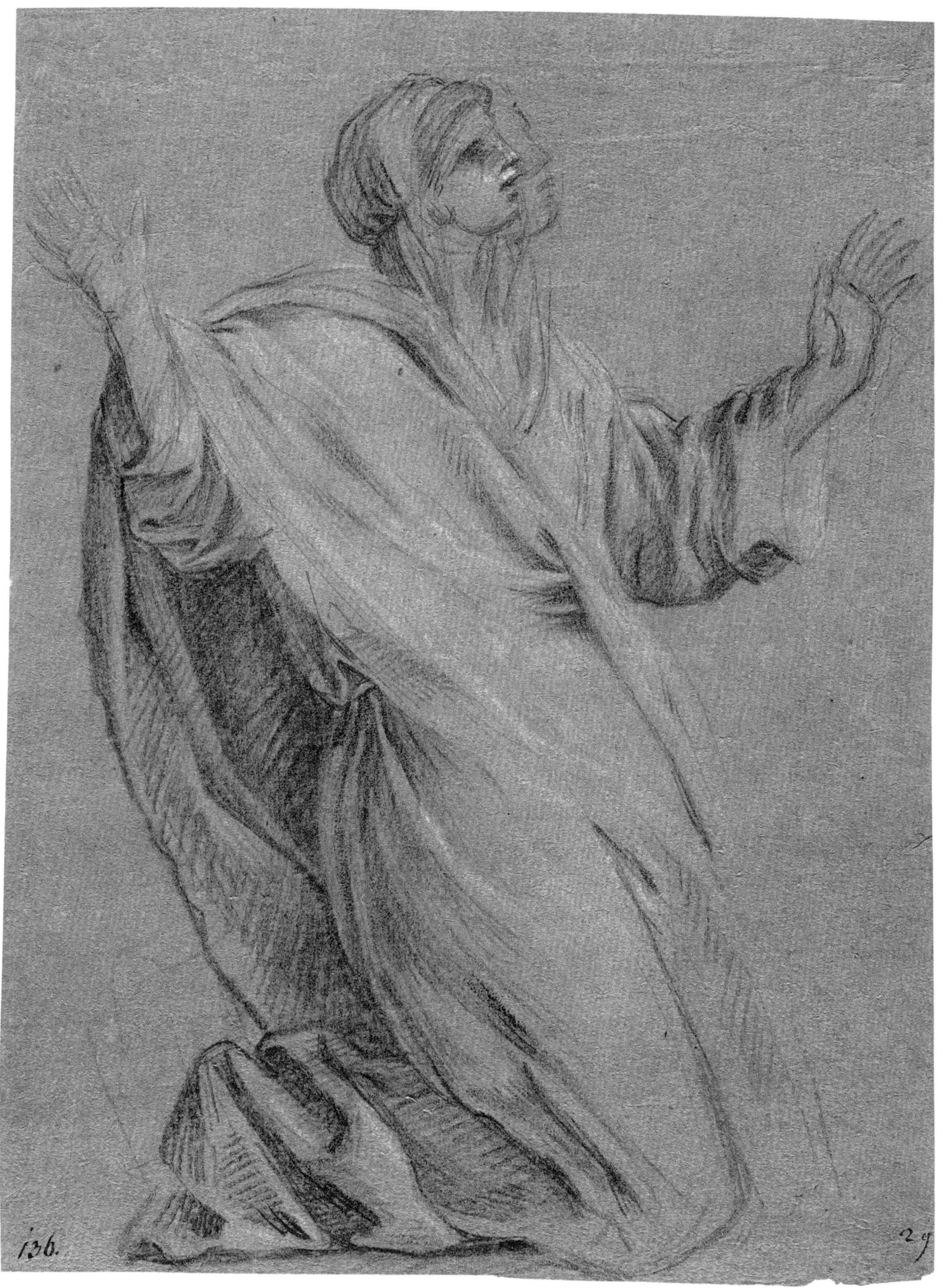

136.

NOTES

1. Inv. no. D 1805 7; Mérot 1987, as above, no. 106, fig. 321.
2. British Museum, inv. no. 1911-9-26-1.
3. Anthony Blunt, *French Drawings in the Collection of His Majesty the King*, Oxford and London, 1945, p. 30, no. 145, not repr. Both drawings are repr. Merot 1987, as above, nos. D.24-41, D.240, figs. 319–20.
4. Inv. nos. 3068, 30666, 30669, and 30687 respectively. See Jean Guiffrey and Pierre Marcel, *Inventaire général des Dessins du Musée du Louvre et du Musée de Versailles: Ecole française*, vol. IX, Paris, 1921, nos. 9184, 9185, 9186, repr.
5. Rosenberg 1970.
6. Mérot 1987, as above, nos. D. 162, 337, D. 379, 340, D. 396, pp. 215ff.

gray paper. The darker paper sets off the figure and beauty of Le Sueur's drapery studies. The Crocker's study of a kneeling woman remained unconnected until 1978, when Marguereite Sapin recognized that it was one of the artist's preparations for the *Sacrifice of Manoah*, the painting commissioned by Monsieur du Lis in 1650 and now in the Musée des Augustins, Toulouse (fig. 24).[1] The story, which is taken from the Old Testament (Judges 13: 20), tells of the angel—by tradition the archangel Gabriel—who appeared to the hitherto childless Manoah and his wife to foretell the birth of Samson, who would deliver the Israelites from their enemies the Philistines. In the painting, Samson's father Manoah and his wife kneel before an altar as the angel departs upward in the light of its blaze. The figure of the wife is placed behind the kneeling figure of Manoah, who occupies the immediate foreground. In the Crocker drawing, there is a pentimento in the head of the woman, who now starts slightly back as if in astonishment, adding dramatic intensity to her reaction. There are at least three other studies for this work, including a figure study of a man in prayer (Manoah) in the British Museum (fig. 25).[2] The other studies are sketches in black chalk and include a compositional sketch in a Parisian private collection and a sketch for the angel at Windsor, first mentioned by Blunt.[3]

In his preliminary survey of the Sacramento drawings in 1970 Pierre Rosenberg accepted the Crocker study as Le Sueur's, recognizing its similarity in style to several examples of the artist's work in the Louvre, including *Study of a Vestal Virgin* and three studies of a *Virgin and Child*,[4] all worked up in black and white chalk on brownish-gray paper. However, Rosenberg rejected the Crocker's other drawings attributed to Le Sueur.[5] More recently Alain Mérot included all four Crocker drawings as autograph in his monographic study of the artist.[6]

CD

INSCRIPTIONS: verso, black chalk, lower left: *Dughet fec.*; verso, graphite, lower left corner: *w…we*

MARKS: verso, lower left corner: Lugt 1008 (Falckeisen & Hubner, Zürich, listed as Füssli in Lugt)

PROVENANCE: Falckeisen & Hubner, Zurich; Edwin Bryant Crocker, by 1871; gift of his widow Margaret to the Museum, 1885

LITERATURE: Crocker 2004, no. 12; Marco Chiarini, "Gaspard Dughet 1615–1675," *Cahiers du dessin français*, no. 7, 1990, no. 32, pp. 8, 16; Boisclair 1986, no. 311, pp. 265, 377; Marie-Nicole Boisclair, "Gaspard Dughet, sa conception de nature et les fresques du palais Colonna," *RACAR*, vol. XIII, 1986, fig. 4c; Susan J. Bandes, "Gaspard Dughet's Frescoes in the Palazzo Colonna, Rome," *The Burlington Magazine*, vol. CXXIII, 1981, pp. 77–88; Crocker 1981, no. 8, repr.; Crocker 1979, no. 12; Reno 1978, no. 5,

33. Gaspard Dughet, *Landscape with Two Figures*, n. d.

Black and white chalks with touches of white on blue-green paper; verso: Pastoral landscape in pen and brown ink, brush and gray wash. 42.3 × 29.7 cm Crocker Art Museum, E.B. Crocker Collection 1871.353

GASPARD DUGHET (1615–1675) was born in Rome, the son of a French father and an Italian mother. Although he traveled in Italy, notably to Milan and Florence, he never left the peninsula. Sometimes he is known as Gaspard Poussin after his famous brother-in-law Nicolas Poussin, in whose studio he worked between 1631 and 1635. It was Nicolas Poussin who encouraged him to go out of Rome into the immediate countryside and make landscapes. Dughet owned two houses in Rome, and perhaps the landscape around Frascati and Tivoli provided him with the views he sought, for he had houses in both towns. He painted landscapes with a light and fresh naturalism, receiving commissions from many ecclesiastical and private patrons, notably the Colonna family, and he also worked for the Borghese late in his career.

This remarkably fresh drawing is one of six by Dughet in the Crocker Art Museum, all executed in black and white chalk on blue paper. It appeared on the cover of the issue of *Master Drawings* in which Pierre Rosenberg discussed French drawings in the Crocker

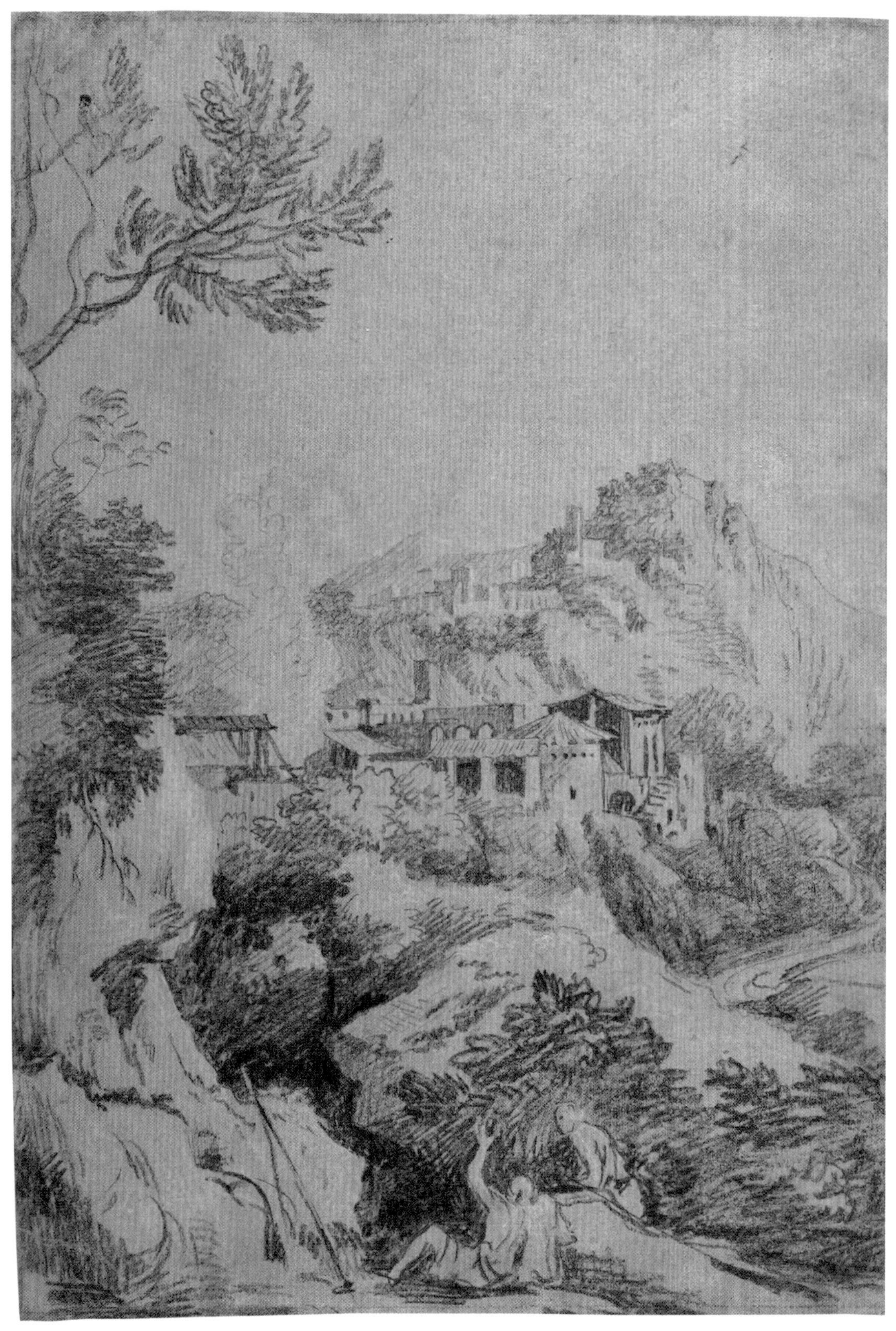

repr.; Marco Chiarini, "Un nouveau dessin apparenté aux gouaches de la galerie Colonna," *Bulletin of the National Gallery of Canada*, vol. XXII, 1973, p. 18; Crocker 1971, no. 61, pp. 25, 102; Rosenberg 1970, p. 32; Marco Chiarini, "Gaspard Dughet, Some Drawings Connected with Paintings," *The Burlington Magazine*, vol. CXI, 1969, p. 754 n. 21; Crocker 1959, no. 5; Trivas 1940a, no. 51, pp. 8, 18

NOTES

1. Rosenberg 1970, figs. 1, 2, pls. 22a-b, 23, and 24.
2. Boisclair 1986, cat. no. 311, fig. 346.
3. Rosenberg 1971, fig. 22a; Boisclair 1986, cat. no. 302, fig. 343.
4. Inv. no. FP 4708; Boisclair 1986, cat. no. 308, fig. 348.
5. Inv. no. 14960; repr. Chiarini 1990, as above, no. 37; also repr. Couturier 2004, no. 8.
6. Rosenberg 1970, p. 32, under no. 5.
7. Patricia Eshagh, writing in Robbin *et al.* 2004, mentions the hypothesis that the artist may have made these highly finished drawings afterwards as presentation sheets for potential clients.

INSCRIPTIONS: verso of mount, dark-brown ink, upper center: *Le Serpent d'Airan / a la plume Lave de Bistre / reaussé de Blanc sur papier Bistré*

MARKS: none discernible

PROVENANCE: Carl Freiherr Rolas du Rosey, before 1864; his sale, Leipzig, Rudolph Weigel, June 13, 1864, no. 5699; Edwin Bryan Crocker, Sacramento, by 1871; gift of his widow Margaret to the Museum , 1885

LITERATURE: Breazeale 2008, p. 214; Breazeale *et al.* 2008, no. 36; Teresa L. Martinelli, *The Drawings of Charles Le Brun and his Circle in the E. B. Crocker Art Museum: Their Role in Artistic Production*, unpubl. M. A. thesis, University of California,

Art Museum, while the other Dughet drawings were illustrated but not discussed in the same article.[1] All six appear to have been made more or less at the same time but only two of them connect with the artist's trompe-l'oeil frescoes in the so-called Gaspard Dughet room located in the summer rooms on the ground floor of the Palazzo Colonna, Rome, on which the artist was occupied in 1667–68. The present drawing is clearly connected to *Landscape with a Village on the Side of a Mountain*, one of the frescoes in the Palazzo Colonna,[2] while another Crocker drawing is connected to *Landscape with Two Men Conversing on a Road*, also painted at the Palazzo Colonna.[3] Engravings were made in the same sense by J. Cunego and F. Giuntotardi after the frescoes. There is another drawing connected to the Colonna project now in the Kunstmuseum, Düsseldorf.[4]

The use of black and white chalk on colored papers seems to be a technique that Dughet adopted in the 1650s and 1660s. Dughet drawings executed in this medium are rare in American collections. Aside from the group of six in the Crocker there is one sheet in the National Gallery of Canada, which is also connected with decorations in the Palazzo Colonna.[5] In European collections the Kunstmuseum, Düsseldorf, has the finest and largest group, including eight drawings, two of which are connected to paintings. There are four sheets in the British Museum, London, while Berlin, Budapest, and Hamburg each have one drawing in this technique.[6]

The similarity of Dughet's chalk drawings to the connected paintings is so close that it may be wondered if the drawings were made as *modelli* for the proposed painting or as record drawings after the completed work.[7] The number of unconnected chalk drawings that survive, however, indicates that they are most likely *modelli* prepared for the patron's approval, rather than record drawings.

CD

34. Nicolas Loir, *The Brazen Serpent*, n. d.

Pen and dark-brown ink, brush and brown washes and white opaque watercolor over traces of red chalk (squared for transfer in red chalk?), laid down, 39.2 × 53.3 cm. Crocker Art Museum, E. B. Crocker Collection 1871.425

ALTHOUGH *Moses and the Brazen Serpent* entered the Crocker collection under the name of Nicolas Loir (1624–1679), it did not appear in the literature of art until 1970, when Pierre Rosenberg mentioned it in passing in his article on the Crocker's French drawings.[1] With some reservation he supported the Loir attribution, while wondering if François Verdier should be considered. The story, taken from the Old Testament (Numbers 21: 4–9), tells how God punished the Israelites with a plague of poisonous snakes for speaking out against God and Moses. After many Israelites died, the people relented and God told Moses to make a serpent out of brass and display it on a post. Those Israelites who were bitten would only be cured if they looked upon the image. Those who refused to look would perish. Because of its obvious parallel to the Crucifixion, the subject was frequently painted.

Loir was trained in the studio of Sebastien Bourdon and in many ways his style recalls that of his master. In 1647 he went to Rome for a period of two years and was much struck with—among other things—Raphael's paintings and those of Nicolas Poussin.

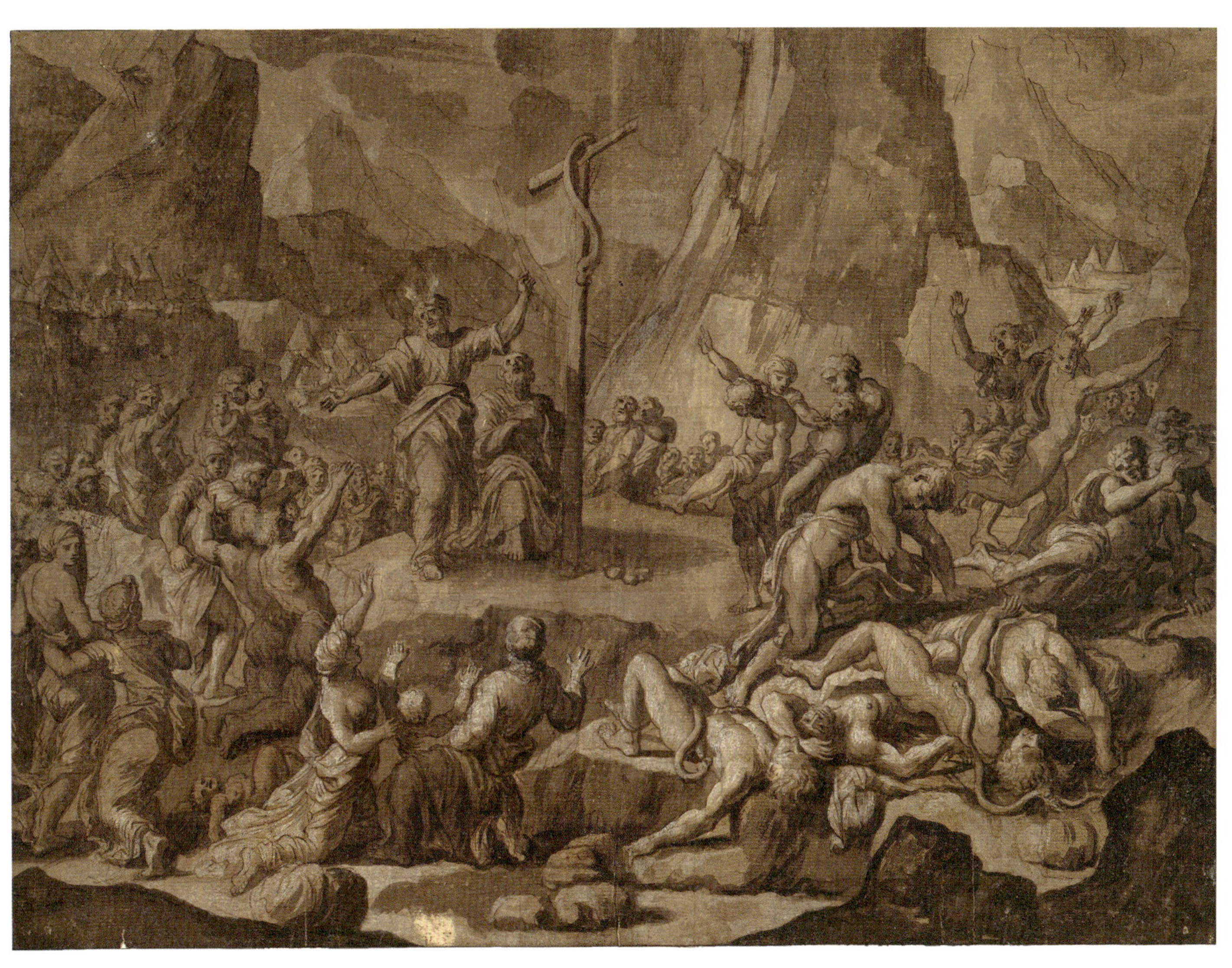

Davis, 1987, no. 3, as Circle of Le Brun;
Howard *et al.* 1973, no. 13; Crocker
1971, no. 69; Rosenberg 1970, p. 39;
Rolas du Rosey sale, Rudolph Weigel,
Leipzig 13 June 1864, no. 5699

NOTES

1. Rosenberg 1970, p. 39, under no. 11.
2. Howard *et al.* 1973, no. 13.
3. Rediscovered in 1506 on the Esquiline Hill
   and acquired by Pope Julius II, it was
   much studied and admired by artists. It is
   now in the Vatican Museums.
4. *The Language of the Nude*, 2008, no. 36.
5. Now in the J. Paul Getty Museum;
   Breazeale *et al.* 2008, fig. 51.
6. The painting is now in the Bristol City
   Museum and Art Gallery. For both
   drawing and painting see Breazeale *et al.*
   2008, no. 25, fig. 46.
7. Moana Weil-Curiel, "A Propos de Nicolas
   Loir (1623-1679)," *Revue du Louvre*, no. 50,
   2000, pp. 54–58.

The present composition is in many ways constructed like a Poussin, densely populated with figures in movement. It has been compared with Poussin's *Rape of the Sabine Women*.[2] One of the authors of the 1973 Crocker catalogue directed by Seymour Howard also sees the influence of the *Laocoön*, the famous Hellenistic sculptural group which Loir would very likely have seen in Rome.[3]

Quite recently Christine Giviskos has thoroughly studied the drawing in a Crocker catalogue.[4] Although in his time Loir received recognition and was occupied with many important commissions and work, he remains a rather unfamiliar artist in our time. He was selected to paint the *May* of Notre-Dame in 1650, depicting *Saint Paul and the False Prophets*, and he was especially well known in connection with his work in the Tuileries Palace and at Versailles. He was also elected to the Académie Royale in 1663.

Giviskos observed that Loir's composition owed something to Bourdon's *Israelites Dancing around the Golden Calf*,[5] where the figure of Moses with the Tables of the Law is similarly placed to the left of the center. Loir probably also knew Le Brun's painting of the Brazen Serpent, for which the Crocker has a study, the figure of a man trying to escape from the snakes at the far right of Le Brun's composition.[6]

Although it has been suggested that the work might well be by François Verdier or be by an artist in the circle of Charles Le Brun, it seems, as its old ascription indicates, to fit with what we know of the style of Loir, who was given to densely peopled compositions in the manner of Poussin and Bourdon. In addition to painted and graphic works in the Louvre, there are also concentrations of his drawings in other museums, notably in Berlin and the British Museum. His figures are often bulky and energetic in their movement and gestures. Although the present work was squared for transfer and is fully worked up as a final compositional sketch or *modello*, the painting for which it was prepared is not known.

Although in his own time Loir received recognition and was occupied with many important commissions, it is curious that he remains relatively unknown now. The closest thing to a real study of him is that of Moana Weil-Curiel,[6] who wrote about Loir at the time of the large Bourdon exhibition in Montpellier. It is possible that many of Loir's works have been confused with those of other artists, such as Bourdon, whose work his style most closely resembles.

CD

35. **Claude Gillot,** *Scene of Sorcery*, n. d.

Pen and black and dark grey ink, brush and red washes; verso: sketches of animal caricatures in pen and black and dark grey ink, red chalk, 21 × 32.9 cm. Crocker Art Museum, E. B. Crocker Collection 1871.397

INSCRIPTIONS: black chalk, lower right (signed?): *Gillot*

MARKS: verso, graphite, lower left corner: circle and stroke

PROVENANCE: possibly sale, Paris, Lebrun fils, December 23, 1771, no. 543 ("*une diablerie de Gillot*");[1] Edwin Bryant Crocker, by 1871; gift of his widow Margaret to the Museum, 1885

LITERATURE: Howard et al. 1983, no. 19; Crocker 1979, no. 12; Reno 1978, no. 19; Steadman and Osborne 1976, no. 30; Crocker 1971, no. 78; Rosenberg 1970, no. 13; Crocker 1964, no. 397; Crocker 1959, no. 7

FOR SOME TIME this subject was believed to represent the Temptation of Saint Anthony, but more recently students of French art, noticing the greater attention given to witchcraft, have interpreted the subject as a scene of sorcery.[2] It has been remarked that in his *Sabbaths* Gillot shows something of the verve and imaginative breadth of Callot, whose work he would have known. Gillot (1673–1722) was an active printmaker, producing some 225 prints, which have been the subject of Bernard Populus's monographic study.[3] The artist would likely have known Callot's famous etchings of the *Temptation of Saint Anthony* but he never rendered the subject himself. Probably the confusion of the subject with the Temptation occurred because of the bespectacled figure in a monk's habit who is sprawled on a raft in the foreground of this highly charged fantastic scene. Equipped with all the accoutrements of black magic, including books, candles, mortar and pestle, skull, and crossed bones, and accompanied by a cat, he consults a book or document. He is most likely a sorcerer conjuring a spell which has brought forth the convocation of witches and Bosch-like grotesque creatures that are to be seen all around and above him. Some of the witches in the Crocker drawing—especially the one on a broomstick—occur in his etchings of *Witches' Sabbaths* (see fig. 26), making it likely that he executed the present drawing around the same time that he was working on these.[4] This suggestion is strengthened by the many animal-head studies on the verso of the Crocker drawing, not unlike the heads of some of the fantastic creatures in the Sabbath prints.

Gillot's customary subject matter was genre-based and included scenes from daily life as well as theatrical subjects. His interest in theatre was comprehensive and had always included marionette theatre—which may have influenced his distinctive style of figure drawing, characterized by light, lithe figures with pointed feet and wide-spaced eyes, not unlike puppets. But the artist also had a lifelong interest in the fanciful which went back to his boyhood in Langres, where he was enthralled by the local stories and legends about witches and sorcery. These, too, would fuel his creative imagination and provide him with a repertoire of fantastic subjects, including satyrs, bacchanals, and witches.

Gillot had learned to paint and etch when he entered the studio of Jean-Baptiste Corneille about 1690. By 1710 he had been *agréé* by the Académie, where he was received five years later as a history painter. It is said that Corneille left him a drawing of a satyr that he had made after the Carracci. There may have been other drawings of this sort of subject which to a degree would have influenced the young artist's taste in subject matter. As we know, he made various etchings depicting the lives of satyrs and also produced etchings of mythic bacchanals and witches' Sabbaths. Populus mentions that Gillot was influenced in this by the stories he had heard when he was a boy, one of which was 'The Candle of Chiropa'.[5] This story was actually produced in 1695 in Langres as a

NOTES
1. According to Bernard Populus, *Claude Gillot (1673–1722), catalogue de l'œuvre gravé*, Paris, 1930, p. 84.
2. Rosenberg 1970.
3. Populus 1930, as in note 1.
4. This impression inv. no. 1866-4-7-31.
5. Populus 1930, as in note 1, p. ?.

6. Paulette Choné, François Moureau, Philippe Quettier, Eric Varnier, *Claude Gillot (1673-1722), Comédies, Sabbats et autres sujets bizarres*, exh. cat. Musée de Langres, Langres, 1999, pp. 72ff.

7. Marianne Roland Michel, "Gillot, Claude," in *Grove Dictionary of Art*, www.oxfordartonline.com, *s. v.*

theatrical piece and ballet by the Jesuits, who staged a production in the *collège* at Langres where had Gillot studied before he left for Paris.[6] It is now generally agreed that most of these etchings of fantastic subjects were most probably executed by Gillot between 1700 and 1710.[7] However, the two etchings of the witches' Sabbath were not printed until after Gillot's death, having been completed by the engraver Jean Audran.

After the death of Corneille in 1705 Watteau entered Gillot's studio, where he remained until 1709. While there he absorbed some of Gillot's subject matter, especially his *commedia dell'arte* theatrical subjects, as well as something of his manner, including his style of figure drawing.

CD

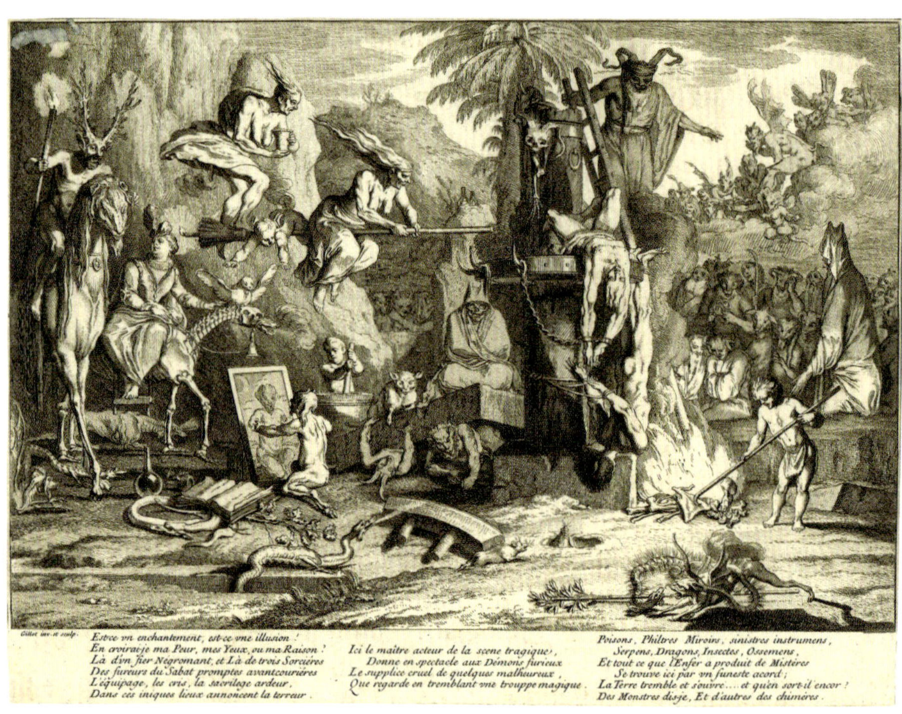

FIGURE 26 Claude Gillot, *Les sabbats*, n. d. Etching and engraving, 24.0 × 32.2 cm. British Museum, London, inv. no. 1866-4-7-31

Verso of cat. no. 35

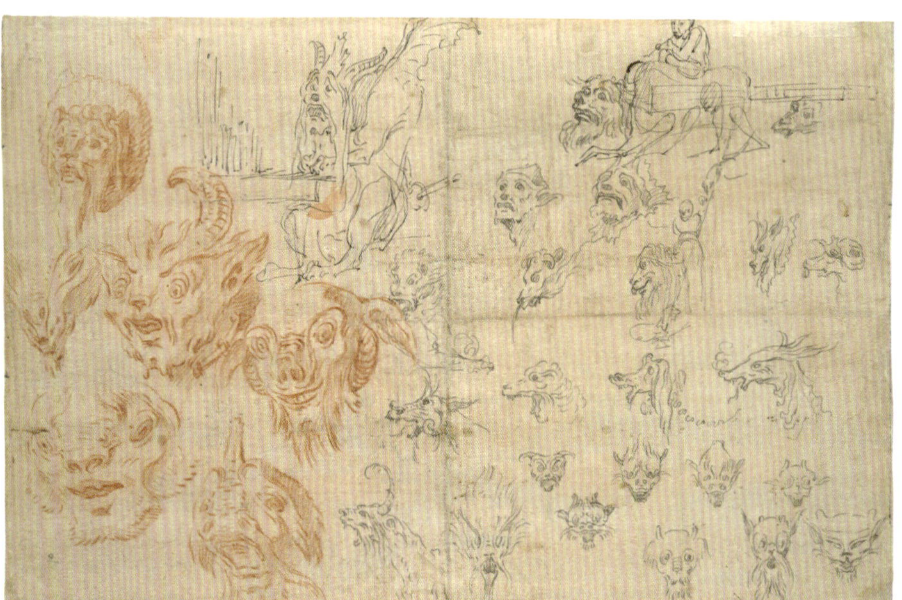

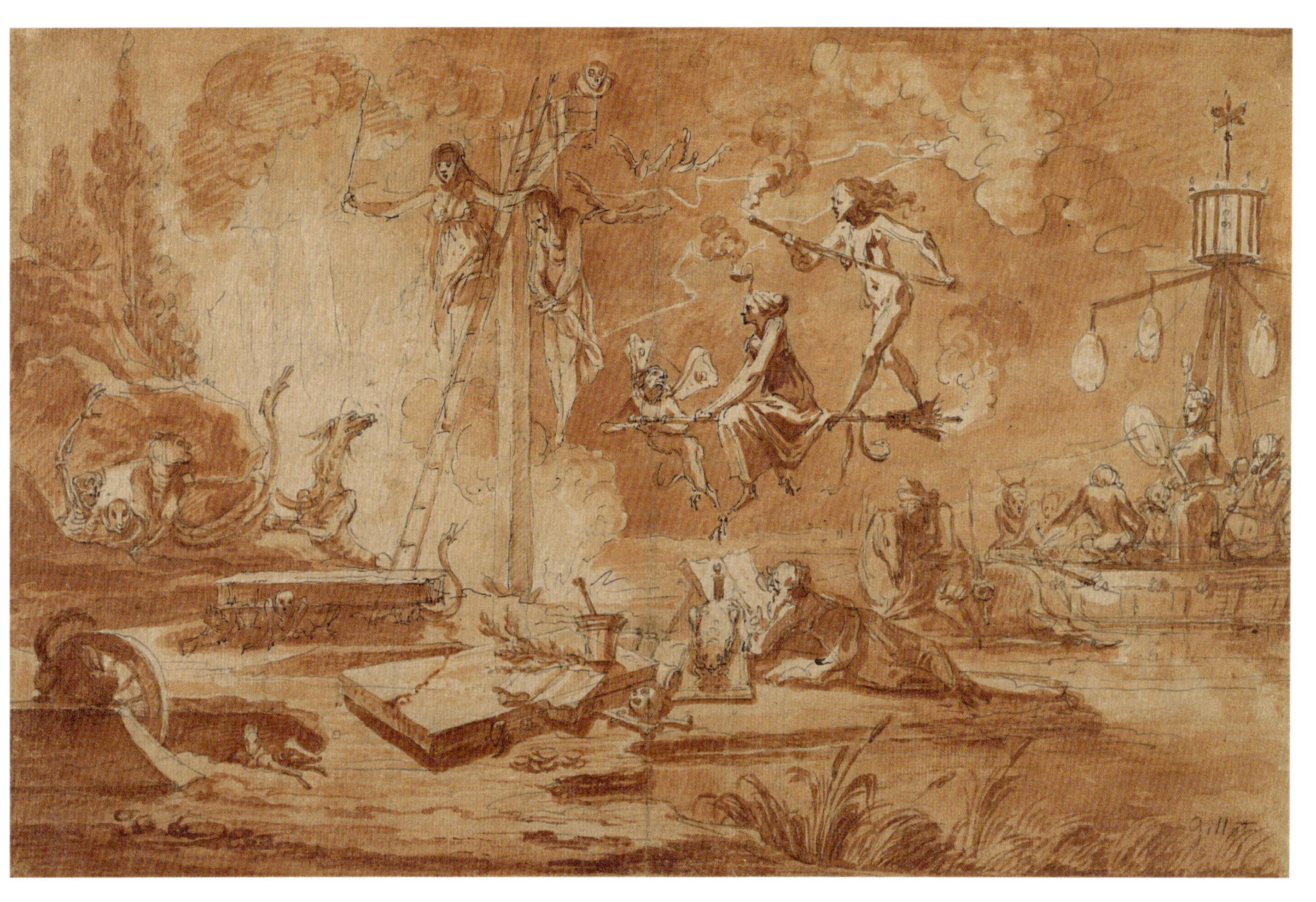

36. François Boucher, *The Birth of Venus*, n. d.

Black and white chalks and charcoal on beige laid paper, 32.6 × 44.9 cm.
Crocker Art Museum, E. B. Crocker Collection 1871.401

INSCRIPTIONS: black chalk, lower right, signed: *Boucher*; verso, black chalk, lower left: *Guriel* [?]; verso, graphite, center right: *6/"*

MARKS: verso, lower left corner: Lugt 2315 (Stiglmeier)

PROVENANCE: Johann Stiglmeier, Straubing, before 1856; Edwin Bryant Crocker, Sacramento, by 1871; gift of his widow Margaret to the Museum, 1885

LITERATURE: Breazeale 2008, p. 214; Breazeale et al. 2008, no. 40; Perrin Stein and Martin Royalton Kisch, *French Drawings from the British Museum, Clouet to Seurat*, exh. cat. Metropolitan Museum, New York, and British Museum, London, 2005, p. 122 under no. 47; Alastair Lang, *The Drawings of François Boucher*, exh. cat. Frick Collection, New York, and Kimbell Art Museum, Fort Worth, 2003, p. 27; Lydia Beauvais, *Charles le Brun 1619–1680, Inventaire général des dessins, école française*, Musée du Louvre, Paris, 2000, under no. 1142; Alistair Laing, "La Re-Naissance de Vénus: une oeuvre des débuts de Boucher retrouvée à Paris," *Revue de l'Art*, no. 103, 1994, pp. 77–81; Ruda 1992, no .18; George R. Goldner with the assistance of Lee Hendrix and Gloria Williams, *European Drawings, I. Catalogue of the Collection*, J. Paul Getty Museum Collection Catalogues, Malibu, 1988, under no. 59; Beverly Schreiber Jacoby, *François Boucher's Early Development as a Draughtsman 1720–1734*, New York, 1986, no. III.C; Ruda 1985, p. 6; Denys Sutton, exh. cat. Tokyo Metropolitan Museum of Art and Kunamoto Prefectural Museum; Tokyo, 1982, no. 91; Clisby 1979, no. 3; Sotheby's, London, June 20–21, 1978, under lot 62; Alexandre Ananoff, *François Boucher*, Lausanne and Paris, no. 180/2; Regina Shoolman Slatkin, *François Boucher in North American Collections: 100 Drawings*, exh. cat. National Gallery of Art, Washington, 1979, p. xvii and no. 54; Howard et al. 1972, no. 20, as follower of Boucher; Crocker 1971, checklist p. 148; Rosenberg 1970, p. 39; Crocker 1964, p. 95 and p. 22

THIS DRAWING BY BOUCHER (1703–1770) is a compositional study for a painting of the early 1730s, *The Birth of Venus*, which presently hangs in the dining room of the Rumanian Embassy in Paris (fig. 27). Before being rediscovered in the embassy in the rue Saint Dominique the painting was for many years believed lost. This former *hôtel particulier* was built by Hippolyte Destailleur in the late nineteenth century for the comtesse

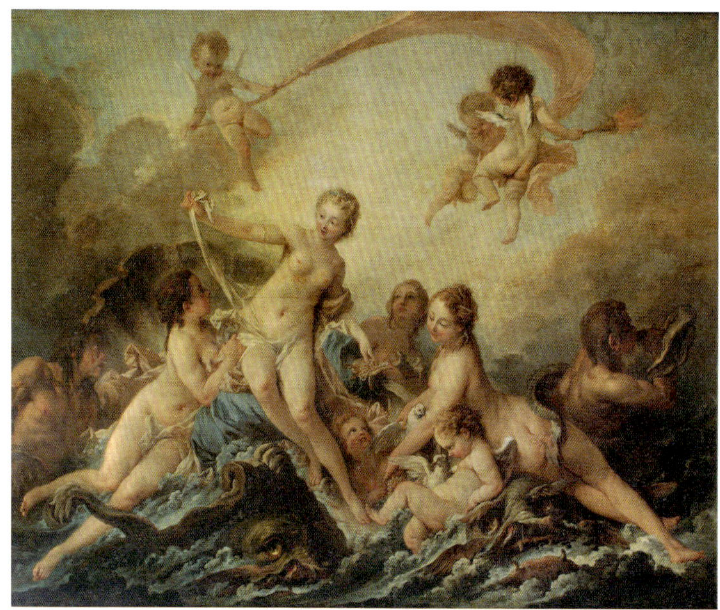

FIGURE 27 François Boucher, *The Birth of Venus*, 1734. Oil on canvas. Rumanian Embassy, Paris

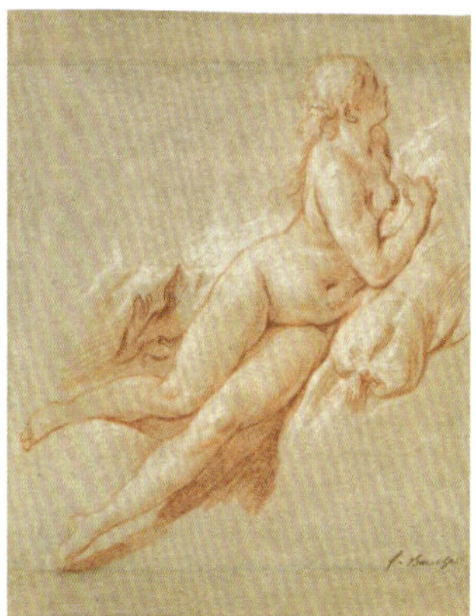

FIGURE 28 François Boucher, *Reclining Female Nude, c.* 1734. Red and white chalks on oatmeal paper, 31 × 24.6 cm. J. Paul Getty Museum, Los Angeles

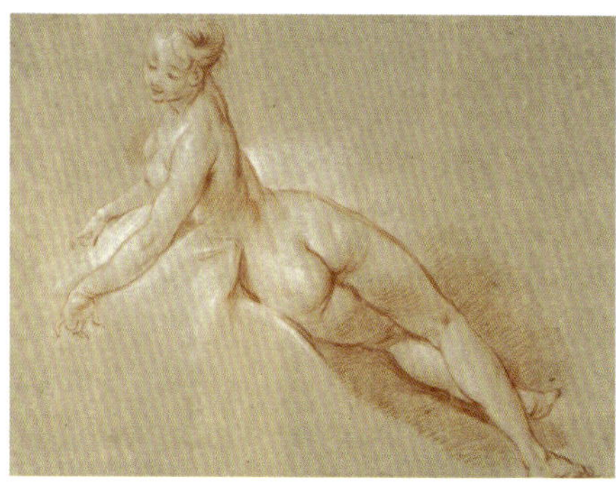

FIGURE 29 François Boucher, *Study of a Reclining Female Nude, c.* 1734. Red and white chalks on oatmeal paper, 24.9 × 35.2 cm. British Museum, London

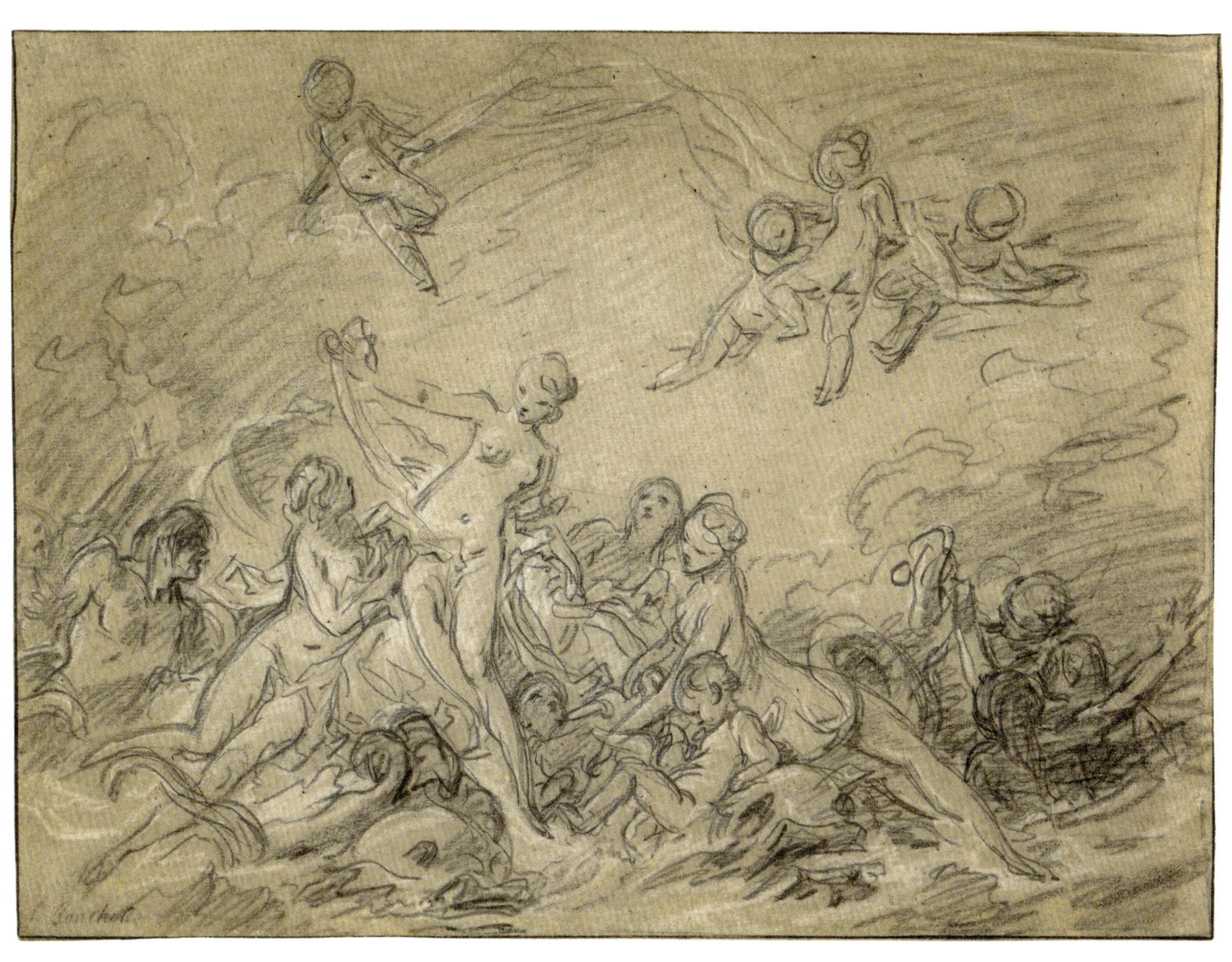

NOTES

1. Laing 1994, as above, no. 103, pp. 71–81, where the painting is shown in reverse.

2. Georges Brunel, *Boucher*, New York, 1986, pp. 58–71. Brunel found François Derbais's estate inventory of 1743: *François Derbais, rue Poissonière, salle de billard, inventaire après décès*, 2 Mar. 1743, Archives Nationales, Minutier Central, LIX, p. 230.

3. Repr. in Brunel 1986, figs. 21, 22, 29 and 30.

4. Jacoby 1986, as above, III.C.1, who convincingly points out the similarity of handling in several other drawings of this period. In addition to the *Nessus and Dejaneira* (IIIC2) Jacoby also mentions the similarity to his illustrations for the *Œuvres de Molière* of about the same time. The illustration closest to the *Birth of Venus* manner seems to me to be the design for the *Prologue de Psyché* in the Musée Fabre, Montpellier, repr. Jacoby 1986, III.D.24.

5. Von Hirsch sale, London, Sotheby's, June 20–21, 1978, lot 62 , repr.

6. Goldner 1988, as above, no. 59, repr.

7. Inv. nos. 84.GB.21 and SL 5223.26 respectively.

8. Stein 2005, as above, no. 47, repr.

9. Breazeale et al. 2008, no. 40.

de Béarn, who also owned the painting. The newly rediscovered work and its fascinating story were published by Alastair Laing in 1994.[1]

The painting was part of a commission which Boucher received soon after his return from Italy in 1731 for François Derbais.[2] Derbais commissioned a suite of paintings to decorate the billiard room in his *hôtel* in the rue Poissonière. The project seems to have occupied Boucher for nearly three years. The other paintings which were part of the Derbais commission are now in three other collections: two, *The Rape of Europa* and *Mercury Confiding the Infant Bacchus to the Nymphs*, are in the Wallace Collection, London, while *Venus Asking Vulcan for Arms for Aeneas* is in the Louvre; still another, *Aurora and Cephalus*, is in the Musée des Beaux-Arts, Nancy.[3]

As can be seen, the Crocker drawing is a work of sudden inspiration, executed rapidly in black chalk heightened with white. In it Boucher has completely worked out all the main compositional elements of the painting. In the light touch of the chalk and the distinctly lithe figure style, it is consistent with other drawings of the early 1730s. As Beverly Schreiber Jacoby has remarked, the Venus is "the mirror image of Dejaneira" in his *Nessus and Dejaneira* and the drawing exhibits a great deal of youthful bravura and exuberance.[4] In addition to the Crocker drawing Boucher made at least three figure drawings connected with the painting. The study for the central figure of Venus, formerly in the collection of Baron Robert von Hirsch, is in a private collection.[5] Studies for the two nereids at either side of Venus are also known: the nereid at her left is in the Getty Museum[6] while the nereid on the right is in the British Museum (figs. 28 and 29).[7] After laying out the composition in the Crocker drawing, as both Perrin Stein[8] and Christine Giviskos note,[9] Boucher would have made the figure studies of Venus and the two nereids from an elaborately posed studio model, probably the same one for all three figures. These studies were executed in detail in red chalk, heightened with white, on light-brown paper.

The final arrangement of the composition follows the Crocker drawing almost exactly. Only a few compositional elements in the drawing are not included in the painting as finally realized. In the painting the shell form to the left of Venus is developed and the goddess is depicted wearing pearls and holding more in her hand as well. The nereid on the left holds also hold pearls in her hand while the other nereid assists Venus with the white drapery she is holding in her raised right hand. The principal figures are supported by a dolphin seen below in the foamy waves of the sea, while a triton looks on from the left. The commission from Derbais was an important one for Boucher and both Laing and Bailey point out that the artist hoped other commissions would come as a result of clients seeing his paintings in Derbais's house.   CD

37. François Guérin, *Portrait of Mme de Pompadour and her Daughter Alexandrine d'Etiolles*, n. d.

Black and white chalks with touches of red chalk on blue laid paper, laid down to heavy cream laid secondary support, 23.9 × 19 cm. Crocker Art Museum, E. B. Crocker Collection 1871.403

INSCRIPTIONS: none discernible

MARKS: none discernible

PROVENANCE: Marquis de Marigny; Edwin Bryant Crocker, by 1871; gift of his widow Margaret to the Museum, 1885

LITERATURE: Hans Sontag, "'Ines' und 'Mimi,' die Lieblingshunde der Marquise de Pompadour, 2008 aus Meissener Porzellan zu neuem Leben erweckt," *Keramos*, vol. CC, April 2008, p. 23; Jones 2002, pp. 42, 166, no. 10; Salmon 2002, no. 28, p. 30; Helge Siefert in Salmon 2002, p. 28; Crocker 1979, no. 22; Albertina 1975, pp. 31f. under no. 52; Crocker 1971, no. 95; Rosenberg 1970, p. 31; Schulz 1968, no. 8; Crocker 1959, no. 8 (dated incorrectly as after 1791); Otto Benesch, "Two drawings dedicated to Madame de Pompadour," *Gazette des Beaux-Arts*, series 6, vol. XXII, 1950, pp. 125–29; Benisovich 1945, pp. 31–42

NOTES

1. Guérin's dates come from Jones 2002, as above.
2. Although it is the property of the Bayerische Hypothek und Wechselbank it is on deposit at the Alte Pinkothek.
3. Repr. in Salmon 2002, p. 407, fig. 1.
4. Inv. no. NG 6440; Siefert 2002, as above.
5. Alden Rand Gordon, *French Inventories I: The Houses and Collections of the Marquis de Marigny*, The Provenance Index of the Getty Research Institute, Los Angeles, 2003, p. 295, no. 807 note 96.

THIS APPEALING DRAWING is a study for François Guérin's portrait of *Mme de Pompadour and her Daughter, Alexandrine d'Etiolles* in the Rothschild collection, Château de Prigny, Switzerland. François Guérin (1711–1792),[1] a student of Charles-Joseph Natoire (1700–1777), was a specialist in portraits of women and children. Here he emulated his contemporary Boucher, who painted Mme de Pompadour many times. In particular his portrait owes a good deal to Boucher's representation of Mme de Pompadour seated and reading a book in her *salon* which is now in Munich,[2] as well as to Drouais's portrait of her in the National Gallery, London (fig. 30).[3] Like Boucher's portrait, Guérin's shows Madame de Pompadour in formal dress and seated in her study or *salon*, a mirror reflecting her from behind, her book in hand, her little dog Mimi at her feet. But in Guerin's painting she sits on a divan with a dog seated beside her, her dress and pose more frontal and closer to Drouais's portrait of her. At lower right Guérin has added her daughter, Alexandrine d'Etiolles, sitting on a footstool playing with her pet bird, who has hopped out of his little cage onto her finger. Mme de Pompadour's other little King Charles spaniel, Ines, sits before her.

The compositional Crocker drawing is quite sketchy. It shows that originally Guérin thought to set the scene outside and to position Alexandrine on the left rather than the right. He has even indicated a garland of flowers suspended above by some winged cherubs. Also, Mme de Pompadour is dressed in a sort of *negligée* rather than the elaborate dress she wears in the finished painting. Mme de Pompadour gestures gracefully with her right hand towards the child in the sketch whereas she pets her little dog Mimi in the painting. In the drawing only one of the little dogs is shown and is seated on a cushion held by a kneeling servant, seen to the right of Alexandrine. The servant is eliminated in the painting, but the dog, Ines, remains.

Alexandrine's father was Charles-Guillaume Le Normant d'Etiolles, whom Jeanne-Antoinette Poisson (1721–1764), the future Madame de Pompadour, *maîtresse en titre* of Louis XV, married in 1741 and from whom she was separated in 1745. Alexandrine was born in 1744 and had entered the convent school of the Assumption in Paris by 1750. She died in 1754 at the age of ten. It stands to reason that Mme de Pompadour and Alexandrine never sat to Guerin, for Alexandrine would not have been alive when Guérin's picture, so indebted to Boucher's and Drouais's works of 1756 and 1764, was painted.

Helge Siefert dates Guérin's painting to after 1764,[4] because Mme de Pompadour wears the same costume that she wears in Drouais's portrait, and her expression and pose are also similar. Siefert also thinks it might date to some time after Mme de Pompadour's death. However, it seems likely that Mme de Pompadour herself commissioned it, since after her death Guérin's portrait passed, along with her other possessions, to her brother, the Marquis de Marigny.[5]

6. Benesch 1950, as above
7. With Derek Johns.

After seeing the Crocker drawing, Benesch reattributed two charming drawings in the Albertina, formerly given to Chardin on the basis of old inscriptions, to Guérin.[6] Each drawing in the Albertina depicts a lady with her child. In one case the child plays on the floor with a birdcage and in the other the lady is drawing the child. Tradition has it that these drawings were made for Mme de Pompadour.

Aside from a famous bust by Saly and some miniature portraits, very few portraits of Alexandrine d'Etiolles are known. There exists, however, a half-length portrait alternately given to Guérin and Boucher which represents the child feeding a bird in a cage.[7]
CD

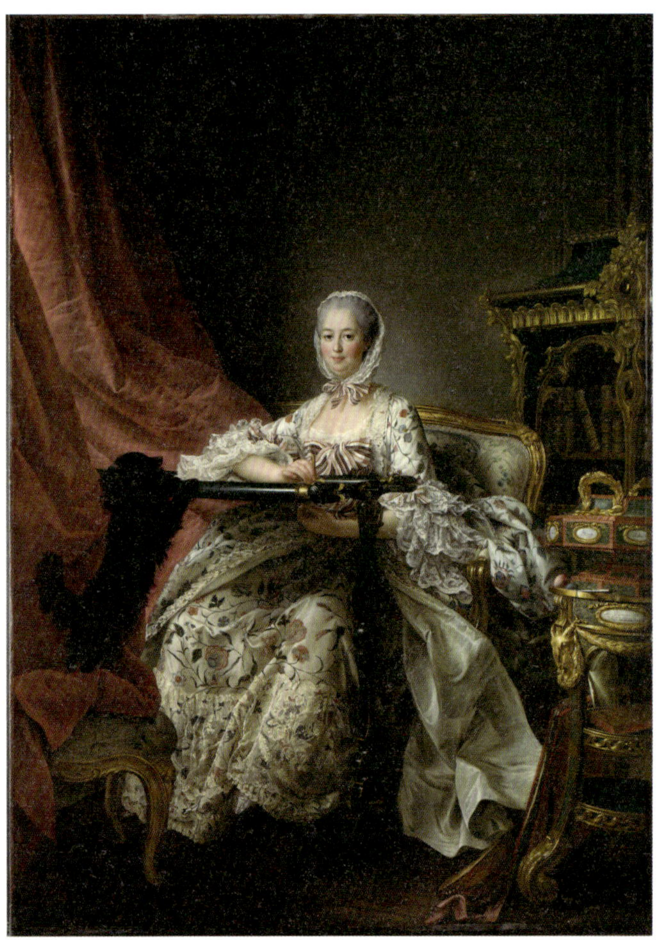

FIGURE 30 François-Hubert Drouais, *Mme de Pompadour at her Tambour Frame*, 1763–64. Oil on canvas, 217 × 156.8 cm. National Gallery, London

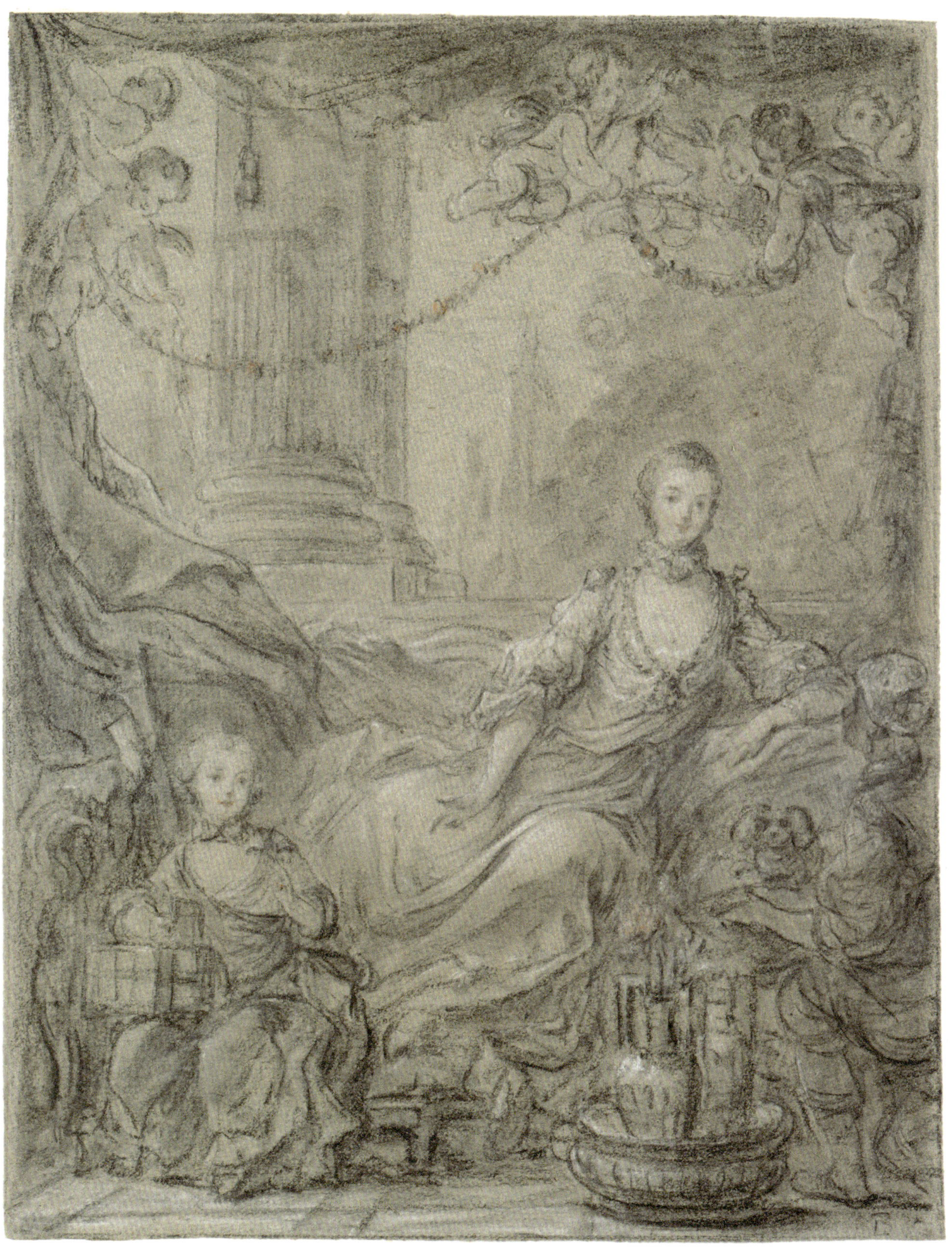

38. Jean-Honoré Fragonard, *An Italian Park*, 1786.

Brush and point of brush and brown washes over black chalk, laid down, 24.1 × 36.9 cm. Crocker Art Museum, E. B. Crocker Collection 1871.407

INSCRIPTIONS: brown ink, lower right, signed and dated: *Frago 1786*

MARKS: none discernible

PROVENANCE: Edwin Bryant Crocker, by 1871; gift of his widow Margaret to the Museum, 1885

LITERATURE: Pierre Rosenberg, *Fragonard*, exh. cat. Grand Palais, Paris, and Metropolitan Museum of Art, New York, 1987, no. 302; Eunice Williams, *Drawings by Fragonard in North American Collections*, exh. cat. National Gallery of Art, Washington; Fogg Art Museum, Cambridge; Frick Collection, New York, 1978, no. 52; Reno 1978, no. 7; Steadman and Osborne 1976, no. 24; Crocker 1971, no. 88; Rosenberg 1970, no. 16; Schultz 1968, no. 5; Ananoff 1963, vol. II, no. 947; Crocker 1964, no. 407; Crocker 1959, no. 6; Trivas 1940b, p. 137; Trivas 1940a, checklist p. 20, no. 63a; Henle 1940, no. 35

THIS LARGE DRAWING, executed from memory or imagination, is rendered almost entirely in transparent light-brown washes—sometimes layered—over a very faint underdrawing in black chalk. It is a good example of Fragonard's superb facility for representing a subject using only brush and wash set off by the white of the paper. This technique is in some ways reminiscent of the drawing style of Giambattista Tiepolo, an artist whose work Fragonard (1732–1806) was familiar with and admired. Since the Crocker drawing was made as late as 1786, this view in a park must represent the artist's recollection of a scene from one of his two sojourns in Italy, which had ended twelve years before, or a scene invented from fantasy.

Fragonard won the Prix de Rome in 1755 and stayed at the French Academy, then located on the Corso, until 1761. During his time there he became friendly with Hubert Robert and the abbé de Saint-Non. Robert went there at about the same time as Fragonard in the company of Robert de Stainville, the future duc de Choiseul. Although not officially a *pensionnaire*, Robert was given a room at the French Academy and was able to stay in Rome until 1763. It was on this first trip to Italy that both Robert and Fragonard developed a lifelong interest in outdoor subjects, an interest encouraged by the then Director of the French Academy in Rome, Charles-Joseph Natoire, who also drew many views of parks and Italian gardens. Fragonard spent a summer at the Villa d'Este with the abbé de Saint-Non. The abbé was beginning to collect material later

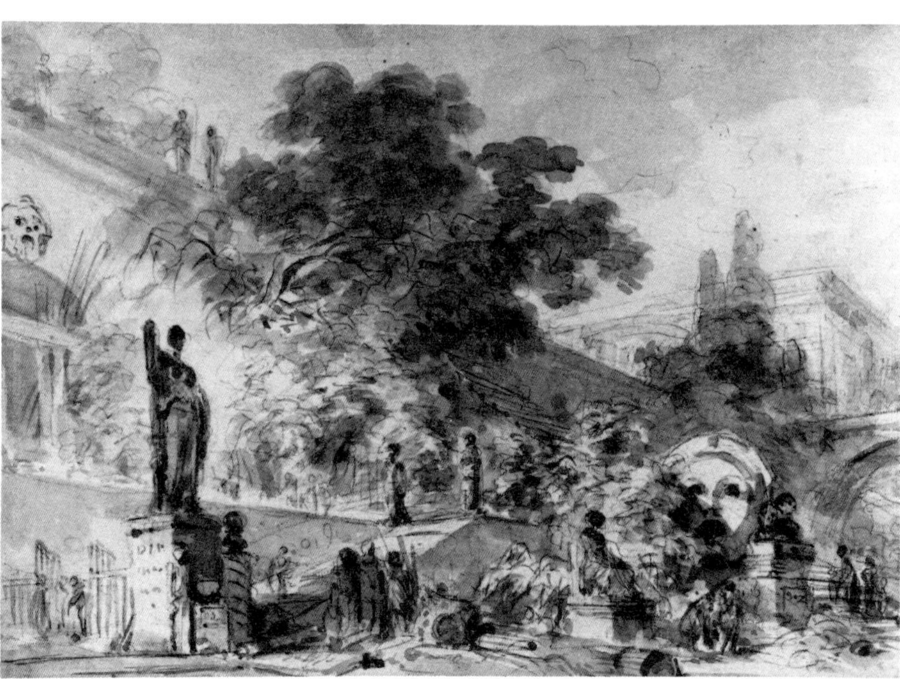

FIGURE 31 Jean-Honoré Fragonard, *An Imaginary Italian Garden*, n. d. Brush and brown wash over black chalk, 29.8 × 42.2 cm. The Morgan Library and Museum, New York

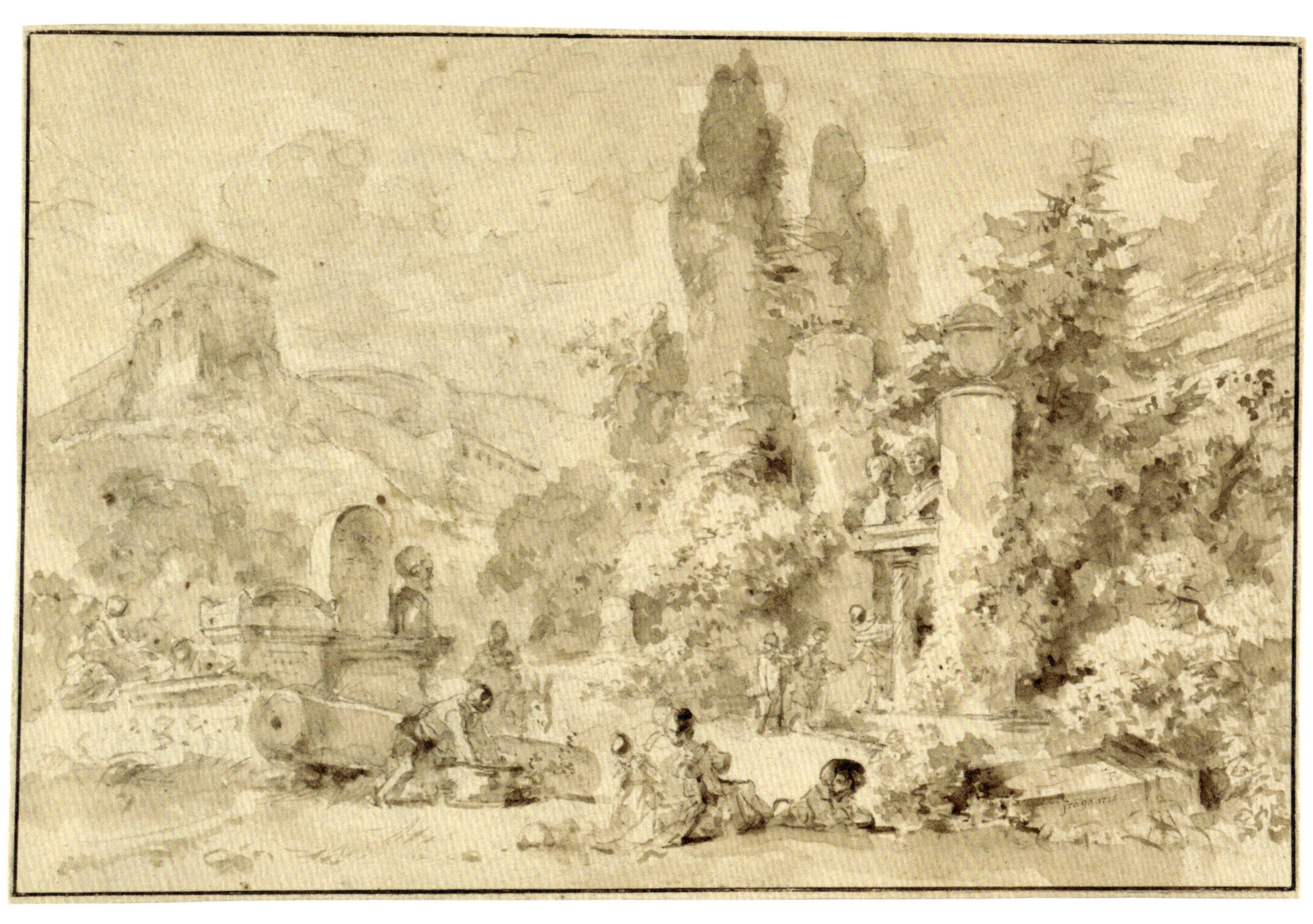

NOTES

1. Inv. no. Thaw Collection 2001.59; Felice Stampfle and Cara Denison, *Drawings in the Collection of Mr. and Mrs. Eugene Victor Thaw*, New York, 1975–76, no. 36.
2. Williams 1978, as above, no. 52, repr.
3. Rosenberg 1987, as above.

published as his *Voyages pittoresques*, and invited Fragonard to accompany him on his leisurely way back to Paris. During his time at the Villa d'Este Fragonard drew many views in red chalk for which he is justly celebrated. He also drew many studies of paintings, sculptures, and art objects that he and Abbé saw on the trip back to Paris.

Later, in 1773-74, Fragonard accompanied his friend and patron Bergeret de Grancourt to Italy again, making both paintings and drawings of the picturesque people and places they visited. In the years following he continued to paint and draw Italian subjects, but many of these late drawings of Italian subjects are *capricci* rather than real views. One in the Morgan Library in New York dates to the late 1770s or early 1780s, *An Imaginary Italian Garden* (fig. 31).[1] It, too, is an invention taken from Fragonard's memory of Italian parks and scenery and is executed on a fairly large scale, somewhat larger than the Crocker drawing, but also in brush and brown wash—with this difference, that the Morgan sheet bears a pronounced underdrawing in black chalk which carries almost as much weight in the design as the brush and wash.

Eunice Williams has described the Crocker drawing as primarily a study of light effects on ancient Roman monuments, and she was especially interested by the fact that it is one of the few dated drawings made after Fragonard's last trip to Italy in 1773–74. It shows that—contrary to some scholars' ideas on the subject—Fragonard was still very much in control of his art and drew and painted with as much brilliance at this period of his life as ever. Williams also dismisses Ananoff's idea that the Crocker drawing is a late reworking of another drawing by the master, since that drawing is in an unrelated style.[2] A list of other comparable drawings is given in Pierre Rosenberg's Fragonard exhibition catalogue of 1987-88. These include the Morgan drawing, a drawing in the Stanford museum and a drawing sold at Sotheby's, London, November 26, 1970, lot 74. Rosenberg remarked that another drawing of a very similar subject was sold in Paris in 1981, of the authenticity of which he was not certain.[3]   CD

39. Pierre Peyron (?), *Young Man Asleep in a Chair*, n. d.

Red and white chalks, laid down, 31.7 × 24.1 cm. Crocker Art Museum, E. B. Crocker Collection 18781.450

INSCRIPTIONS: pen and brown ink, lower right, signed: *Peyron ft*

MARKS: none discernible

PROVENANCE: Edwin Bryant Crocker, by 1871; gift of his widow Margaret to the Museum, 1885

LITERATURE: Pierre Rosenberg and Udolpho van de Sandt, *Pierre Peyron 1744-1814*, Paris, 1983, no. X 20; Crocker 1979, no. 32 (as *Woman Asleep in Chair*); Crocker 1971, no. 92, repr. (as *Woman Asleep in Chair*); Rosenberg 1970, p. 39 (as *Man Asleep on his Elbows*); Crocker 1959, no. 10 (as *Woman Asleep in Chair*)

PIERRE PEYRON (1744–1814) won the Prix de Rome in 1773 in competition with his slightly younger contemporary Jacques-Louis David. David won the next year and both artists set out for Rome in 1775. While the artists were in Rome Peyron's avowed preference for classical subjects influenced his contemporaries to turn away from the Rococo style towards Neoclassicism. Even his rival David would later acknowledge his formative role, saying "Peyron opened my eyes." Peyron returned to Paris in 1782 and was *agréé* by the Académie Royale in 1783 and appointed Inspecteur Général of the Gobelins factory. By 1787 he was received as a full member of the Académie. He exhibited his *Death of Socrates* at the Salon but it was eclipsed by David's version of the same subject. Although his post at the Gobelins was abolished during the Revolution, Peyron continued to receive commissions, including official commissions, especially under the First Empire.

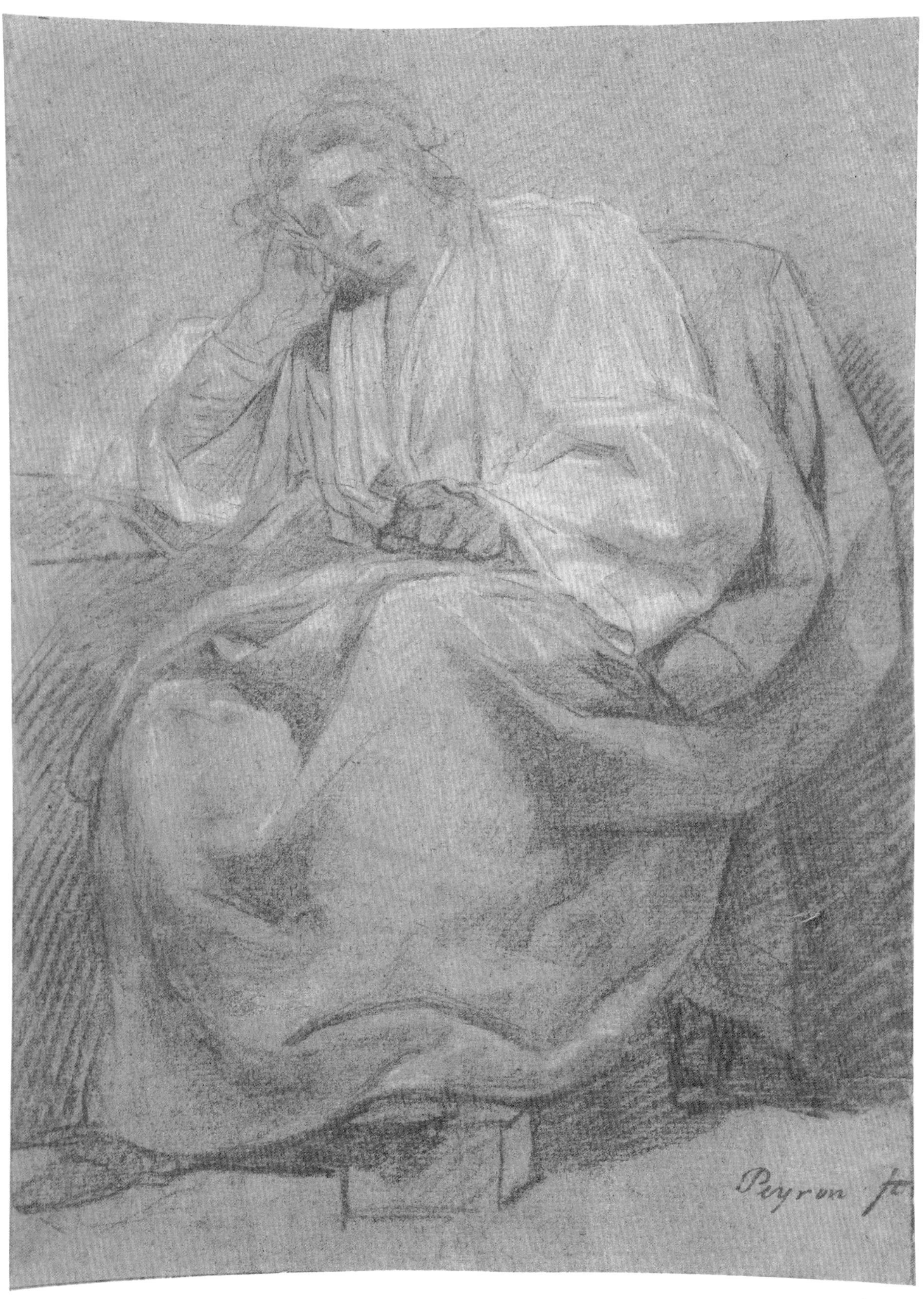

Peyron f.

NOTES
1. Rosenberg 1970, note 11.
2. Rosenberg and Van de Sandt 1983, as
   above.
3. *Ibidem*; see figs. 214, 215, and 217 for
   signatures for comparison.

Pierre Rosenberg was the first to recognize that the figure represented here is a young man rather than a woman.[1] For many years this drawing has been described as a *Woman Asleep in a Chair*, but it is clearly an academy study of a young man, probably a studio model, posed with his head leaning on his right hand, sitting with one foot resting on a block. His closed left hand holds an unidentified object and rests in his lap. The figure is covered in draperies arranged to resemble classical dress. Poses like this are common in the work of Peyron, who often depicted some important figure enthroned on a stepped dais. Occasionally the figure is depicted sitting in this manner, one foot on a step and the other on the floor. Although Rosenberg did not question that the signature was autograph in 1970, he later changed his mind, and included the drawing in a list of rejected drawings at the back of his 1983 monograph on the artist written with Van de Sandt, stating that his doubts had increased since 1970.[2] It is true that the style of drawing is very different from Peyron's other drawings and indeed no other academy of this sort by the artist is known. Usually he executes rather elongated, small-headed figures in a quick and assured manner, often in pen and ink or brush and wash.

Yet might not the technique of the Crocker drawing and the paraphernalia shown in the drawing, such as the block on which the model's left foot is raised, be explained as conditioned by the genre of academy figures, which were an institution of the academy? Life classes were held in the academy daily and the figures were always drawn painstakingly in red chalk with white heightening on white paper or in black chalk on blue paper. The fact remains that even though the figure in classical dress fits well with the overwhelmingly Neoclassical subject-matter for which Peyron is known, the style of the drawing does not match any of the examples provided in Rosenberg and Van de Sandt's monograph. However, the artist's signature, which is quite close to known examples and seemingly genuine, is difficult to explain if the drawing is excluded from his oeuvre on grounds of its unusual style.[3]

CD

40. Hubert Robert, *Massacre of the Innocents*, 1796

Red chalk, 20.7 × 18.5 cm. Crocker Art Museum, E. B. Crocker Collection 1871.410

INSCRIPTIONS: red chalk, lower left corner: D'AN IV

MARKS: none

PROVENANCE: Edwin Bryant Crocker, by 1871; gift of his widow Margaret to the Museum, 1885

LITERATURE: Crocker 1971, p. 150, as David; Rosenberg 1970, under no. 11, p. 39, as Hubert Robert (?)

BECAUSE THE INSCRIPTION on this drawing was interpreted as the signature of Jacques-Louis David, it was kept under his name for some years. However, Pierre Rosenberg suggested the name of Hubert Robert (1733–1808), effectively dismissing the David attribution.[1] While Rosenberg suggested Robert's name only tentatively, subsequent scholars—including Victor Carlson and Jean-Pierre Méjanès—have independently confirmed the Robert attribution.[2] According to Carlson, the assured manner of drawing indicates that the Crocker sheet is a mature work, most likely executed late in Robert's career.

While Robert routinely drew in red chalk, the subject matter of this drawing is atypical for him. It is a copy from a painting, and the artist is not known for making copies of paintings. Here he copied two figures from Guido Reni's *Massacre of the Innocents*, painted

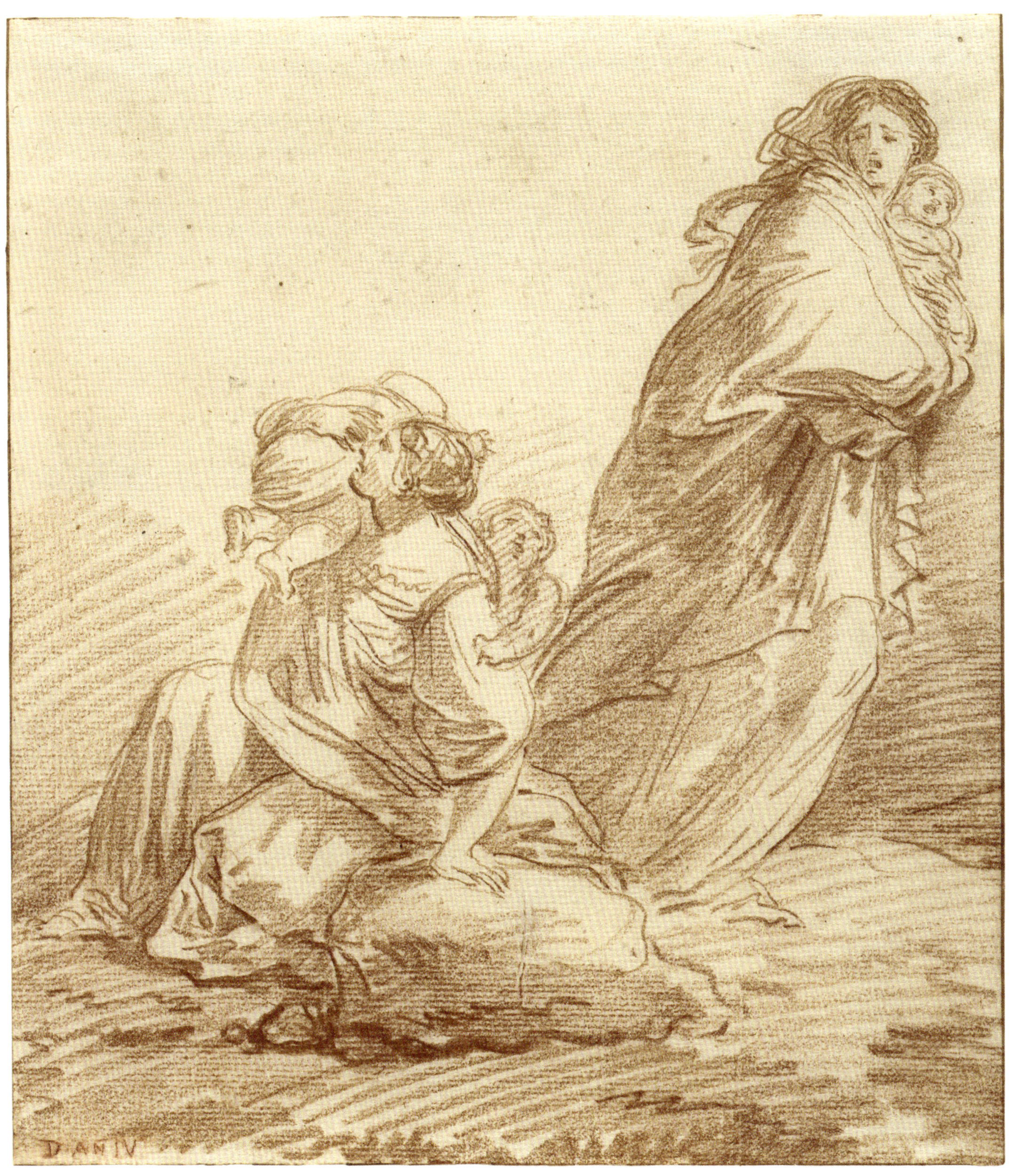

NOTES

1. Rosenberg 1970, as above.

2. Carlson in conversation; Méjanès in an undated note in the Crocker curatorial files.

3. Victor Carlson, *Hubert Robert: Drawings and Watercolors*, exh. cat. National Gallery of Art, Washington, 1978, p. 18.

4. The Academy emphasized the study of the works of artists such as Michelangelo, Vignola, Domenichino and Raphael, as well as those of the ancient Greeks.

5. Stephen Pepper, *Guido Reni, A Complete Catalogue of his Works*, New York, 1984, p. 225.

in 1611 for the family of the conte Berò for their chapel in the church of San Domenico, Bologna. While Robert was in Rome for eleven years, it is not known that during his stay he ever traveled to Bologna. He traveled to Naples with the abbé de Saint-Non in 1760 and visited Florence in 1763. His Italian sojourn overlapped for a number of years with that of Fragonard but, unlike Fragonard, Robert never went back to Italy a second time.

Although not officially a *pensionnaire*, Robert was allowed to stay at the French Academy, thanks to the intervention of his patron the duc de Choiseul.[3] It was stipulated, however, that he must participate in the academy's regular program of instruction.[4] Like the other young artists, he responded to the experience of Rome in many sketches and drawings of the monuments and people in and around the city. As a matter of course, he made drawings of antique statues—more often than not, however, as notations of objects seen in a particular place that he visited. His genius was as a painter of architecture and landscapes; he was particularly attracted to the city of Rome and its environs and ruins, and these became his preferred subject matter when he returned to Paris. He was known by his contemporaries as "Robert des Ruines."

During the 1790s Hubert was a member of the committee to organize and direct the museum of the Louvre. While he may already have known Reni's *Massacre of the Innocents* from the many engravings made after it, it seems certain that he saw the painting in 1796 when the French took it from Bologna and brought it to Paris.[5] In his official capacity at the Louvre, he could hardly have missed seeing it at first hand. The inscription on the drawing can in fact clearly be read as the date 1796, written as Revolutionary year IV. Robert only depicted the poses of two of the women in the painting—the fleeing woman who looks over her shoulder with an expression of fright and another woman who is seen crouching in the left foreground, trying to protect her child. The artist probably chose these figures in particular for their poses, possibly to use in one of his own compositions.

CD

41. Jean-Auguste-Dominique Ingres, *The Actor Brochard in Costume*, n. d.

Graphite, brush and black ink, on cream rough-wove paper, diam. 9.5 cm.
Crocker Art Museum, E. B. Crocker Collection 1871.459

INSCRIPTIONS: pen and black ink, at margin counter-clockwise from shoulder, signed: *Ingres fils*

MARKS: verso, graphite, lower left corner: circle and stroke

PROVENANCE: Edwin Bryant Crocker, by 1871; gift of his widow Margaret to the Museum, 1885

LITERATURE: Hans Naef, in Gary Tinterow and Philip Conisbee, eds., *Portraits by Ingres, Images of an Epoch*, exh. cat. Metropolitan Museum of Art, New

THIS EARLY PORTRAIT DRAWING by Ingres (1780-1867) was exhibited under the title *Head of a Warrior* as entry no. 1 in the exhibition held on the centenary of Ingres's death in 1967 at the Fogg Art Museum.[1] The exhibition was arranged chronologically and the organizers believed it to be the earliest of three portrait drawings in the show, executed by the artist before he left for Paris to study with Jacques-Louis David in 1797. Ingres was born in Montauban in 1780. He studied first with his father, an artist, and then in Toulouse with the painter Guillaume-Joseph Roque and the sculptor Jean-Pierre Vigan. It was probably through arrangement with his teacher Roque, who was a friend of David, that the artist went expressly to Paris to study with him.

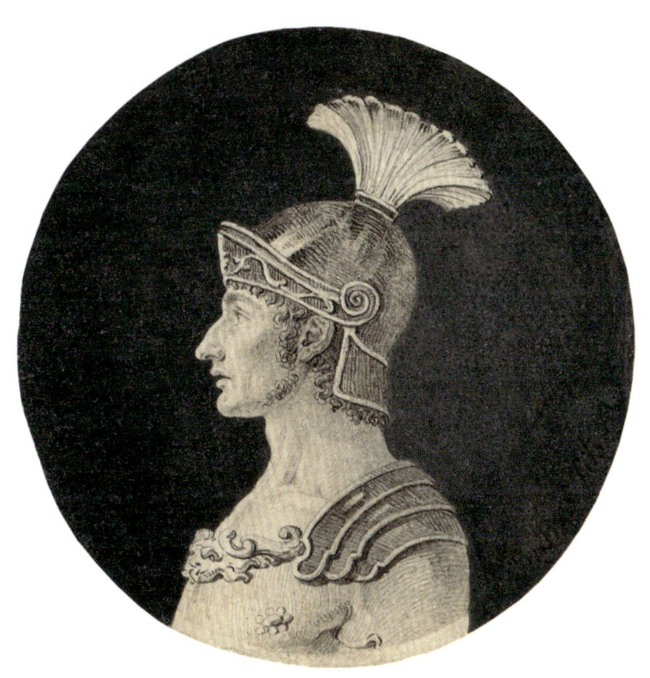

York; National Gallery, London; National Gallery of Art, Washington, 1999, no. 16, and under no. 15; Ruda 1992, no. 69; Crocker 1979, no. 16; Reno 1978, no. 8; Hans Naef, *Die Bildniszeichnungen von J.-A.-D. Ingres*, Bern, 1977, vol. I, no. 12 and pp. 42–44; Crocker 1971, no. 98; Rosenberg 1970, p. 31; Hans Naef, "Ingres' fruhe Profilbilnisse in Medallionform," *Pantheon*, vol. 28, no. 3, May–June 1970, no. 7 and pp. 226–27, 235, fig. 3; Agnes Mongan and Hans Naef, *Ingres Centennial Exhibition 1857–1967, Drawings, Watercolors and Oil Sketches from American Collections*, Cambridge, 1967, no. 1

NOTES
1. Mongan and Naef 1967, as above, no. 1.
2. Naef 1970, pp. 221–36, cat. no. 7. Naef had already tentatively advanced this identification in 1967.
3. *Ibidem*; now in a North American private collection.
4. Naef 1999, as above, no. 15.
5. Naef 1977, as above.
6. *Ibidem*, I, pp. 35–51.
7. *Ibidem*, cat. nos. 6,10,15, figs. 5, 6, 12.
8. *Ibidem*, cat. no. 3, fig. 3.

The subject of the Crocker drawing was identified by Hans Naef as a portrait of the actor Monsieur Brochard on the basis of another Ingres portrait of the very same man wearing contemporary dress,[2] identified by the artist in an inscription on the back of the drawing (fig. 32).[3] Since this drawing is both signed and dated 1796, there is no reason to doubt that the Crocker drawing of Brochard in Roman armor dates from the same year. Given the fact that, as seen on the inscription in fig. 32 and in an 1883 auction catalogue, Brochard was often described as a skillful interpreter of Molière, Hans Naef has proposed that in the Crocker drawing the actor may be dressed for Molière's *Amphitryon*, which is about a Theban general.[4] The rendering of the Crocker drawing is unusual in that Ingres has set off the pencil portrait in relief with a dark ink wash, almost like an antique cameo, and unlike any other surviving early portrait by the artist.

Before the 1967 centennial catalogue the drawing was apparently generally unknown—except at the Crocker, which had always kept it under the name of Ingres—but since 1967 Hans Naef has written about it several times, most extensively in his four-volume comprehensive study of Ingres's pencil portraits.[5] Here, as in all the early medallion portraits, the artist signed himself *Ingres fils* to distinguish his work from that of his father. This was before he left for Paris. After 1797 he signed his name simply *Ingres*.

According to Naef's account of Ingres's medallion-style portraits,[6] a fairly small number survive, and most of them were executed before he left Toulouse. Of the four Ingres medallion portraits in the United States, which include the *Portrait of a Boy* in the Morgan Library and Museum, the *Portrait of a Man* in the National Gallery of Art, Washington, and the *Portrait of a Man* in the Fogg Art Museum,[7] only the subject of the drawing in the Crocker has been identified. The artist had established the style in which it is drawn as early as 1792, when he was only twelve years old, as may be seen in the profile portrait drawing of his father, Jean-Marie-Joseph Ingres, now in the Musée Ingres, Montauban.[8]

CD

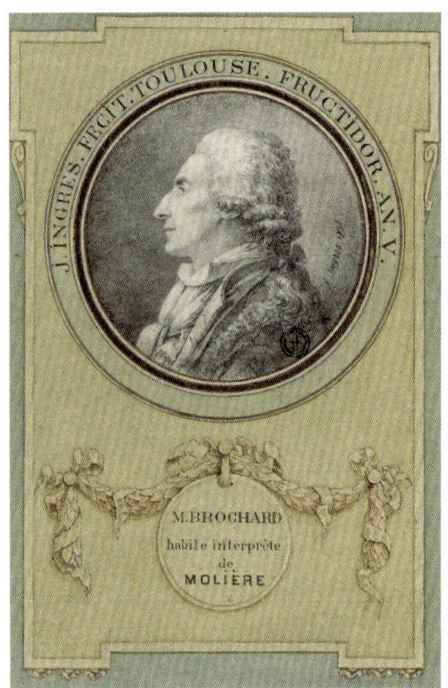

FIGURE 32 Jean-Auguste-Dominique Ingres, *Portrait of the Actor Brochard*, 1796. Graphite, diam. 7.9 cm. Private collection, USA

DRAWINGS FROM CENTRAL EUROPE

 Albrecht Dürer, *Female Nude with a Staff,* 1498

Pen and dark-brown ink, 31 × 22 cm. Crocker Art Museum, E. B. Crocker Collection 1871.3

INSCRIPTIONS: dark-brown ink, lower center, monogrammed and dated: AD [ligatured] 1498; brown ink, lower left corner, numbered (vertically): 81; verso, graphite, lower right: F O/ I; verso, dark-brown ink, lower right corner: 60

MARKS: verso, lower center, erased: Lugt 2314 (Stiglmeier)

PROVENANCE: Johann Stiglmeier, Straubing, before 1856; Edwin Bryant Crocker, Sacramento, by 1871; gift of his widow Margaret to the Museum, 1885

LITERATURE: Breazeale 2008, pp. 207, 211; Breazeale et al. 2008, cat. no. 45, pp. 134–36; *Durero y Cranach, Arte y humanismo en la Alemania del Renacimiento,* exh. cat. Thyssen-Bornemisza Collection, Madrid, 2007, cat. no. 41, p. 218; Bodo Brinkmann, ed., *Hexenlust und Sündenfall: Die seltsamen Fantasien des Hans Baldung Grien,* exh. cat. Städel Museum, Frankfurt, 2007, cat. no. 21, p. 80, fig. 43; Kaufmann 2004, pp. XIV, XVIII, 5–7; Klaus Albrecht Schroeder and Maria Luise Sternath, eds., *Albrecht Dürer,* exh. cat. Albertina, Vienna, 2003, p. 242; Anne Röver-Kann, *Albrecht Dürer: Das Frauenbad von 1496,* exh. cat. Kunsthalle, Bremen, 2001, p. 24, fig. 2.8; Anne-Marie Bonnet, '*Akt' bei Dürer,* Cologne 2001, p. 92, fig. 44; Rainer Schoch, ed., *Albrecht Dürer, Das druckgraphische Werk,* vol. 1, Munich 2001, p. 66, pl. on p. 67; Flagg 1999, pp. 3–11, 16; Ruda 1992, no. 21; Hutchison 1991, pp. 55–56 ; Jane Campbell Hutchison, *Albrecht Dürer: A Biography,* Princeton, 1990, p. 71; Ruda 1985, p. 5, fig. 3; Jacqueline and Maurice Guillaud, *Albrecht Dürer 1471–1528. Gravures Dessins,* exh. cat. Centre Culturel du Marais, Paris, 1978, cat. no. 141; Matthias Mende, *Albrecht Dürer, Das Frühwerk bis 1500,* Herrsching am Ammersee, 1976, frontispiece; Feinblatt 1976, p. 150, no. 172; Walter L. Strauss, *The Complete Drawings of Albrecht Dürer,* New York, 1974, vol. 1, no. 1498/2; Axel Janeck, "Dürer Colloquium Nürnberg: Lisa Oehler, Die Aktzeichnungen W. 85 (Paris, Louvre) und W. 947 (Sacramento, Crocker Art Gallery)," *Kunstchronik,* vol. 25, 1972, pp. 206–08; *1471 Albrecht Dürer 1528,* exh.

ELEGANTLY TWISTING herself to the left, the nude young woman in this drawing appears to be studying the drapery cascading down from the long staff she holds at her side. The figure is composed of fine and closely spaced lines that become increasingly dense and crosshatched in the shadows giving form to the breasts, belly, shoulders and head. The light source comes from the upper left, and the variegations between light and dark give this rotating figure an almost three-dimensional effect.

This delicate drawing by Albrecht Dürer (1471–1528), the first to enter an American collection, was created in the early stages of his remarkable career. Born in Nuremberg in 1471, Dürer received his early training from his father, a goldsmith, and the painter and woodcut designer Michael Wolgemut. After his apprenticeship, he went on a *Wanderjahr,* traveling to many cities including Basle, Frankfurt, and Colmar to learn the techniques and styles employed by his fellow artists. From the autumn of 1494 to the spring of 1495, Dürer was in Italy, where he visited Venice, Padua, and Mantua. By 1495, Dürer was a master in his own right running a large workshop in Nuremberg. During the late 1490s, he worked incredibly hard to build a market for his own painted and printed works—

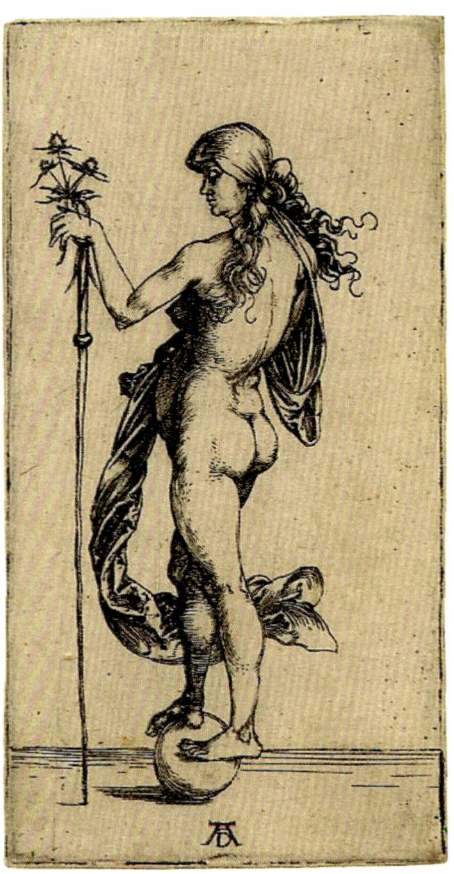

FIGURE 33 Albrecht Dürer, The Small Fortune, *c.* 1496. Engraving, 12.0 x 6.6 cm. British Museum, London

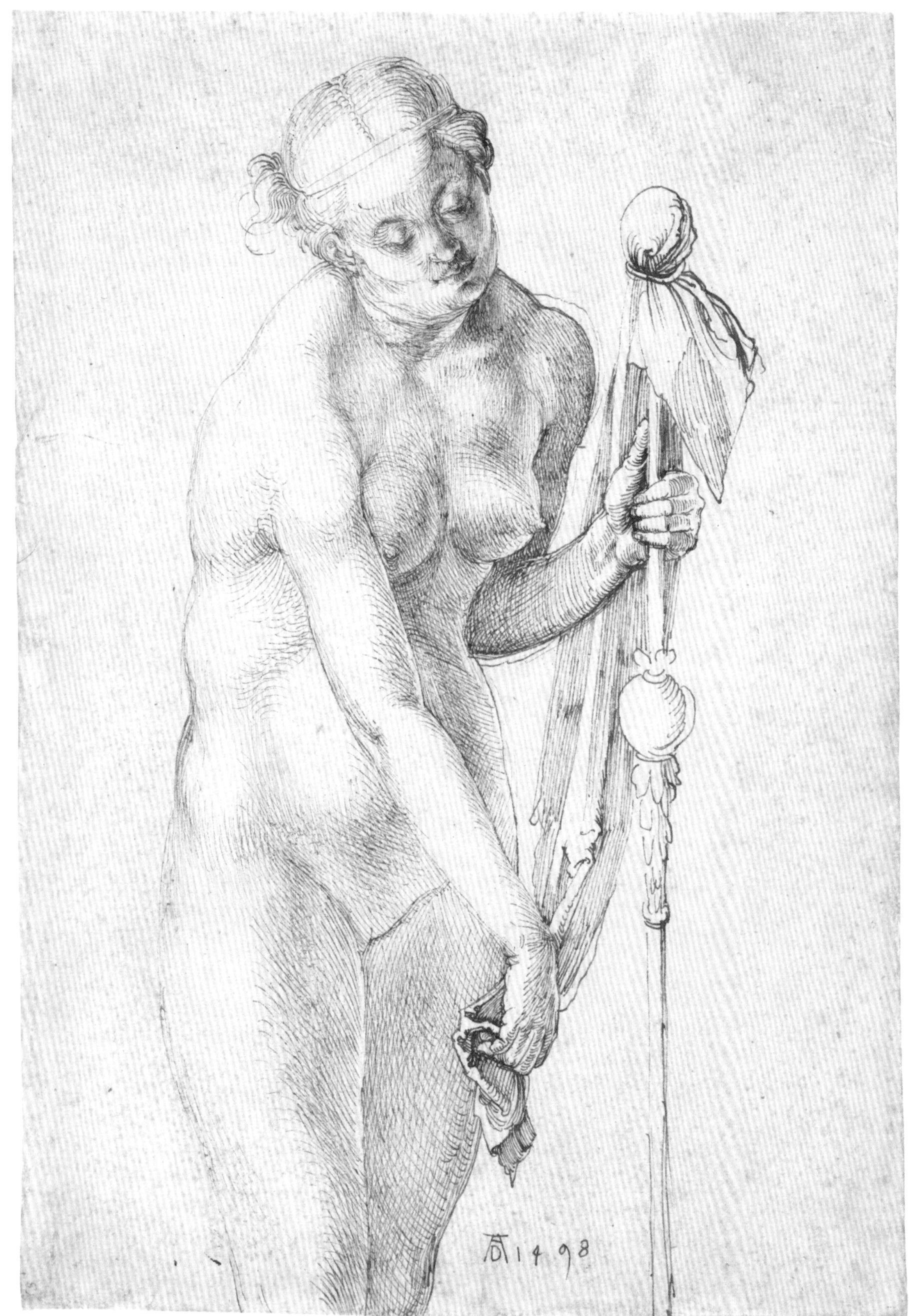

cat. Germanisches Nationalmuseum, Nuremberg, 1971, no. 458; Crocker 1971, no. 7, p. 2; Talbot and Levenson 1971, no. v, pp. 34–36; Joanna Eagle, "'Hand-drawings' by Germany's Greatest Artist," *Smithsonian*, May 1971, pp. 44–45, ill. p. 42; White 1972, p. 167; Crocker 1964, no. 3, p. 37; Crocker 1959, "German School," no. 4; Friedrich Winkler, *Albrecht Dürer, Leben und Werk*, Berlin, 1957, p. 95; Felice Stampfle, *Drawings and Prints by Albrecht Dürer*, The Pierpont Morgan Library, New York, 1955, pp. 3–4; Hans Tietze, *Dürer als Zeichner und Aquarellist*, Vienna, 1951, pl. 16; Hans Tietze, *European Master Drawings in the United States*, New York 1947, p. 58; Erwin Panofsky, *Albrecht Dürer*, Princeton, 1943, handlist no. 1181; Trivas 1940, p. 137; Friedrich Winkler, *Die Zeichnungen Albrecht Dürers*, vol. IV, Berlin, 1939, no. 947, p. 110; Crocker 1939, no. 3; Alfred Neumeyer, "Albrecht Dürer, Study of a Nude Female Figure," *Old Master Drawings*, vol. 13, 1938, pp. 16–17; Harry Noyes Pratt, "The E. B. Crocker Collection of Old Master Drawings," *Prints*, vol. 8, 1937, pp. 27, 30; Tietze and Tietze-Conrat 1937–38, vol. 2, no. 127a

NOTES

1. To name just two examples among many: Talbot and Levenson 1971, p. 34; Neumeyer 1938, as above, p. 17.
2. Hutchison 1991, p. 55.
3. Talbot and Levenson 1971, p. 36.
4. Fritz Koreny, *The Robert Lehman Collection, VII, Fifteenth to Eighteenth Century European Drawings*, New York, 1999, p. 40.
5. As noted by several scholars, the group includes the following drawings: *Naked Woman* of 1493 in the Musée Bonnat, Bayonne; *Female Nude with Staff* of 1495 in the Louvre, Paris; *Women's Bathhouse* of 1496 in the Kunsthalle, Bremen; and the aforementioned *Fortune in a Niche* in the Lehman Collection, Metropolitan Museum of Art, New York.
6. This impression British Museum inv. no. 1855-7-14-36.
7. Dürer may also have been exposed to Mantegna's engraving of *Four Women Dancing* of c. 1497 (Hind 21).
8. Inv. no. 6652.

publishing his first edition of the woodcut *Apocalypse* series in 1498. It is during this fruitful period that Dürer created the *Female Nude with a Staff*.

Many scholars have considered this work a drawing from life, as it shows signs of Dürer working through the proportions of the hips and the left shoulder and arm.[1] On the other hand, Jane Campbell Hutchison more recently points out that the shape and torsion of the torso relate to Praxiteles's lost *Aphrodite of Knidos* (c. 350 BC), known in the sixteenth century through many Hellenistic and Roman copies.[2] The drawing does seem poised ever so delicately between the real and the ideal, as Talbot and Levenson aptly note about a related drawing in the Lehman Collection of *Fortuna in the Niche* of 1498.[3]

Life drawings of nudes as studies of the human figure are among the earliest independent drawings from the fifteenth century and become a central theme of the Renaissance.[4] Dürer's drawing is one of the first such drawings north of the Alps and is part of a group of works produced during the 1490s that focuses on the female nude.[5] Also part of this grouping are several prints including *Four Naked Women* of 1497; *The Dream of the Doctor* of 1498; and the *Small Fortune* from c. 1497. The last engraving (fig. 33) has all of the elements of the Crocker drawing, but instead of an idyllic figure in contrapposto it shows a more aged woman with a notably Gothic figure—rounded stomach, high waist, elongated proportions—seen from behind.[6] Although the context of the figure is different, Neumeyer's contention that the Crocker drawing is a preparatory study for the nude female in *The Dream of the Doctor* has been widely accepted.

Dürer was first introduced to mathematical perspective and proportions by the itinerant Italian artist Jacopo de' Barbari, whose own engravings of *Victory and Fame* and *Vanity* (Hind 26 and 18) betray an interest in the female nude and ideal proportions.[7] This drawing was created in the period just after Dürer's return from his first trip to Italy. Dürer, the insatiable student, would have been well acquainted with Leon Battista Alberti's *Della pittura* and Cennini's *Trattato della pittura*, as well as other Quattrocento theories of proportion, and even with the canon of proportions developed by Vitruvius. Like the Lehman *Fortuna*, the bulging and steep neck muscles of the figure in the Crocker drawing seem to be based on geometric studies of the female body, as seen in Dürer's *Nude Woman with a Staff* in the National Gallery in Ottawa, an early study for the 1504 *Adam and Eve*.[8]

FS

43. **Master of Mühldorf**, *The Annunciation*, 1514

Pen and black ink, grey wash, and white opaque watercolor, on cream laid paper prepared with brownish-red, 20.8 × 15 cm. Crocker Museum of Art, E. B. Crocker Collection 1871.11

INSCRIPTIONS: pen and black ink, upper right corner: W [monogram]/ 1514

MARKS: none

PROVENANCE: Franz Graf von Sternberg-Manderscheid; his sale, Dresden, November 10, 1845, lot 593 (as German Monogrammist); Rudolf Weigel, before 1847, *Kunstlagerkatalog*, no. 16785, with date of 1515; Edwin Bryant Crocker, Sacramento, by 1871; gift of his widow Margaret to the Museum, 1885

LITERATURE: Kaufmann 2004, pp. 22–23; Flagg 1999, checklist p. 16; Rowlands 1993, mentioned under no. 487, pp. 226–27; Ruda 1992, no. 37; John Rowlands, *The Age of Dürer and Holbein: German Drawings 1400–1550*, London, 1988, discussed under no. 124; Reno 1978, no. 11; Feinblatt 1976, no. 178, pp. 148–49; Isolde Hausberger, *Der Meister von Mühldorf: Der Maler Wilhelm Pätzsold*, Mühldorf am Inn, 1973, pp. 94–96; Crocker 1971, no. 19; Charles Talbot and Alan Shestack, *Prints and Drawings of the Danube School*, exh. cat. Yale, New Haven, 1969, no. 75; Schulz 1968, no. 24; Franz Winzinger, "Unbekannte Werke des Meisters von Mühldorf," *Zeitschrift des deutschen Vereins für Kunstwissenschaft*, vol. XXII, nos. 1–2, 1968; Franz Winzinger, *Albrecht Altdorfer Graphik*, Munich, 1963, p. 18; *Five Centuries of Drawings*, exh. cat. Museum of Fine Arts, Montreal, 1953, no. 97; Annemarie Henle, *Master Drawings, An Exhibition of Drawings from American Museums and Private Collections*, San Francisco, 1940, no. 68; Crocker 1939, no. 11; F. Bruillot, *Dictionnaire des Monogrammes*, 1832–34, vol. I, no. 3176

FIRST IDENTIFIED as by the Master of Mühldorf by Ernst Buchner in 1938, this was the only drawing attributed to the Master prior to Winzinger's reappraisal and expansion of the artist's oeuvre.[1] In fact, Winzinger's other attributions of both prints and drawings to the Master are based on the Crocker image and its similarity to paintings on two wings and the predella of an altarpiece of the *Passion*, dated 1511.[2] The most similar image stylistically, the *Virgin of Altötting*, is also executed in pen and black ink heightened with white opaque watercolor on brownish paper.[3] This drawing shows the Virgin heavily draped and luxuriously adorned standing on a sphere and surrounded by angels. It represents a local type of the Virgin in glory seen in the Holy Chapel at Altötting, close to Mühldorf.

Instead of the heavenly scene of the *Virgin of Altötting*, Mary is here seated in a dramatically rendered interior space that seems to be at once bedchamber and church. The beamed ceiling leads the eye into the depths of the right half of the drawing—this pull to the right is reinforced by the announcing angel's gesture towards Mary.[4] Behind Gabriel the architectural appears to be more ecclesiastical, with the three windows symbolically placed above the main doorway. This drawing is often compared to various works by Albrecht Altdorfer, most frequently his night scenes, but it is really quite similar to his conception of space in the 1513 woodcut of the *Annunciation* (fig. 34).[5] In this drawing, Mary is seated in her bedchamber reading at a candlelit desk below a circular window—also seen in the Crocker drawing. Both images include deep perspectival settings, though with awkward results. In place of Altdorfer's disproportionately large figure of Gabriel, the Master of Mühldorf's column acts as a visual barrier to the space of the unfolding narrative.

In the upper right corner of the drawing is the Master's complicated monogram. John Clarke (in *Prints and Drawings of the Danube School*, 1969) identified the Master of Mühldorf's monogram as that of Wilhelm Beinholt, whose gravestone is preserved in the parish church of Mühldorf.[6] Isolde Hausberger (1973) understood the monogram differently and, citing a misreading of the gravestone, named the Master of Mühldorf Wilhelm Pätzsold in her monograph on the artist. Kaufmann agreed with Hausberger's designation of the monogram as WP and not WB, but was reluctant to designate the Master as Pätzsold.

FS

NOTES

1. Alfred Neumeyer, cited in a note on the old mount of the drawing: Buchner's letter of December 18, 1938.

2. The altarpiece was probably made for the Salvatorkirche, Ecksberg, but is now in the parish church of St. Lorenz near Altmühldorf, near Mühldorf.

3. British Museum, inv. no. 1949-4-11-122. Rowlands 1993, as above, removes *The Annunciation* (1519; British Museum inv. no. 1879.1213.37) from Winzinger's group and attributes it to an unknown south Bavarian artist, probably in the region around Regensburg.

4. Winzinger relates Gabriel's gesture in the drawing to two other works by the Master of Mühldorf, *The Entry of Christ* from the Altmühldorf altarpiece and the *Saint George* painting from the Mühldorf Rathaus.

5. This impression British Museum, London, inv. no. 1895-1-22-351; Talbot and Shestack 1969, as above, p. 75; repeated Kaufmann 2004, p. 22.

6. Talbot and Shestack 1969, as above, p. 74.

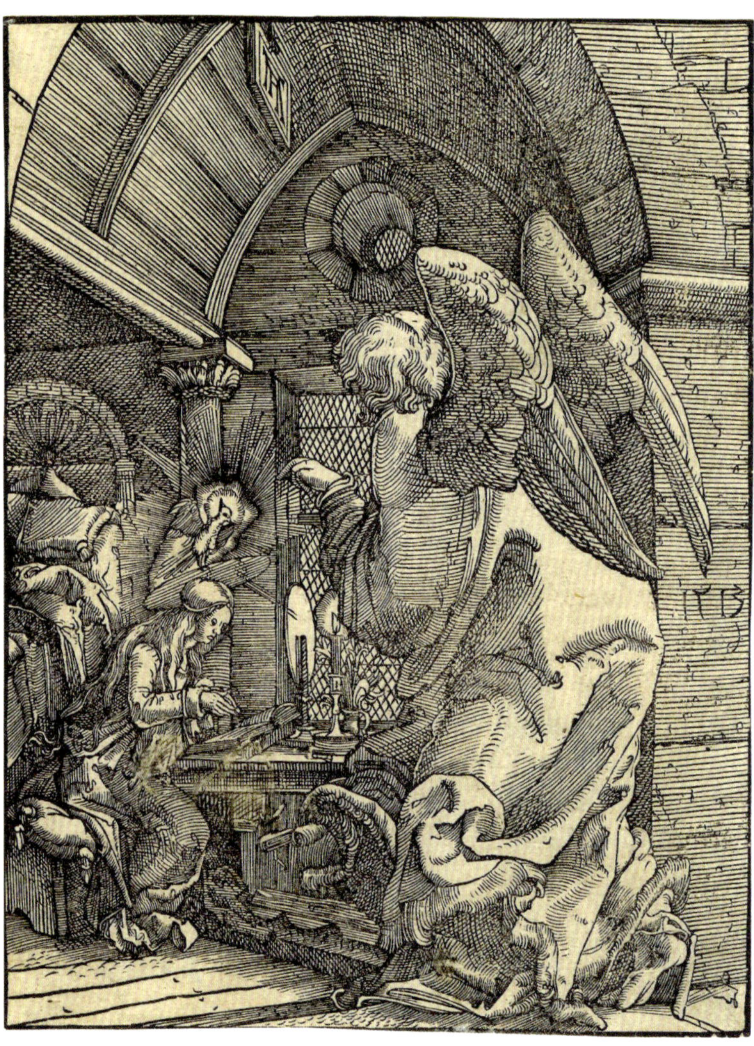

FIGURE 34 Albrecht Altdorfer, *The Annunciation*, 1513. Woodcut, 12.2 × 9.5 cm. British Museum, London

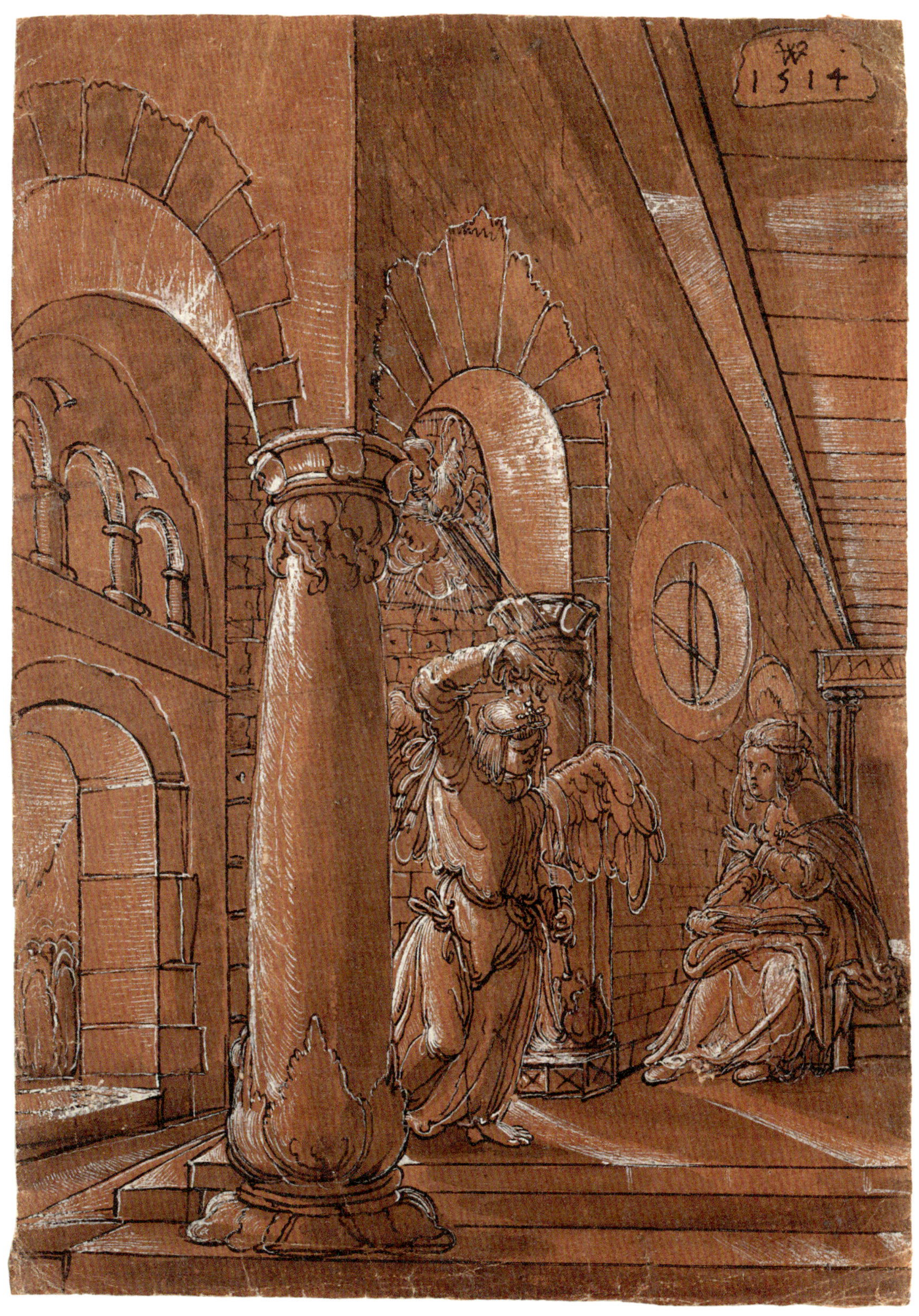

44. Michael Herr, *Witches' Sabbath; verso: Sketch of Figural Group*, n. d.

Pen and black ink with grey wash, over black chalk and graphite; verso: black chalk and graphite.
32 × 41 cm. Crocker Art Museum, E. B. Crocker Collection 1871.28

INSCRIPTIONS: graphite, lower right corner: *n. 3* [?]; verso, black chalk, lower margin, signed: *Michl Herr*; verso, lower right corner: *Herr/ 104/ -* ; upside down: *5*

MARKS: none

PROVENANCE: possibly Matthäus Merian collection, or unknown Nuremberg collector.(1) Edwin Bryant Crocker, Sacramento, by 1871; gift of his widow Margaret to the Museum, 1885

LITERATURE: Kaufmann 2004, pp. 47–49; Silke Gatenbröcker, *Michael Herr (1591–1661): Beiträge zur Kunstgeschichte Nürnbergs im 17. Jahrhundert*, Münster, 1996, cat. no. Z 266, pp. 463–65; Ruda 1992, cat. no. 11; Silke Gatenbröcker, Rolf Bidlingmaier, Achim Riether, *Michael Herr 1591–1661, ein Künstler zwischen Manierismus und Barock*, Metzingen, 1991, pp. 38–40; Kaufmann 1985, p. 88; White 1972, p. 167; Crocker 1971, no. 54 (as Joseph Heinz [*sic*] the Younger)

NOTES

1. Gatenbröcker 1996, as above, p. 464 n. 511.
2. This impression British Museum inv. no. 1880-7-10-388. The etching is inscribed: *Michael Herr inuent: M. Merian fecit 1626.*
3. See Christoph Michel, "'Luxe de Croyance?' Goethe und die Mythen," in *Mythen-Symbole-Metamorphosen in der Kunst seit 1800: Festschrift für Christa Lichtenstern zum 60. Geburtstag*, eds. Helga and J. Adolf Schmoll, Regina Maria Hillert, Berlin, 2004, p. 100 n. 54.
4. Gerhild Scholz Williams, *Ways of Knowing in Early Modern Germany: Johannes Praetorius as a Witness to his Time*, Burlington, 2006, p. 86.
5. Riether in Gatenbröker, Bidlingmaier and Riether, as above, p. 38.
6. Gatenbröcker 1996, as above, nos. Z 47, *Zauberkreis mit allerlei phantastischen Figuren* (c. 1621–26), Staatliche Museen Preußischer Kulturbesitz, Kupferstichkabinett, Berlin, inv. no. KdZ 10440, and Z 52, *Hexenkeller* (c. 1628), Städtisches Kunstmuseum Spendhaus, Sammlung Ziegler, inv. no. 678.
7. As Kaufmann noted, Herr's drawing demonstrates Germany's continuing fear of witches into the seventeenth century.
8. Previously the drawing had been assigned to Joseph Heintz the Younger by Alfred Neumeyer, and was published as Heintz in Crocker 1971, no. 54.

A CHIM RIETHER connected this drawing with Matthäus Merian the Elder's etched broadsheet *Zauberey* (Witchcraft), first published in 1626 (fig. 35).[2] The etching was later published in Cebes Thebanus's *Die Kunstreiche Tafel* (Frankfurt, 1638), and again as the title page to Johannes Praetorius's *Blockes-Berges Verrichtung* (Leipzig and Frankfurt, 1668).[3] Merian's etching illustrates the celebration of Walpurgis night, the annual witches' Sabbath held on the highest peak, the Blocken, of the Harz Mountains in central Germany on the evening of April 30.[4] Merian's image could also be entitled *The Dance on the Blocksberg*, as an inscription on the print specifies the location of the large revelry. For centuries the site was the gathering place of a veritable demonic extravaganza, where Satan's subjects and witches were said to practice their black arts in the vast and mystifying landscape.

Herr's drawing is much more abstract than Merian's etching and differs in some of the details. Using broad and sweeping strokes, Herr creates a chaotic scene of humans and demons flying, mixing brews, dancing, and generally carousing. The figures are not defined beyond general shapes and characteristics, and there is much evidence of Herr's working process. Corrections and revisions are made directly to the sheet—as seen in the area around the cauldron. It does, however, represent only the earliest preliminary sketch for the print,[5] and is grouped together with two other drawings that illustrate similar subjects, also created in the mid 1620s.[6] The drawings are executed in the same style and, although compositionally different, contain all of the same elements—the large bubbling cauldron, gallows, witches riding broomsticks, and wizards studying magic texts. Many of these insidious activities are described in the infamous *Malleus Maleficarum* (The Hammer of Witches), which was being published as late as 1669.[7]

Kaufmann first published this drawing as the work of Michael Herr (1591–1661) in 1985, after discussion with Heinrich Geissler in 1982.[8] This attribution was confirmed in the 1992 Flint catalogue on the authority of a conversation between Jeffrey Ruda and Werner Schade in 1990.

FS

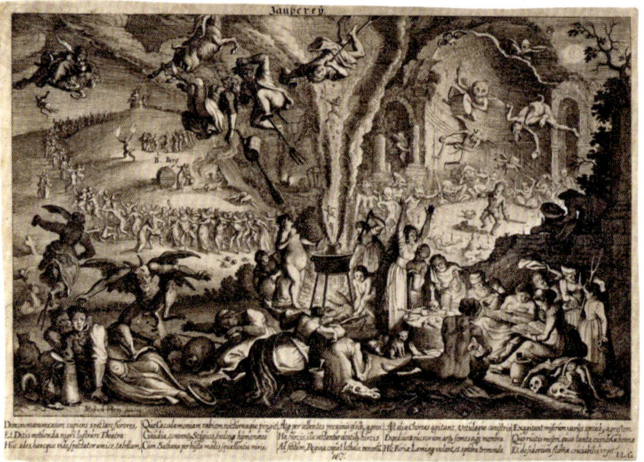

FIGURE 35 Matthias Merian the Younger, *Zauberey*, 1626. Engraving with text, 28.2 x 32.5 cm. British Museum, London

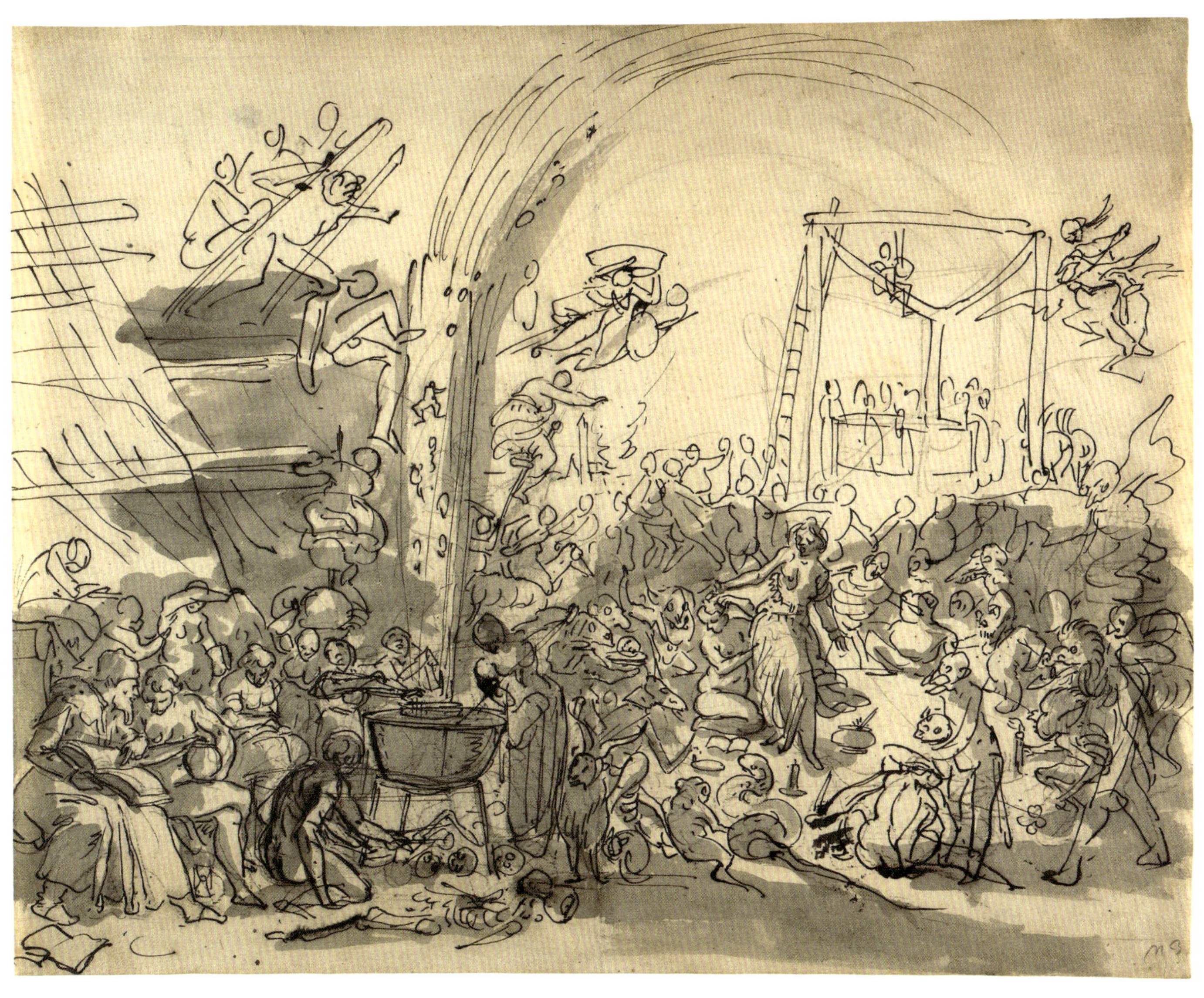

45. **Hermann Weyer**, *Hercules Being Shown the Mountainous Road to the Temple of Immortal Fame in the Company of Minerva and Bellona*, n. d.

Brush and grey wash, pen and black ink with white opaque watercolor, on tan paper covered with yellow wash; verso: pen and black ink with grey wash, 31.2 × 19.3 cm. Crocker Museum, E. B. Crocker Collection 1871.601

INSCRIPTIONS: pen and black ink, upper right, signed and dated: 1612 [with stroke above] /; *HE W* [HE elided]

MARKS: none

PROVENANCE: Edwin Bryant Crocker, Sacramento, by 1871; gift of his widow Margaret to the Museum, 1885

LITERATURE: Kaufmann 2004, pp. 83–84; Kaufmann 1985, p. 111 ; Howard et al. 1972, cat. no. 23, p. 27–28; Crocker 1971, checklist p. 166

NOTES
1. In Howard *et al.* 1972.
2. Jan Filedt Kok, "Jan Harmensz. Müller as Printmaker–I," *Print Quarterly*, vol. XI, 1994, p. 233 n. 37.
3. *Ibidem*, p. 233.
4. Howard *et al.* 1972, p. 28.

KAUFMANN AND OTHERS[1] have recognized that the recto of this drawing depicts the story of Hercules at the Crossroads and copies an engraving by Jan Muller after a design by Bartholomaeus Spranger. Jan Piet Filedt Kok further demonstrates that a red-chalk drawing highlighted with lead white now in the Wallraf-Richartz Museum, Cologne, most likely served as the model for Muller's engraving.[2] He also notes that two proof impressions of the engraving were heavily reworked (or corrected) in pen and brown ink, grey wash, and lead white—closely corresponding to Spranger's drawing style and chosen media.[3]

Weyer's double-sided drawing is also executed in pen and wash with white highlights. It has been argued that this technique corresponds to chiaroscuro woodcuts popular at the time, and may have been used for drawings that would serve as models for prints; yet no extant prints have been found that relate to Weyer's drawings.[4] Perhaps the style and media chosen by Weyer had more to do with a stylistic affinity between his work and the artist he was copying—in this case Spranger. This makes sense if Weyer was in fact compiling these double-sided drawings into sketchbooks simply to collect and study important works of art.

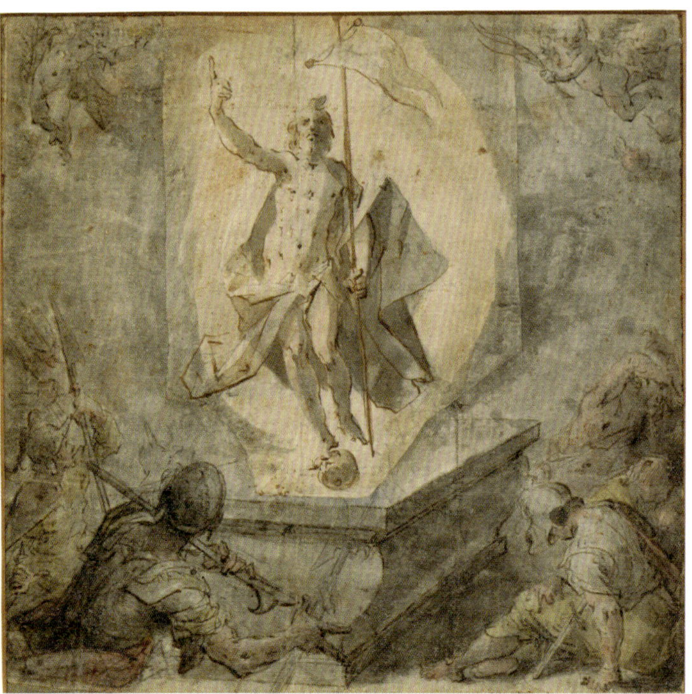

FIGURE 36 Hans von Aachen, *The Resurrection*, n. d. Pen and brown ink, brush and grey wash and red, pinkish, yellowish watercolor. Moravská Galerie, Brno

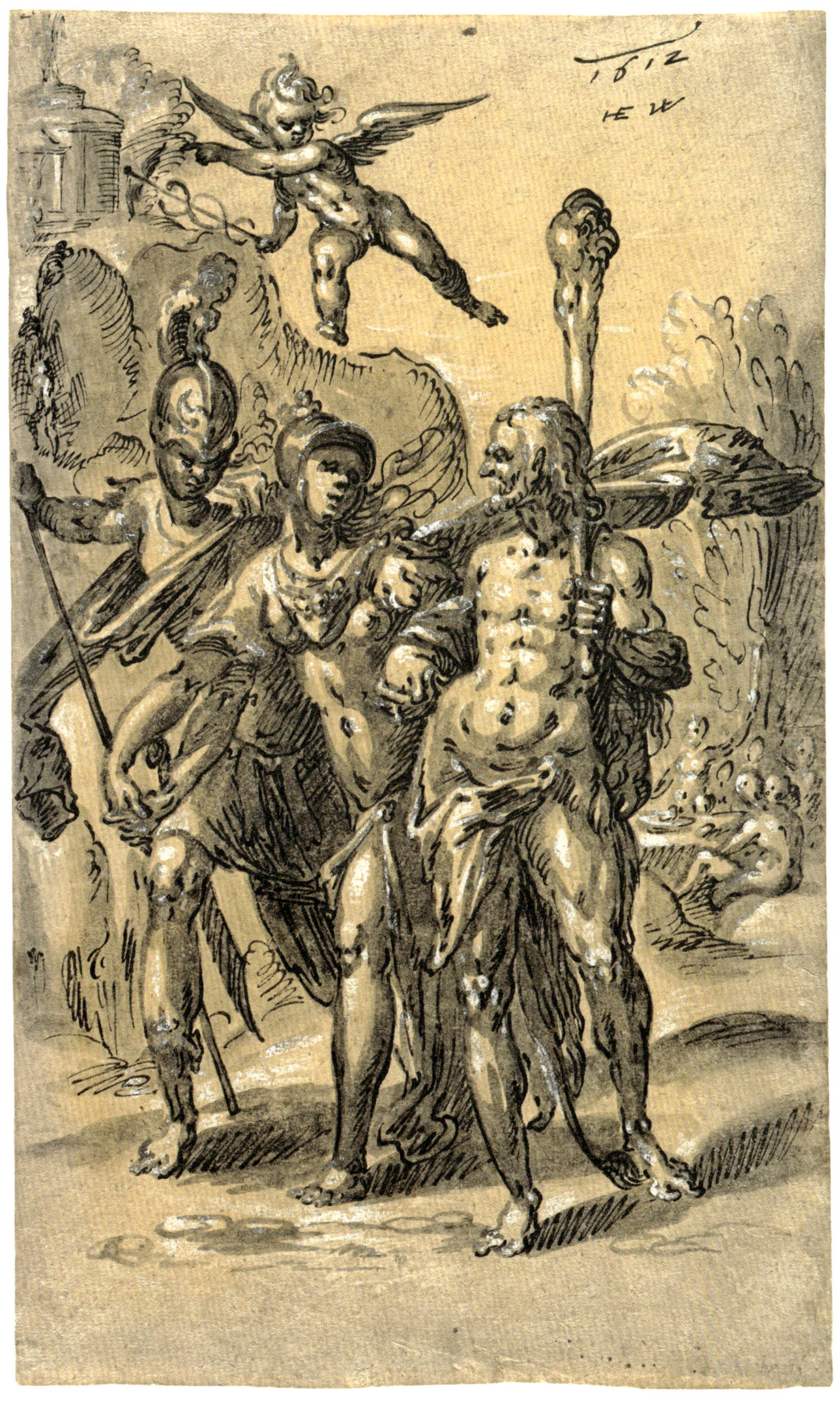

5. Lubomír Konečný, "Climbing the Rocky Path: Or, The Rudolfine Artist in Quest of Fame," in *Rudolf II, Prague and the World: Papers from the International Conference Prague, 2–4 September 1997*, eds. Lubomír Koneány, Beket Bukovinská, Ivan Muchka, Prague, 1998.

6. K. Oberhuber, *Die stilische Entwicklung im Werk Bartholomäus Sprangers*, unpubl. PhD diss. University of Vienna, 1958, cat. no. 42, pp. 147–48, 282–83: "Herkules von Minerva und Bellona (Mars) geleitet."

7. Vienna, Kunsthistorisches Museum, Gemäldegalerie, inv. no. 1133.

8. Prague, Národní galerie v Praze, inv. no. O 1574.

9. Brno, Moravská Galerie, inv. no. B7302; there is also a copy in the Wallraf-Richartz Museum, inv. no. Z. 5663.

10. Von Aachen's drawing was the model for the central panel of a triptych meant for the All Saints' Chapel in Prague Castle, for which Spranger and Heintz did the interior wings and Hans Vredeman de Vries and von Aachen did the exterior. See Van Mander 1994, I, p. 326.

11. Eliška Fučiková also notes in regards to the Müller epitaph that Spranger's Resurrection type stems from the influence of von Aachen, who most likely was himself influenced by Italian prints such as Parmigianino's etching from *c.* 1528–29. See Eliška Fučiková, *Die rudolfinische Zeichnung*, Hanau, 1987, under 1.18, p. 141. For other examples of Spranger's Resurrection scenes on epitaphs see the Epitaph of Michael Peterle, Saint Stephen's Church, Prague.

Very little is known about the artist's life aside from his birthdate of 1596. His father (d. 1621) and brother (1608–1666), both named Hans, were active as portrait painters in Coburg. It remains unclear whether the Coburg Weyers were related to the Nuremberg artist Gabriel Weyer (1576–1632), who also worked in the Mannerist style of Dutch artists like Spranger. Hermann Weyer died around 1621.

While the source of the recto is widely accepted, the identity of the left-most figure of the central grouping has remained debatable. Kaufmann contends that Mars and Minerva are leading Hercules towards the virtuous path, whereas Lubomír Konečný believes the figure represents Virtue, and furthermore that Hercules's quest is symbolic of Rudolfine artists' desire for fame.[5] I believe that Konrad Oberhuber's identification of the individual as Bellona is correct.[6] The similarity of this figure with Spranger's figure of Bellona in the painting *Triumph of Wisdom* (*c.* 1595) is unmistakable.[7] Both wear roman togas, helmets with feathers in the back, and carry swords. Although the figure could easily be either Mars or Bellona, it is widely accepted that the painted figure is Bellona.

Spranger's *Triumph of Wisdom* can also be connected to the verso of the Weyer drawing. Its composition is extremely similar to Spranger's triangular arrangement of the figures in his Resurrection panel of the Nicholas Müller epitaph (National Gallery, Prague).[8] The verso of Weyer's drawing shows a comparable scene with Christ standing triumphant in contrapposto carrying a banner and holding up his left hand to the heavens. These details, along with the soldiers being awakened and running from their revelation, are also evident in a preparatory sketch of the *Resurrection* by Hans von Aachen (fig. 36).[9] According to Karel van Mander, the von Aachen drawing was part of a collaborative project with Spranger.[10] In appears likely that it also inspired Spranger's own conception of the scene of the Resurrection, which he used repeatedly on epitaph monuments.[11]

Weyer's drawing thus combines two very different kinds of imagery that in Rudolfine imagery were in fact closely allied—the triumph of virtue/wisdom/art and Christ's triumph.

FS

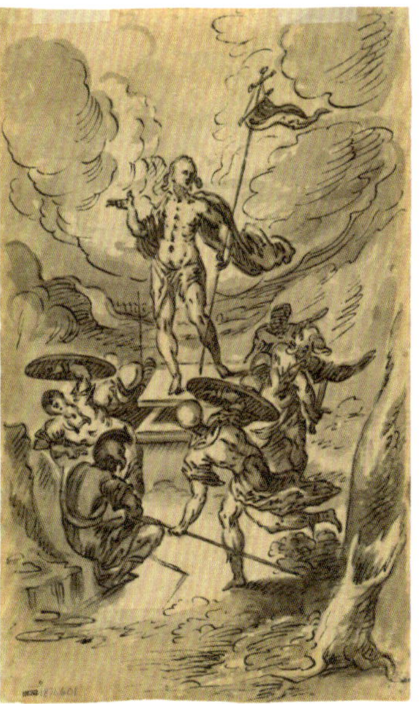

Verso of cat. no. 45

46. **Johann Georg Bergmüller**, *Saint Martin Appealing to the Virgin*, 1715

Pen and dark-brown ink, brush and brown and greyish-brown washes and blue, pink, brownish-red, magenta watercolor, white, pinkish, red opaque watercolor, over black chalk, 34.2 × 30.2 cm. Crocker Art Museum, E. B. Crocker Collection 1871.60

INSCRIPTIONS: brown ink, lower left corner, signed: *Joh. Georg Berckhmiller fecit Año 1715*; brown ink, center right, on shield: *QUIS UT DEUS*

MARKS: center bottom margin: Lugt 2237 (Rolas du Rosey)

PROVENANCE: Prince Carl zu Schwarzenberg, Vienna, before 1820; his sale, Leipzig, Rotthes Collegium, November 8, 1826 (catalogue dated October 25, 1826), no. 3018; Carl Freiherr Rolas du Rosey, before 1862; his sale, Leipzig, Weigel, June 13, 1864, no. 5072; Edwin Bryant Crocker, Sacramento, by 1871; gift of his widow Margaret to the Museum, 1885

LITERATURE: Breazeale 2008, p. 211; Josef Strasser, *Johann Georg Bergmüller 1688–1762, die Zeichnungen*, exh. cat. Salzburger Barockmuseum and Staatliche Graphische Sammlung, Munich, 2004–05, no. Z9; Kaufmann 2004, p. 96; *300 Jahre Pfarrkirche St. Martin Tannheim, Festschrift zum Jubiläum im Jahre 2002*, Tannheim, 2002, pp. 73–74, 106; Alois Epple, "Das Hochaltarbild in der Pfarrkirche in Tannheim," *Der Spiegelschwab*, no. 3, 1990; *Meister der Zeichnung*, exh. cat. Germanisches Nationalmuseum, Nuremberg, 1992, under no. 85; Kaufmann 1989, no. 8; Howard *et al.* 1983, no. 35; Steadman and Osborne 1976, no. 7; Kent Sobotik, *Central Europe 1600–1800*, exh. cat. Ringling Museum of Art, Sarasota, 1972, no. 61; Crocker 1959, no. 2; *Age of Elegance: The Rococo and its Effects*, exh. cat. Baltimore Museum of Art, Baltimore, 1959, no. 260; Lawrence 1956, no. 6; Crocker 1939, no. 46; Rosey sale, Leipzig, Weigel, June 13, 1864, no. 5072; Schwarzenberg sale, Leipzig, November 8, 1826, no. 3018

O NE OF THE RELATIVELY FEW watercolors in the Crocker collection, this drawing by the painter Johann Georg Bergmüller proposes a visually arresting solution to the challenge of a multi-figured altarpiece. Perhaps a contract drawing, its tumbling diagonals and unifying color align each of the gracefully handled saints in a clear narrative, seen here before changes likely requested by the altarpiece's patron.

Bergmüller was born in 1688 in the town of Türkheim, a seat of the Bavarian Wittelsbach court. Though he surely learned the rudiments of art from his father, a cabinetmaker and sculptor, he was noticed by Duke Maximilian Philipp, who sponsored his study in Munich under Johann Andreas Wolff beginning in 1702. By 1708, the nineteen-year-old Bergmüller received his first commission from another member of the Wittelsbach family, Prince Johann Wilhelm of the Palatinate, moving to his court in Düsseldorf to complete frescoes for the church of Saint Hubert, now destroyed. Three years later, the Wittelsbachs sponsored another trip, this time to the Netherlands *"mehrers perfection ieben [sic],"*[1] to perfect his art. Settling in Augsburg in 1713, the artist found a niche as history painter, becoming the leader of the painters' guild in 1722, the Catholic director of the city's painting academy in 1730, and court painter in 1739. His many frescoes in Augsburg—for the Cathedral, the churches of Heilig-Kreuz and St. Anne, and the Bishop's Palace—are mainly destroyed, though churches in Diessen, Ochsenhausen, Steingaden and other surrounding towns preserve them. Bergmüller's altarpieces are scattered more widely throughout southern Germany, from Konstanz to Biberach to Dillingen. He worked also as a printmaker, especially of thesis prints (prints made on the occasion of an academic degree). He died in 1762.

Evidence is scant that Bergmüller ever went to Italy. Rather, his Italianate clarity of composition and skill in handling the human form must derive from his training under Wolff, his study of prints, and later, the pressures of keeping up with advances in art as the director of an academy ideally situated between north and south. He wrote a treatise on the human figure as early as 1723.[2]

This skill in handling the figure and its expression in large compositions is in ample evidence in the Crocker drawing. The main episode of Saint Martin at left appealing to the Virgin above is in no way disturbed by the activities of the other saints, Michael at right casting out a demon, Mary Magdalen kissing the foot of the Christ Child, and Saints George and Catherine (?) adoring the Child from left and right. A bolt of lightning departs from Saint Michael's hand to divide the scene in halves, travelling down to the earthly realm shared by the hell-bound demon above and the beggar who gratefully receives Martin's cloak below. At the pinnacle of the composition and not visible in reproduction, the figure of God watches over all.

The Crocker drawing dates from 1715, in the early years of Bergmüller's maturity. The hand and spelling of the inscription is shared by a second drawing of Saint Martin

NOTES

1. Strasser 2005, as above, p. 11.
2. *Anthropometria sive statura hominis a navitate ad consummatum aetatis incrementum ad dimensionsum & proportionum Regulas discriminata,* Augsburg, 1723.
3. Inv.no. Hz. 4043.
4. Epple 1990, as above.
5. *300 Jahre ... Festschrift 2002,* as above, pp. 73–74.
6. See Breazeale 2008, pp. 205–26.

now in the Germanisches Nationalmuseum.[3] The similarity of subject once created some confusion, since the Crocker drawing is conected with neither this drawing nor the related altarpiece of 1712 in the town of Merching, but rather with the altarpiece completed in 1716 for the church of Tannheim (fig. 37), as discovered by Alois Epple in 1990.[4]

The altarpiece, likely because of changes requested by the patron, loses some of the drawing's narrative clarity. The squawking goose who has given away Saint Martin's hiding-place intrudes at left, while the former grace of the lower-right quadrant is disturbed by the reversed position of Saint Martin's hands, the illogical presence of a socle or altar, and the melodrama created both by Saint Michael's lightning-bolt tracing his motto *Quis ut deus* formerly on his shield and by the flaming mouth of hell. According to Epple, an early restorer, repairing the altarpiece to obviate moisture damage, may have changed some of the latter areas.[5]

Like many drawings in the Crocker collection, this one belonged to the noble Prussian general, art historian, and collector Freiherr Carl Rolas du Rosey, the sale of whose estate took place in 1864, only six years before the drawing entered the Museum. It is part of a larger group from the stock of Rudolf Weigel, a member of a longstanding family of dealers in Leipzig.[6]

WB

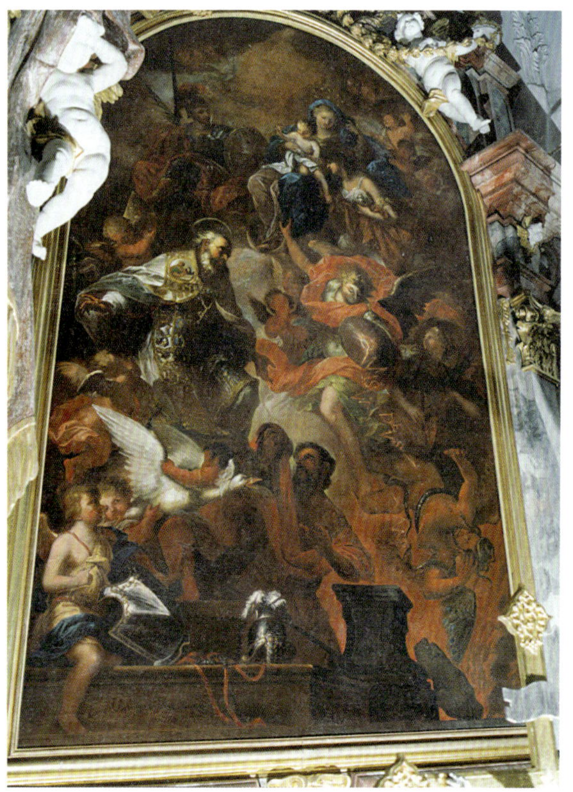

FIGURE 37 Johann Georg Bergmüller, *Saint Martin Appealing to the Virgin,* 1716. Oil on canvas, 500 × 300 cm (approx). Pfarrkirche St. Martin, Tannheim

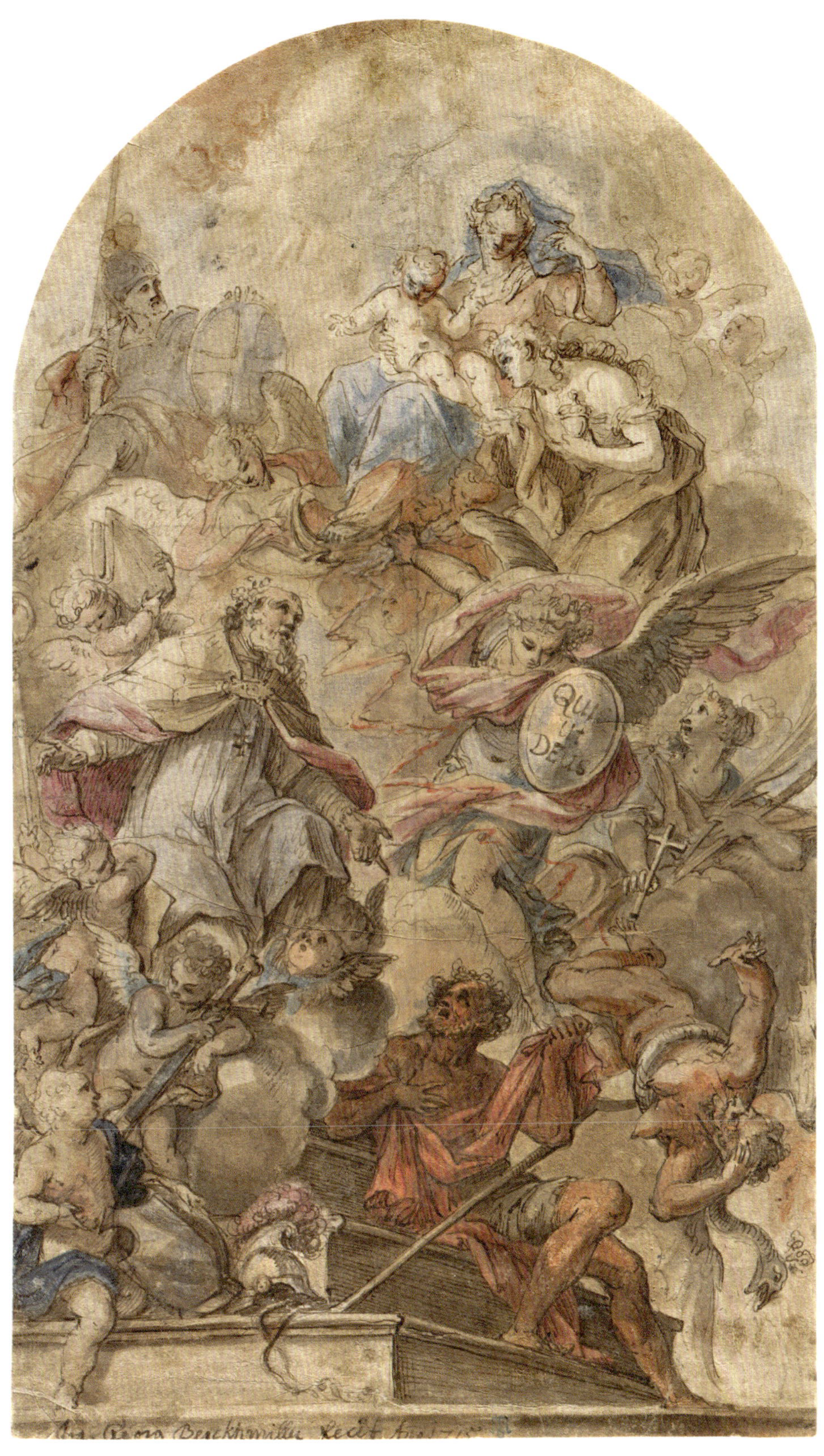

QVIS
VT
DEVS

47. **Johann Wolfgang Baumgartner,** *Lazarus and the Rich Man,* n. d.

Pen and dark-brown and grey ink, brush and point of brush and greyish washes and white opaque water-color on blue laid paper, 18.1 × 29.4 cm. Crocker Art Museum, E. B. Crocker Collection 1871.77

INSCRIPTIONS: none

MARKS: verso, graphite, lower left: circle and stroke

PROVENANCE: Edwin Bryant Crocker, Sacramento, by 1871; gift of his widow Margaret to the Museum, 1885

LITERATURE: Kaufmann 2004, pp. 91–92; Steadman and Osborne 1976, no. 67; Schulz 1968, no. 87; Lawrence 1956, no. 65; Scheyer 1949, no. 144; Crocker 1939, no. 64

NOTES
1. *Saurs allgemeines Künstlerlexikon, sub voce.*
2. Inv. no. 1362; Mareike Hennig, *Mit freier Hand, Deutsche Zeichnungen vom Barock bis zur Romantik aus dem Städelschen Kunstinstitut,* exh. cat. Städel Museum, Frankfurt, 2003, no. 20a.

IN THE EIGHTEENTH CENTURY the southern German city of Augsburg witnessed the flowering of a uniquely German expression of the irrational in architecture, painting and prints. One of the proponents of the so-called Augsburg Rococo, Johann Wolfgang Baumgartner, incorporated its flourishes even in moralizing religious subjects such as this scene of *Lazarus and the Rich Man.*

The place of Baumgartner's birth in 1709 is undocumented but is thought to be Kufstein in the Tyrol. His origins were humble, his first training being as a blacksmith, probably under his father. Apprenticed in Salzburg, he trained as a *Hinterglasmaler,* a painter of decorative scenes on the reverse of glass panels. His *Wanderjahr* was spent in Austrian lands, including Bohemia and Hungary, and a reference to *"Welschland"* may refer to time in Italy otherwise undocumented.[1] In 1733 he settled in Augsburg with his wife, attaining full citizenship and guild membership only in 1746. He began to receive commissions for major frescoes and altarpieces only in later years, with works in the Wallfahrtskirche Heilige Kreuz in Bergen near Neuberg in 1757–58 and frescoes of the Twelve Months in the garden pavilion of the Prince-Bishop of Constance at the Neue Residenz in Meersberg.

Baumgartner was a friend of many Augsburg artists, especially those around the Academy. He may well have known Johann Georg Bergmüller, also represented in this exhibition, and had as pupils Gottfried Bernhard Götz and Johann Evangelist Holzer.

The preponderance of Baumgartner's surviving works are drawings, which served for devotional prints, *Thesenblätter* (prints made on the occasion of a completed academic degree), calendars, narrative series and book illustrations. Unusually, and logically for a *Hinterglasmaler* used to working in reverse, some of his preparatory works for prints were done in oils. Perhaps because of his early work as a blacksmith, he was especially attuned to ornament and rocaille, which came to dominate his fictive spaces and style.

In the Crocker drawing, Baumgartner divides the space between the loggia where the rich man holds his banquet and the mound in the foreground at left where Lazarus sits begging, dogs licking his sores in accordance with the biblical passage (Luke 16: 19–31). The situation will be reversed after their deaths, Lazarus being taken to Abraham's bosom and the rich man tortured instead. Baumgartner employs his most elaborate style for the rich man's palace, with a swooping balustrade at left where silver riches are displayed, graceful, curving parapets and stairs, and a billowing curtain above the rich man's throne. A drawing of *Christ in the House of the Tax Collector* now in Frankfurt[2] demonstrates the artist's facility with figures, their gestures and rhythms, while the architecture, showing awareness of Venetian models, is more restrained. The same rhythm of gesture is present in the Crocker *Lazarus,* which moreover shows beggar and rich man framing the composition in echoing poses, their heads emphasized by the empty fields of Baroque ornaments behind them. Such narrative clarity is especially appropriate for

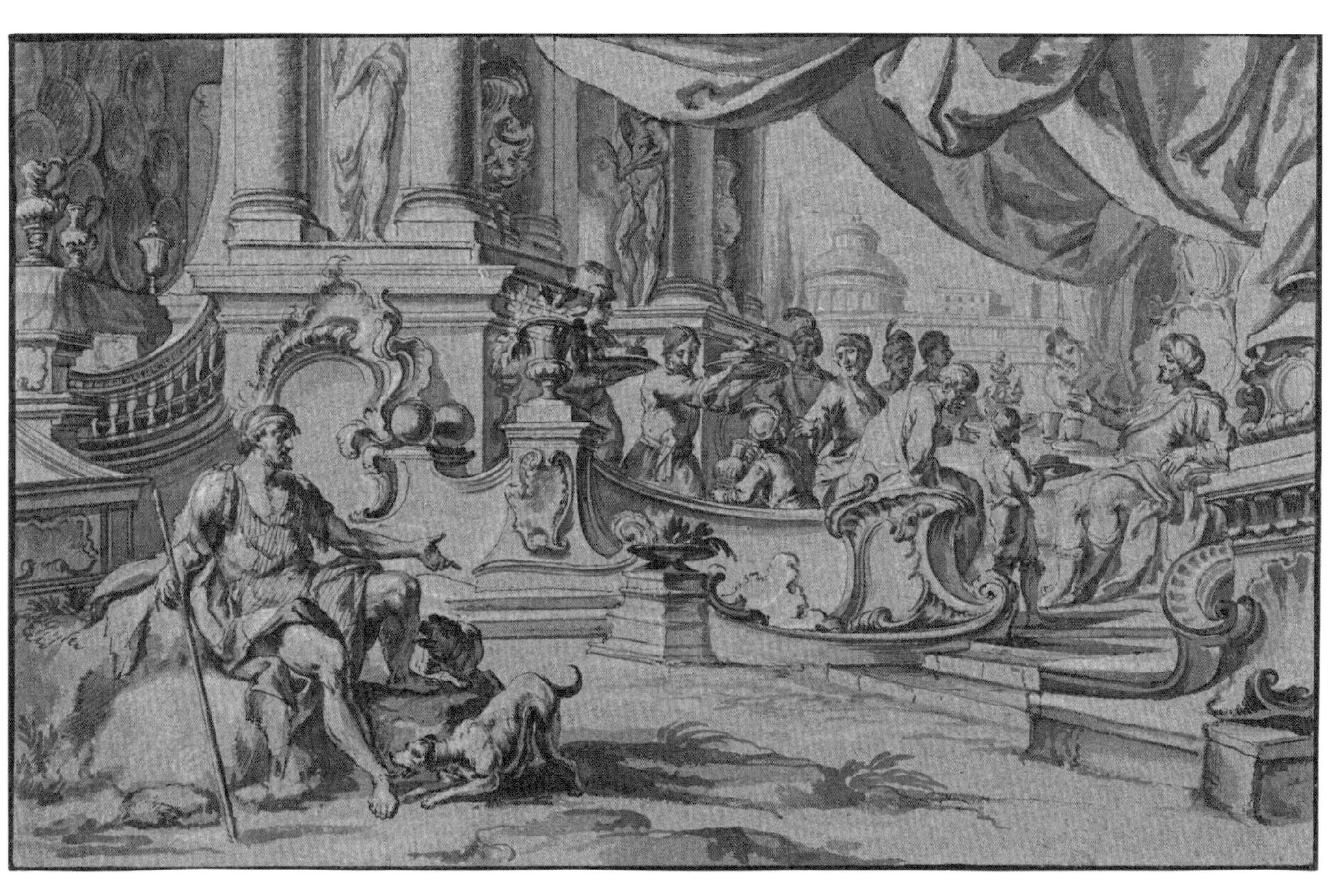

3. Letter and note in Crocker curatorial files.
4. Hennig 2003, as above (note 2), p. 65, under no. 20.

religious prints and, in fact, the verso of the Crocker drawing is dusted for transfer with red chalk.

Long known as the work of Januarius Zick, the name under which it entered the collection, the Crocker drawing was first attributed to Baumgartner by Bruno Bushart in 1976, an opinion confirmed by Thomas Le Claire in 1992.[3] Though no print depicting the Crocker composition has yet been found, it seems best to date it in the 1740s, when Baumgartner was occupied with religious illustration, including the plainer *Engelbrechtschen Bibelfolgen* of 1743, to which Baumgartner contributed drawings.[4]   WB

48. Georg Melchior Kraus, *Young Woman Eating*, n. d.

Red chalk, brush and brownish wash and bluish-grey watercolor on cream laid paper, 40.1 × 27.4 cm.
Crocker Art Museum, E. B. Crocker Collection 1871.1068

INSCRIPTIONS: graphite, lower right corner: *G. M. Kraus*; verso, graphite, lower left corner: *E- / 1 / Kraus Weimar*

MARKS: none

PROVENANCE: Edwin Bryant Crocker, Sacramento, by 1871; gift of his widow Margaret to the Museum, 1885

LITERATURE: Kaufmann 2004, p. 127; Kaufmann 1989, no. 80; Crocker 1971, checklist p. 154; Scheyer 1949, no. 87

NOTES

1. Johann Wolfgang von Goethe, *Dichtung und Wahrheit*, vol. IV, Book 20, quoted in Christina Kröll, *Der Maler Georg Melchior Kraus*, exh. cat. Goethe-Museum, Düsseldorf, 1983, p. 30.
2. Though the date of the artist's birth has been posited as 1737, the date of 1733 is based on the account of his close friend Bertuch and seems most reliable; see Kröll 1983, as above note 1, p. 4.
3. Wolfgang Huschke, "Der Maler Georg Melchior Kraus (1737–1806), ein Frankfurter Landesmann Goethes in Weimar, Herkunft und Familienkreis," in *Festschrift für Heinz F. Friederichs*, Neustadt, 1980, p. 127.
4. Städel Museum, inv. nos. 6104 and 6102 respectively; see Edmund Schilling and Kurt Schwarzweller, *Städelsches Kunstinstitut Frankfurt am Main, Katalog der deutschen Zeichnungen, Alte Meister*, Munich, 1973, nos. 1646 and 1648.

"Er war ein heiterer *Lebemann, dessen leichtes erfreuliches Talent in Paris die rechte Schule gefunden hatte*" (He was a cheerful, pleasure-seeking man whose graceful and delightful talent had found its best training-ground in Paris).[1] Goethe's words about his friend Georg Melchior Kraus ring true in the present drawing, which combines the new genre subjects of Greuze with a lively technique.

Born in 1733, Kraus was the son of a tavernkeeper and wine merchant in Frankfurt am Main.[2] This seemingly humble origin is belied by other relationships that had bearing on his choice of profession and his later life: through his mother, he was related to painters at the Saxon court, and Goethe's grandparents served as her godparents.[3] As peripatetic as his forebears, Kraus moved to Kassel for his first training, under Johann Heinrich Tischbein the Elder, then in 1761 to Paris. Here he met François Boucher and Jean-Baptiste Greuze, both of whom influenced his technique and style. Following his return from the French capital in 1766, he travelled in northern Germany and, in 1770–71, Switzerland. He secured an appointment as drawing tutor to a young noblewoman, Jeanette Louise von Stein, and, following her marriage, moved with the household to their lands in Thuringia and later the court city of Weimar. Having met Goethe there by 1774, Kraus became the poet's friend and drawing instructor as well. These years saw the enterprising young artist established as director of the new Herzogliche Freie Zeichenschule in 1775. After his appointment he turned to landscape more and more and made a drawing trip to the Harz mountains in Goethe's company in 1784. A prolific printmaker as well, Kraus drew on his sharp eye for landscape and costume, providing illustrations for Friedrich Justin Bertuch's *Journal des Luxus und der Moden* from 1786 until his death in 1806.

The Crocker *Young Woman Eating* reflects the training Kraus received in France, especially in the vigorous use of red chalk, reinforced at key points and hatched with slashing parallels. The handling is similar to other drawings of single figures dated to the Paris period, for example the *Man Reading* and *Seated Woman* now in Frankfurt,[4] though both of these are in black and white chalk on blue paper. The subject is simple: a bonneted

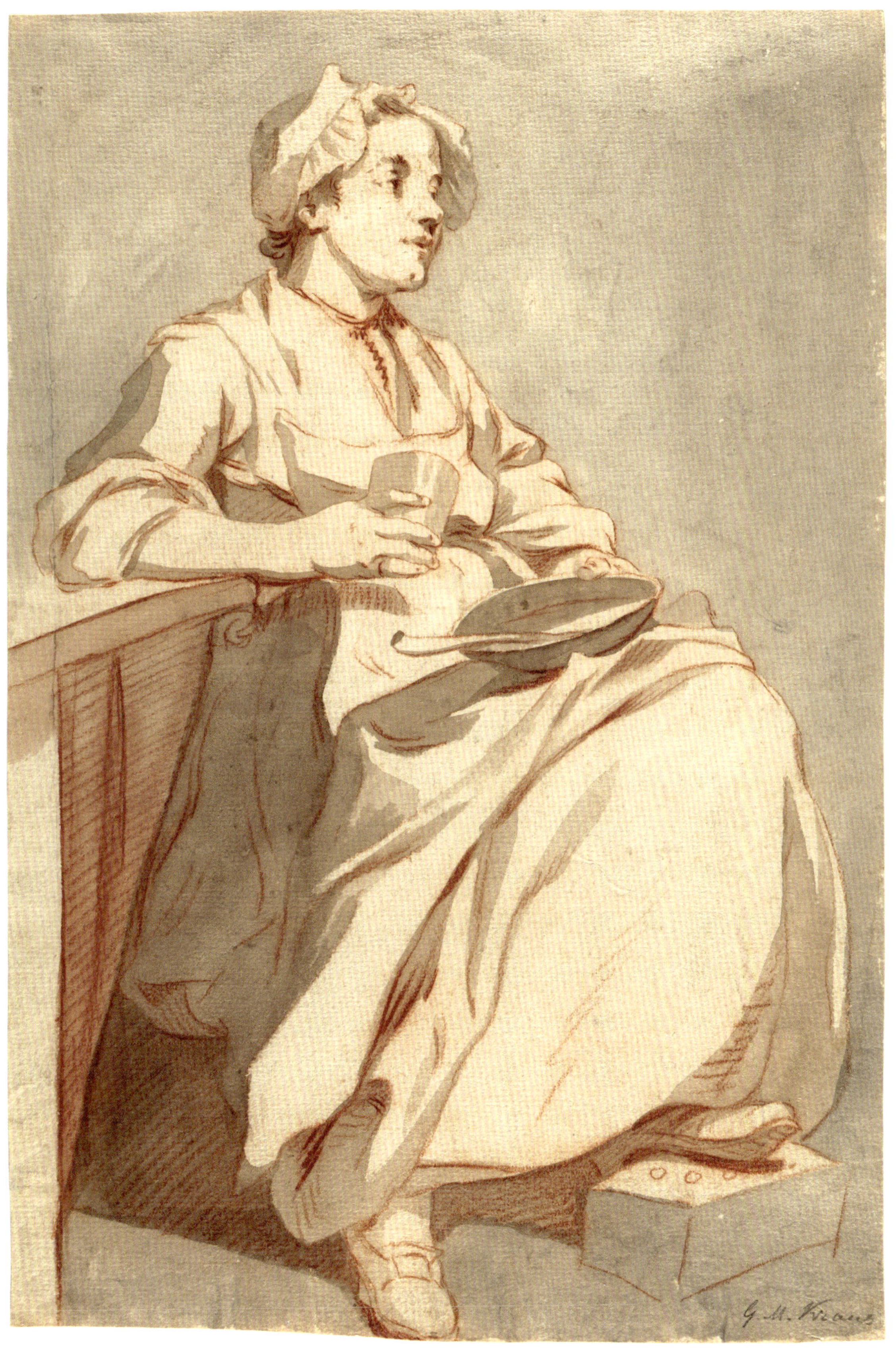

5. Museen für Kunst und Kulturgeschichte der Hansestadt Lübeck, Sammlung Dräger/Stubbe; see Thorsten Albrecht et al., *Zum Sehen geboren, Handzeichnungen der Goethezeit und des 19. Jahrhunderts, die Sammlung Dräger/Stubbe*, Leipzig, 2007, pp. 170–77.

young woman, her elbow propped on a table and her foot on a charcoal-heated foot-warmer, holds glass and plate over her apron as she gazes into the middle distance, seemingly about to speak. Her costume and demeanor reflect the lower middle classes as depicted by Greuze, though without the latter's moralizing tone.

Kraus's watercolor in Lübeck of a *Mother with Three Children* (fig. 38)[5] is closer in theme to Greuze. In this scene of family life, the German artist replicates the Crocker figure, though transforming it through changes in detail and setting. The matron's head is now closer to profile, the footwarmer has become a footstool, the glass has disappeared, and her youngest child now reaches into her lap to play with the dish. The neutral background has now become a rustic kitchen where the family is surrounded by piles of clothes, firewood, and onions hanging from a shelf. As in the Crocker drawing, the tone of the watercolor is greyish-blue.

It seems, then, that the Crocker drawing is preparatory to the Lübeck watercolor, being a spontaneous single-figure study done from a model that the artist then incorporated into a larger composition. The watercolor is dated *1766* in the artist's hand, so the Crocker red chalk, similarly signed but not dated, must have been done near that time, late in the period of Kraus's Paris training.   WB

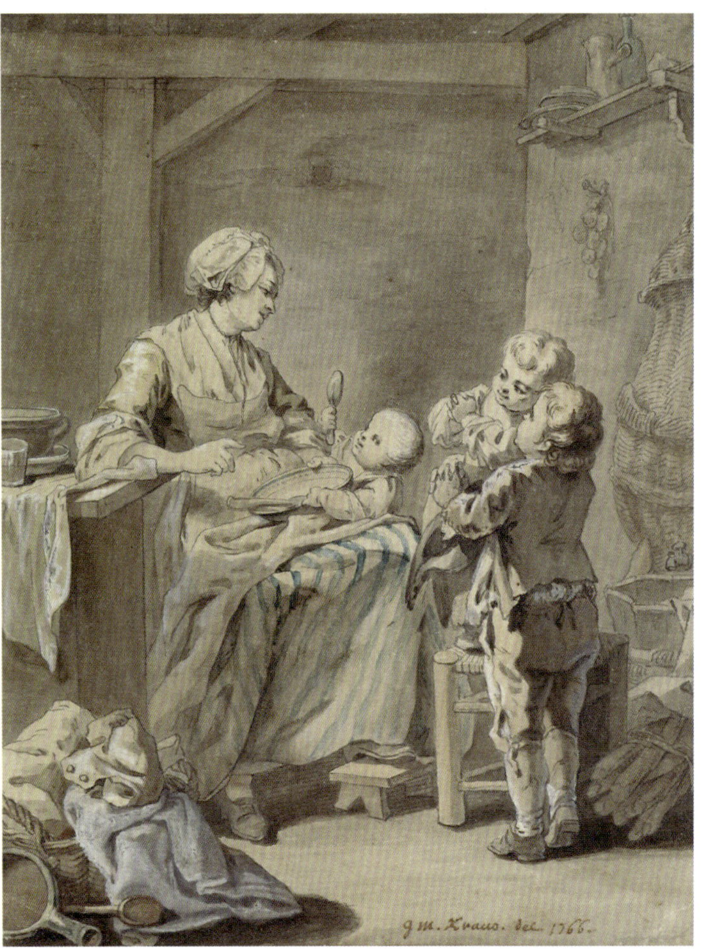

FIGURE 38 Georg Melchior Kraus, *Mother with Three Children*, 1766. Watercolor, 20.4 × 16.6 cm. Museen für Kunst und Kultur-geschichte der Hansestadt Lübeck, Lübeck, Sammlung Dräger/Stubbe

49. Johann Eleazer Zeisig, called Schenau, *Self-Portrait*, 1773

Black, white and red chalks on brown laid paper, 20.3 × 16.5 cm. Crocker Art Museum,
E. B. Crocker Collection 1871.1067

INSCRIPTIONS: black chalk, lower
right, signed: *Schenau se ipse del. 1773*

MARKS: none

PROVENANCE: Edwin Bryant Crocker,
by 1871; gift of his widow Margaret to the
Museum, 1885

LITERATURE: Breazeale 2008, p. 211;
Kaufmann 2004, pp. 161–62; Kaufmann
1989, no. 66; Crocker 1971, checklist p. 163;
Scheyer 1949, no. 121

JOHANN ELEAZER ZEISIG, called Schenau from his birthplace of Groß-Schönau, now
Velký Šenov in the northern Czech Republic, was born in 1737. His father, a weaver,
recognized his talent for drawing and sent the twelve-year-old boy to Dresden for training. There, Schenau was apprenticed to the portrait painter Johann Christian Beßler.
Eventually he came to the studio of the painter Charles-François de Silvestre, who was
forced to return to France in 1756, taking Schenau with him. Settling in Paris, the
twenty-year-old Schenau soon joined the group of German artists living there, one of
whom, the printmaker Johann Georg Wille, became a pivotal figure in his life. Wille
took the young artist under his wing, following his developing skills as well as intro-
ducing him to Christian Ludwig von Hagedorn, the future director of the Dresden
Kunstakademie. Schenau met and studied with Chardin and Greuze as well, both of
whom influenced his choice of genre and portrait painting as his first career.

In 1765, the German artist opened his own studio in Paris, supplying a ready market
there until 1770. Hagedorn's call to Dresden had come two years earlier, but poor health
had prevented travel. In 1773, Schenau received a major commission, the portrait of the
Saxon princely family, and became director of the drawing and painting school at the
Meissen porcelain manufactory. The following year he was named Professor at the
Dresden Kunstakademie. The artist's production soon followed this double path: at the
same time as he produced light, charming scenes of children and lovers at Meissen, he
created history paintings in a grand style for Dresden, like his reception-piece *Priamus,
Achilles and the Body of Hector*. Schenau became co-director of the Kunstakademie in 1776,
sharing the post with Giovanni Battista Casanova until the latter's death in 1795. He
gave up the Meissen directorship the following year. Never in good health, he died
in 1806.

Schenau's self-portrait shows his technical ability in the extremely sensitive use of
three chalks on brown paper. Manufactured to be darker than the tone of flesh, the
paper provides a neutral background from which the figure emerges. The smoothness of
the skin, blushed and highlighted in precise red and white chalk, contrasts with the hair
and costume, where a variety of vigorous hatchings create volume. The inscription
makes clear that the drawing is a self-portrait, being interpreted "Schenau himself drew
himself, 1773."

The drawing may be related to a painting Schenau completed in 1773 (fig. 39).[1]
Entitled *Das Kunstgespräch* (The art discussion) it is, according to the diary of the printmaker Daniel Chodowiecki, simultaneously group portrait and allegory. At the table sit
the patron Thomas, Freiherr von Fritsch and the Dresden Academy founder Christian
Ludwig von Hagedorn, observed at left by Painting, Sculpture and Poetry in the persons
of Adrian Zingg, Anton Graff and, in the center, Schenau himself.[2] A 1772 drawing of
Schenau by Heinrich Füger now in Weimar,[3] clearly depicting the same sitter as in the

NOTES
1. Dresden, Gemäldegalerie Alte Meister,
inv. no. 3161; see Harald Marx, "'… den
guten Geschmack einzuführen.' Zum 250
Geburtstag von Johann Eleazar Zeisig,
genannt Schenau," *Dresdner Kunstblätter*,
vol. XXXII, no. 1, 1988, pp. 10–18, at p. 11.
The date given in the caption to the
reproduction is incorrect; the text
contains the correct date of 1773.
2. Ibidem, p. 12.
3. Schloßmuseum, inv. no. KK 512, repr.
ibidem p. 14.

Crocker drawing, has been proposed as the model for the central figure at left. Though the figure raises its index figure to the chin as in the painting, the costume is less formal and the hairstyle completely different. The Crocker drawing, while omitting the hand, is closer in shading and hairstyle to the figure in *Das Kunstgespräch*. While Schenau may have had reason to use a drawing by another artist as the basis of his self-portrait in the painting, it seems unlikely that he would have omitted to make his own drawing during his preparations. Though it is difficult to determine the exact relationship between painting and drawing, surely it is not coincidence that one of the artist's most sensitive drawings, posed similarly to the self-portrait in *Das Kunstgespräch*, should have been done at the same date.

WB

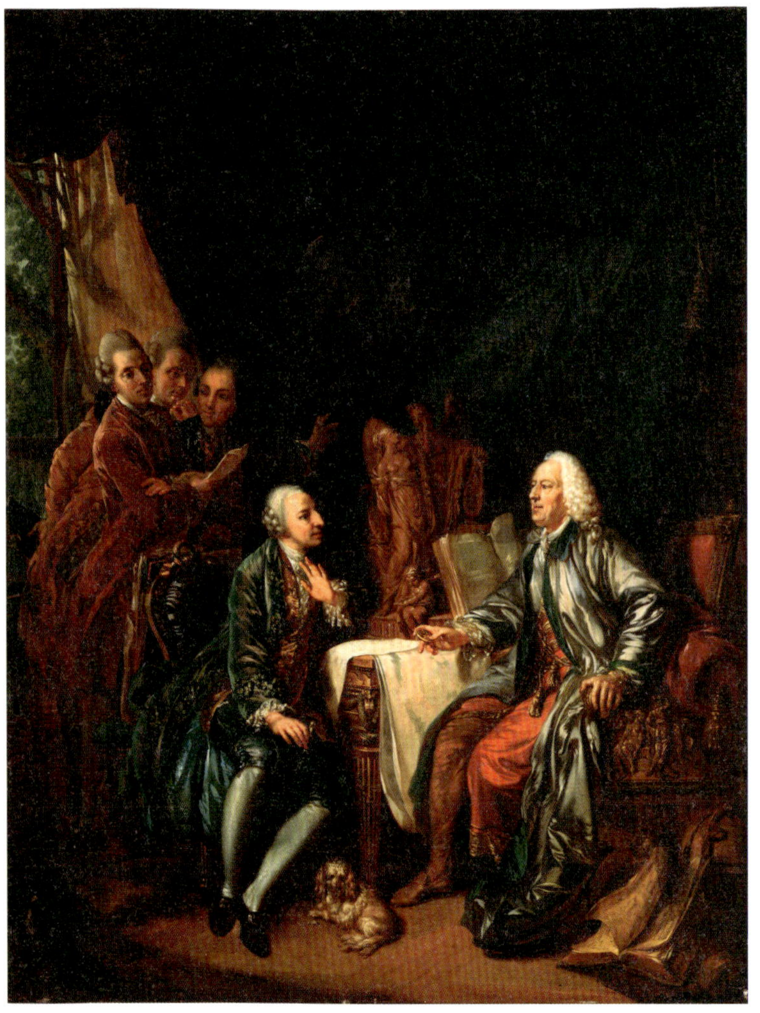

FIGURE 39: Johann Eleazer Zeisig, called Schenau, *Das Kunstgespräch*, 1773. Oil on canvas, 80 × 63.5 cm. Dresden, Gemäldegalerie Alte Meister

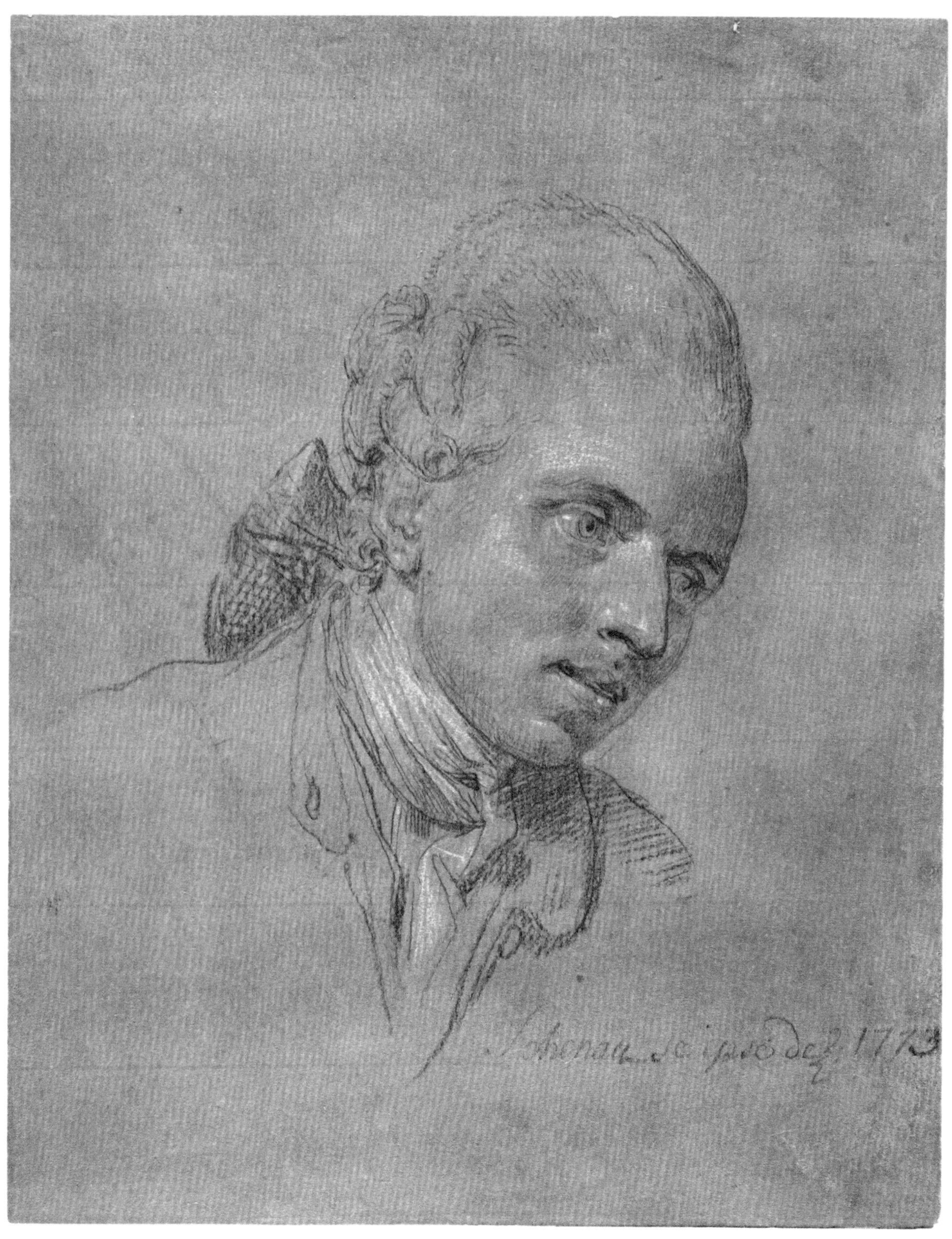

50. **Franz Schüz,** *View of the Münster Valley,* 1780

Black chalk, charcoal, white chalk on blue laid paper, 30.2 × 20.9 cm. Crocker Art Museum,
E. B. Crocker Collection 1871.1073

INSCRIPTIONS: dark-brown ink, across bottom margin: *gegend aus dem Münsterthal / seinem Freund zum Andencken von Franz Schüz 1780 / gezeichnet in Genf.*

MARKS: none

PROVENANCE: Edwin Bryant Crocker, Sacramento, by 1871; gift of his widow Margaret to the Museum, 1885

LITERATURE: Kaufmann 2004, pp. 168–69; Crocker 1971, checklist p. 163

NOTES
1. The Albertina has surely the largest collection of Schüz's drawings; see Maren Gröning and Marie Luise Sternrath, *Die Deutschen und Schweizer Zeichnungen des späten 18. Jahrhunderts*, Vienna, 1997, nos. 788–814; nos. 814 and 807 represent scenes at the Saint Gotthard Pass and the Isole Borromee respectively.

ONE OF FRANZ SCHÜZ's most engaging landscapes, the Crocker *View of the Münster Valley* depicts a mountain pass in a vertical format, unusual for the artist. Dated 1780, it was completed the year before the artist's death.

The short-lived Schüz was born in 1751 in Frankfurt am Main. He was the son of Christian Georg Schütz the Elder, also a painter, from whom he received his early training. Little is recorded of his activities until the age of twenty-six, when he met Gideon Burckhard, a merchant and patron living in Basle. Schüz became the merchant's protégé, accompanying him on a long trip through the canton of Uri, Lugano and the lake country of northern Italy, and Milan in 1777–78. Drawings record many of the views the two encountered, including the Saint Gotthard Pass and the Isole Borromee on the Lago Maggiore.[1] Still enjoying Burckhard's support, in 1780 the artist moved to Geneva, where he died of tuberculosis the next year.

Only a very few oil-paintings survive by Schüz. Though he provided designs for etchers as well, his main output was landscape drawings. The Crocker drawing shows well the artist's skill in manipulating black and white chalk, especially in the distant mountains and sky, where delicate transitions between the two are very effective in depicting cloud formations. Relying very little on graphic shorthand, Schüz captures the different textures of vegetation, rock and water. As often in his drawings, he includes a fisherman and child in the left foreground to enable the eye to comprehend the scale of the scene beyond.

In addition to recording the artist and date, the inscription at center of the lower margin indicates that the drawing was planned as a finished work of art, as it seems many of Schüz's drawings were, and as a gift. It is unfortunate that the artist does not indicate which friend he dedicates the drawing to, though it is perhaps Burckhard himself. At right, the phrase *gezeichnet in Genf* tells us that it was created in Geneva, where artist and patron had moved earlier in the year. This raises the question of whether the drawing was created on the basis of sketches no longer extant. Whether or not such sketches existed, the arrangement of bridge, mountains and stream seems calculated to create a coherent, visually pleasing whole, while the foreground tree at left and the bushes at right are planned to frame the view and draw the eye into the distance.

The inscription *gegend aus dem Münsterthal* at left identifies the view, though rather deceptively, as there are many valleys known by this German name. One is in the Tirol, at the opposite end of Switzerland from Geneva and well beyond the canton of Uri, the town of Lugano and the route to Milan that the artist is recorded as having taken in 1777–78. A more likely place for the view's origin, especially given the relatively low mountains, is the Münsterthal or Val de Munster on the Fecht river in Alsace, not far from Geneva where the drawing was made. To this writer, the fact that few if any drawing by Schüz survive that can be documented as scenes east of Canton Uri is persuasive.

WB

Gegend aus dem Münsterthal.
Seinem freund zum Andenken. obn: Franz Schütz 1780   gezeichnet in Genf.

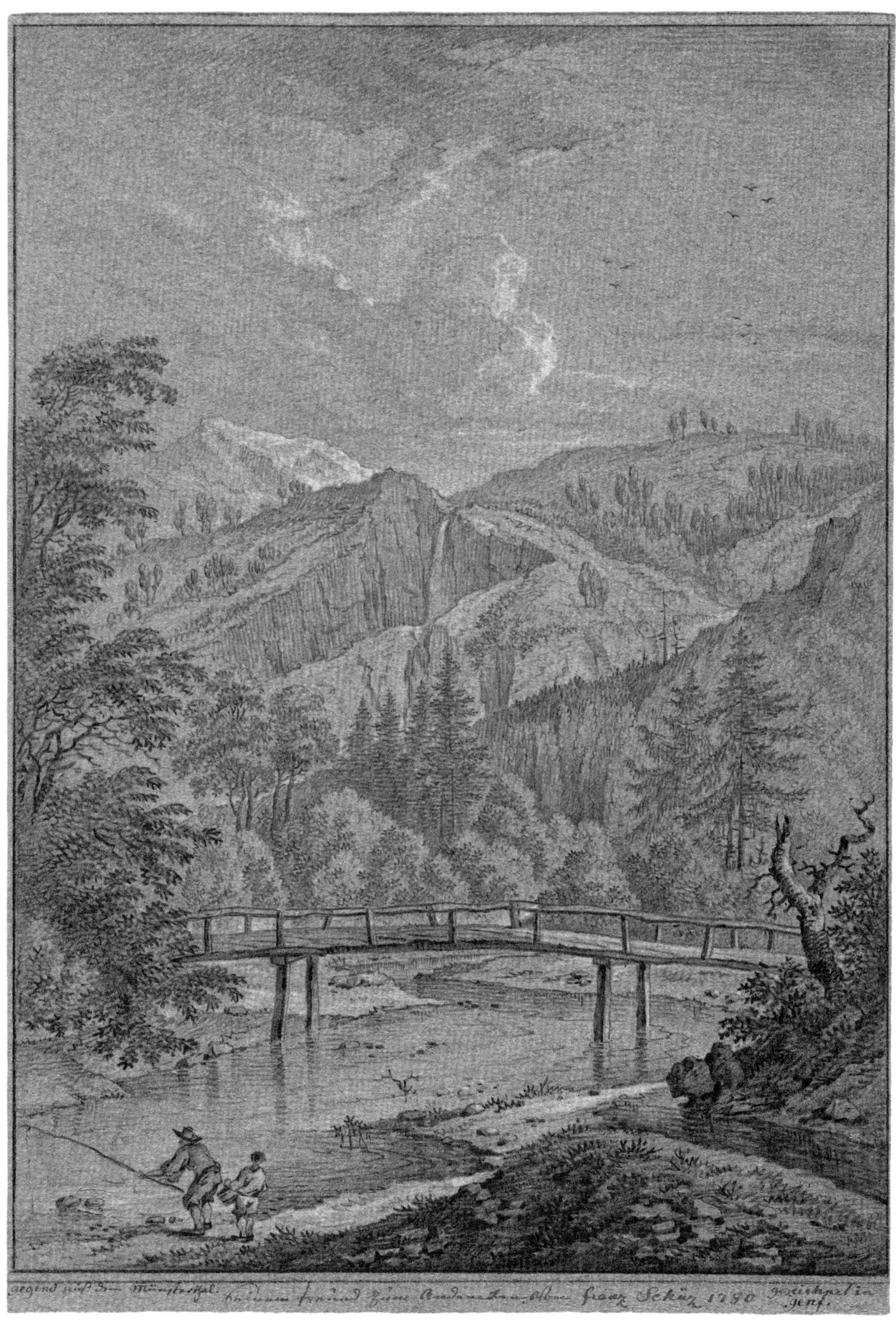

151

 # Adrian Zingg, *A View of the Elbe River and the Bastei Rocks in the Sächsische Schweiz, Saxony,* n. d.

Pen and black and dark-brown ink, brush and brown washes on off-white wove paper, 39.1 × 31.1 cm.
Crocker Art Museum, purchased with funds provided by Anne and Malcolm McHenry, 2006.12

INSCRIPTIONS: verso, graphite, at center: 115356 / 1; verso, graphite, lower right corner: 562; verso, upper right, graphite: 562; verso, green chalk, upper center: *Adr. Zing / Dresden 18. Jhrt.*

MARKS: verso, in black, lower left corner: Lugt 324 (Becker); verso, in blue, lower left: Lugt 2841a (Heumann)

PROVENANCE: W. G. Becker, Dresden, before 1813; Carl Heumann, Chemnitz, before 1945; Thomas Le Claire; Museum purchase, 2006

LITERATURE: Thomas Le Claire, *Master Drawings, Recent Acquisitions, Catalogue XVII,* 2005, no. 17

A RECENT ACQUISITION, this engaging landscape by Adrian Zingg brings a new artist to the Crocker's collection of drawings by professors at the Dresden Kunstakademie. Zingg's conception of landscape, elaborated during his time as a young artist in Paris, was a key development leading to the Romantic depiction of nature.

The son of a gunsmith, Adrian Zingg was born in 1734 and learned the rudiments of etching, also used to decorate weapons, from his father. He then studied with the printmaker Johann Rudolf Holzhalb in Zurich and moved to Bern at the age of twenty-three to study with Johann Ludwig Aberli, a printmaker who specialized in landscape. Aberli accompanied the young Zingg in 1759 to Paris, where he introduced him to Johann Georg Wille. Wille took the Swiss artist under his wing, as he had so many others, including the painter Schenau represented in this exhibition. Over the next seven years Wille directed Zingg's studies and secured him commissions, including etching landscapes by other artists. Christian Ludwig von Hagedorn, it seems at Wille's recommendation, called Zingg to lead the printmaking department at the Dresden Kunstakademie in 1764, though he arrived only in 1766. In Dresden Zingg met his countryman Anton Graff, with whom he made a trip to the district along the Elbe river the same year.[1] The rugged landscape prompted the two artists to give the area the name "Sächsische Schweiz" or Saxon Switzerland, which it preserves today. Admitted as a foreign member to the Vienna academy in 1767 and to the Berlin academy in 1787, Zingg received the title of Professor at Dresden only in 1803. The author of two textbooks on landscape published in 1805 and 1811, Zingg died in 1816.

Zingg worked very much in an etcher's style, his landscape drawings being made most often in detailed black ink with wash added only after the line drawing was complete. To produce more than one version of the same scene, in fact, he sometimes saved time by etching a large plate before adding the wash in the same way as to a drawing. In creating the Crocker drawing, Zingg used an extremely fine pen to create the outlines of rocks, land masses, and distant mountains, with more robust lines only in the foreground foliage. The masterful gradations of wash create the masses of stone and land, with fine detail in the farmsteads below. The scene depicted, the limestone rock formation surrounding the pillar known as the Bastei, or bastion, is located near the town of Rathen. Zingg unusually chooses to depict it from a neighboring promontory rather than from the plain lying along the riverbed. After the artist's death, in 1824, a pedestrian bridge was constructed for access to the formation.

Zingg's skill for landscape was developed under Wille, whose habit of taking his students on week-long sketching trips in the countryside was decisive for his technique. According to his friend Daniel Chodowiecki, Zingg made the bones of his final drawings in nature, sketching them in graphite, then going over them with ink and wash in the studio, finally adding staffage and trees to complete the composition.[2]

NOTES

1. A sketchbook containing 54 drawings records this trip, Dresden Kupferstichkabinett inv. no. Ca 1991-1; see Bärbel Muller, "Ein neuerworbenes Skizzenbuch Adrian Zinggs im Dresdner Kupferstichkabinett," *Dresdner Kunstblätter,* vol. XLV, no. 1, 1997, pp. 24–27.

2. *Ibidem,* p. 26.

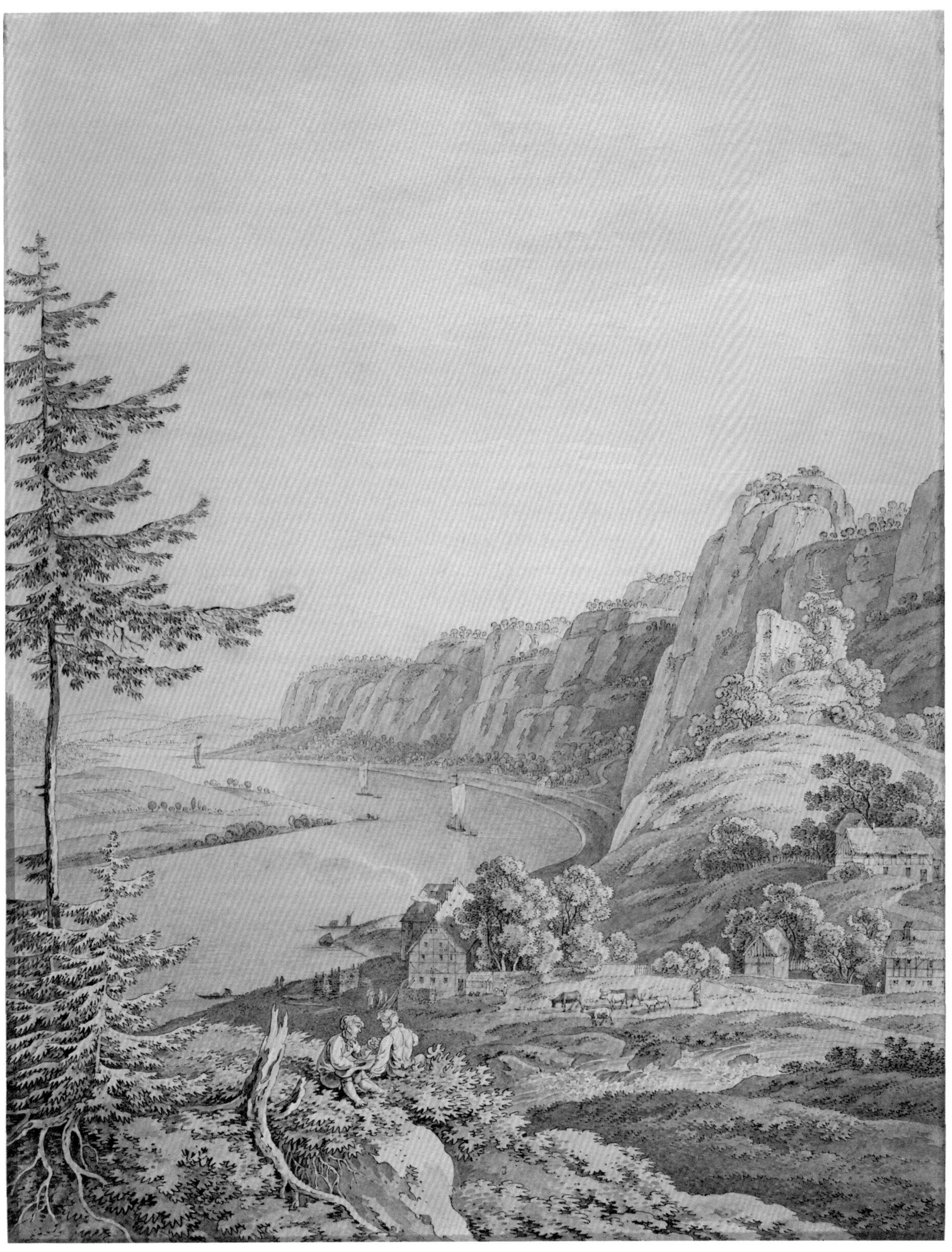

Though any graphite on the Crocker drawing has since been erased, something of the same technique may be present here: the precise view of the Bastei formation and the river flowing along its base is accompanied by details that can only have been added to complete the composition—like the shepherd and flocks, the figures perched on the foreground hill, and the boats sailing along the Elbe. The large tree at left likewise provides a counterweight to the mass of rock opposite. Zingg's drawing records one of the principal monuments along the present-day "*Malerweg*" (Painter's way), a route with picturesque views along the Elbe from Pillnitz to Dečin, which has its origin in his sketching trips to the Elbsandsteingebirge with students from the Dresden Academy.   WB

52. Domenico Quaglio the Younger, *The Neuthor, Ulm*, 1815

Black chalk on cream wove paper, 43.3 × 31.1 cm. Crocker Art Museum, E. B. Crocker Collection 1871.1051

INSCRIPTIONS: black chalk, bottom margin at left: *Neuthor in Ulm. D. Quaglio*

MARKS: none

PROVENANCE: Edwin Bryant Crocker, Sacramento, by 1871; gift of his widow Margaret to the Museum, 1885

LITERATURE: Breazeale 2008, p. 212; Kaufmann 2004, pp. 232–34; Crocker 1971, checklist p. 160; Scheyer 1949, no. 106

THOUGH ITS ORIGINS lay in the Val d'Intelvi just north of Como in Lombardy, by the late eighteenth century the Quaglio family of artists had settled in Germany, where Domenico Quaglio the Younger was born in 1787. Domenico was one of the most important members of his family, who had been court artists around Europe from the early seventeenth century.

Domenico's father Giuseppe had settled in 1778 in Munich, where he was a theater and scene painter. At his knee the young artist learned perspective, a skill which was to remain important throughout his career, as he concentrated more and more on

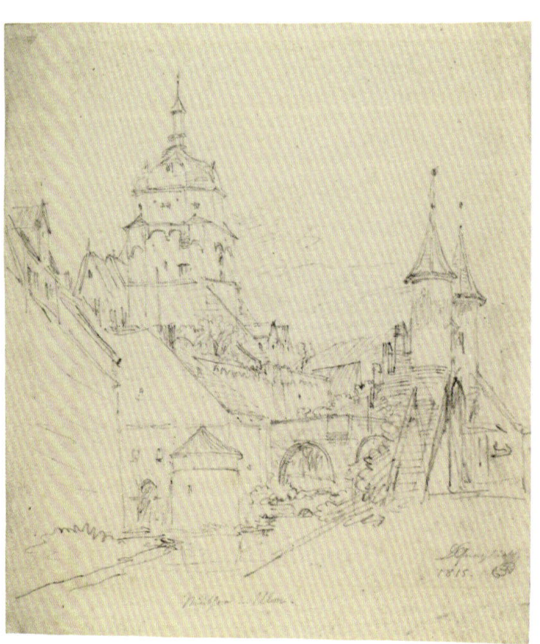

FIGURE 40: Domenico Quaglio the Younger, *The Neuthor in Ulm*, 1815. Black chalk, 28.3 × 26.3 cm. Germanisches Nationalmuseum, Nuremberg

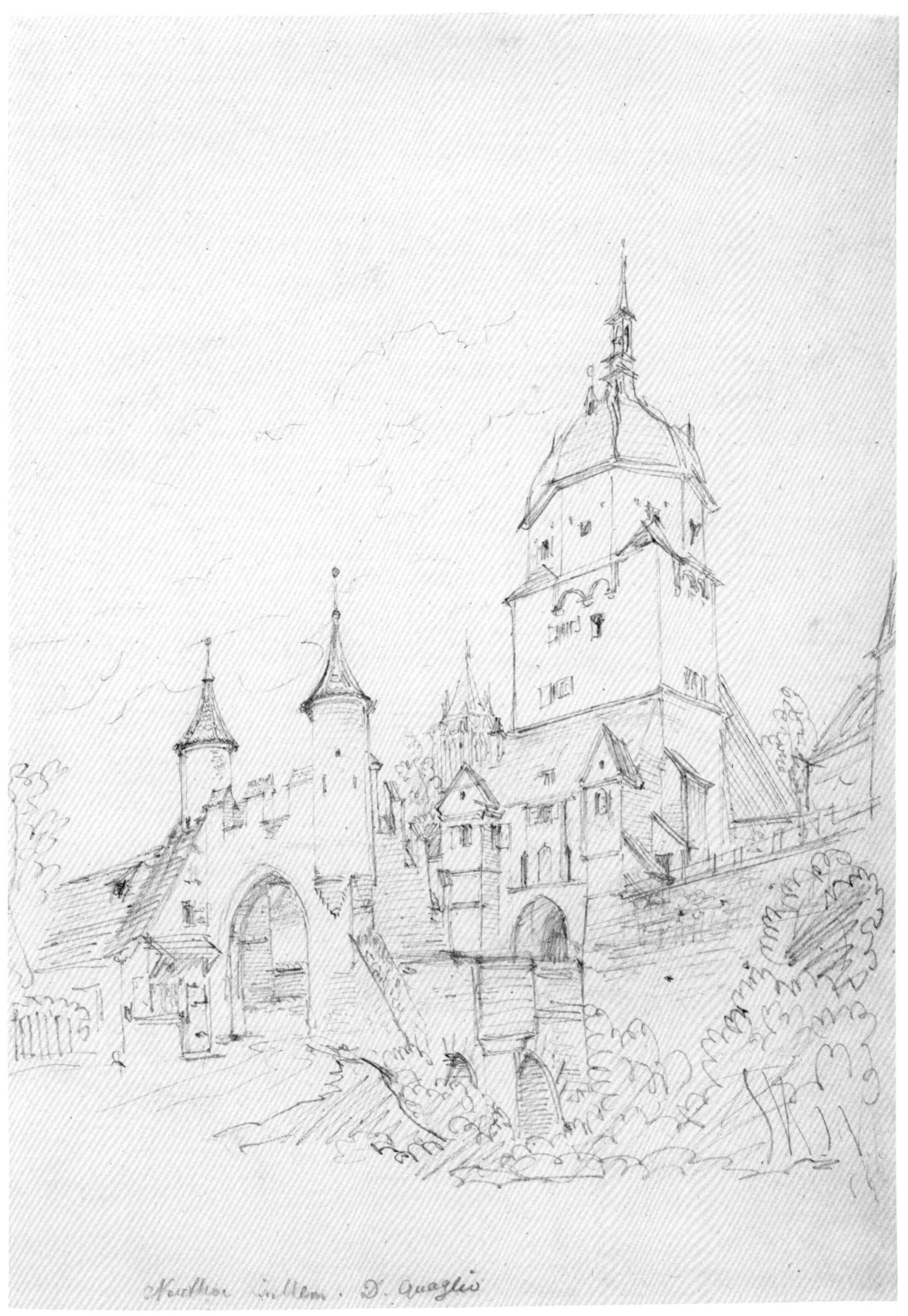

Neuthor in Mem. D. Quaglio

NOTES
1. Inv. no. Hz 2267; see Brigitte Trost, *Domenico Quaglio 1787–1837, Monographie und Werkverzeichnis*, Munich, 1973, no. 44.
2. *Ibidem*, pp. 35–38.
3. *Ibidem*, p. 34.

architecture. His father's training was supplemented by the teachings of Johann Michael Mettenleiter and Carl Hess in the field of printmaking. In 1803, at the age of sixteen, Domenico became a decorative painter and was appointed the scene painter for the Munich court theater five years later. In 1811, a series of his views of Munich scenes was published. From this point he became especially interested in medieval architecture, a passion which took him on trips throughout southern Germany and into Austria in following years. Having become a founding member of the Munich Kunstverein in 1823, Quaglio by 1829 had so developed his skill in architectural printmaking that an English patron, Henry Gally Knight, sponsored a sketching trip and print series. In 1833, the Bavarian Crown Prince Maximilian, for whom Quaglio had long served as drawing tutor, commissioned him to renovate the castle of Hohenschwangau together with the architect Georg Friedrich Ziebland. Quaglio's historical knowledge was essential to the project and, in fact, he gave up all other activity to concentrate on Hohenschwangau. He died in 1837 in the midst of the renovations, which were completed by Moritz von Schwind.

The Crocker drawing shows a dynamic view of a medieval monument in the Danube city of Ulm—the Neuthor or new city gate, which has now been destroyed. Quaglio depicts it diagonally to the picture plane, which, aside from being the most attractive view, allows for a more complete view of the towers, walkways, and moat. The drawing was most likely done at the scene, given the quick, gestural use of the portable medium of graphite to depict the forms, which contrasts with the even more gestural shorthand used for the trees and sky.

Another drawing of the same monument, signed similarly and dated 1815, is in the Germanisches Nationalmuseum in Nuremberg (fig. 40).[1] It is even more gestural than the Crocker drawing—very much a sketch—and is smaller. The view in the Nuremberg drawing is less inspired, showing the city gate from the side and giving little idea of the building's complexity, as the Crocker drawing does.

These two drawings record an otherwise undocumented visit to Ulm in 1815, a year in which Quaglio also visited the Altmühltal with its many fortresses, Rothenburg, Nuremberg, and Bamberg to sketch castles and ruins.[2] Such trips were often packed with activity: the previous September and October the artist had visited Augsburg, Tittmoning, Neuötting, Burghausen and Salzburg.[3] They also supplied Quaglio with a variety of architectural motifs that he used in print series in following years. Few of these drawings have the casual, personal quality of the Crocker Neuthor in Ulm, which may have been done as a personal memento of an attractive scene. WB

53. Joseph Karl Stieler, *Portrait of Balthasar Speth,* 1820

Charcoal and white chalk on brown wove paper, 37.9 × 29.6 cm. Crocker Museum,
E.B. Crocker Collection 1871.1053

IN 1828, STIELER was commissioned to paint the now canonical portrait of Johann Wolfgang von Goethe.[1] He received this commission by enticing Goethe with a beautiful portrait of the actress Fräulein von Hagen. Johann Peter Eckermann relates a conversation with Goethe: "'That is worth something,' said [Goethe], after we had observed [Fräulein von Hagen's portrait] for some time, 'is it not? Stieler is no fool. He employed this beautiful morsel as a bait for me, and, whilst by such arts he induced me to sit, he flattered me with the hope that, under his pencil, another angel would appear, whilst he was only painting the head of an old man.'"[2] Stieler was already famous as a portraitist with royal patronage and as co-founder of the Kunstverein in Munich.

Stieler (1781–1858) began his career as a painter of portraits in miniature and executed his first large-scale portrait paintings under the tutelage of F. H. Füger in Vienna (1800). From Vienna, Stieler traveled to Poland, and ended up in Paris training with the renowned Neoclassical portrait-painter François Gérard. Stieler traveled to Italy between 1810 and 1812, and would have been exposed to the work of the Nazarenes. After his Italian sojourn, Stieler returned to Munich and received commissions from the Bavarian court to create portraits of some of the most famous men and beautiful women of his time. In addition to these imperial portraits, Stieler is also known for his more intimate painted portraits of the bourgeoisie. In both cases his drawings capture striking and expressive features, and often betray his method of sketching from life.

In the Speth portrait, evidence of Stieler's rapid technique can be seen in the pentimenti found in the cursory middle-class costume. Though not as highly finished as some of his preparatory sketches for paintings (as in the case of his drawing of Goethe),

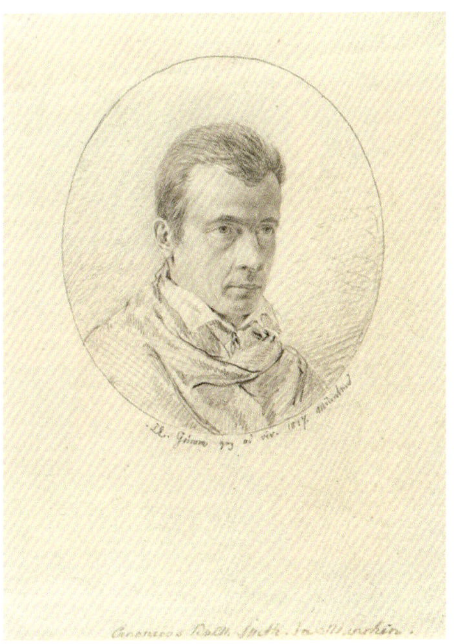

FIGURE 41 Ludwig Emil Grimm,
Portrait of Balthasar Speth, 1817.
Graphite on cream wove paper,
19.2 × 16.1. Crocker Art Museum,
E. B. Crocker Collection

3. Preparatory sketch of Goethe, Staatliche
Graphische Sammlungen, inv. no. 44337.

4. Kaufmann 2004, p. 250.

5. See Balthasar Speth, *Die Kunst in Italien*,
Munich, 1819–23. In a recent auction
there was a painting by Speth, painted in
the Baroque style, of the *Madonna and
Child* in watercolor and gouache on ivory
(Neumeister Kunstauktionen, November
30, 2005, lot 715a).

6. There is also another drawing of Speth in
a private collection catalogued by Ingrid
Koszinowski and Vera Leuschner: *Ludwig
Emil Grimm. Zeichnungen und Gemälde*,
Marburg, 1990, vol. II, cat. P141, p. 78.
Grimm also etched a portrait after this
drawing that was published in the
Munich *Künstlerunterhaltung* (Ludwig
Emil Grimm, *Erinnerungen aus meinem
Leben*, with additions by Adolf Stoll,
Leipzig, 1913, no. 69); for Grimm's
relationships with Speth and Stieler see
this work, pp. 486–87.

7. Inv. no. 1871.1052.

8. Etching, 1827.

9. Sketch, 1830; Brüder Grimm-Museum,
Kassel.

10. Sketch, 1837; private collection.

the Speth drawing is delicately highlighted in white chalk and signed with Stieler's full name and dated—designating it as a finished work in its own right.[3]

Kaufmann rightly believes that "elements of the artist's style found in the work may lead to a reinterpretation of his portraiture."[4] Rather than this representing a combination of his French and English manners or a midway point between his courtly and bourgeois portrait styles, the Speth portrait appears to be part of a more Romantic tradition of representing friends and colleagues—*Künstlerfreundschaftsbilder*—developed a decade earlier by the Nazarene painters Friedrich Overbeck and Carl Philipp Fohr in Rome.

In addition to being a member of the Cathedral chapter and court preacher, Balthasar von Speth (1774–1846) was also an art critic, amateur artist, and collector. He wrote extensively on seventeenth-century Italian art as well as on the work of his own contemporaries.[5] Speth operated in the same social networks as Stieler, known to be his acquaintance; a mutual friend, Ludwig Emil Grimm, also created several portraits of him.[6] A graphite portrait by Grimm, which is also in the Crocker (fig. 41), identifies the sitter as Speth and claims that it was completed *ad vivum* in 1817.[7] Grimm, the younger brother to the famous philologists Jakob and Wilhelm, executed many portraits of his circle of well-known friends, for example Heinrich Heine,[8] Niccolò Paganini,[9] and Clemens Brentano.[10]

FS

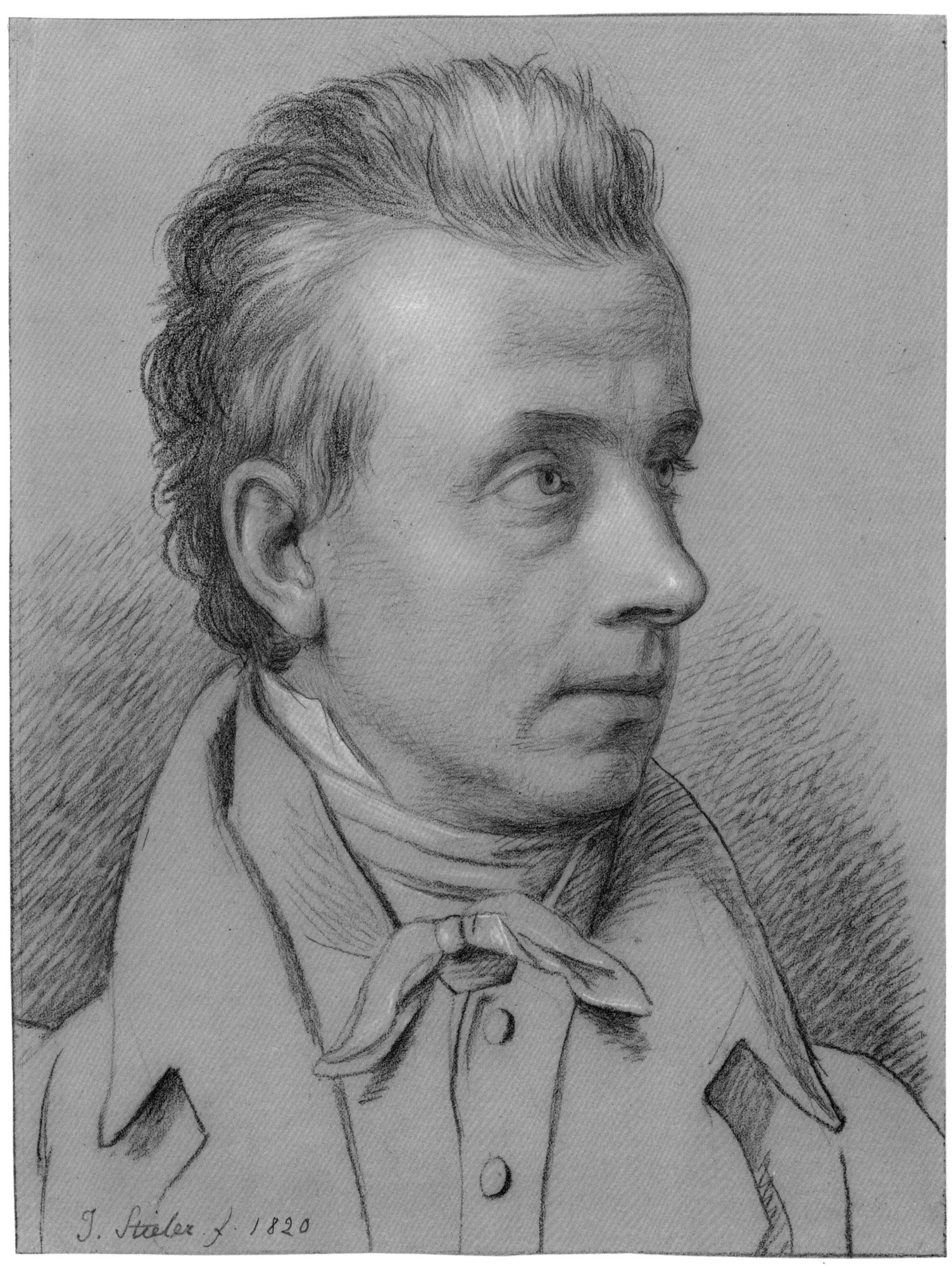

J. Stieler f. 1820

54. **Franz Xaver Rektorzik**, *Landscape with a Cliff*, n. d.

Pen and black ink, watercolor, and opaque watercolor on beige wove paper, 43.2 × 55.4 cm.
Crocker Art Museum, E. B. Crocker Collection 1871.1272

INSCRIPTIONS: pen and dark-brown ink, lower right corner, signed: *Nach der Natur. F. Rektorzik. Brünn*

MARKS: none

PROVENANCE: Edwin Bryant Crocker, Sacramento, by 1871; gift of his widow Margaret to the Museum, 1885

LITERATURE: Kaufmann 2004, p. 236; Crocker 1971, checklist p. 160

NOTES

1. A comparison can be made with the gentians in Franz Xavier Petter's *Woodland Flowers*, 1860, Niederösterreichisches Landesmuseum, Vienna. For more on the flowers in this work see Geraldine Norman, *Biedermeier Painting 1815–1848: Reality Observed in Genre, Portrait and Landscape*, New York, 1987, p. 50.
2. Kaufmann 2004, p. 236.
3. Moravská Galerie, Brno, inv. nos. B11518, B10808; British Museum, London, inv. no. 1866-11-10-1111.

First TRAINED by his father, the Brno painter Ignaz Rektorzik, Franz Xaver Rektorzik (1793–1851) went on to study with the sculptors Ignaz Weidlich, Bartolomeo Girardoni, and Antonio Arrigoni. Although Franz Xaver remained an amateur draughtsman and printmaker, this landscape shares many affinities with *vedute* created by Austrian Biedermeier artists such as Rudolf Alt, Franz Steinfeld, Ferdinand Georg Waldmüller, and Friedrich Gauermann.

Biedermeier artists often went on sketching trips in their local environs and sketched directly from nature. As a group they exhibited a great interest in realistically representing the diversity of everyday life and the environment. In the Biedermeier style, Rektorzik's vigorous drawing demonstrates a delicate handling of light and creates the illusion of a closely observed nature in its wealth of details. In his inscription Rektorzik asserts that it was done *nach der Natur*, and pays close attention to the treatment of light, the small details of the leaves on the trees of the vast forest, and the beautiful blue flowers found scattered throughout the scene—most likely gentians.[1] Rektorzik shows incredible dexterity with watercolor, rendering the landscape as two distinct regions by shifting the palette: in the forest along the right edge, he uses muted tones of green to suggest atmospheric perspective as the trees get closer to the horizon, whereas, in the foreground, he uses more vibrant reddish-browns, tans, blues, and greens.

While the drawing demonstrates directness in reproducing nature, it also includes a figure and cow, which appear to be anecdotal and were probably incorporated later to create an idyllic effect. Rektorzik combines the Biedermeier interests in rendering atmospheric effects and in accurately describing their local environment; his watercolor most likely depicts a region of southern Moravia, where, as Thomas DaCosta Kaufmann notes, comparable terrain can be found near the Austrian border.[2]

This drawing is similar in style to other drawings by the artist in Brno, as well as to a signed etching that shows the same lush treatment of the treetops in a mountainous landscape with cows and figures walking along a path.[3]　　　　FS

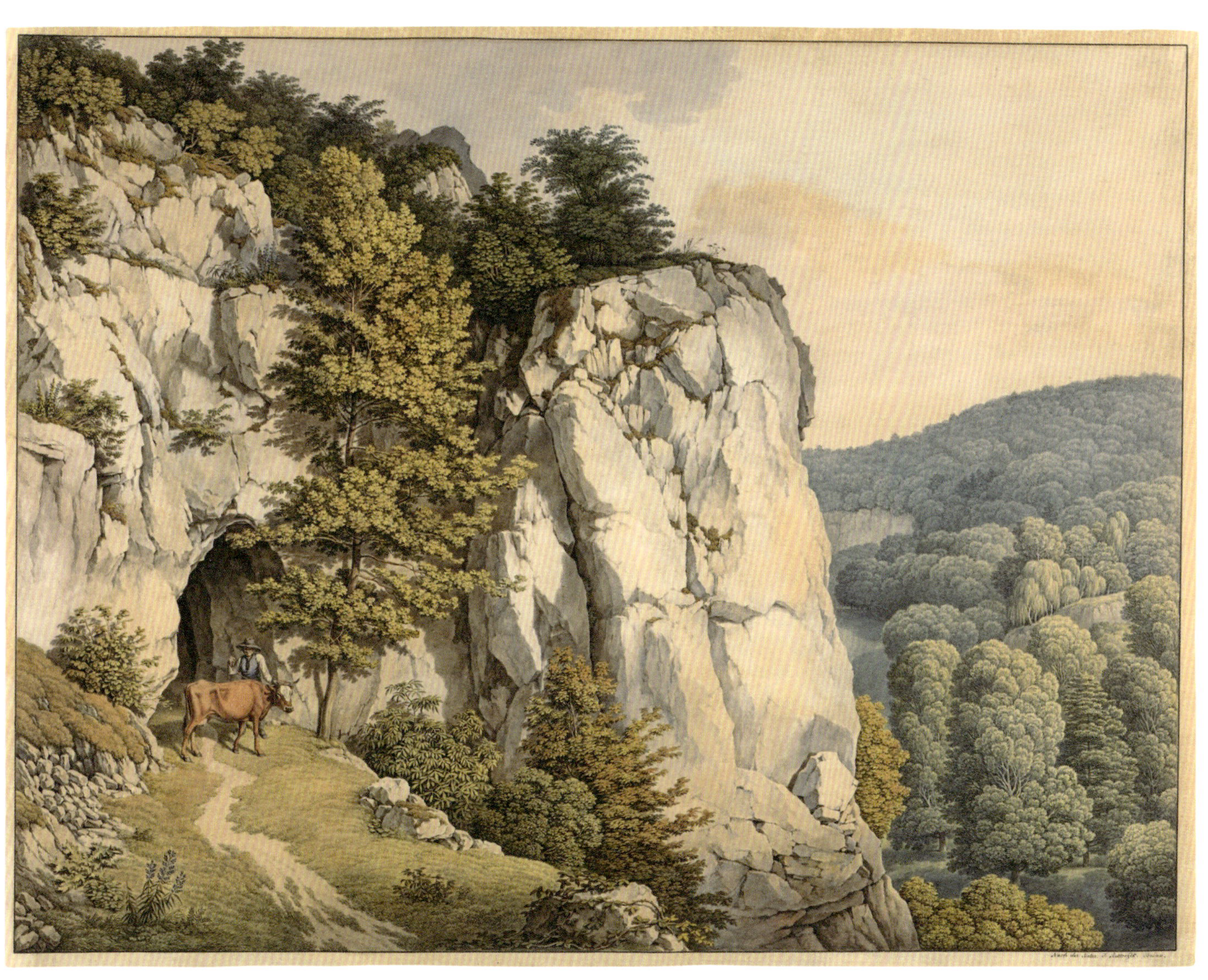

55. Moritz Daniel Oppenheim, *Portrait of a Man with an Open Collar*, n. d.

Graphite on cream wove paper, 27.2 × 21.2 cm. Crocker Art Museum Purchase, 1973.49

INSCRIPTIONS: verso, graphite: *22./8/ 22./26.4/9.6*

MARKS: on fragment of old mat: *Nachlass/Moritz Oppenheim* (not in Lugt)

PROVENANCE: before 1973; Crocker Art Museum purchase

LITERATURE: Kaufmann 2004, p. 230

NOTES

1. For a discussion of the Lentulus letter, see Joseph Koerner, *The Moment of Self-Portraiture*, Chicago, 1993, pp. 103–04. For a full discussion of the origins, editions, and reception of this text, see Ernst von Dobschütz, *Christus-bilder. Untersuchung zur christlichen Legende*, 2 vols., Leipzig, 1899.
2. Translation from Michael Baxandall, *Painting and Experience in Fifteenth Century Italy: A Primer in the Social History of Pictorial Style*, Oxford, 1972, p. 57.
3. Portrait of Overbeck by Friedrich Olivier, now in the Staatliche Kunstsammlungen, Dresden; Rehbenitz's *Self-Portrait* now in the same collection; Fohr's *Self-Portrait* now in the Kurpfälzisches Museum, Heidelberg.
4. This style of execution is evident in many of Oppenheim's drawings from the 1820s. Some interesting examples include *The Nude Man*, c. 1822 (Museum Hanau, Schloß Philippsruhe); *After the Fall*, 1822–24 (Israel Museum, Jerusalem); and *Moses and Aaron before Pharaoh* (Israel Museum, Jerusalem).
5. Israel Museum, Jerusalem, inv. no. 1882-23.
6. Georg Heuberger and Anton Merk, eds., *Moritz Daniel Oppenheim: Die Entdeckung des jüdischen Selbstbewusstseins in der Kunst*, Cologne, 1999, p. 16. For Justi, see *Grundlage zu einer Hessischen Gelehrten-, Schriftsteller und Künstler-Geschichte vom Jahre 1806 biz zum Jahre 1830*, Marburg, 1831.
7. Israel Museum, Jerusalem, inv. no. P541-8-58.

THIS DELICATE BUT CAREFULLY WORKED graphite drawing portrays an unknown man in the guise of Jesus Christ as he was described in the legendary Lentulus letter.[1] A product of monastic culture around 1300, the letter's vivid description inspired many Northern artists, including Albrecht Dürer in his conception of Christ. The letter tells of Christ's almond-shaped eyes, wide forehead, thick full beard, and hair parted in the center flowing down in curls to his shoulders, in the manner known as Nazarene.[2] This manner inspired a group of German artists working in the early nineteenth century in Rome to call themselves "Nazarenes" and ape Christ's appearance. Variations of this can be seen in portraits of Friedrich Overbeck, Carl Philipp Fohr and Theodor Rehbenitz.[3]

Born in the Jewish ghetto of Hanau outside of Frankfurt, Moritz Daniel Oppenheim (1800–1882) benefited from the liberalization of German culture brought about by the French occupation under Napoleon. He was able to attend the Hanau Academy of Drawing and to travel extensively as a journeyman—to Munich, Paris, Florence, Naples, and Rome. Even though Oppenheim arrived in Rome shortly after the Nazarenes disbanded, there was still a large and active community of German Romantics. He was greatly influenced by their style of describing figures with strong graphic outlines and an absence of internal structuring or cross-hatching.[4] He was also very interested in their philosophy regarding a brotherhood of artists.

The Crocker drawing is very similar to another by Oppenheim of a fellow artist he met in Rome, Friedrich Müller, of 1822–23.[5] Unlike the *Portrait of a Man with an Open Collar*, Müller's is found in one of several sketchbooks Oppenheim used almost as a diary during his stay in Italy and contains an inscription that tells the name of the sitter, which is typical of his sketchbook. Although there are differences in scale and detail between this drawing and the Müller portrait, one can assume the Crocker drawing was created during the same period. The two portray similarly styled men sketched from life, and expand on the concept of *Kunstlerfreundschaftsbild* (artist's friendship image) developed a decade earlier by Overbeck and Fohr.

In 1831, Karl Wilhelm Justi published a description of Oppenheim, presumably written by his first teacher, then the director of the Hanau Academy, Conrad Westermayr. Westermayr remarks that from the beginning of his career Oppenheim made powerful and beautiful life drawings and had a great interest in portraiture.[6] It was for his talents in the latter genre that Oppenheim was celebrated both by his colleagues and the critics; and, as a result of his reputation, Oppenheim eventually became portraitist to the world-renowned Rothschild family. Unlike his more formal painted portraits, *Portrait of a Man with an Open Collar* displays the naturalism and intimacy apparent in his early portrait drawings. Similar to his first *Self-Portrait* of c. 1819, the Crocker drawing shows the unknown man abstracted from his surroundings with the focus on his physiognomy and psyche.[7]

FS

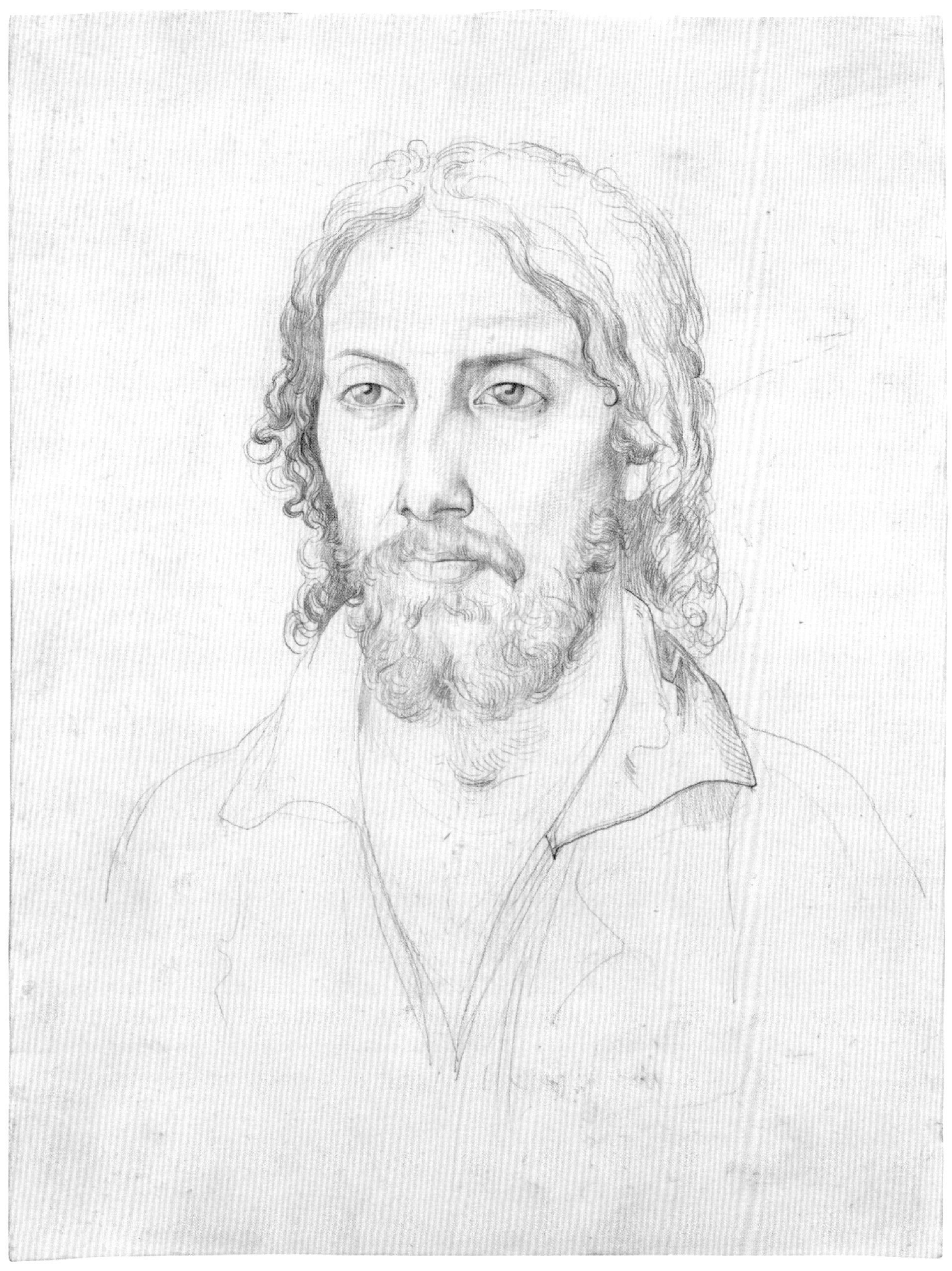

56. Carl Adalbert Hermann, *Allegory of the Nativity*, 1835

Graphite and brush and bluish, yellowish, tan watercolor on two pieces of superimposed cream wove paper, tracery possibly contemporary with drawing, 29.4 × 27.9 cm. Crocker Museum, E. B. Crocker Collection 1871.1036

INSCRIPTIONS: graphite, lower right, monogrammed and dated: *1835*; graphite, inscribed on banderole: GLORIA.IN. EXCELSIS.DEO.ET.IN.TERRA.PAX. HOMINIBUS.BONAE.VOLUNTATIS; graphite, inscribed in the lower margin: NOX.NATIVITATIS.CHRISTI

MARKS: none discernible

PROVENANCE: Edwin Bryant Crocker, Sacramento, by 1871; gift of his widow Margaret to the Museum, 1885

LITERATURE: Kaufmann 2004, pp. 211–12; Crocker 1971, checklist p. 153

NOTES
1. Mitchell Benjamin Frank, *German Romantic Painting Redefined: Nazarene Tradition and the Narratives of Romanticism*, Burlington, 2001, p. 81.
2. For more on this bible see *Julius Schnorr von Carolsfeld: Die Bibel in Bildern und andere biblische Bilderfolgen der Nazarener*, exh. cat. Clemens-Sels-Museum, Neuss, 1982, and Sepp Hollweck, *Und alsbald krähte der Hahn: Gedanken zur Passion nach Bildern von Julius Schnorr von Carolsfeld*, Mödling, 1988.

BORN IN OPPELN (NOW OPOLE), Silesia, Hermann (1791–1845) probably first trained with Joseph Bergler in Prague. He then went on to study at the Dresden Academy under the painter and printmaker Moritz Retzsch. During his tenure in Dresden, he became interested in German Romantic writers such as the Schlegels, Wackenroder, and Tieck. This fascination would continue throughout his career. After Dresden, he returned home briefly in 1814, only to leave again to become a member of the Berlin Academy. While there, he received a Prussian government fellowship that sent him to Rome in 1817, where he joined the German Romantic painters known as the Nazarenes. Hermann remained in Rome until 1820, when he returned home, eventually becoming a teacher of art history at the Magdalena and Elisabeth Gymnasium in the Silesian capital of Breslau (now Wroclaw).

First published as by Carl Adalbert Hermann by Kaufmann in 2004, this signed and dated drawing demonstrates a decidedly Nazarene style of draughtsmanship. Although the drawing was executed more than a decade after his Nazarene activities, Hermann retains their Romantic style, creating forms through an economy of sharp graphic lines that reject any kind of sensuality—even as he demonstrates the angels' beauty. While Hermann uses some parallel lines to create tone, the addition of watercolor clarifies his tranquil and ideal vision of the heavenly realm. Indeed, Hermann's scene is ideal and not historical. According to the inscriptions, Christ is shown on the evening of the Nativity surrounded by angels singing his praises, but he is also shown as the Man of Sorrows before the Crucifix triumphant over earthly sin. The drawing achieves what Mitchell Benjamin Frank called "equal parts historical authority and originality."[1]

The drawing with its framing of Gothic tracery has the appearance of something intended for reproduction, as it may well have been. One of the collaborative projects undertaken by the Nazarenes was an illustrated Bible, in which a drawing such as this was likely intended to be included. The project was first proposed in 1811 by Johann Friedrich Overbeck. By 1835 he was the last among the original group to remain in Rome, and was less and less able to work on the Picture Bible owing to his work on an increasingly large number of commissions. Work did continue on the Bible as a collaborative project of the Brotherhood of Saint Luke, much of it being done by Julius Schnorr von Carolsfeld.[2] Many of Carolsfeld's images for the Old and New Testaments, like Hermann's complicated allegorical narrative, are re-imaginings of the biblical stories rather than conventional representations.

FS

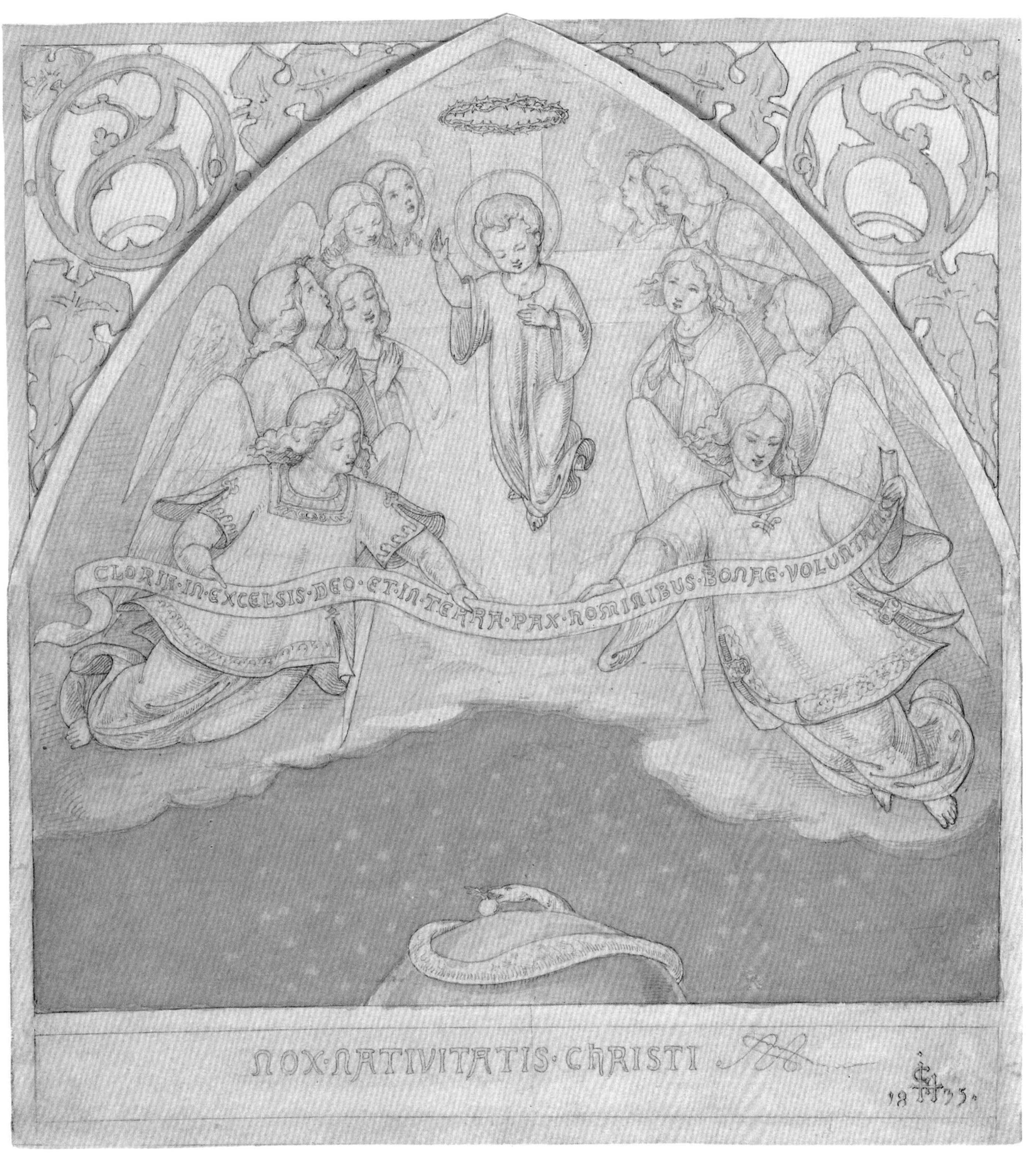

GLORIA·IN·EXCELSIS·DEO·ET·IN·TERRA·PAX·HOMINIBUS·BONAE·VOLUNTATIS
NOX·NATIVITATIS·CHRISTI
1855

BIBLIOGRAPHY

Albertina 1975
   Gedächtnisausstellung Otto Benesch, exh. cat. Vienna, 1975
Ananoff 1963
   Alexandre Ananoff, *L'Œuvre dessiné de Jean-Honoré Fragonard*, 2 vols, Paris, 1961–63
Bagni 1992
   Prisco Bagni, *I Gandolfi, affreschi dipinti bozzetti disegni*, Bologna, 1992
Benesch 1973
   Benesch, Otto, *The Drawings of Rembrandt*, 2nd. edn., London, 1973
Bevers 2006
   Holm Bevers, *Rembrandt: Die Zeichnungen im Berliner Kupferstichkabinett*, Berlin, 2006
Bevers et al. 1991
   Holm Bevers et al., *Rembrandt, the Master and His Workshop, Drawings and Etchings*, exh. cat. Berlin, 1991
Bionda 1983
   R. W. A. Bionda, "Een album amicorum van Jacobus Smies," *Jaarboek van het Genootschap Amstelodamum*, vol. LXXV, 1983, pp. 92–105
Bohr 1958
   Russell Bohr, *The Italian Drawings in the E. B. Crocker Art Gallery Collection, Sacramento, California*, unpubl. Ph.D. diss., University of California at Berkeley, 1958
Boisclair 1986
   Marie-Nicole Boisclair, *Gaspard Dughet, sa vie et son œuvre 1615–1675*, Paris, 1986
Bolten 2007
   Jaap Bolten, *Abraham Bloemaert c. 1565–1651: The Drawings*, n. p., 2007
Breazeale 2007
   Breazeale, William, "Nature and a New Drawing by Otto Marseus van Schrieck," *Master Drawings*, vol. XLV, no. 4, Winter 2007, pp. 527–33
Breazeale 2008
   Breazeale, William, "Old Masters in Old California: The Origins of the Drawings Collection at the Crocker Art Museum," *Master Drawings*, vol. XLVI, no. 2, Summer 2008, pp. 205–26
Breazeale et al. 2008
   William Breazeale, Susan Anderson, Christine Giviskos, and Christiane Andersson, *The Language of the Nude: Four Centuries of Drawing the Human Body*, exh. cat. Crocker Art Museum, Sacramento; London, 2008
Budapest 2007
   Andrea Czére, ed., *In Arte Venustas. Studies on drawings in honour of Teréz Gerszi presented on her eightieth birthday*, Budapest, 2007
Choulant 1852
   Ludwig Choulant, *Geschichte und Bibliographie der anatomischen Abbildung*, Leipzig, 1852
Choulant 1920
   Ludwig Choulant, *History and Bibliography of Anatomic Illustration*, trans M. Frank, Chicago, 1920

Couturier 2004
   Sonia Couturier, *French Drawings from the National Gallery of Canada*, exh. cat. Ottawa, 2004
Crocker 1939
   Drawings by the German Masters in the Edwin Bryant Crocker Collection, Sacramento, California, ed. Alfred Neumeyer, exh. cat. Sacramento, 1939
Crocker 1959
   Drawings of the Masters, exh. brochure, Sacramento, 1959
Crocker 1964
   Crocker Art Gallery, Catalogue of the Collections, Sacramento, 1964
Crocker 1971
   Master Drawings from Sacramento, exh. cat., intro. John Mahey, Sacramento, 1971
Crocker 1979
   French Drawings from the E. B. Crocker Collection, exh. cat. Long Beach, 1979
Davidson 1982
   Jane Davidson, *A Renaissance Collector's Cabinet of Art*, exh. cat. Reno, 1982
Dittrich 1987
   Christian Dittrich, *Van Eyck, Bruegel, Rembrandt, Niederländische Zeichnungen des 15. bis 17. Jahrhunderts aus dem Kupferstich-Kabinett Dresden*, exh. cat. Dresden, 1997
Elsig 2004
   Frédéric Elsig, *Jheronimus Bosch, la question de la chronologie*, Geneva, 2004
Farr and Bradford 1986
   Dennis Farr and William Bradford, *The Northern Landscape: Flemish, Dutch, and British Drawings from the Courtauld Collections*, exh. cat. New York, 1986
Feinblatt 1976
   Ebria Feinblatt, *Old Master Drawings from American Collections*, exh. cat. Los Angeles, 1976
Flagg 1999
   Peter Flagg, *Fate, Fortune, Nemesis, Albrecht Dürer at the Century's End*, exh. cat. Sacramento, 1999
Franklin 2003
   David Franklin, *Italian Drawings from the National Gallery of Canada*, exh. cat. Toronto, Vancouver, and Windsor (Ottawa), 2003
Frensemeier 2001
   Marietta Frensemeier, *Studien zu Adriaen van de Velde (1636–1672)*, Aachen, 2001
Gaignebet 2004
   Claude Gaignebet, *Les Triomphes de Carnival*, exh. cat. Musée de Gravelines, 2004
Goldfarb 1989
   Hilliard Goldfarb, *From Fontainebleau to the Louvre, French Drawing from the Seventeenth Century*, exh. cat. Cleveland, 1989
Harrison 1986
   Jefferson C. Harrison, *French Paintings from the Chrysler Museum*, exh. cat. Norfolk, 1986

Hautekeete 2007
Stefaan Hautekeete et al., *Dessins du siècle d'or hollandaise: La Collection Jean de Grez*, exh. cat. Brussels, 2007

Hildebrecht 2004
Douglas R. Hildebrecht, *Otto Marseus van Schrieck (1619/20–1678) and the Nature Piece: Art, Science, Religion, and the Seventeenth-Century Pursuit of Natural Knowledge*, Ph.D. diss, University of Michigan, Ann Arbor, 2004

Hollstein
F. W. H. Hollstein et al., *Dutch and Flemish Etchings, Engravings, and Woodcuts ca. 1450-1700*, Amsterdam, 1949– ; and *German Engravings, Etchings, and Woodcuts, ca. 1400-1700*, Amsterdam, 1954

Howard 1984
Seymour Howard, "Carracci-School Drawings in Sacramento," *Zeitschrift für Kunstgeschichte*, vol. XLVII, no. 3, 1984, pp. 349–73

Howard et al. 1972
Seymour Howard et al., *Classical Narratives in Old Master Drawings*, exh. cat. Sacramento, 1972

Howard et al. 1973
Seymour Howard et al., *Old Testament Narratives in Master Drawings*, exh. cat. Sacramento, 1973

Howard et al. 1976
Seymour Howard et al., *New Testament Narratives in Master Drawings*, exh. cat. Sacramento, 1976

Howard et al. 1983
Seymour Howard et al., *Saints and Sinners in Master Drawings*, exh. cat. Sacramento, 1983

Hume and Cheke 2004
Julian Pender Hume and Anthony S. Cheke, "The White Dodo of Réunion Island: unraveling a scientific and historical myth," *Archives of Natural History*, vol. XXXI, no. 1, 2004, pp. 57–79

Hutchison 1991
Jane Campbell Hutchison, "Forum: Dürer's Praxitlean Aphrodite," *Drawing*, vol. XIII, 1991, pp. 55–56

Jaffé 2002
Michael Jaffé, *The Devonshire Collection of Northern European Drawings*, London, 2002

Jones 2002
Colin Jones, *Madame de Pompadour, Images of a Mistress*, exh. cat. London, 2002

Katritzky 2006
M. A. Katritzky, *The Art of Commedia: A Study in the Commedia dell'Arte 1560-1620, with Special Reference to the Visual Records*, New York, 2006

Kaufmann 1982
Thomas DaCosta Kaufmann, *Drawings from the Holy Roman Empire 1540-1680: A Selection from North American Collections*, exh. cat., The Art Museum, Princeton University, 1982

Kaufmann 1985
Thomas DaCosta Kaufmann, "A Census of Drawings from the Holy Roman Empire, 1540–1680, in North American Collections," *Central European History*, vol. XVIII, no. 1, March 1985, pp. 70–113

Kaufmann 1989
Thomas DaCosta Kaufmann, *Central European Drawings 1680-1800, a Selection from American Collections*, exh. cat. Princeton, 1989

Kaufmann 2004
Thomas DaCosta Kaufmann, *Central European Drawing in the Collection of The Crocker Art Museum*, Turnhout, 2004

Koldeweij et al. 2001
Jos Koldeweij, Bernard Vermet, with Barbera van Kooij, *Hieronymus Bosch, New Insights into His Life and Work*, exh. cat. Museum Boijmans-van Beuningen, Rotterdam, 2001

Koreny et al. 2002
Fritz Koreny, Erwin Pokorny, and Georg Zeman, *Early Netherlandish Drawings from Jan van Eyck to Hieronymus Bosch*, exh. cat. Rubenshuis, Antwerp, 2002, p. 164

Kurutz 1990
K. D. Kurutz, "Sacramento's Pioneer Patrons of Art, the Edwin Bryant Crocker Family," *Golden Notes*, vol. XXXVI, no. 1, Spring 1990, pp. 1–38

Lawrence 1956
German and Austrian Prints and Drawings of the Eighteenth Century, exh. cat. Lawrence, Kansas, 1956

Liedtke et al. 1995
Walter Liedtke et al., *Rembrandt/Not Rembrandt in The Metropolitan Museum of Art: Aspects of Connoisseurship*, exh. cat. New York, 1995

Luijten et al. 1993
Ger Luijten et al., *Dawn of the Golden Age: Northern Netherlandish Art, 1580-1620*, exh. cat. Rijksmuseum, Amsterdam, 1993

Mauquoy-Hendrickx 1956
Marie Mauquoy-Hendrickx, *L'iconographie d'Antoine van Dyck; catalogue raisonné*, 2 vols., Brussels, 1956

Moir et al. 1977
Alfred Moir et al., *Regional Styles of Drawing in Italy 1600-1700*, exh. cat. Santa Barbara, 1977

Montreal 1953
Five Centuries of Drawings, ed. Regina Shoolman, exh. cat. Montreal, 1953

Neumeyer 1938
Alfred Neumeyer, "Albrecht Dürer," *Old Master Drawings*, vol. XIII, 1938, pp. 16–17

Pignatti 1974
Terisio Pignatti, *Venetian Drawings from American Collections*, exh. cat. Washington, 1974

Pratt 1937
Harry Noyes Pratt, "The E. B. Crocker Collection of Old Master Drawings," *Prints*, vol. VIII, no. 1, October 1937, pp. 26–33

Reno 1978
Master Drawings from the E. B. Crocker Art Gallery at the Church Fine Arts Gallery, University of Nevada, Reno, exh. cat., intro. Sven Loevgren, Reno, 1978

Reznicek 1961
E. K. J. Reznicek, *Die Zeichnungen von Hendrick Goltzius mit einem beschreibenden Katalog*, 2 vols., Utrecht, 1961

Robbin et al. 2004
C. Roxanne Robbin et al., *Drawing in Italy from 1550-1650*, exh. brochure, Sacramento, 2004

Robinson 1977
Franklin W. Robinson, *Seventeenth-century Dutch Drawings from American Collections*, exh. cat. Washington, D.C., 1977

Robinson 1979
William W. Robinson, "Preparatory Drawings by Adriaen van de Velde," *Master Drawings*, vol. XVII, no. 1, Spring 1979, pp. 3–23

Robinson 1993
William W. Robinson, "Some Studies of Nude Models by Adriaen van de Velde," *Donum Amicorum: Essays in Honour of Per Bjurström*, festschrift, Bulletin-Nationalmuseum 1993, pp. 53–66

Rodgers 1978
Malcolm Rodgers, *Sir Peter Lely 1618-1680*, exh. cat. National Portrait Gallery, London, 1978

Röhrl 2000
Boris Röhrl, *History and Bibliography of Artistic Anatomy*, Hildesheim, 2000

Roethlisberger 1969
Marcel Roethlisberger, *Bartholomäus Breenbergh, Handzeichnungen*, Berlin, 1969

Roethlisberger and Bok 1993
Marcel Roethlisberger and Marten Jan Bok. *Abraham Bloemaert and His Sons: Paintings and Prints*, Ghent, 1993

Rollová 1993–94
Anna Rollová, "Pieter Stevens Known and Unknown: New Facts Concerning His Drawings," *Bulletin of the National Gallery in Prague*, vols. III–IV, 1993–94, pp. 117–19

Rosand and Muraro 1976
David Rosand and Michelangelo Muraro, *Titian and the Venetian Woodcut*, exh, cat. National Gallery of Art, Washington, D.C., 1976

Rosenberg 1970
Pierre Rosenberg, "Twenty French Drawings in Sacramento," *Master Drawings*, vol. VIII, no. 1, Spring 1970, pp. 31–39

Rowlands 1993
John Rowlands, *Drawings by German Artists and Artists from German-speaking Regions of Europe in the Department of Prints and Drawings in the British Museum*, London, 1993

Roy 1992
Alain Roy, *Gérard de Lairesse (1640-1711)*, Paris, 1992

Ruda 1985
Jeffrey Ruda, *The World of Old Master Drawings. A Centennial Exhibition at the Crocker Art Museum*, exh. brochure, Sacramento, 1985

Ruda 1992
Jeffrey Ruda, *The Art of Drawing*, exh. cat. Flint, Michigan, 1992

Salmon 2002
Xavier Salmon, *Madame de Pompadour et les Arts*, exh. cat. Versailles, 2002

Saunders and O'Malley 1950
J. B. de C. M. Saunders and Charles O'Malley, *The Illustrations from the Works of Andreas Vesalius of Brussels*, Cleveland, 1950

Schapelhouman and Schatborn 1987
Marijn Schapelhouman and Peter Schatborn, *Land & Water: Dutch Drawings from the 17th Century in the Rijksmuseum Print Room*, Amsterdam, 1987

Schatborn 1985
Peter Schatborn, *Tekeningen van Rembrandt zijn onbekende leerlingen en navolgers*, Amsterdam, 1985

Scheyer 1949
Ernst Scheyer, "Goethe and the Visual Arts," *The Art Quarterly*, vol. XII, no. 144, 1949

Schultz 1968
Jürgen Schultz, *Master Drawings from California Collections*, exh. cat. Berkeley, 1968

Spicer 2004
Joaneath Spicer, *Dutch and Flemish Drawings from the National Gallery of Canada*, Ottawa, 2004

Stampfle 1979
Felice Stampfle, *Rubens and Rembrandt in Their Century, Flemish and Dutch Drawings of the 17th Century from The Pierpont Morgan Library*, New York, 1979

Steadman and Osborne 1976
David W. Steadman and Carol Osborne, *18th-century Drawings from California Collections*, exh. cat. Claremont, 1976

Steensma 1999
Susanna Steensma, *Otto Marseus van Schrieck, Leben und Werk*, Hildesheim and New York, 1999

Talbot and Levenson 1971
Charles Talbot and Jay Levenson, eds., *Dürer in America: his Graphic Work*, exh. cat. Washington, 1971

Ternois 1962
Daniel Ternois, *Jacques Callot, catalogue complet de l'oeuvre gravé*, Paris, 1962

Tietze and Tietze-Conrat 1937-38
Hans Tietze and Erika Tietze-Conrat, *Kritisches Verzeichnis der Werke Albrecht Dürers*, 2 vols., Basle, 1937–38

Trivas 1940a
Numa S. Trivas, *Three Centuries of Landscape Drawing*, exh. cat. Sacramento, 1940

Trivas 1940b
Numa S. Trivas, "Lesser Known American Art Collections. I. The E. B. Crocker Art Gallery of Sacramento, California, U.S.A.," *Apollo*, vol. IV, December 1940, pp. 135–37

Trivas 1942
Numa S. Trivas, *Old Master Drawings from the E. B. Crocker Collection. The Dutch and Flemish Masters*, unpubl. manuscript, Sacramento, 1942

Turner and Stampfle 2006
Jane Shoaf Turner and Felice Stampfle, *Dutch Drawings in The Pierpont Morgan Library, Seventeenth to Nineteenth Centuries*, 2 vols., New York, 2006

Van Mander 1994
Karel van Mander, *The Lives of the Illustrious Netherlandish and German Painters, from the first edition of the Schilder-boeck (1616–1618)*, intro. and trans. Hessel Miedema, Doornspijk, 1994

Vasari, ed. Milanesi
Giorgio Vasari, *Le vite de' più eccellenti pittori, scultori ed architettori*, ed. G. Milanesi, 9 parts in 8 vols., Florence, 1878–86

Vey 1962
Horst Vey, *Die Zeichnungen Anton van Dycks*, Brussels, 1962

Vitzthum 1970
Walter Vitzthum, *A Selection of Italian Drawings from North American Collections*, exh. cat. Regina and Montreal, 1970

Weigel, Kunstlagerkatalog
Rudolf Weigel, *Kunstlagerkatalog*, 35 parts in 5 vols., Leipzig, 1838–66

Westins 1981
Jean K. Westin and Robert H. Westin, *Transformations of the Roman Baroque*, exh. cat. Gainesville, 1981

White 1972
Christopher White, review of Crocker 1971, *Master Drawings*, vol. X, no. 2, Summer 1972, p. 167

White and Crawley 1994
Christopher White and Charlotte Crawley, *The Dutch and Flemish Drawings of the Fifteenth to the Early Nineteenth Centuries in the Collection of Her Majesty the Queen at Windsor Castle*, Cambridge, 1994

LIST OF ARTISTS

Federico Barocci, *Head of an Elderly Man*, cat. no. 3

Fra Bartolommeo, *Angel Playing a Lute*, cat. no. 2

Johann Wolfgang Baumgartner, *Lazarus and the Rich Man*, cat. no. 47

Johann Georg Bergmüller, *Saint Martin Appealing to the Virgin*, cat. no. 46

Giuseppe Bernardino Bison, *Capriccio Landscape with Classical Monuments*, cat. no. 14

Frederick Bloemaert, *Landscape with Tree Trunks and a Shepherd Resting*, cat. no. 25

Circle of Hieronymus Bosch, *Christ Carrying the Cross*, cat. no. 15

François Boucher, *The Birth of Venus*, cat. no. 36

Bartholomaeus Breenbergh, *Temple of the Tiburtine Sibyl at Tivoli*, cat. no. 21

Burgundian School (?), *Two Magistrates with a Shield*, cat. no. 29

Jan Steven van Calcar, *Studies of Human Bones*, cat. no. 16

Jacques Callot, *Martyrdom of Saint Sebastian*, cat. no. 30

Domenico Campagnola, *The Presentation of the Virgin*, cat. no. 4

Simone Cantarini, *Holy Family and Figure Studies*, cat. no. 10

Vittore Carpaccio, *Pope Alexander III Presenting a Ceremonial Umbrella to Doge Sebastiano Ziani at Ancona*, cat. no. 1

Giuseppe Cesari, called il Cavaliere d'Arpino, *Mystic Marriage of Saint Catherine*, cat. no. 8

Agostino Ciampelli, *The Visitation*, cat. no. 7

Pier Francesco Cittadini, *Landscape with Herder and Animals*, cat. no. 11

Donato Creti, *Virgin and Child*, cat. no. 12

Gaspard Dughet, *Landscape with Two Figures*, cat. no. 33

Albrecht Dürer, *Female Nude with a Staff*, cat. no. 42

Anthony van Dyck, *Portrait of Paulus Halmalius*, cat. no. 20

Jean-Honoré Fragonard, *An Italian Park*, cat. no. 38

Giacomo Franco (?), *Musicians in a Gondola*, cat. no. 5

Ubaldo Gandolfi, *Education of the Virgin*, cat. no. 13

Claude Gillot, *Scene of Sorcery*, cat. no. 35

Hendrick Goltzius, *Judith with the Head of Holofernes*, cat. no. 17

François Guérin, *Portrait of Mme de Pompadour and her Daughter Alexandrine d'Étiolles*, cat. no. 37

Carl Adalbert Hermann, *Allegory of the Nativity*, cat. no. 56

Michael Herr, *Witches' Sabbath*, cat. no. 44

Jean-Auguste-Dominique Ingres, *The Actor Brochard in Costume*, cat. no. 41

Georg Melchior Kraus, *Peasant Woman Eating*, cat. no. 48

Gérard de Lairesse, *Expulsion of Hagar*, cat. no. 28

Peter Lely, *Two Clerics, from a Procession of the Order of the Garter*, cat. no. 26

Eustache Le Sueur, *Kneeling Woman seen in Profile, Arms Upraised*, cat. no. 32

Nicolas Loir, *The Brazen Serpent*, cat. no. 34

Master of Mühldorf, *The Annunciation*, cat. no. 43

Pier Francesco Mola, *Christ in the Garden of Gethsemane*, cat. no. 9

Moritz Oppenheim, *Portrait of a Man with an Open Collar*, cat. no. 55

Pierre Patel the Elder, *Classical Landscape*, cat. no. 31

Pierre Peyron (?), *Young Man Asleep in a Chair*, cat. no. 39

Domenico Quaglio the Younger, *The Neuthor, Ulm*, cat. no. 52

Franz Xaver Rektorzik, *Landscape with a Cliff*, cat. no. 54

Rembrandt van Rijn (?), *Liberation of Saint Peter*, cat. no. 23

Hubert Robert, *Massacre of the Innocents*, cat. no. 40

Jan Savery, *Dodo Birds*, cat. no. 19

PHOTOGRAPHIC CREDITS

All photographs besides those listed below are copyrighted by their respective collections.

Figure 7: E. B. Crocker Art Gallery records, reel 1855 frame 489, Archives of American Art, Smithsonian Institution

Figures 8, 13, 18, 20, 22, 24, 29, 33, 34, 35: © Trustees of the British Museum

Figure 9: Réunion des Musées Nationaux/Art Resource, NY

Figure 10: Fine Arts Museums of San Francisco, Achenbach Foundation for the Graphic Arts

Figure 12: Bowdoin College Museum of Art, Brunswick, Maine, Museum Purchase

Figure 14: su concessione del Ministero Beni e Attività Culturali - Archivio Fotografico Soprintendenza BSAE - Bologna

Figure 16: © National Gallery in Prague 2008

Figure 19: Kupferstich-Kabinett, Staatliche Kunstsammlungen Dresden

Figure 21: Kunsthistorisches Museum, Wien

Figure 24: Toulouse Musée des Augustins, photographe Daniel Martin

Figure 30: © National Gallery, London / Art Resource, NY

Figure 31: The Pierpont Morgan Library, New York

Figure 38: © Museen für Kunst und Kulturgeschichte der Hansestadt Lübeck, Sammlung Dräger/Stubbe

Figure 39: Gemäldegalerie Alte Meister, Staatliche Kunstsammlungen Dresden